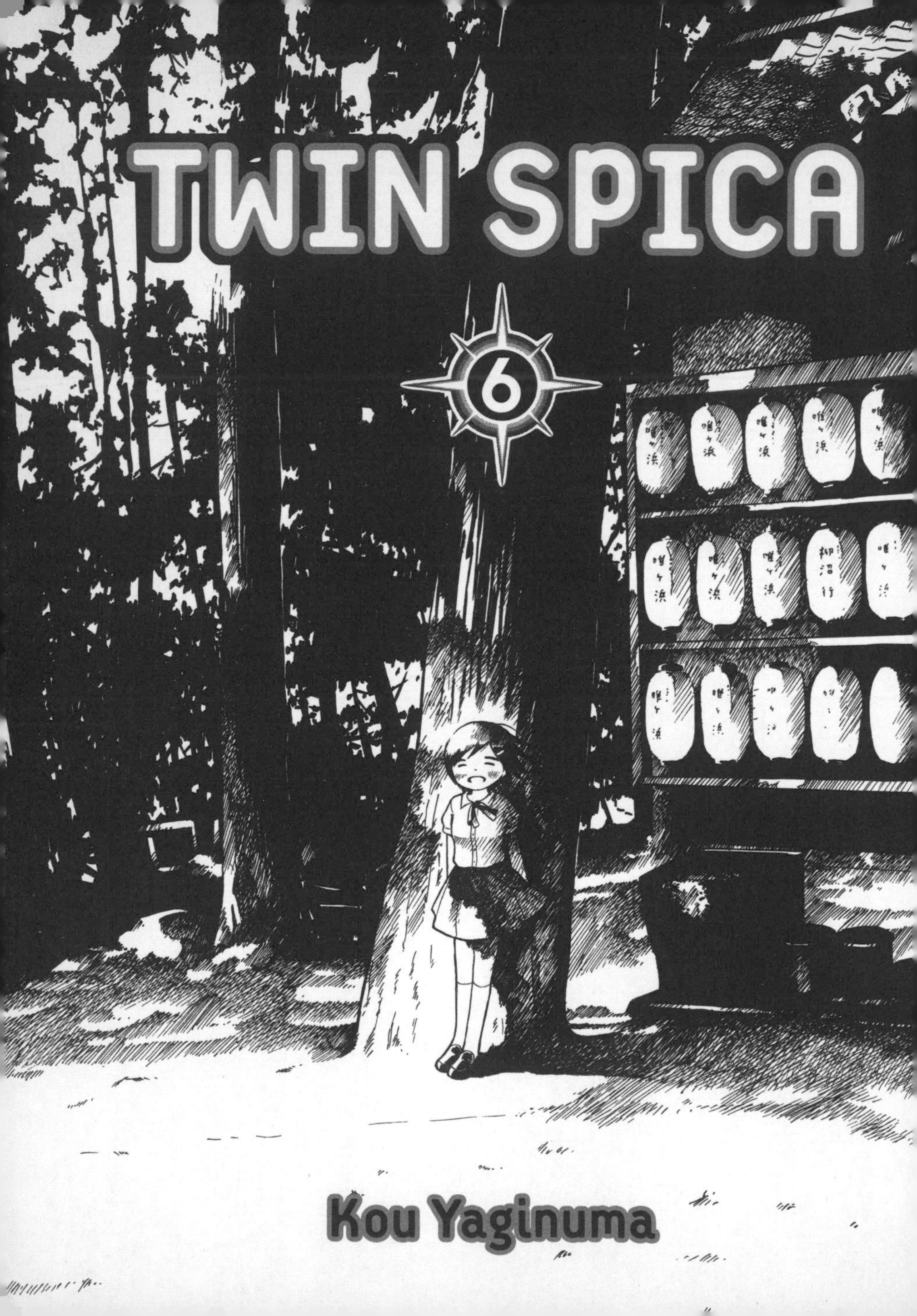
TWIN SPICA
6
Kou Yaginuma

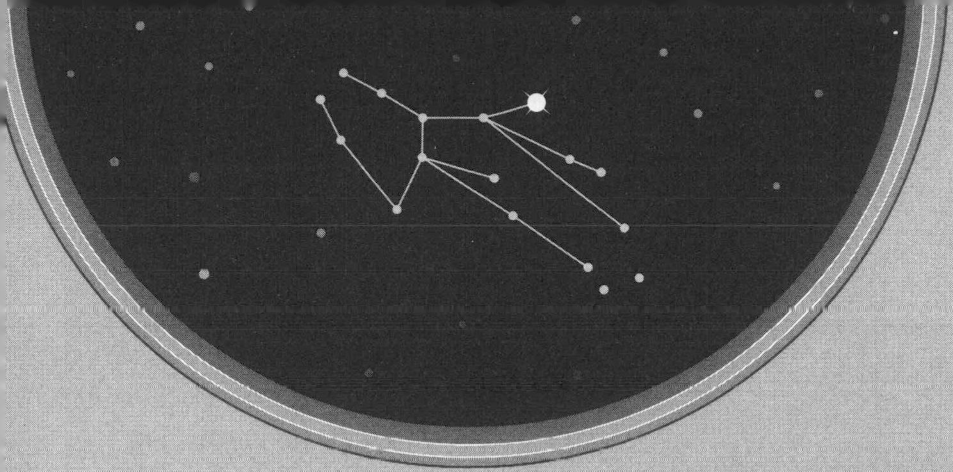

CONTENTS

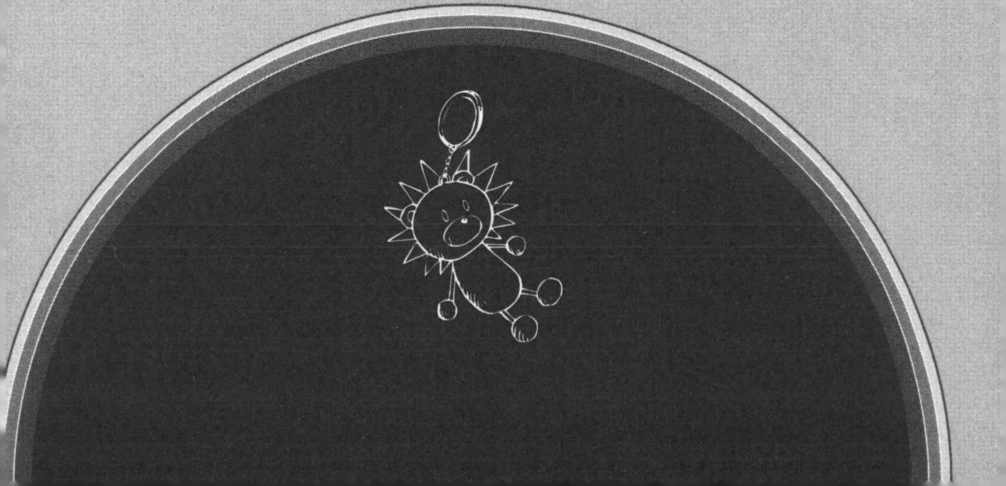

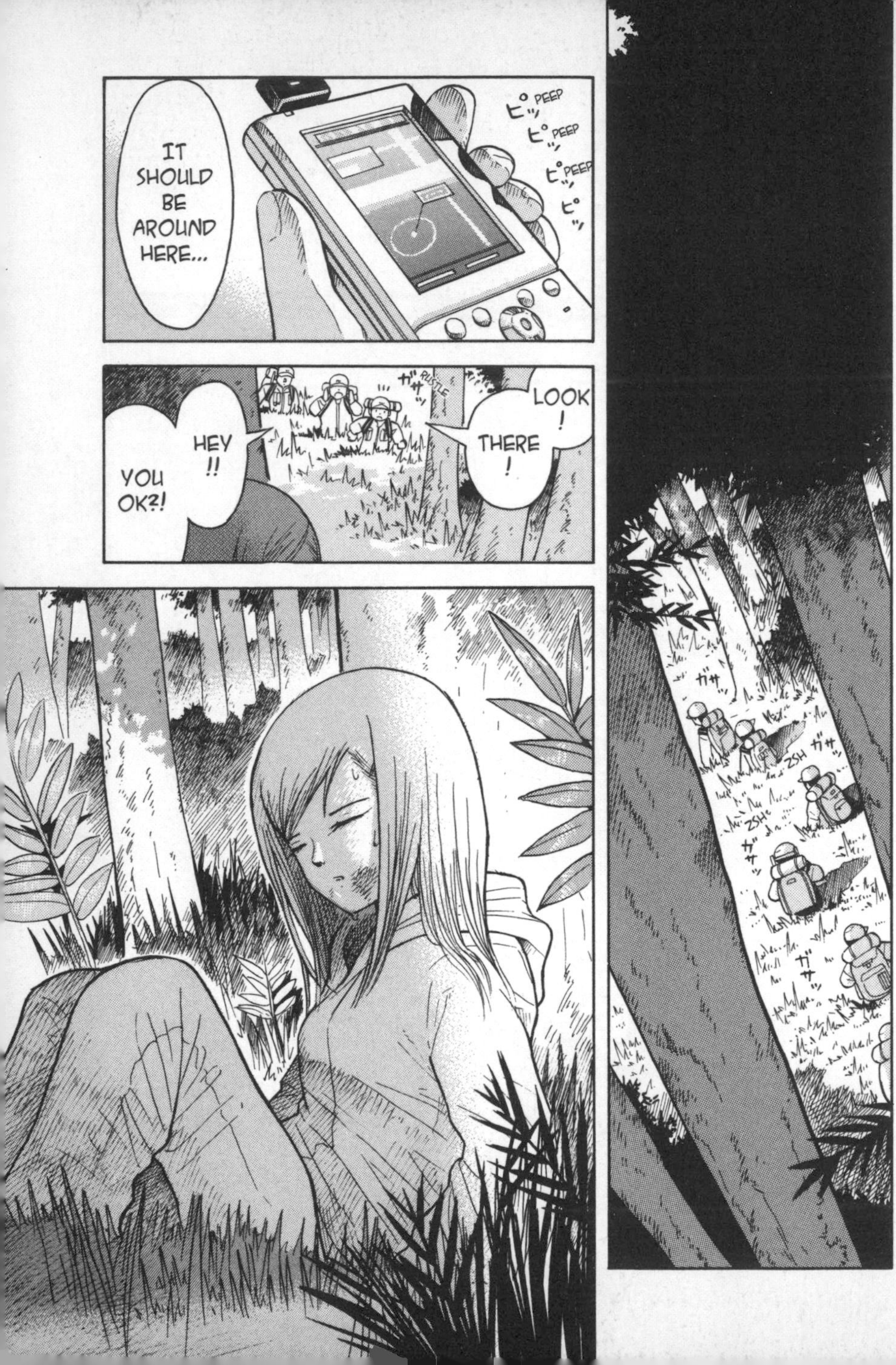
ガサッ
ZSH
ZSH
ガサッ
ガサッ
ピッ PEEP
ピッ PEEP
ピッ PEEP
ピッ
IT SHOULD BE AROUND HERE...
LOOK! THERE!
ガサッ RUSTLE
HEY!!
YOU OK?!

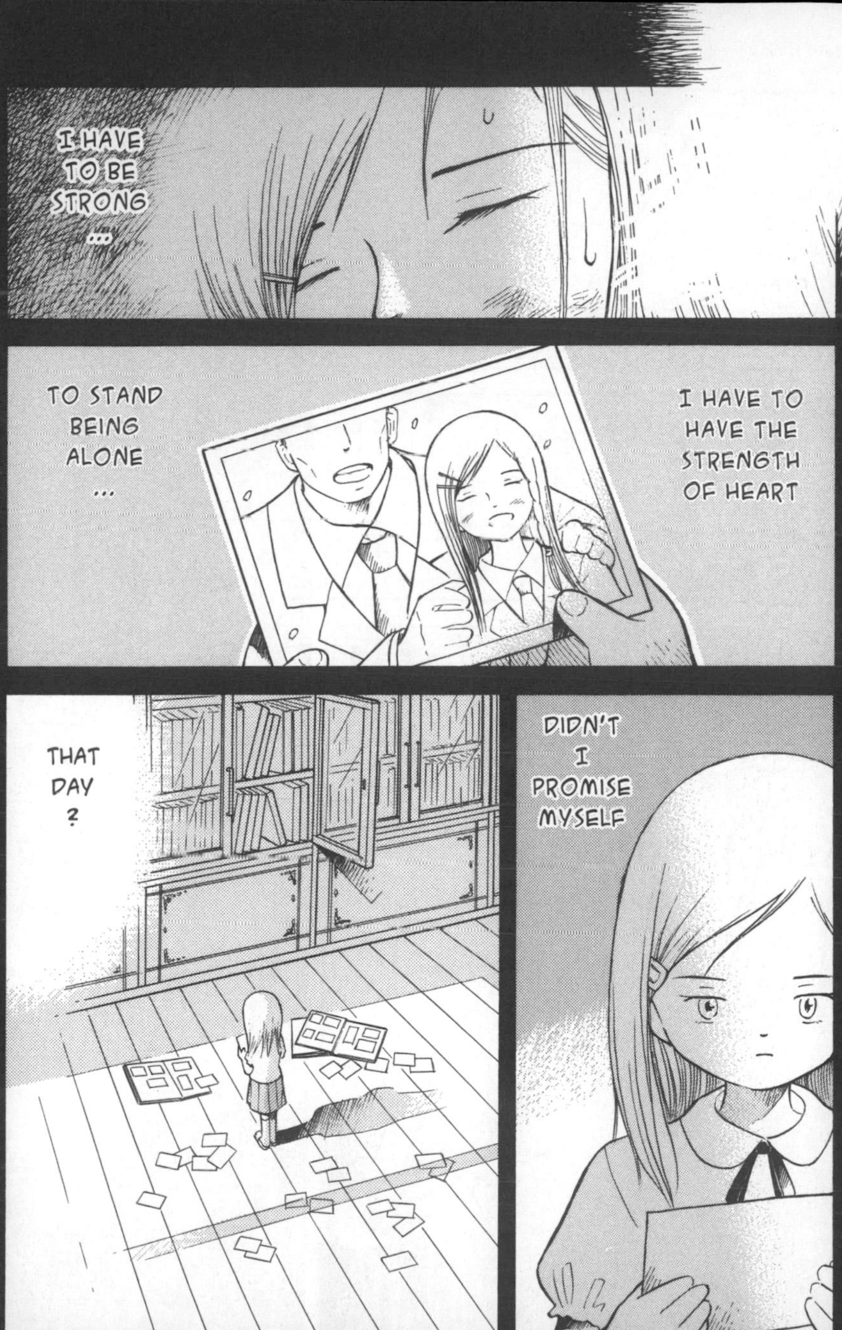
I HAVE TO BE STRONG ...
I HAVE TO HAVE THE STRENGTH OF HEART
TO STAND BEING ALONE ...
DIDN'T I PROMISE MYSELF
THAT DAY ?

MISSION:25

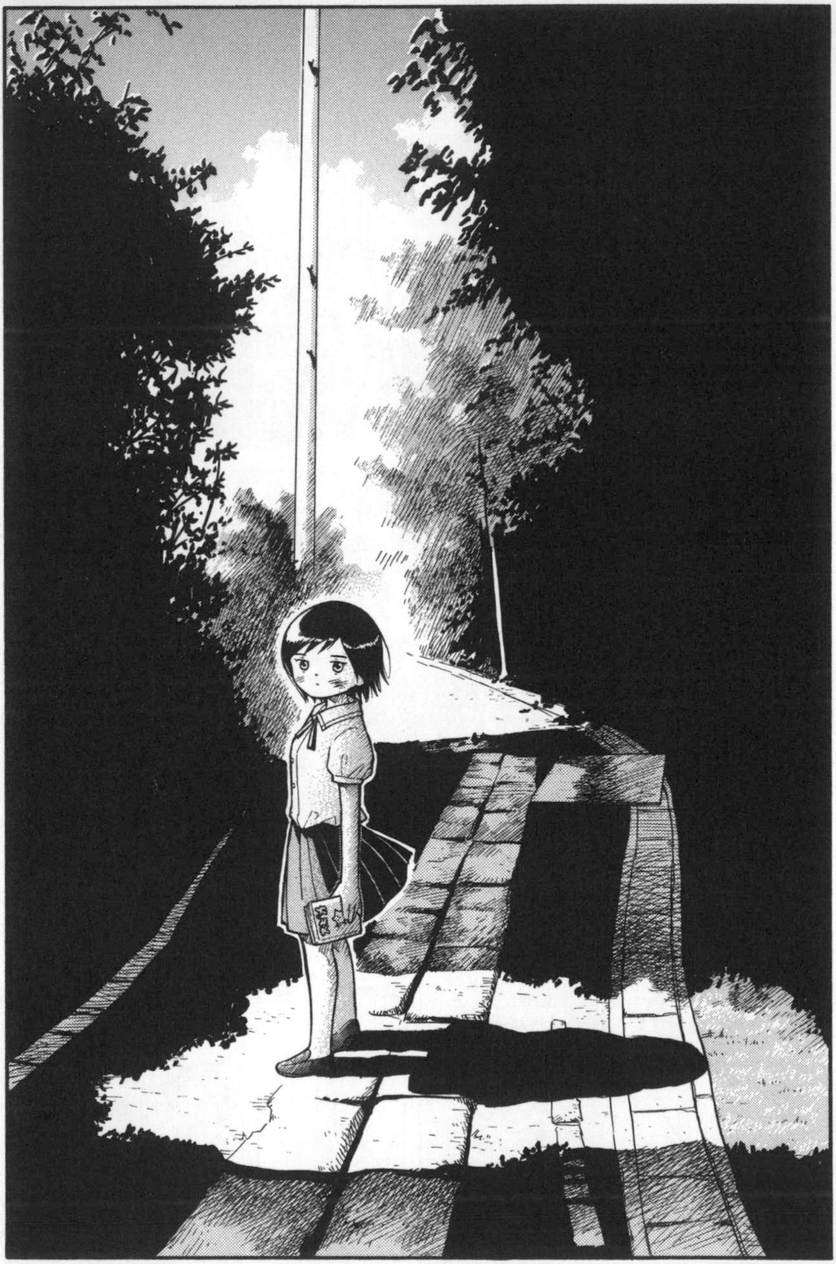

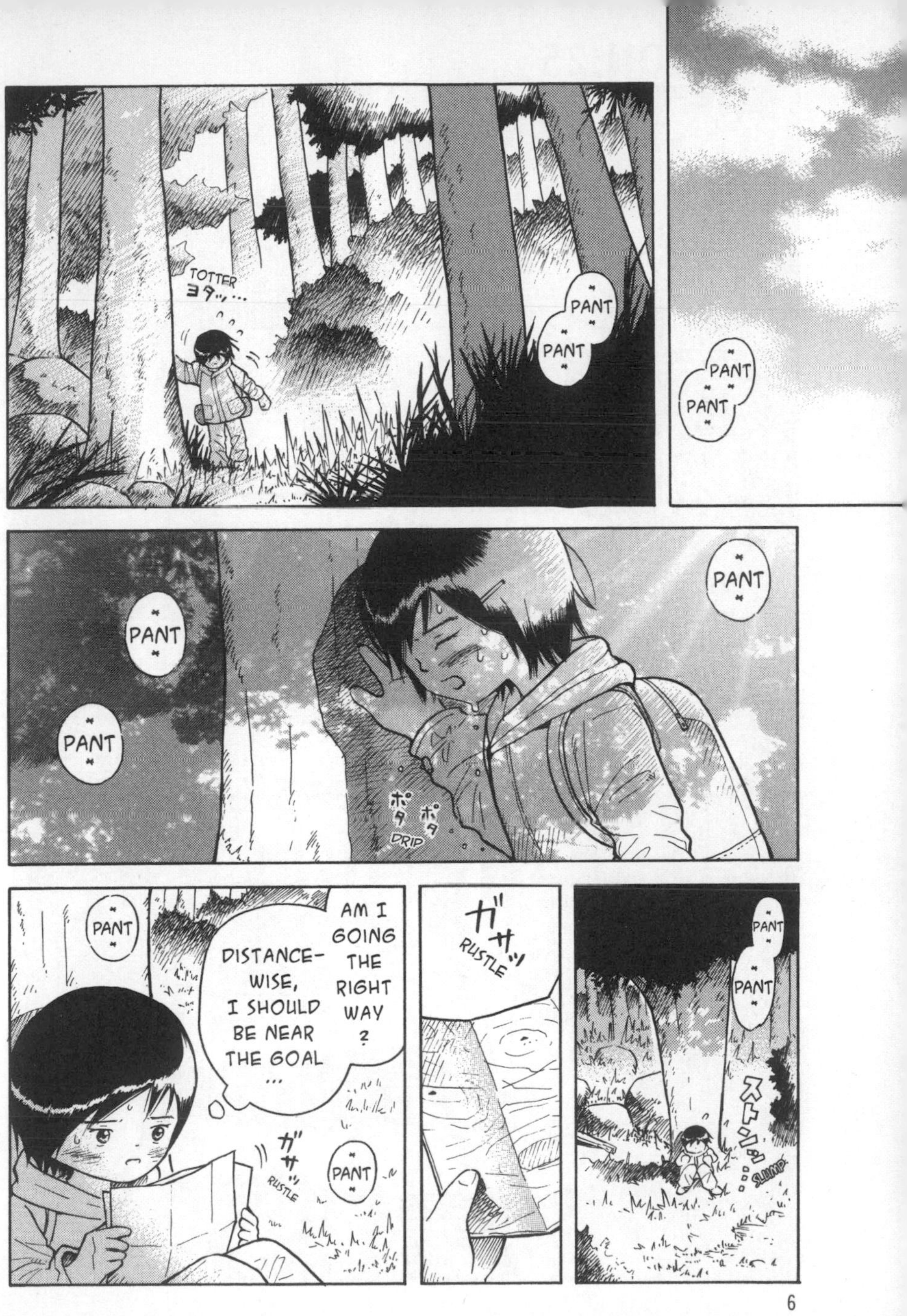
PANT
PANT
PANT
PANT
TOTTER
ヨタッ…
PANT
PANT
PANT
ポタ ポタ
DRIP
PANT
PANT
ストン…
SLUMP
ガサッ
RUSTLE
AM I GOING THE RIGHT WAY ?
DISTANCE-WISE, I SHOULD BE NEAR THE GOAL ...
PANT
PANT
ガサッ
RUSTLE

PANT
PANT
PANT
PANT
ザッ ZSH
PANT
PANT
ザッ ZSH
...
ぎゅるるる GROWL るるる....
ギュッ... GRIP
PANT
ザッ ZSH
ザッ ZSH
PANT
チロチロ.... TRICKLE
!
WATER !
ザッ ZSH...
ザッ ザッ ZSH
ザッ

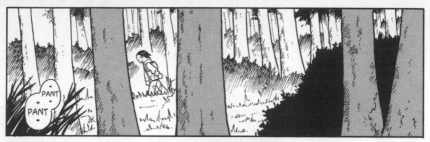

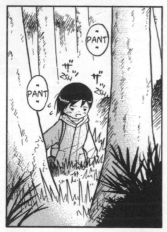

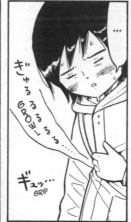

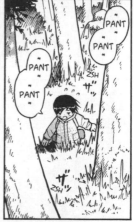

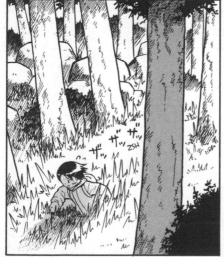

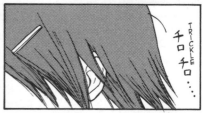

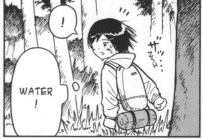

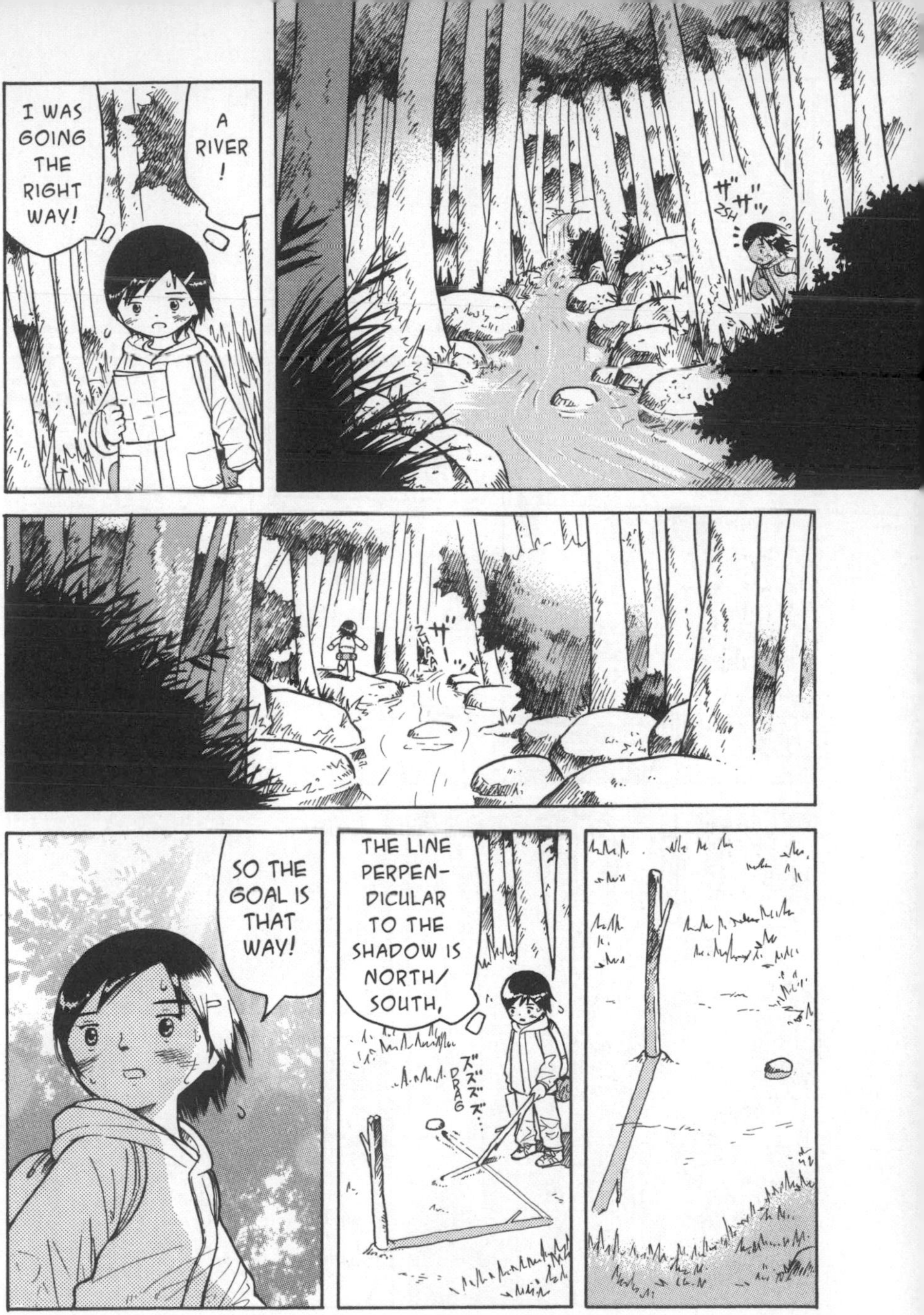
ザザッ
ZSH
A RIVER!
I WAS GOING THE RIGHT WAY!
ザッ
ZHAA
THE LINE PERPEN-DICULAR TO THE SHADOW IS NORTH/SOUTH,
ズズズ…
DRAG
SO THE GOAL IS THAT WAY!

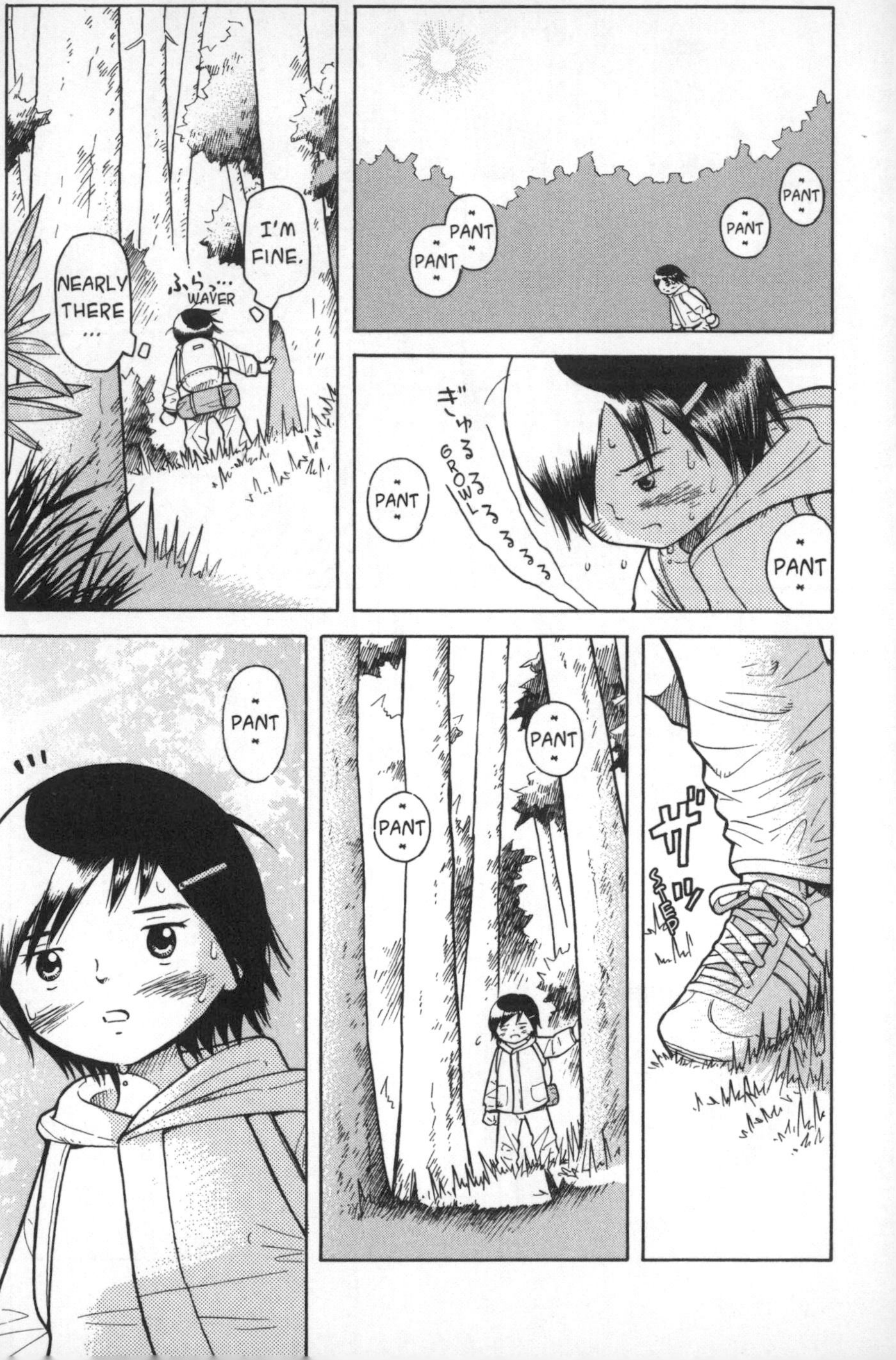
PANT
PANT
PANT
PANT
ぎゅるるるるるる GROWL
PANT
PANT
I'M FINE.
ふらっ… WAVER
NEARLY THERE …
ザッ STEP
PANT
PANT
PANT

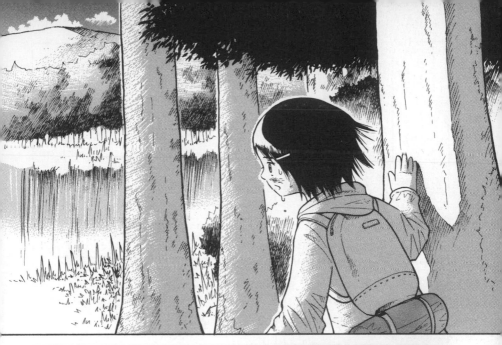

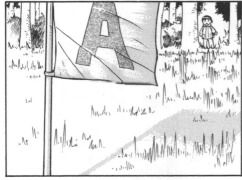

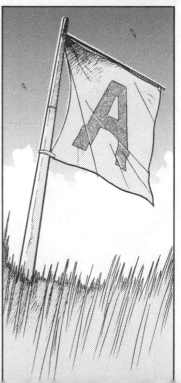

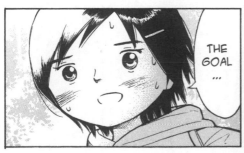

THE GOAL...

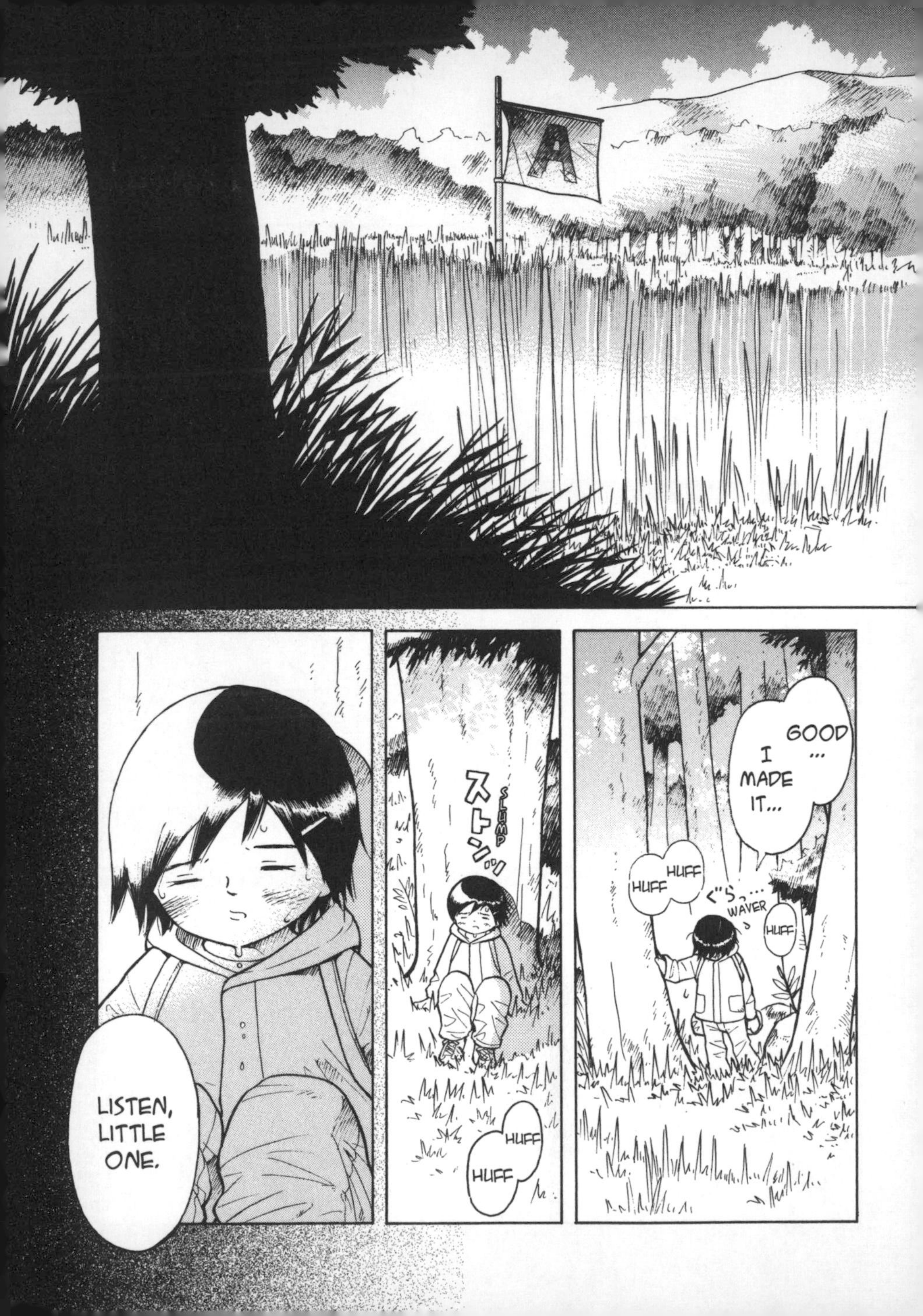
GOOD ... I MADE IT...
HUFF
HUFF
ぐらっ… WAVER
HUFF
ストンッ SLUMP
HUFF
HUFF
LISTEN, LITTLE ONE.

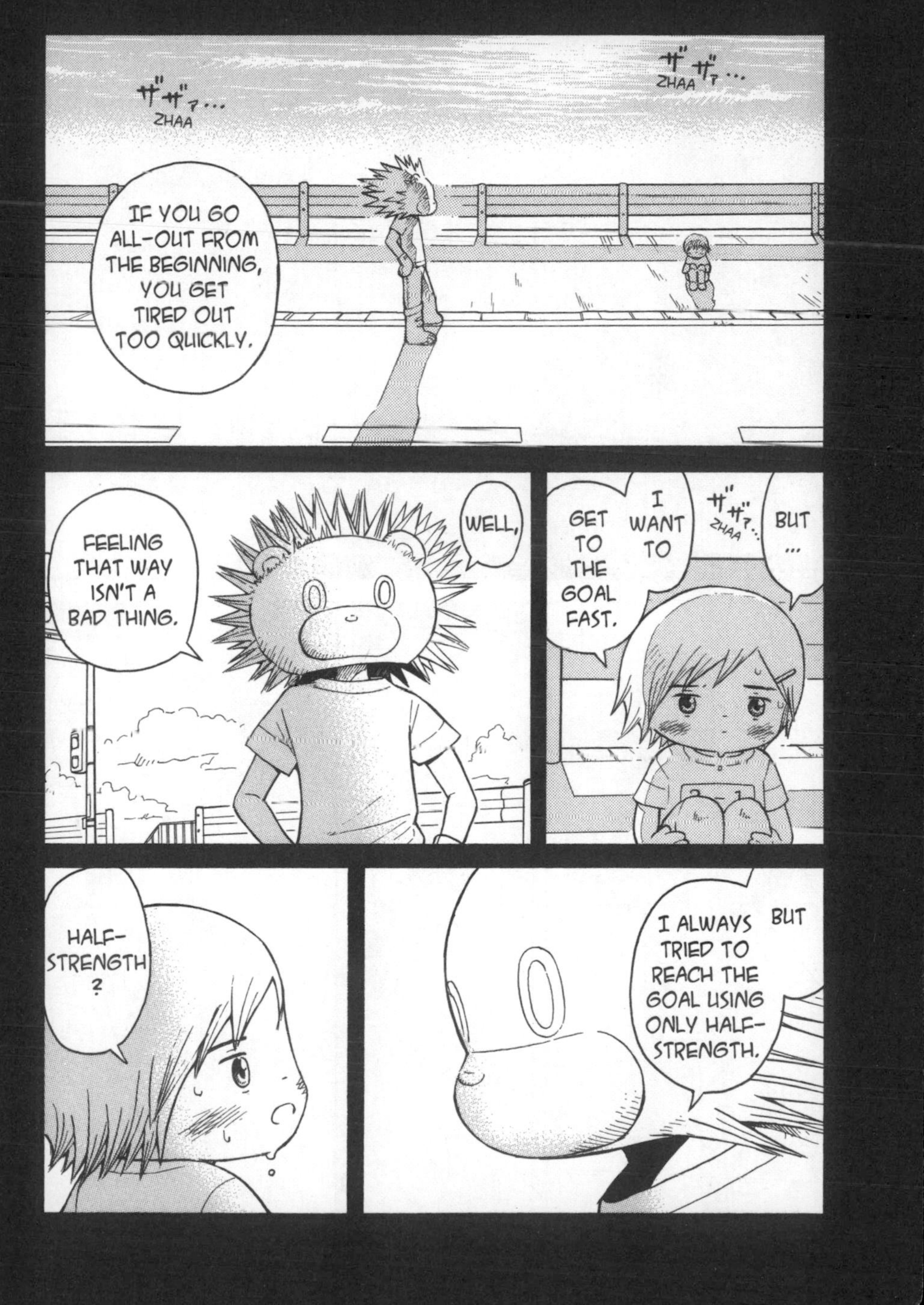
ザザァ…
ZHAA
ザザァ…
ZHAA
IF YOU GO ALL-OUT FROM THE BEGINNING, YOU GET TIRED OUT TOO QUICKLY.
BUT ...
ザザァ…
ZHAA
I WANT TO GET TO THE GOAL FAST.
WELL,
FEELING THAT WAY ISN'T A BAD THING.
BUT
I ALWAYS TRIED TO REACH THE GOAL USING ONLY HALF-STRENGTH.
HALF-STRENGTH?

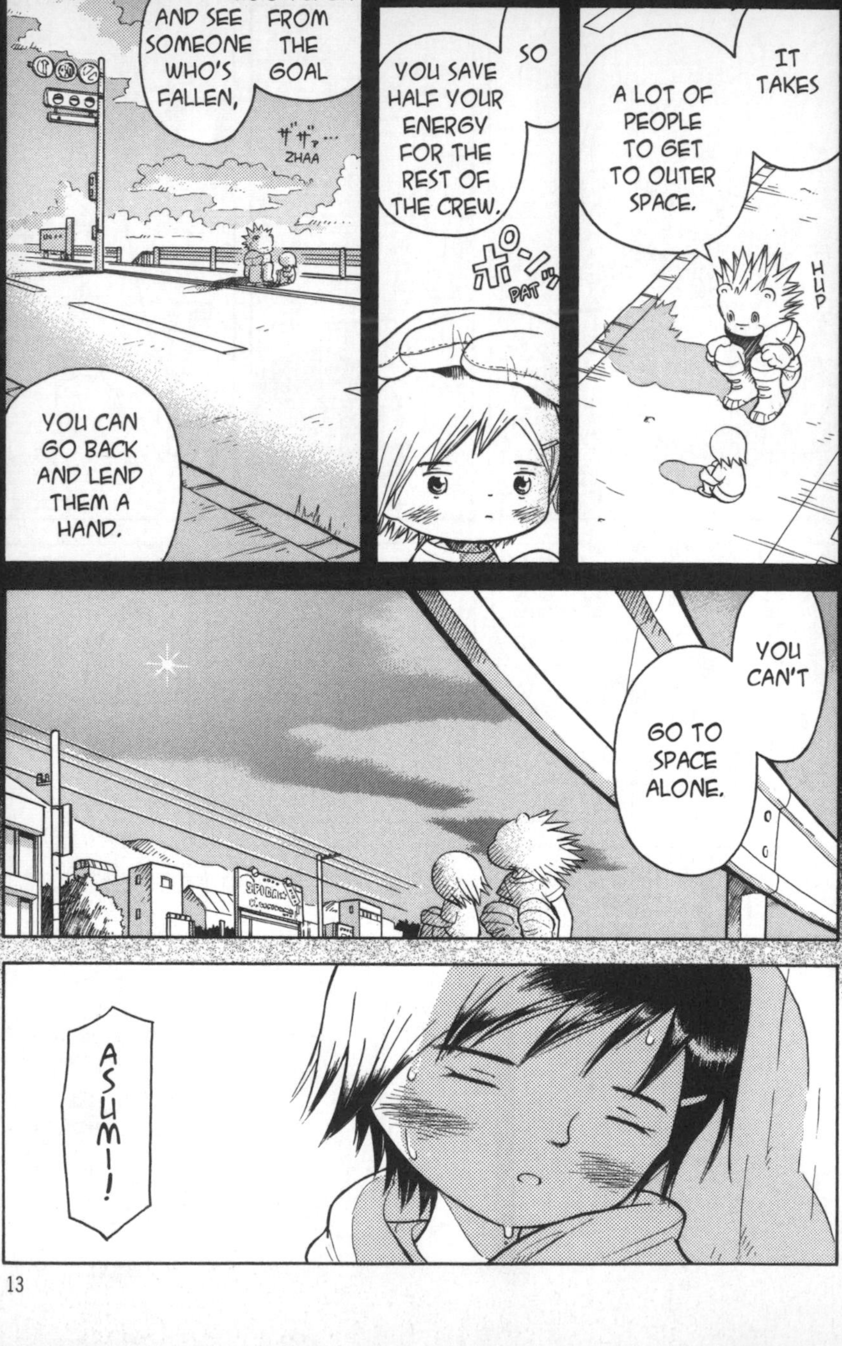
IT TAKES
A LOT OF PEOPLE TO GET TO OUTER SPACE.
HUP
SO
YOU SAVE HALF YOUR ENERGY FOR THE REST OF THE CREW.
PAT
THAT WAY, IF YOU LOOK BACK FROM THE GOAL
AND SEE SOMEONE WHO'S FALLEN,
ZHAA
YOU CAN GO BACK AND LEND THEM A HAND.
YOU CAN'T
GO TO SPACE ALONE.
ASUMI!

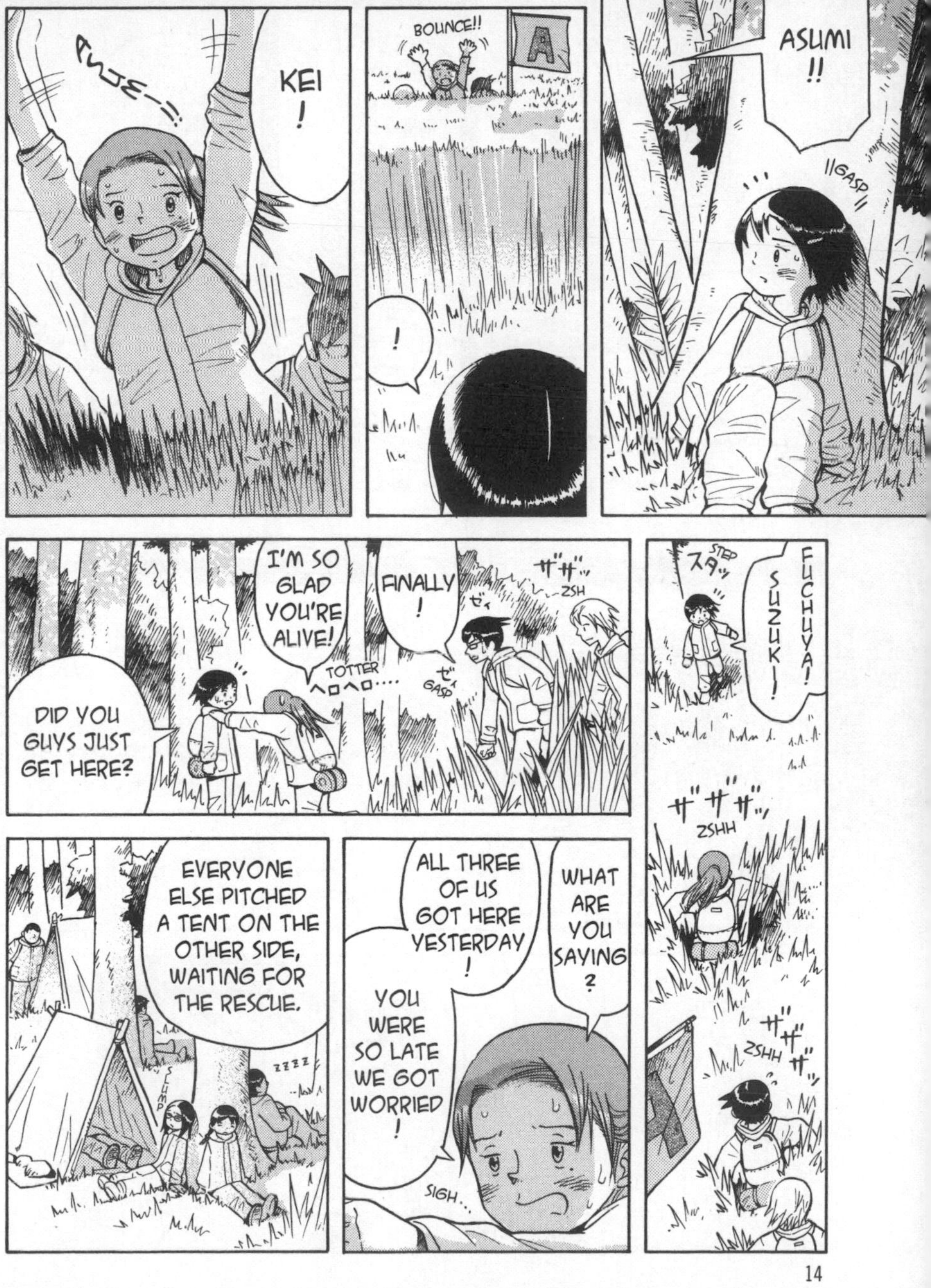
ASUMI !!
GASP
BOUNCE!!
!
KEI !
AWWE—!!
FUCHUYA!
SUZUKI!
STEP
スタッ
ザザザッ
ZSHH
ザザッ
ZSHH
ザザッ
ZSH
ゼイ
GASP
FINALLY !
I'M SO GLAD YOU'RE ALIVE!
TOTTER
ヘロヘロ....
DID YOU GUYS JUST GET HERE?
WHAT ARE YOU SAYING ?
ALL THREE OF US GOT HERE YESTERDAY !
YOU WERE SO LATE WE GOT WORRIED !
SIGH...
EVERYONE ELSE PITCHED A TENT ON THE OTHER SIDE, WAITING FOR THE RESCUE.
ZZZZ
SLUMP

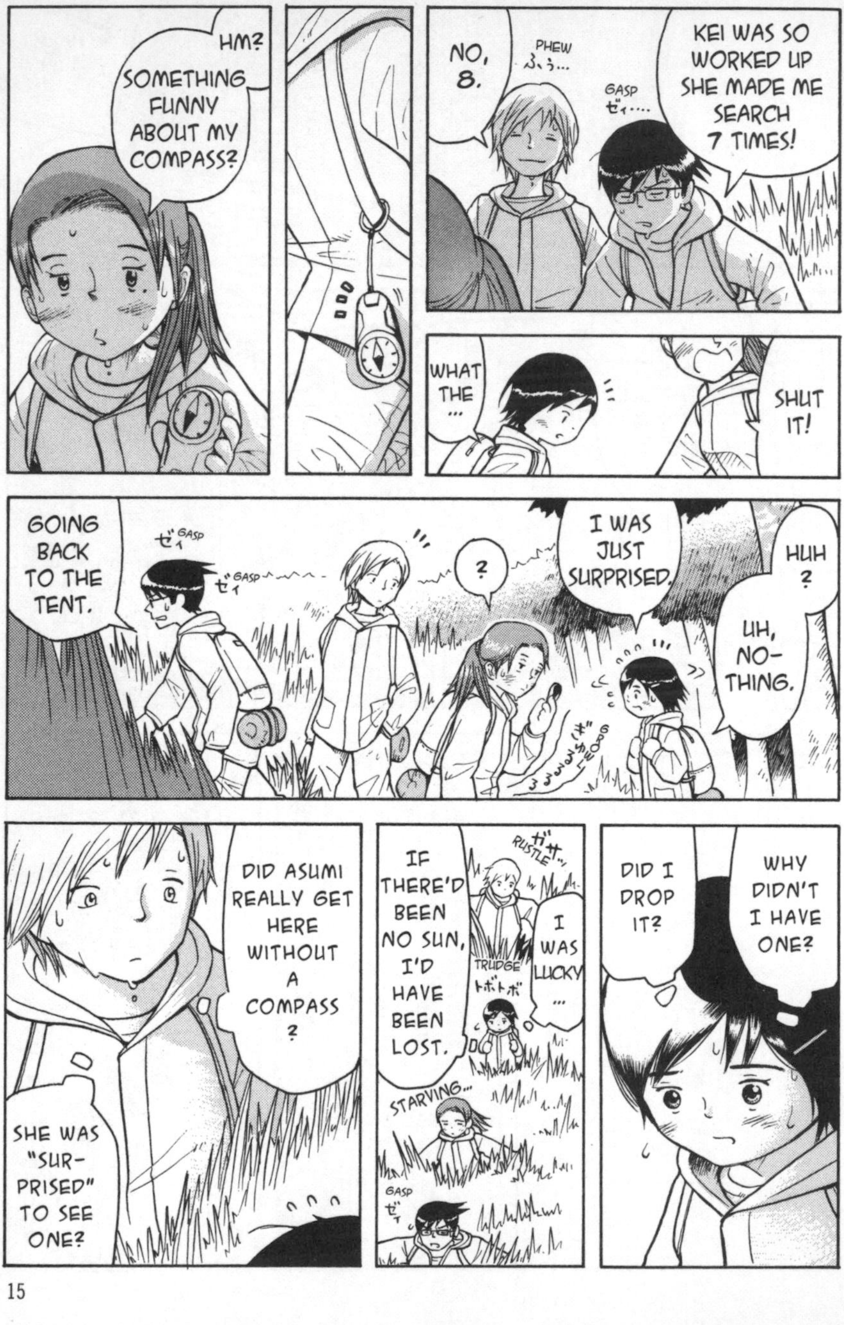
KEI WAS SO WORKED UP SHE MADE ME SEARCH 7 TIMES!
GASP ゼィ....
PHEW ふぅ...
NO, 8.
SHUT IT!
WHAT THE ...
HM? SOMETHING FUNNY ABOUT MY COMPASS?
HUH ?
UH, NO-THING.
I WAS JUST SURPRISED.
?
GASP ゼィ
GASP ゼィ
GOING BACK TO THE TENT.
WHY DIDN'T I HAVE ONE?
DID I DROP IT?
RUSTLE ガサ...
I WAS LUCKY ...
IF THERE'D BEEN NO SUN, I'D HAVE BEEN LOST.
TRUDGE トボトボ
STARVING...
GASP ゼィ
DID ASUMI REALLY GET HERE WITHOUT A COMPASS ?
SHE WAS "SUR-PRISED" TO SEE ONE?

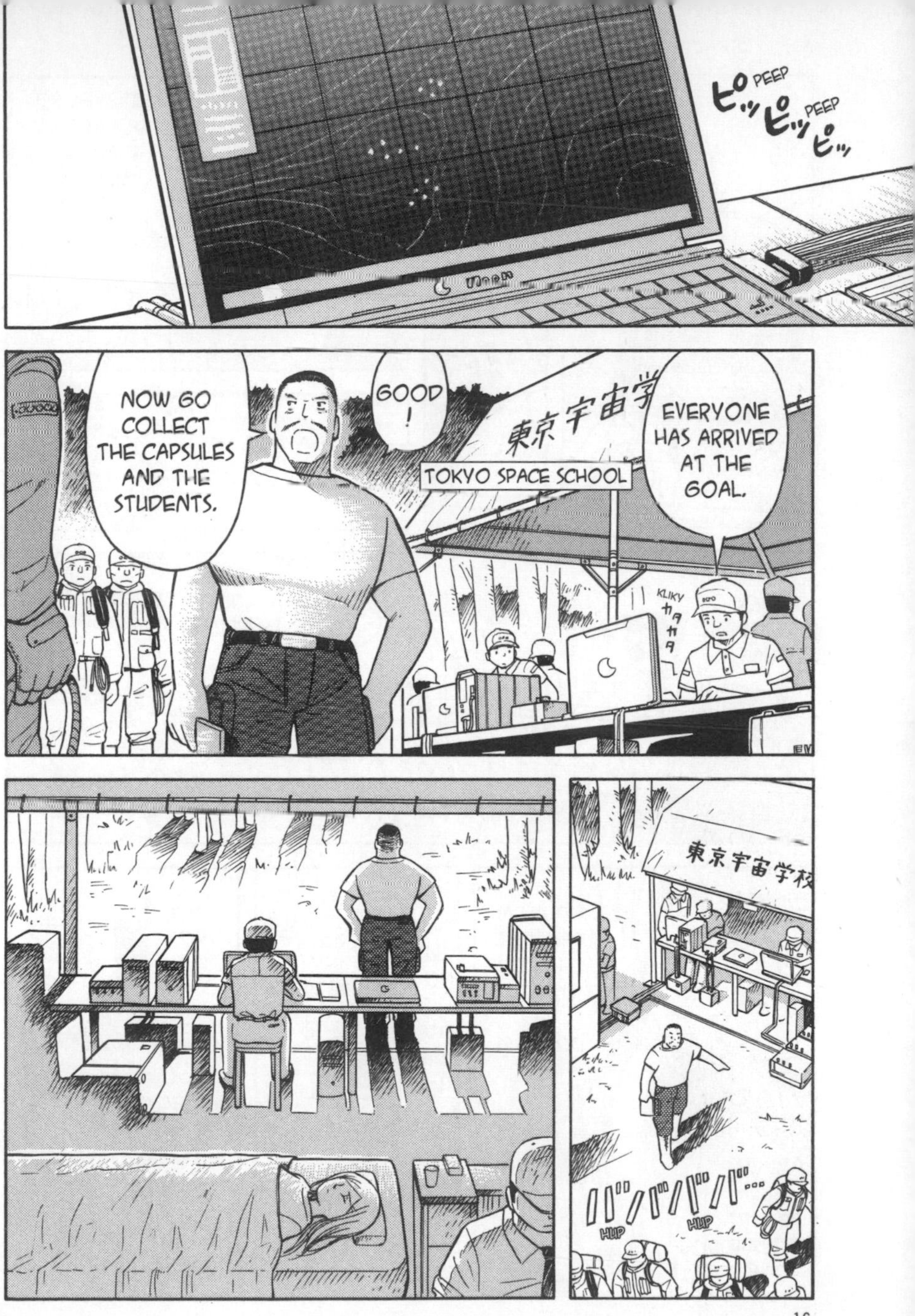
ピッ
PEEP
ピッ
PEEP
ピッ
ピッ
EVERYONE HAS ARRIVED AT THE GOAL.
KLIKY
カタカタ
東京宇宙学
TOKYO SPACE SCHOOL
GOOD!
NOW GO COLLECT THE CAPSULES AND THE STUDENTS.
東京宇宙学校
バババ…
HUP
HUP

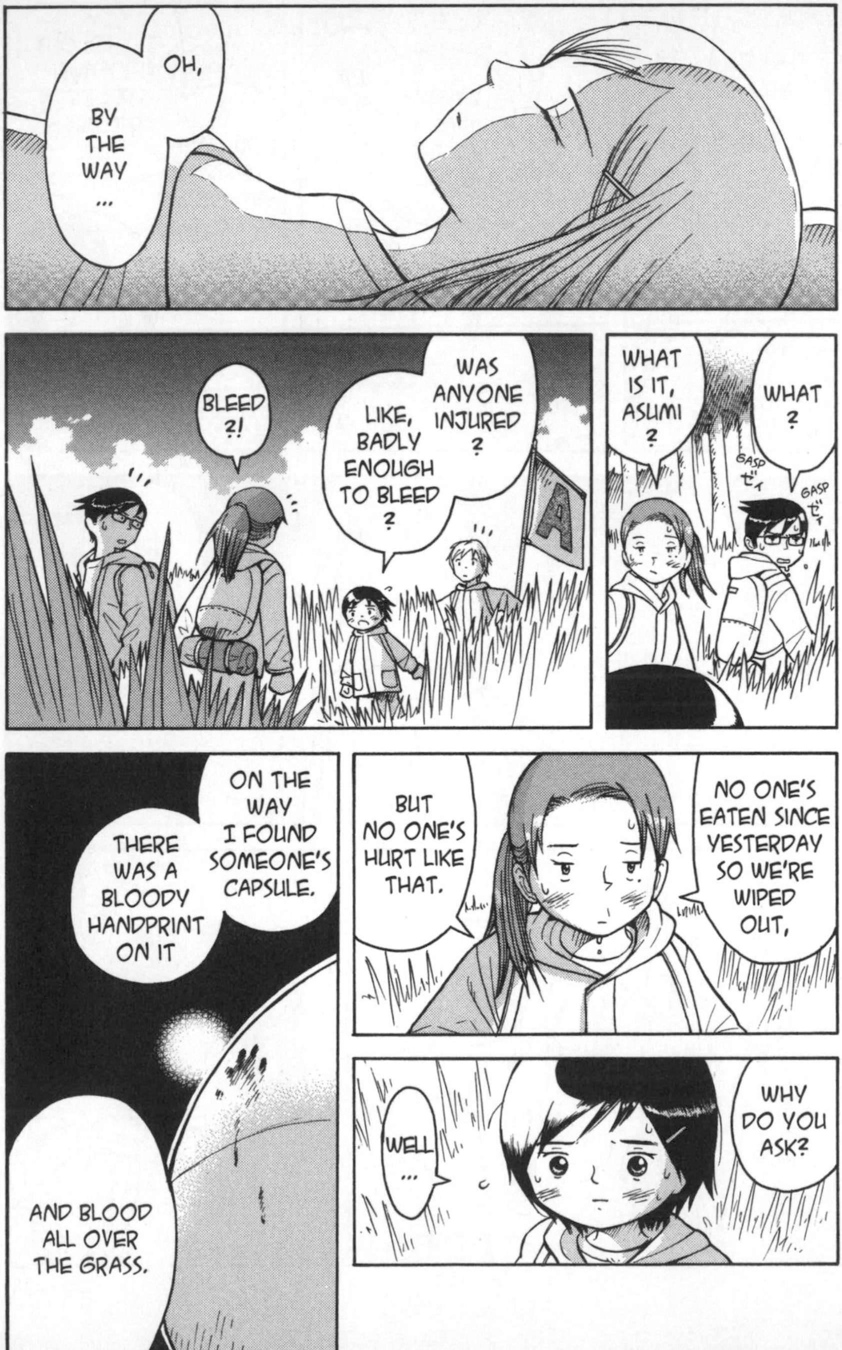
OH,
BY THE WAY ...
WHAT ?
GASP ゼィ
GASP ゼィ
WHAT IS IT, ASUMI ?
WAS ANYONE INJURED ?
LIKE, BADLY ENOUGH TO BLEED ?
BLEED ?!
NO ONE'S EATEN SINCE YESTERDAY SO WE'RE WIPED OUT,
BUT NO ONE'S HURT LIKE THAT.
WHY DO YOU ASK?
WELL ...
ON THE WAY I FOUND SOMEONE'S CAPSULE.
THERE WAS A BLOODY HANDPRINT ON IT
AND BLOOD ALL OVER THE GRASS.

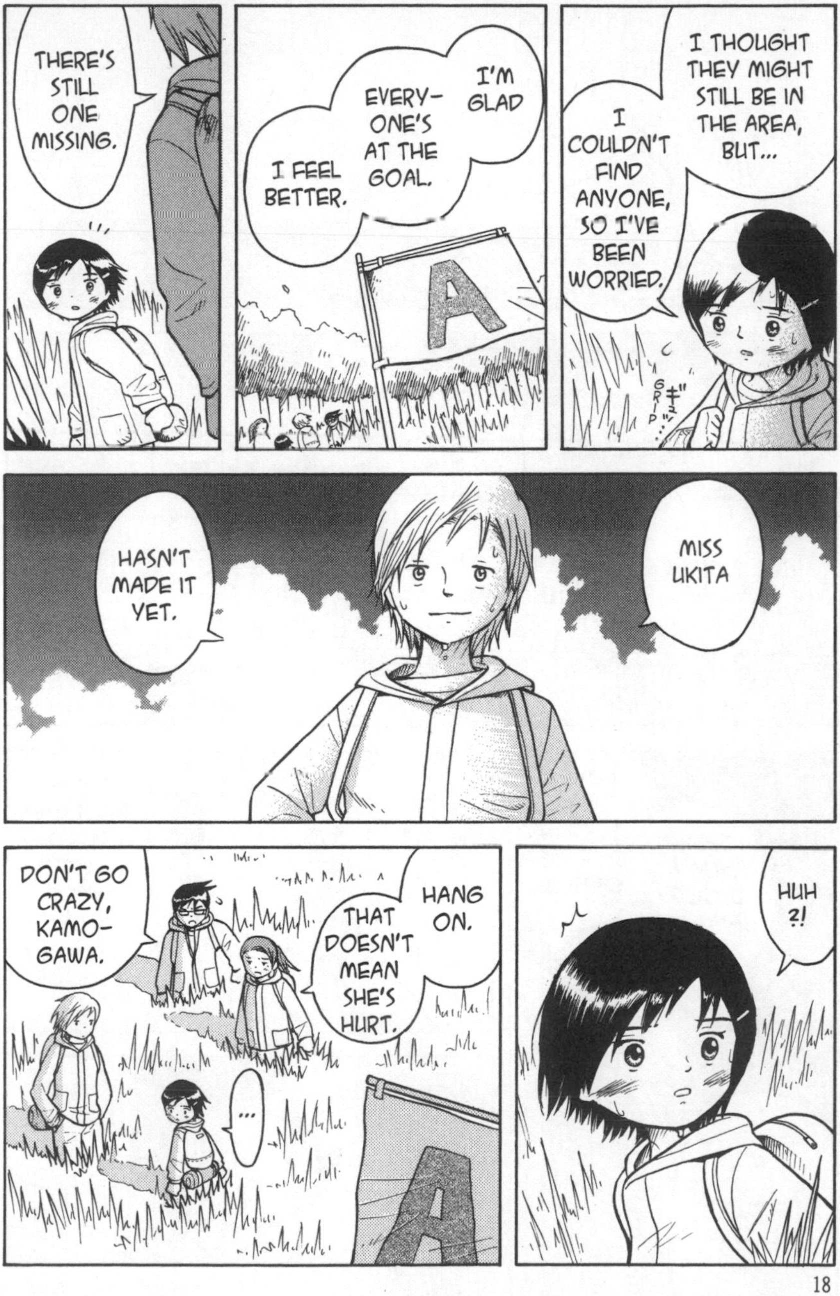

I THOUGHT THEY MIGHT STILL BE IN THE AREA, BUT...
I COULDN'T FIND ANYONE, SO I'VE BEEN WORRIED.
GRIP
I'M GLAD EVERY-ONE'S AT THE GOAL.
I FEEL BETTER.
THERE'S STILL ONE MISSING.
MISS UKITA
HASN'T MADE IT YET.
HUH ?!
HANG ON.
THAT DOESN'T MEAN SHE'S HURT.
DON'T GO CRAZY, KAMO-GAWA.
...

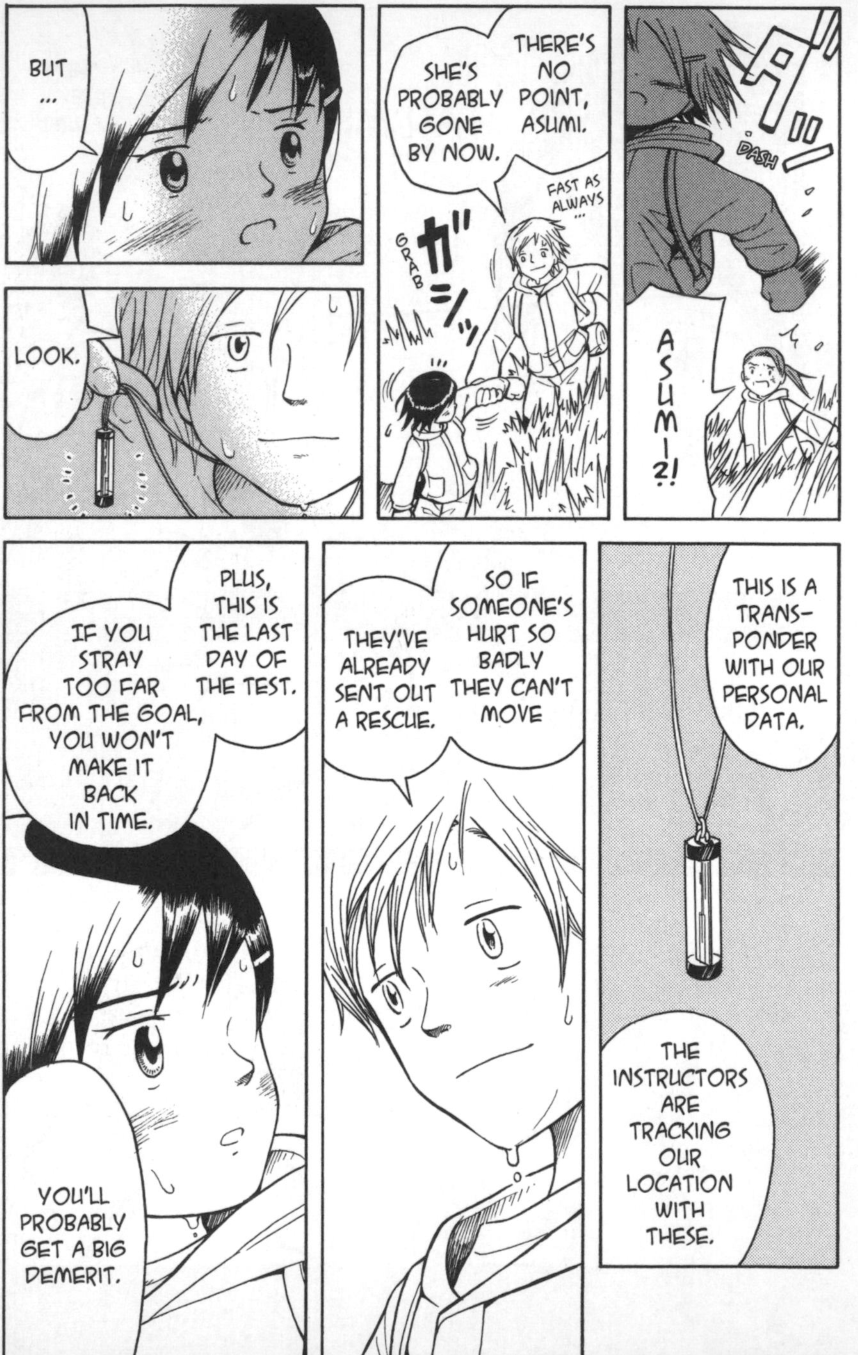
DASH
ASUMI?!
THERE'S NO POINT, ASUMI.
SHE'S PROBABLY GONE BY NOW.
FAST AS ALWAYS ...
GRAB
BUT ...
LOOK.
THIS IS A TRANS-PONDER WITH OUR PERSONAL DATA.
THE INSTRUCTORS ARE TRACKING OUR LOCATION WITH THESE.
SO IF SOMEONE'S HURT SO BADLY THEY CAN'T MOVE
THEY'VE ALREADY SENT OUT A RESCUE.
PLUS, THIS IS THE LAST DAY OF THE TEST.
IF YOU STRAY TOO FAR FROM THE GOAL, YOU WON'T MAKE IT BACK IN TIME.
YOU'LL PROBABLY GET A BIG DEMERIT.

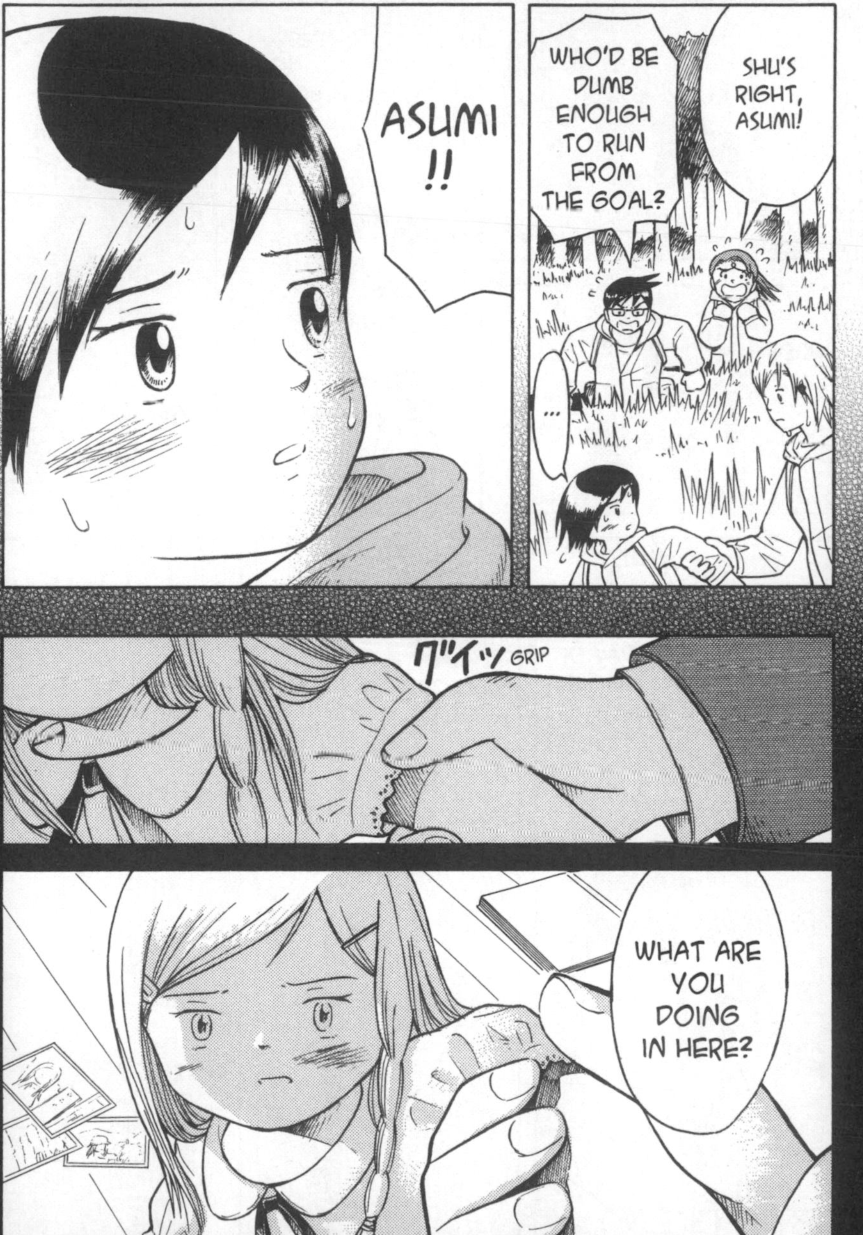
SHU'S RIGHT, ASUMI!
WHO'D BE DUMB ENOUGH TO RUN FROM THE GOAL?
...
ASUMI !!
グイッ GRIP
WHAT ARE YOU DOING IN HERE?

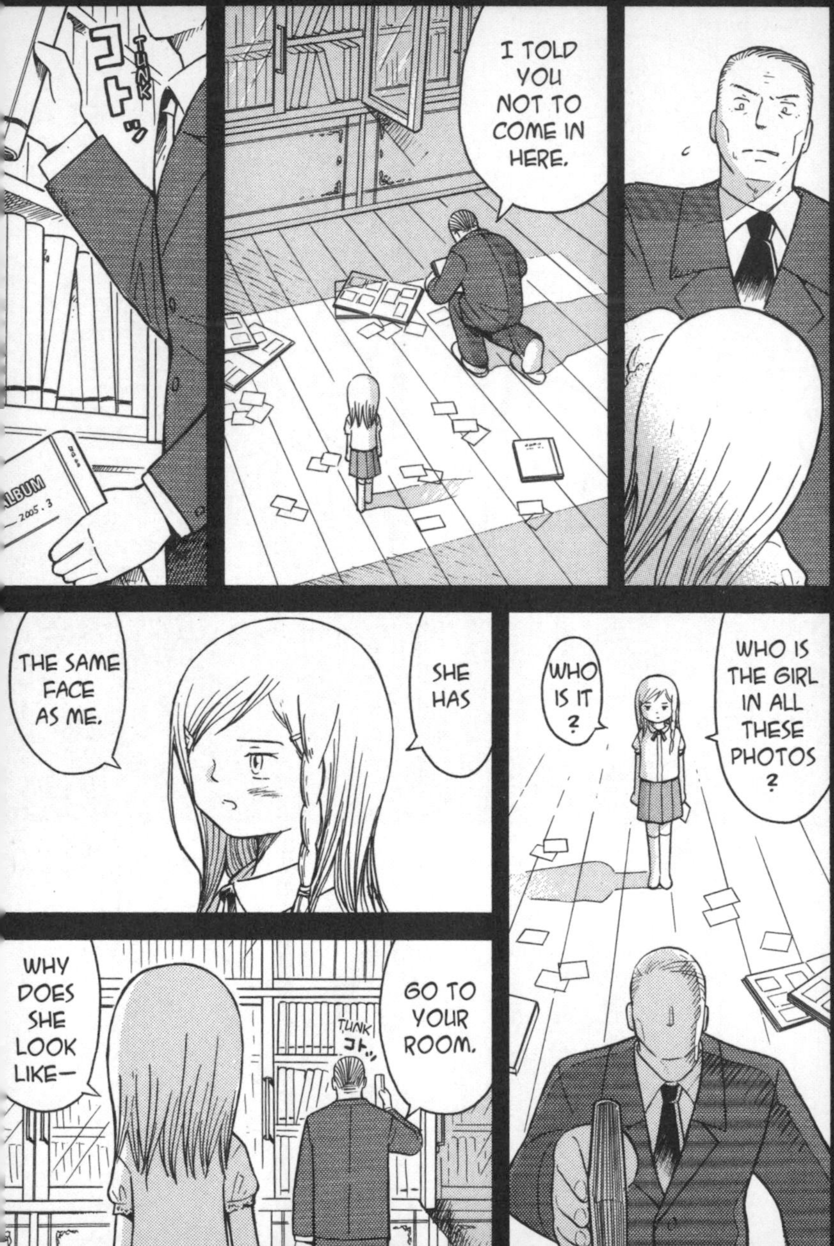
I TOLD YOU NOT TO COME IN HERE.
TUNK
コトッ
ALBUM
2005.3
WHO IS THE GIRL IN ALL THESE PHOTOS?
WHO IS IT?
SHE HAS
THE SAME FACE AS ME.
GO TO YOUR ROOM.
TUNK
コトッ
WHY DOES SHE LOOK LIKE—

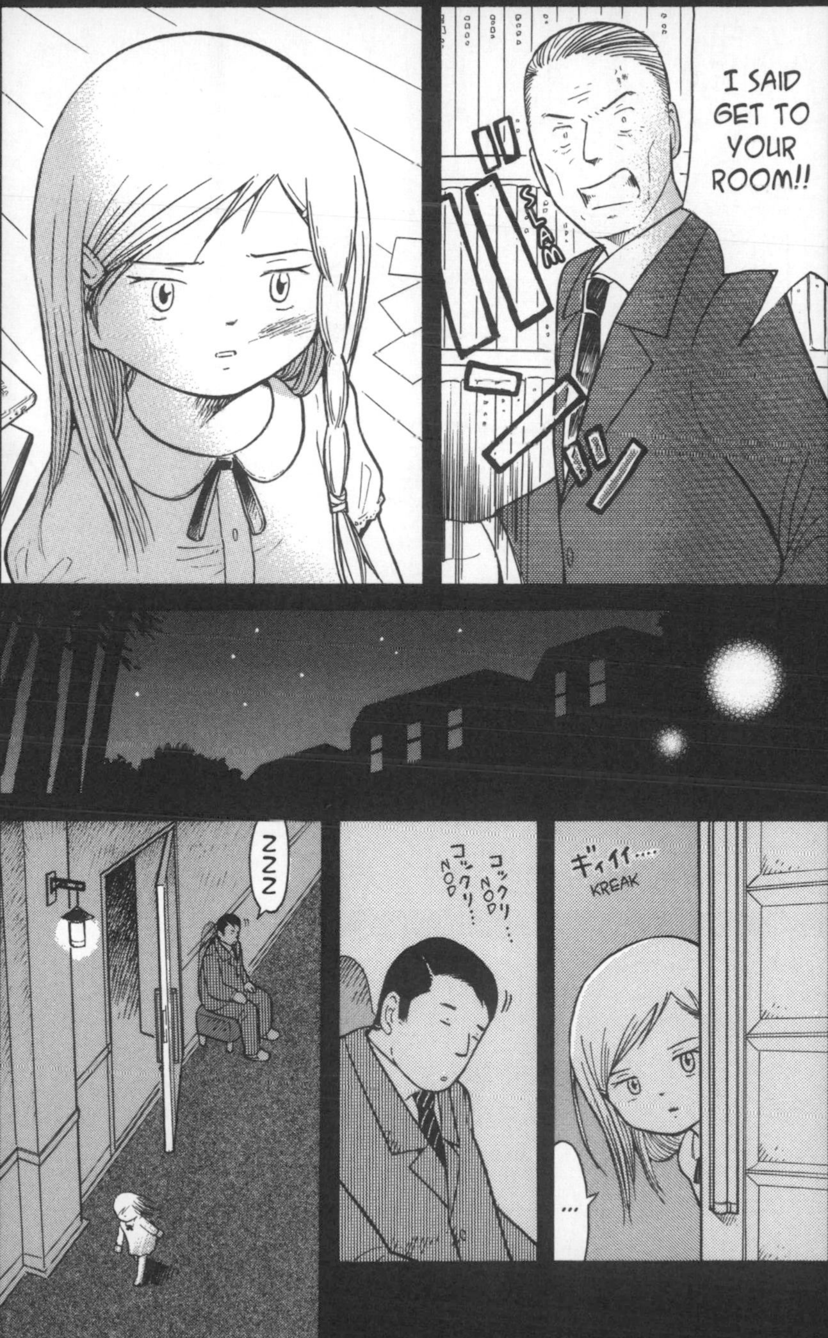
I SAID GET TO YOUR ROOM!!
SLAM
ギィイ…
KREAK
...
コックリ
NOD
コックリ…
NOD
ZZZ

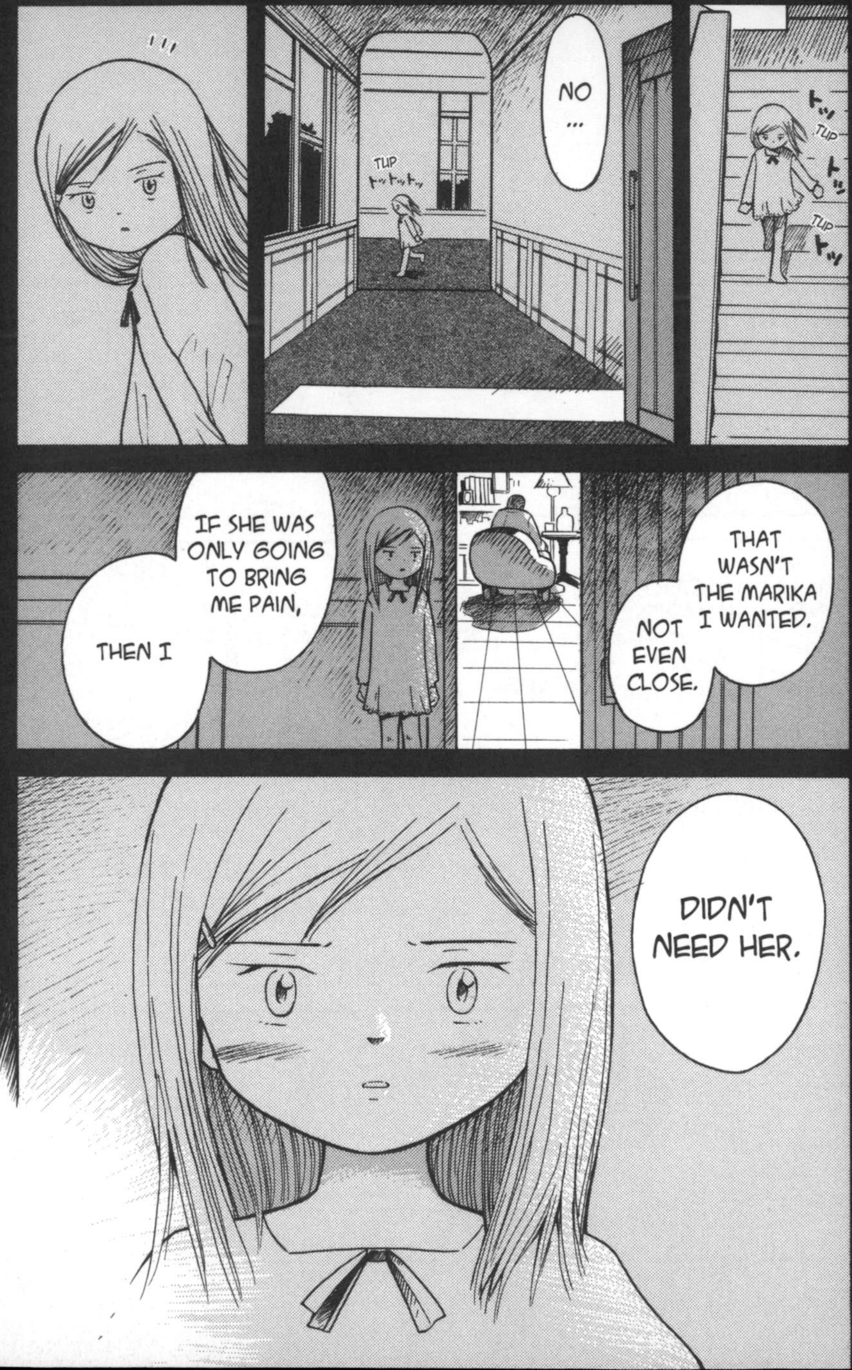
TUP
TUP
NO ...
TUP
THAT WASN'T THE MARIKA I WANTED.
NOT EVEN CLOSE.
IF SHE WAS ONLY GOING TO BRING ME PAIN,
THEN I
DIDN'T NEED HER.

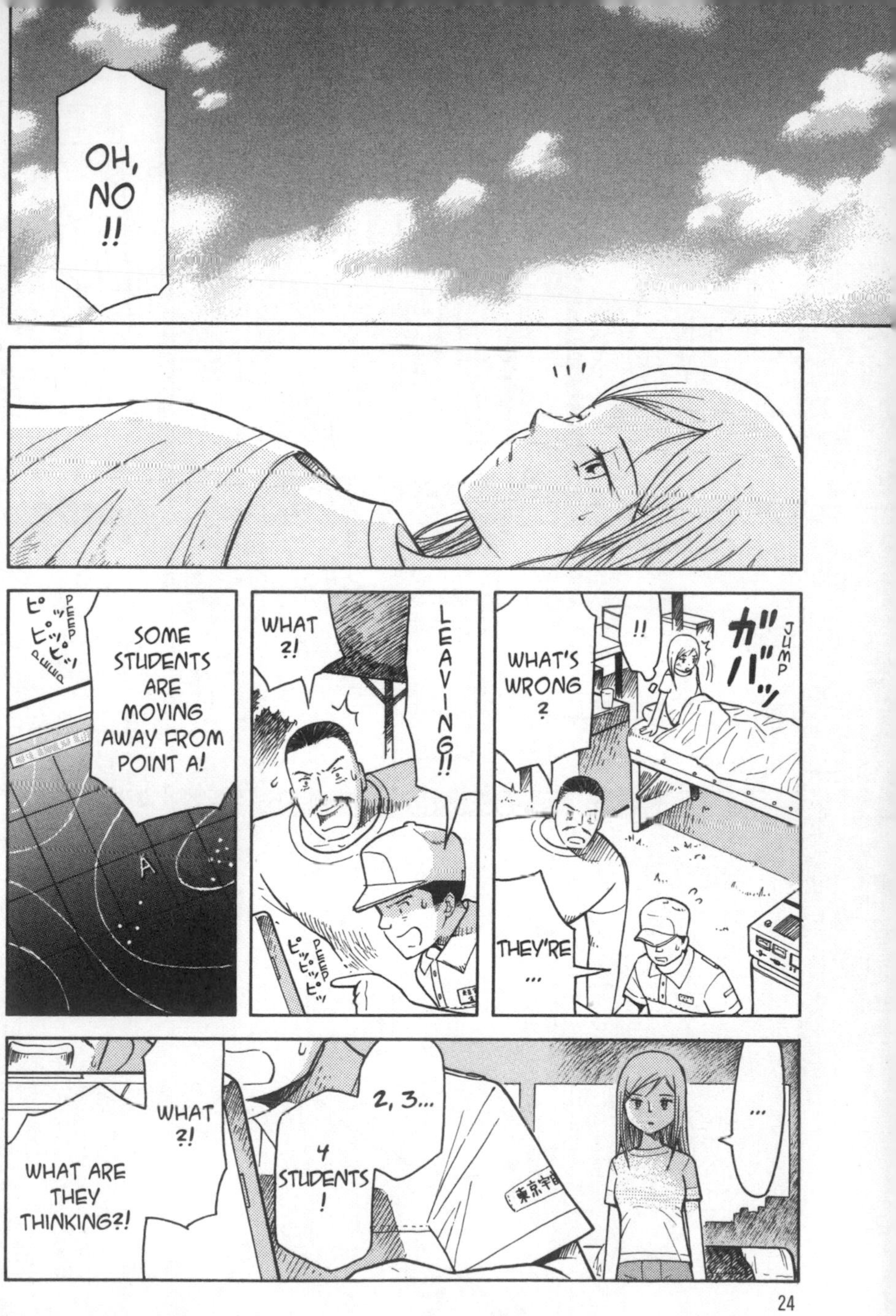
OH, NO!!
ガバッ JUMP
!!
WHAT'S WRONG?
THEY'RE ...
LEAVING!!
WHAT?!
ピッピッピッ PEEP
ピッピッピッ PEEP
SOME STUDENTS ARE MOVING AWAY FROM POINT A!
A
...
2, 3...
4 STUDENTS!
WHAT?!
WHAT ARE THEY THINKING?!

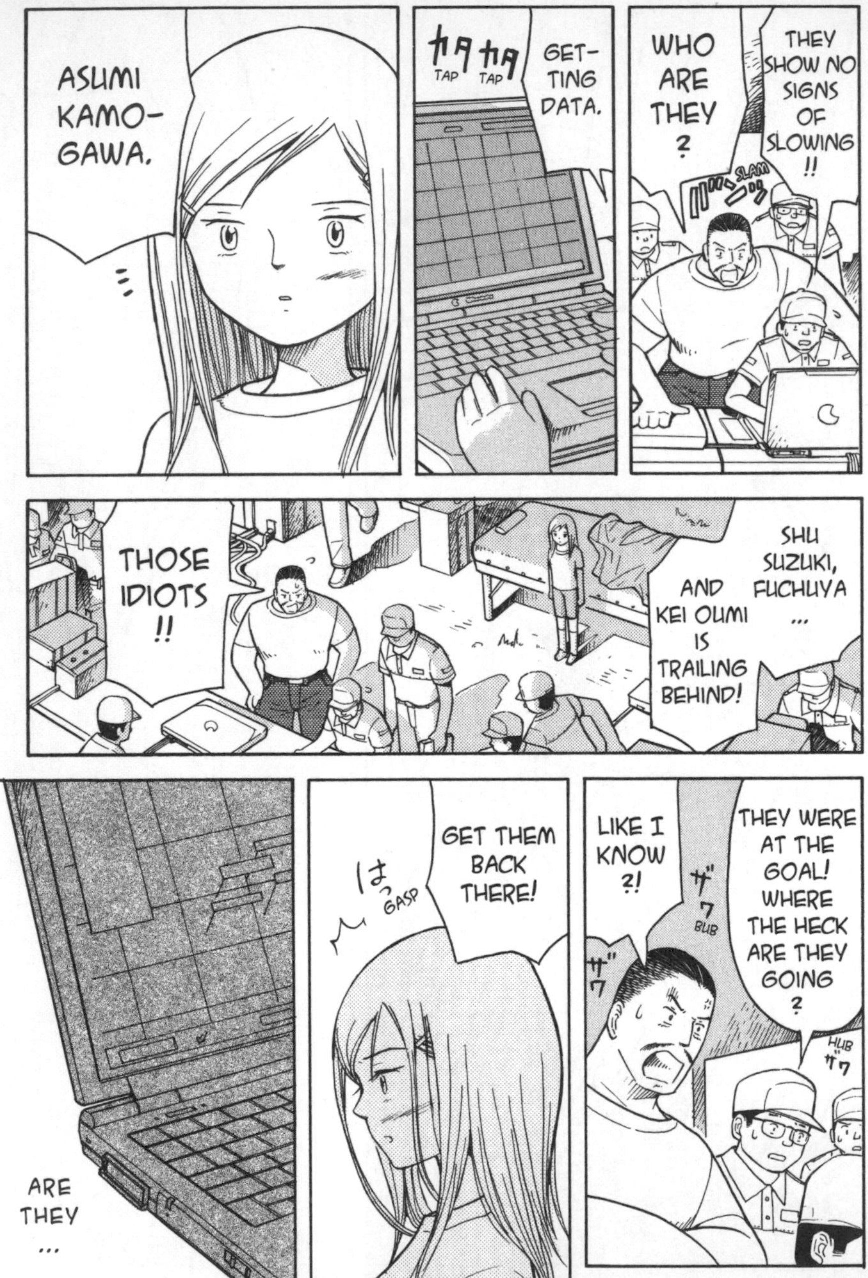
THEY SHOW NO SIGNS OF SLOWING !!
WHO ARE THEY ?
SLAM
カタカタ
TAP TAP
GET-TING DATA.
ASUMI KAMO-GAWA.
SHU SUZUKI, FUCHUYA ...
AND KEI OUMI IS TRAILING BEHIND!
THOSE IDIOTS !!
THEY WERE AT THE GOAL! WHERE THE HECK ARE THEY GOING ?
ザワ
BUB
LIKE I KNOW ?!
HUB
ザワ
GET THEM BACK THERE!
はっ
GASP
ARE THEY ...

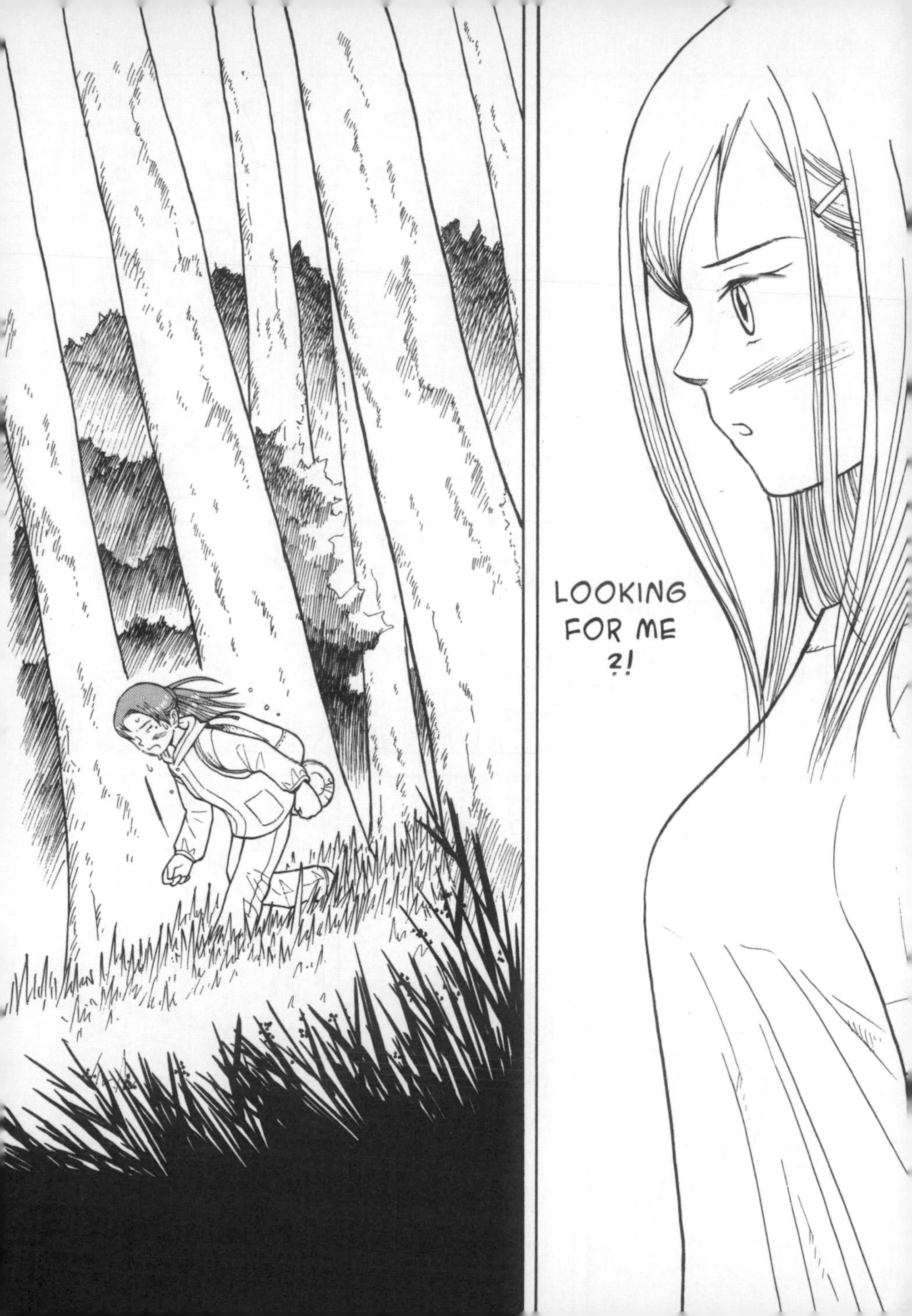
LOOKING FOR ME ?!

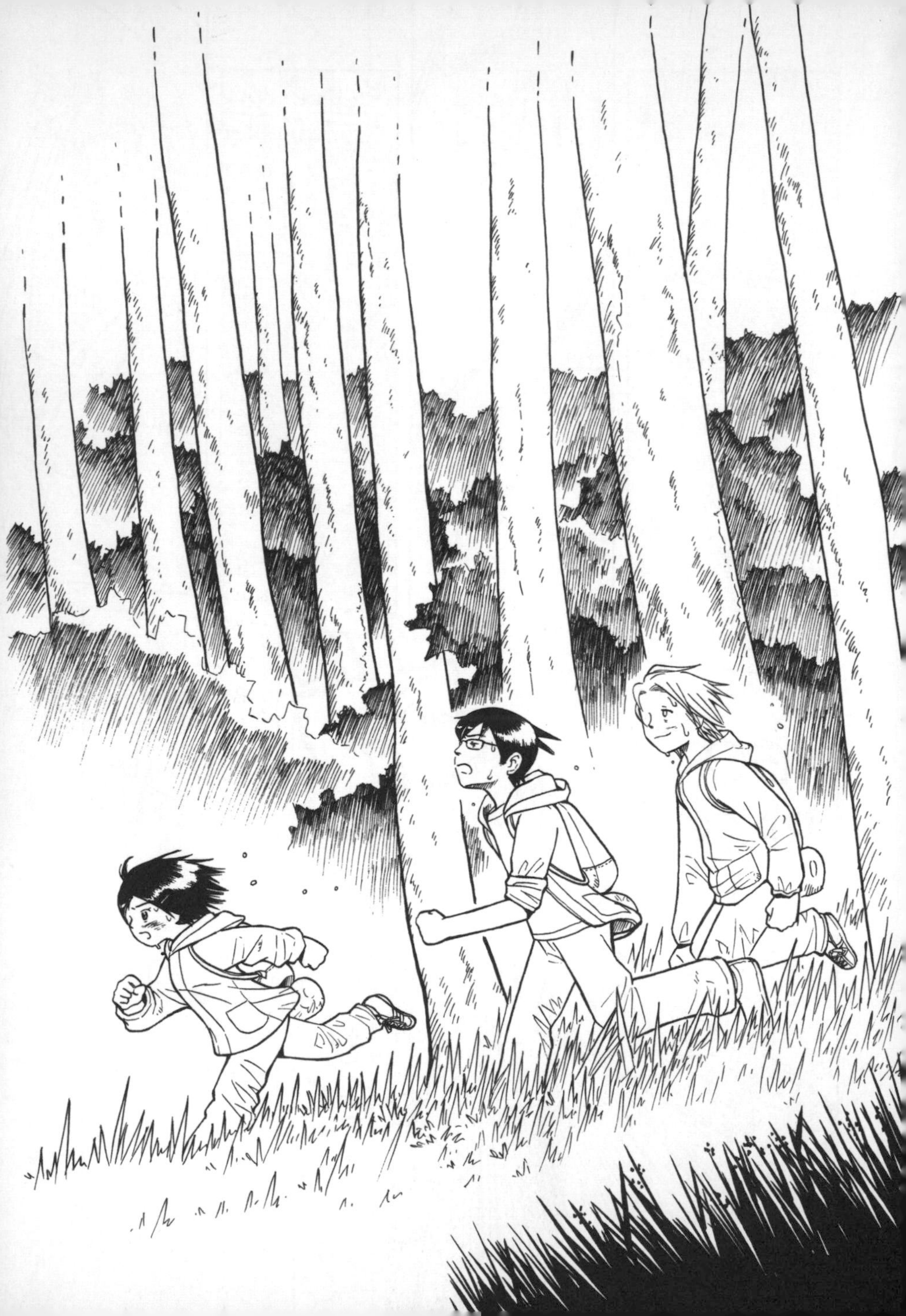

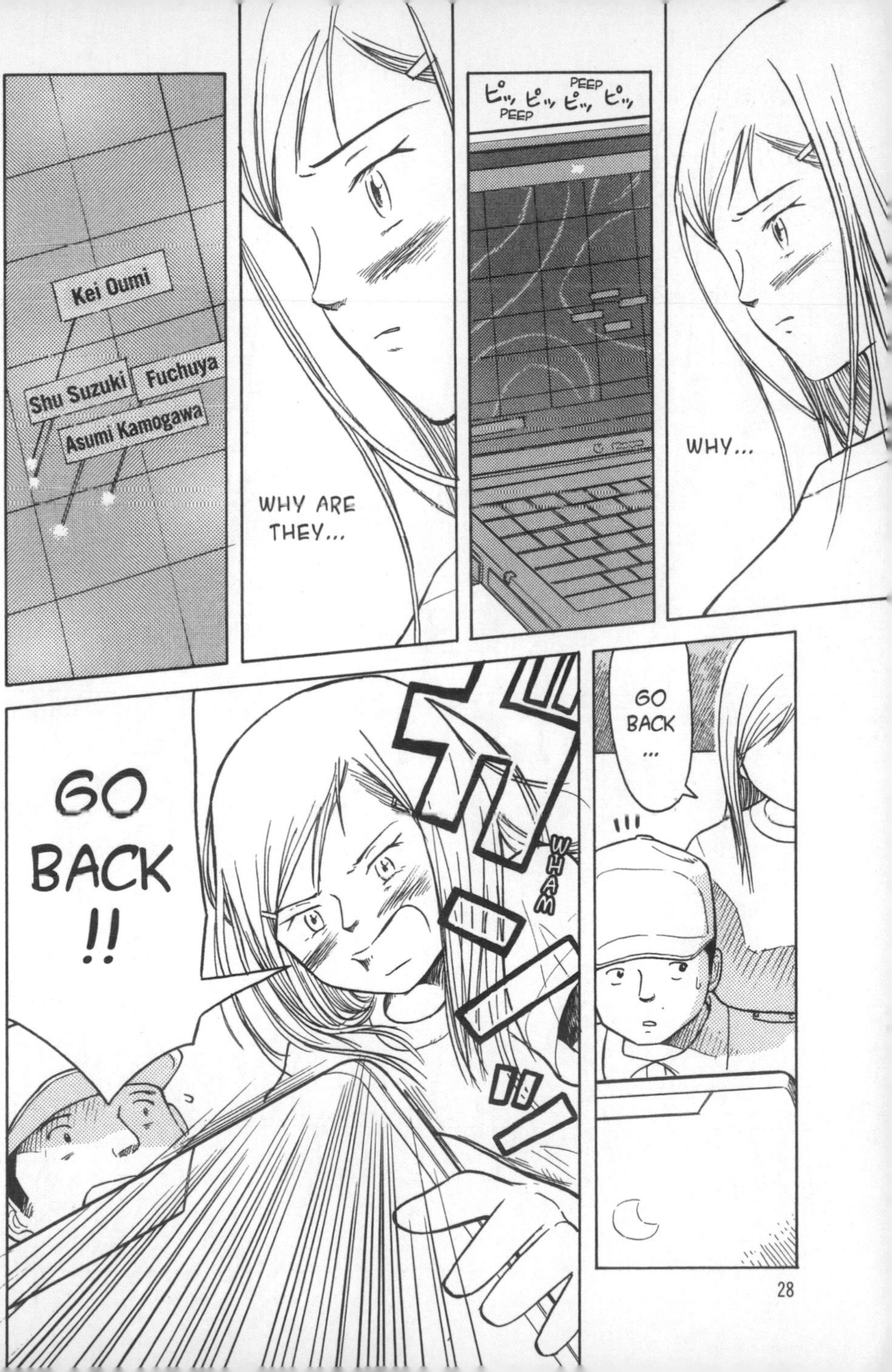
WHY...
ピッ ピッ ピッ ピッ
PEEP
PEEP
WHY ARE THEY...
Kei Oumi
Fuchuya
Shu Suzuki
Asumi Kamogawa
GO BACK ...
!!!
GO BACK !!
WHAM

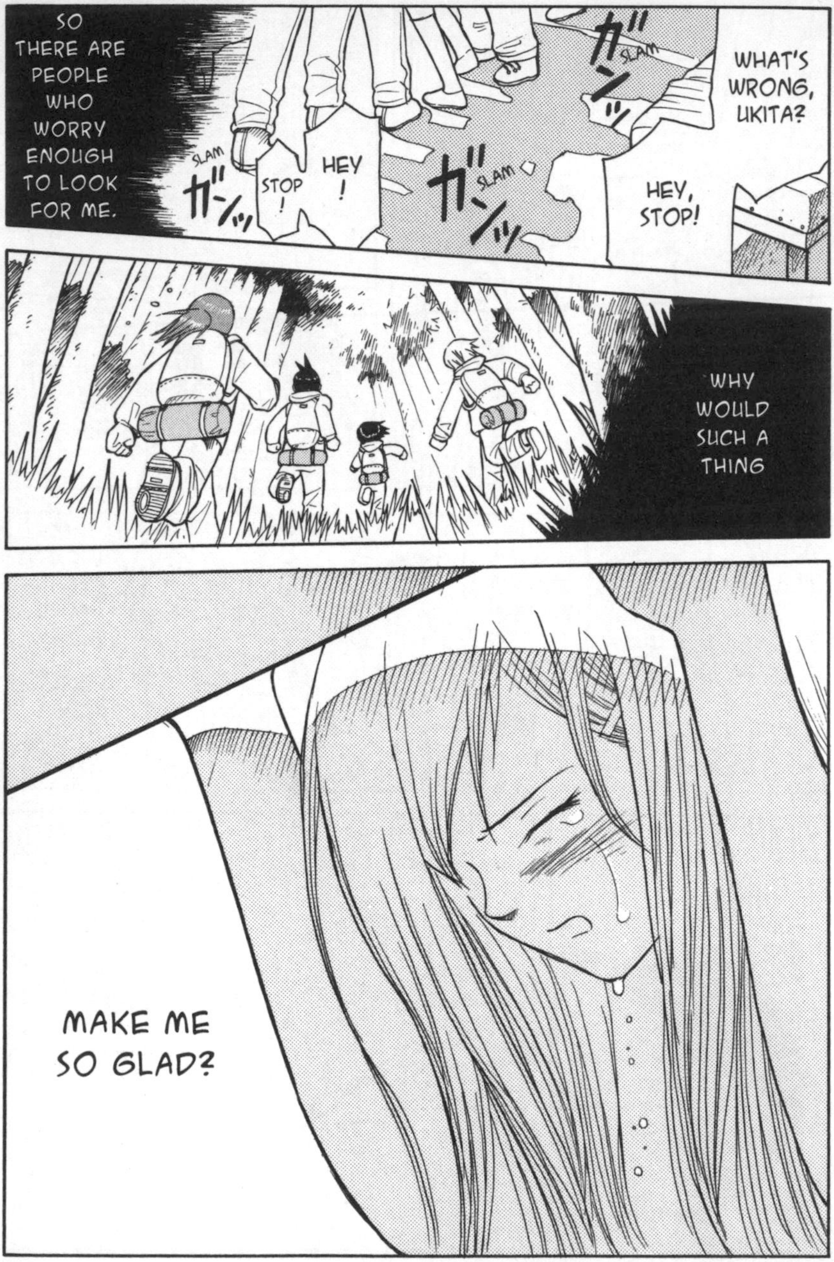
WHAT'S WRONG, UKITA?
SLAM
HEY, STOP!
SLAM
HEY!
STOP!
SLAM
SO THERE ARE PEOPLE WHO WORRY ENOUGH TO LOOK FOR ME.
WHY WOULD SUCH A THING
MAKE ME SO GLAD?

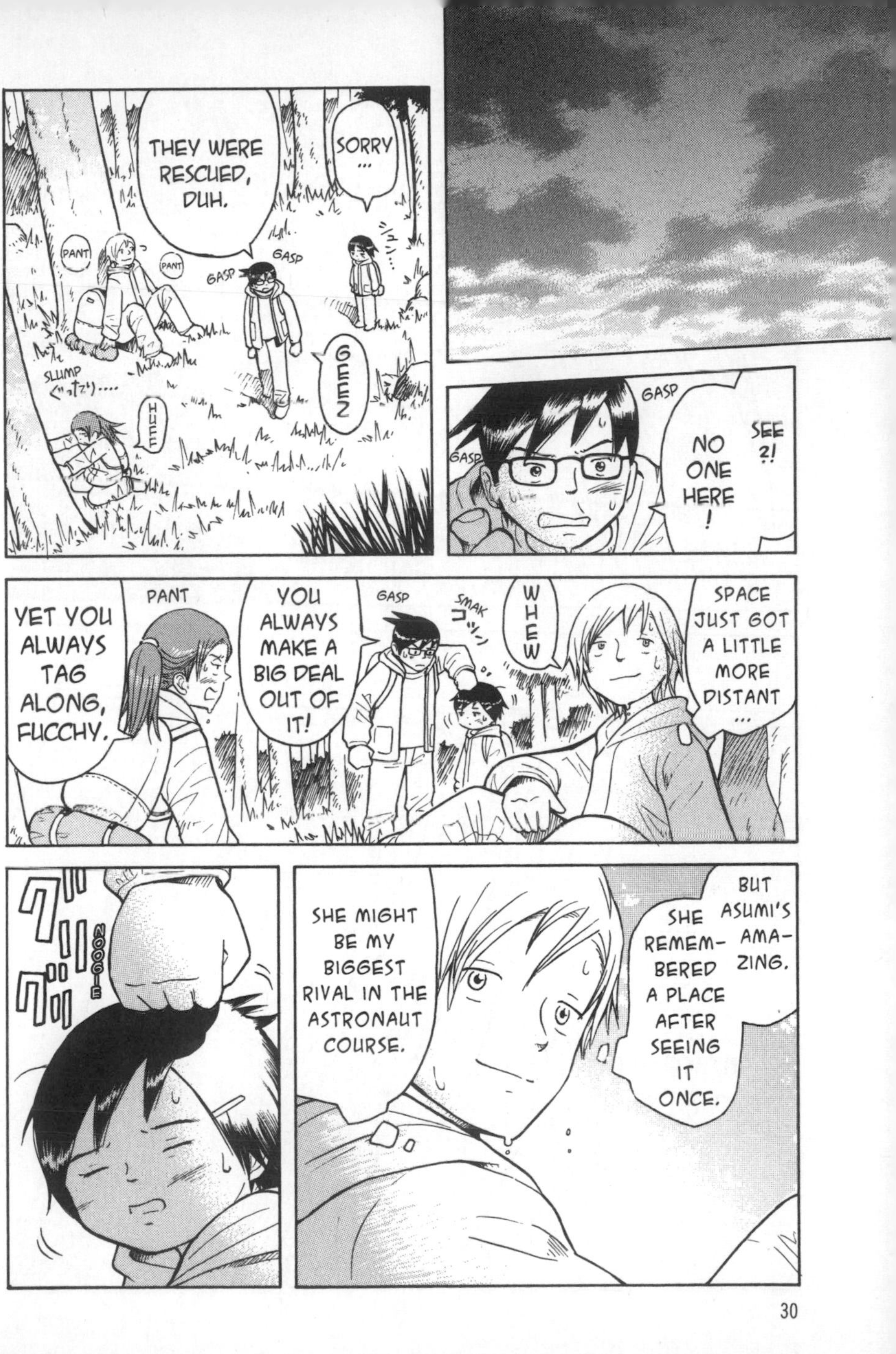
GASP
SEE ?!
NO ONE HERE !
GASP
SORRY ...
THEY WERE RESCUED, DUH.
GASP
GASP
PANT
PANT
GEEZ
HUFF
SLUMP
SPACE JUST GOT A LITTLE MORE DISTANT ...
WHEW
SMAK
GASP
YOU ALWAYS MAKE A BIG DEAL OUT OF IT!
PANT
YET YOU ALWAYS TAG ALONG, FUCCHY.
BUT ASUMI'S AMA-ZING.
SHE REMEM-BERED A PLACE AFTER SEEING IT ONCE.
SHE MIGHT BE MY BIGGEST RIVAL IN THE ASTRONAUT COURSE.
NOOGIE

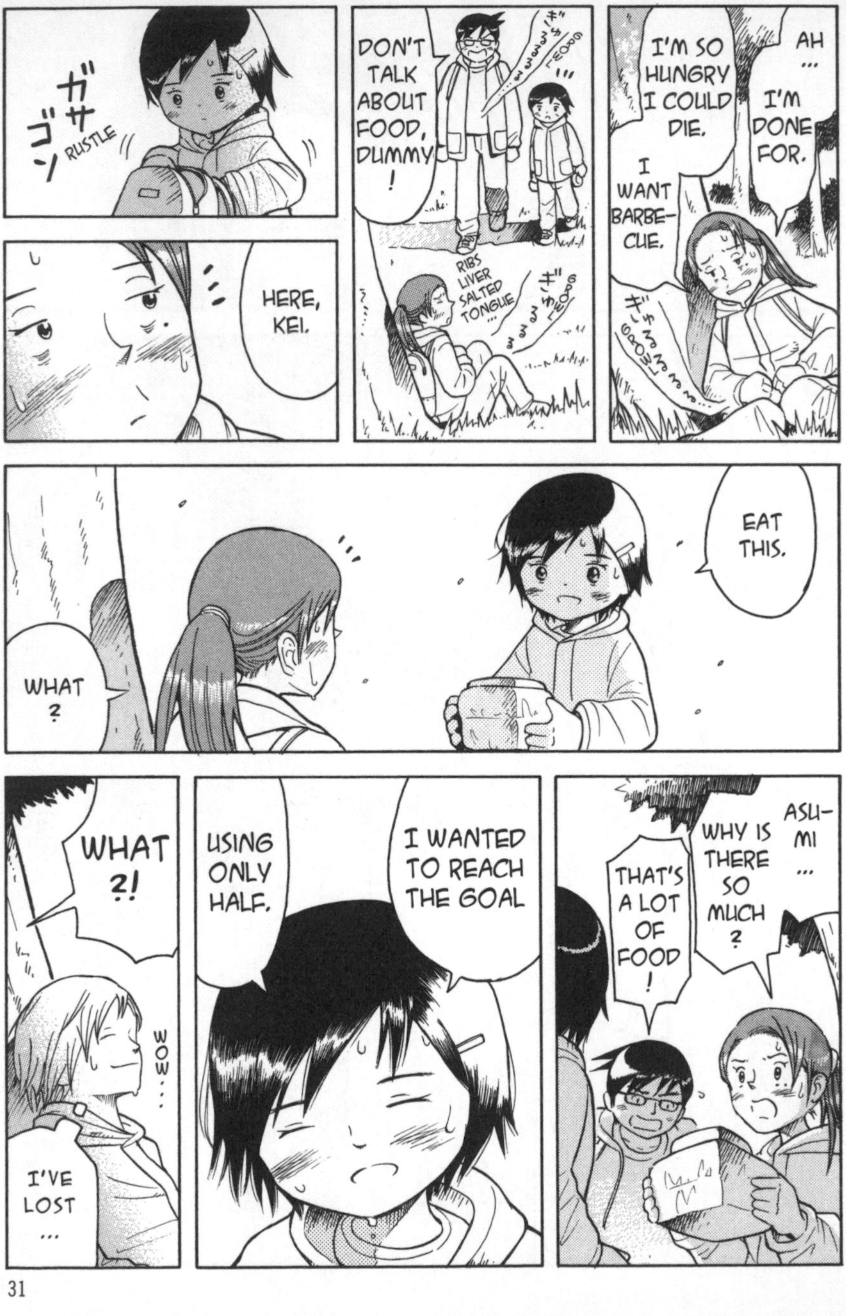
AH ... I'M DONE FOR.
I'M SO HUNGRY I COULD DIE.
I WANT BARBE-CUE.
GROWL
DON'T TALK ABOUT FOOD, DUMMY!
RIBS LIVER SALTED TONGUE ...
GROWL
ガサゴソ
RUSTLE
HERE, KEI.
EAT THIS.
WHAT?
ASU-MI ...
WHY IS THERE SO MUCH?
THAT'S A LOT OF FOOD!
I WANTED TO REACH THE GOAL
USING ONLY HALF.
WHAT?!
WOW...
I'VE LOST ...

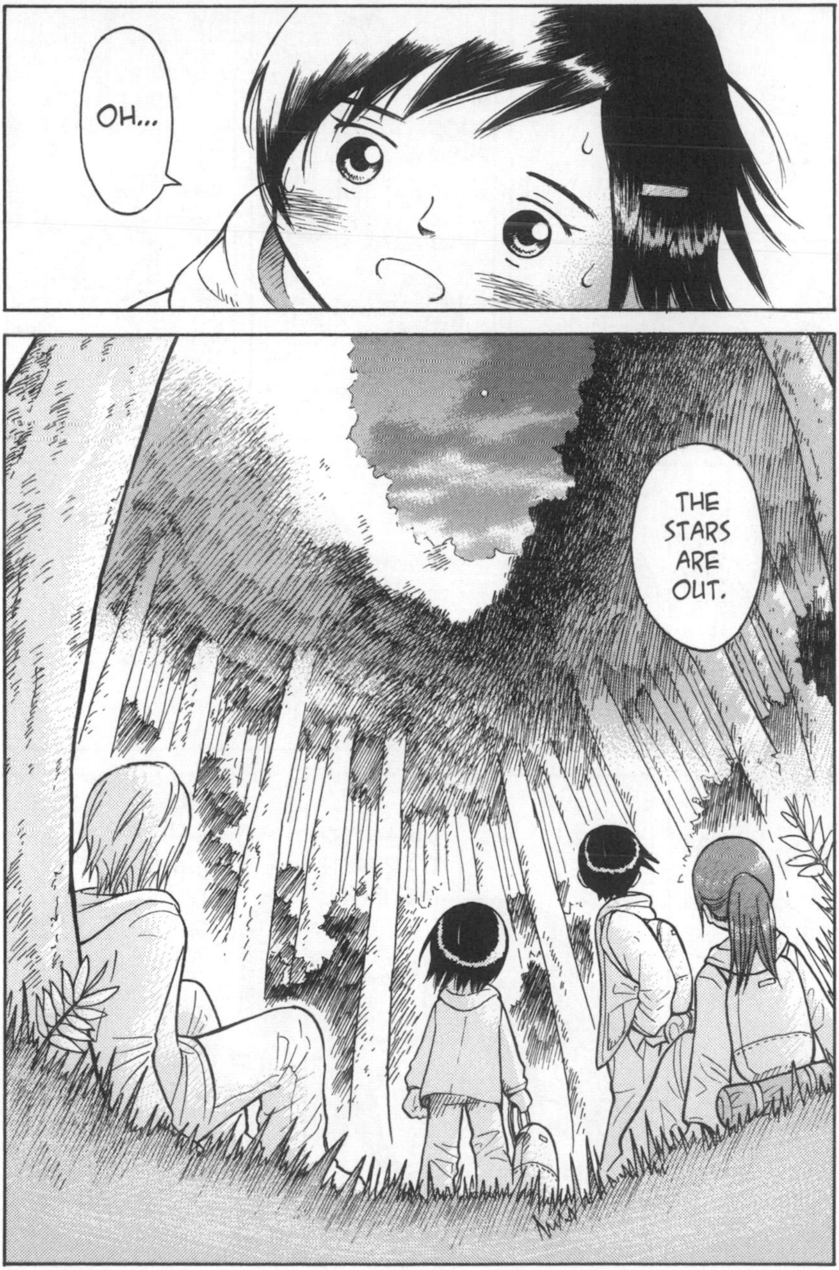
OH...
THE STARS ARE OUT.

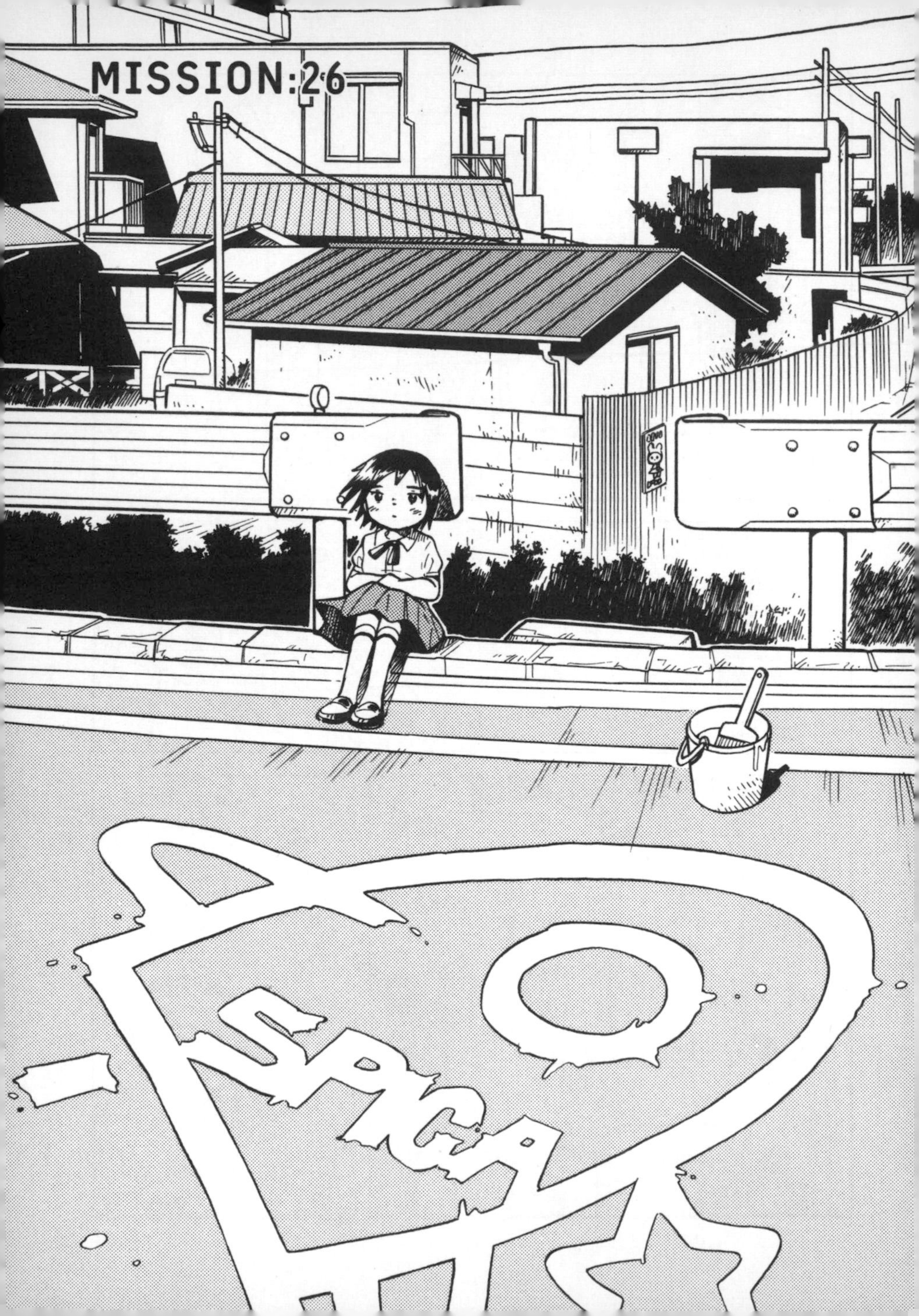
MISSION:26

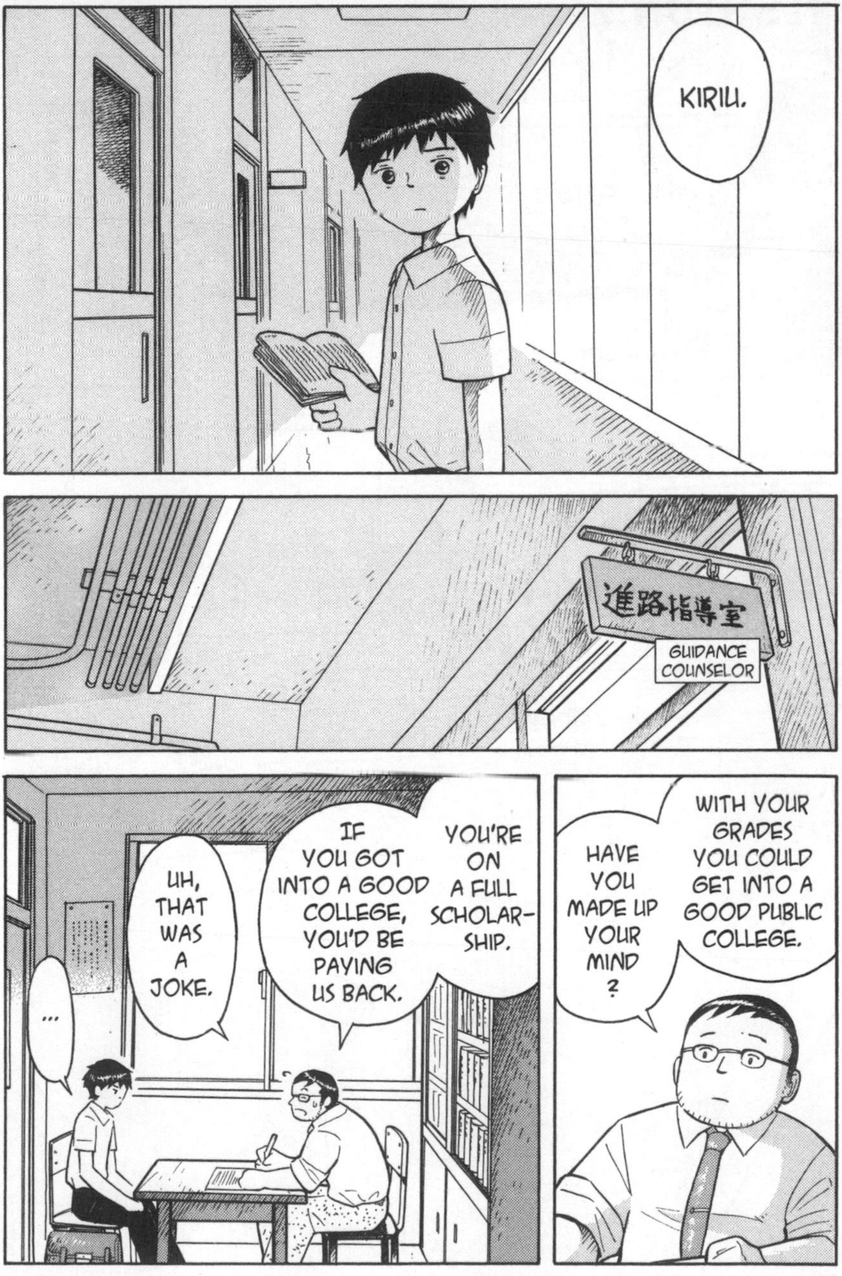
KIRIU.
進路指導室
GUIDANCE COUNSELOR
WITH YOUR GRADES YOU COULD GET INTO A GOOD PUBLIC COLLEGE.
HAVE YOU MADE UP YOUR MIND?
YOU'RE ON A FULL SCHOLARSHIP.
IF YOU GOT INTO A GOOD COLLEGE, YOU'D BE PAYING US BACK.
UH, THAT WAS A JOKE.
...

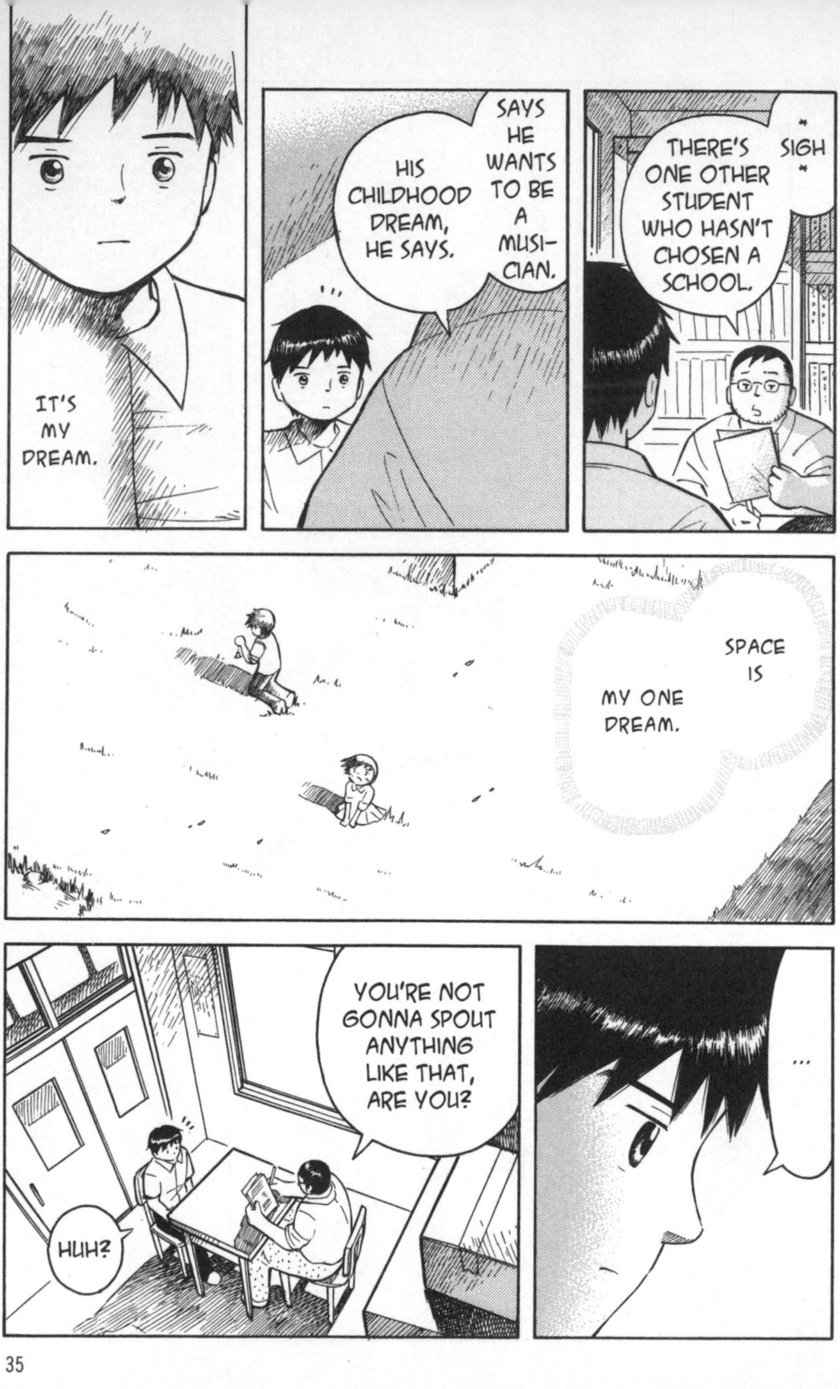
SIGH
THERE'S ONE OTHER STUDENT WHO HASN'T CHOSEN A SCHOOL.
SAYS HE WANTS TO BE A MUSI-CIAN. HIS CHILDHOOD DREAM, HE SAYS.
IT'S MY DREAM.
SPACE IS MY ONE DREAM.
...
YOU'RE NOT GONNA SPOUT ANYTHING LIKE THAT, ARE YOU?
HUH?

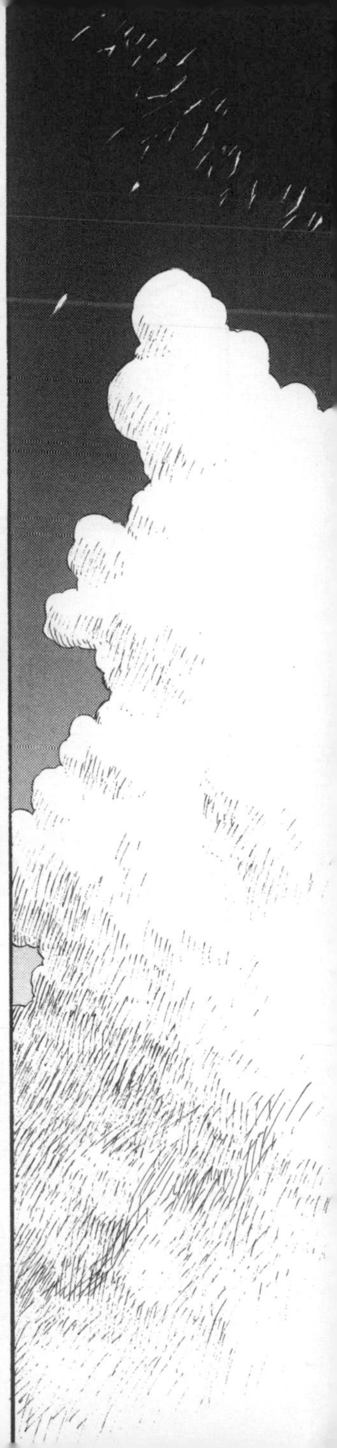

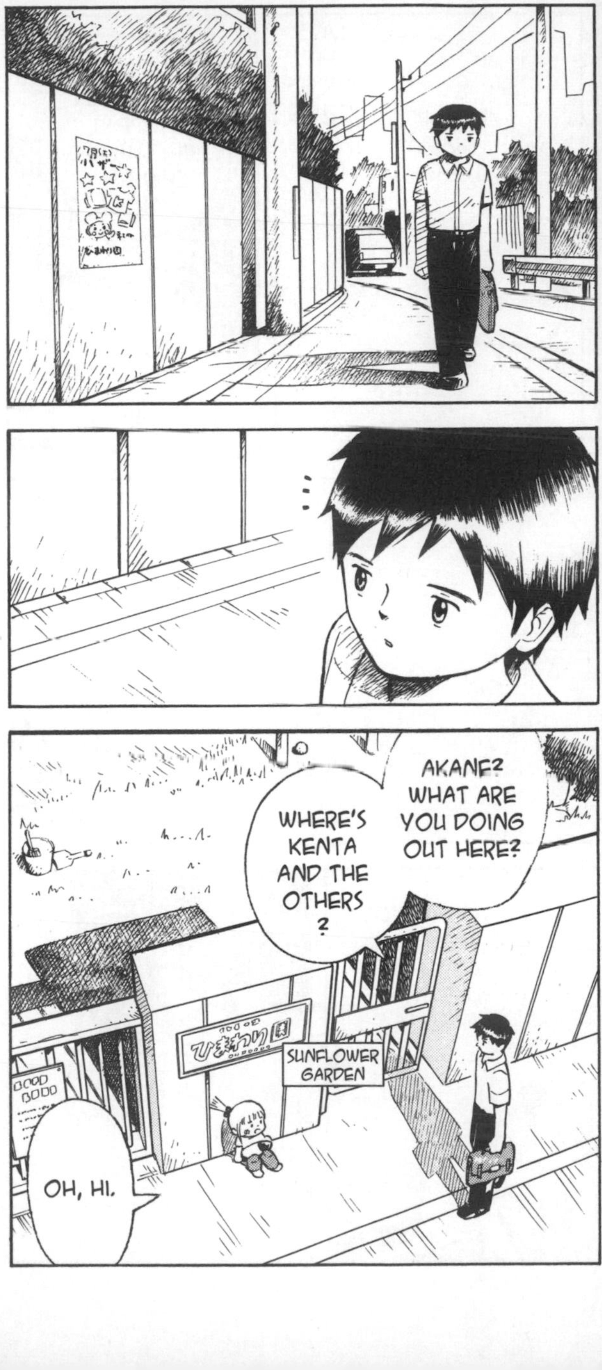
AKANE? WHAT ARE YOU DOING OUT HERE?
WHERE'S KENTA AND THE OTHERS?
ひまわり園
SUNFLOWER GARDEN
OH, HI.

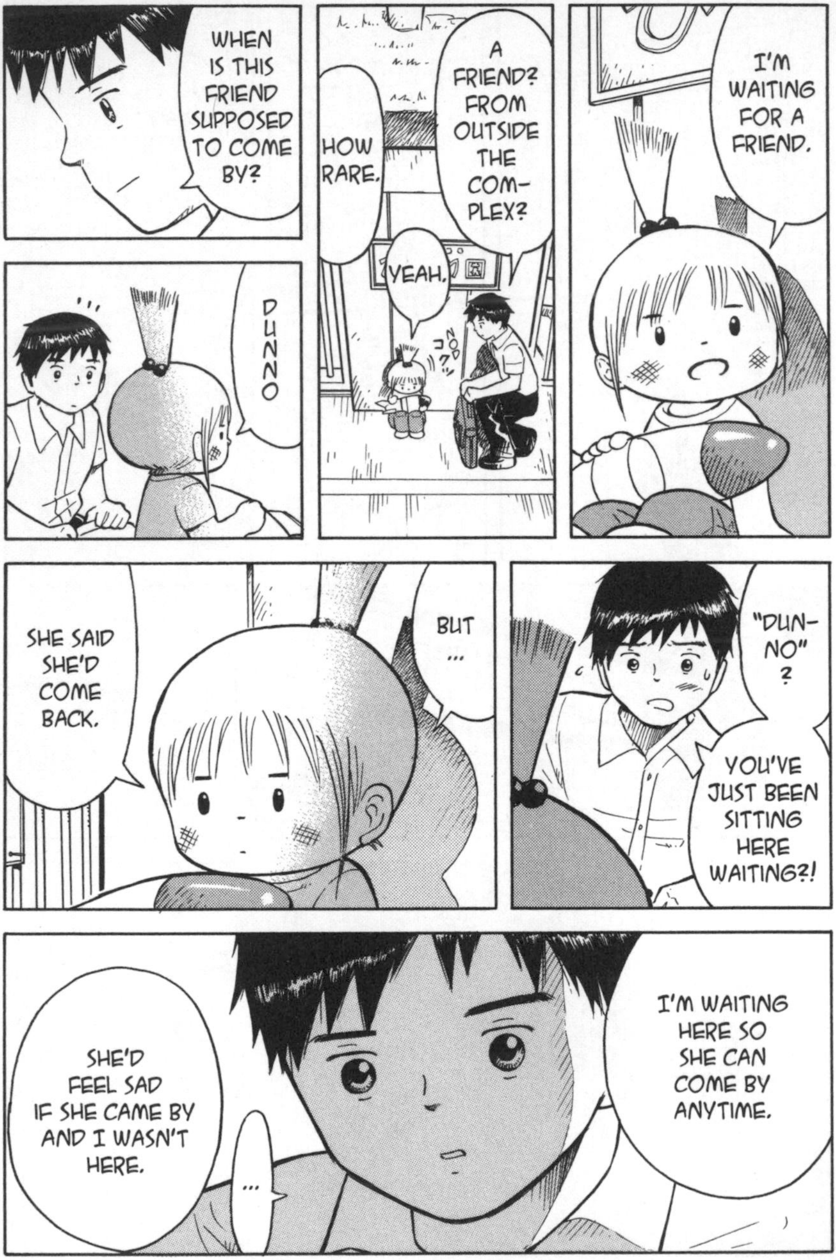
I'M WAITING FOR A FRIEND.
A FRIEND? FROM OUTSIDE THE COM-PLEX?
HOW RARE.
YEAH.
NOD
WHEN IS THIS FRIEND SUPPOSED TO COME BY?
DUNNO
"DUN-NO" ?
YOU'VE JUST BEEN SITTING HERE WAITING?!
BUT ...
SHE SAID SHE'D COME BACK.
I'M WAITING HERE SO SHE CAN COME BY ANYTIME.
SHE'D FEEL SAD IF SHE CAME BY AND I WASN'T HERE.
...

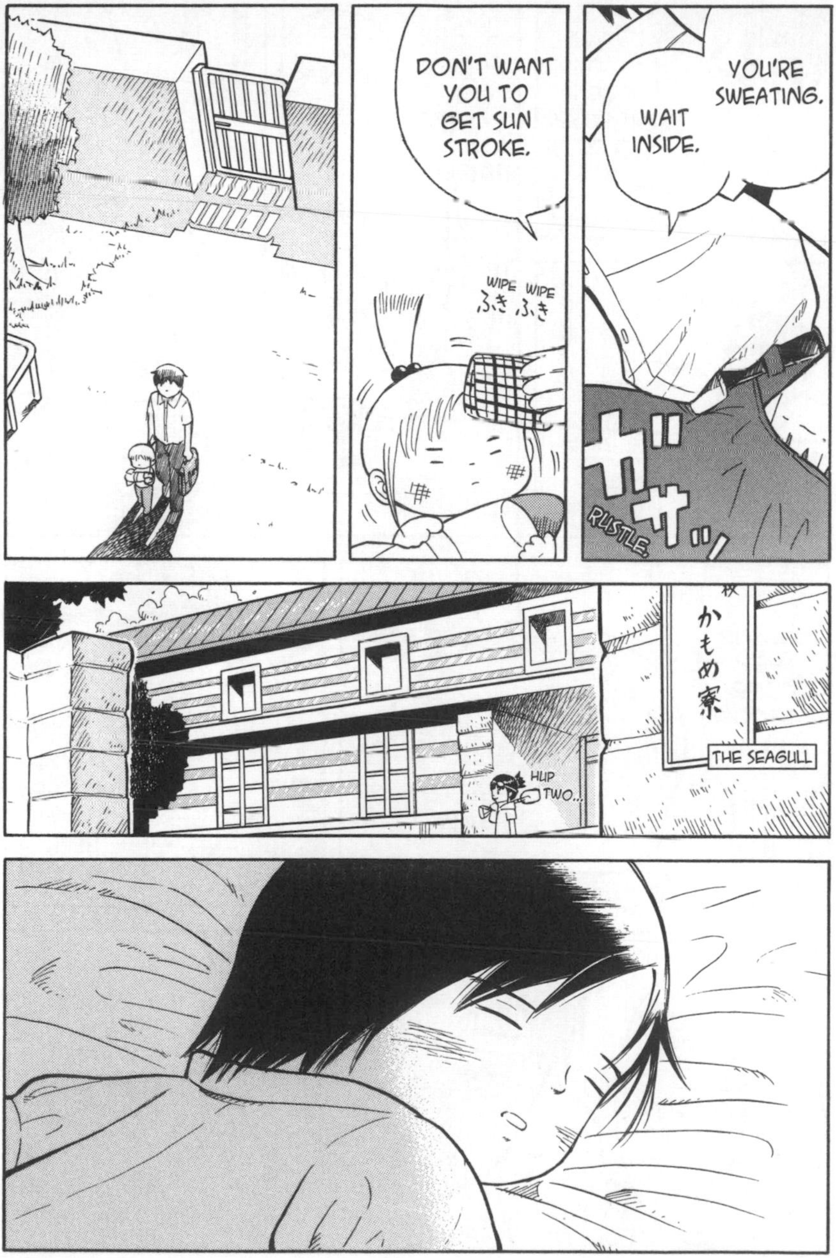

YOU'RE SWEATING.
WAIT INSIDE.
RUSTLE
ガサッ
DON'T WANT YOU TO GET SUN STROKE.
WIPE WIPE
ふきふき
かもめ寮
THE SEAGULL
HUP TWO...

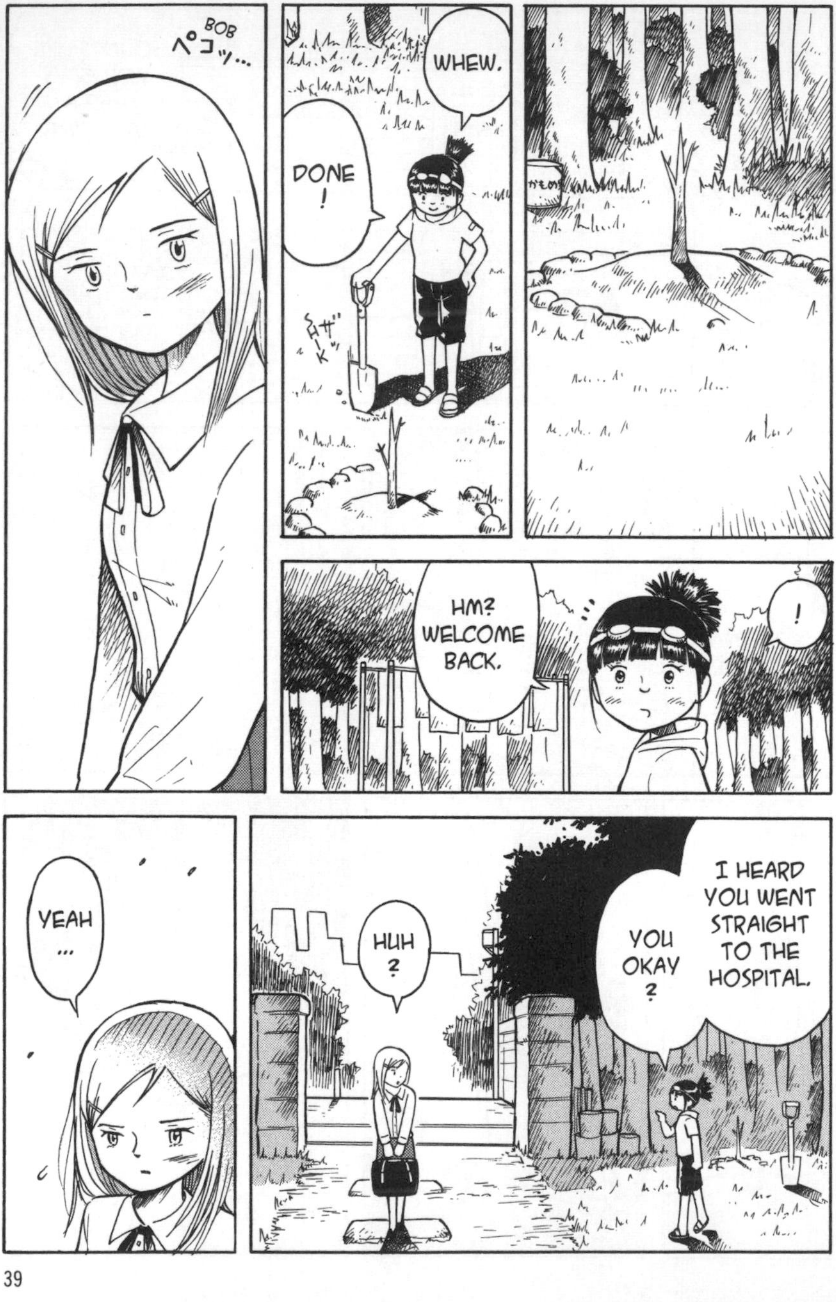
WHEW.
DONE !
SHIK ザッ
!
HM? WELCOME BACK.
BOB ペコッ…
I HEARD YOU WENT STRAIGHT TO THE HOSPITAL.
YOU OKAY ?
HUH ?
YEAH …

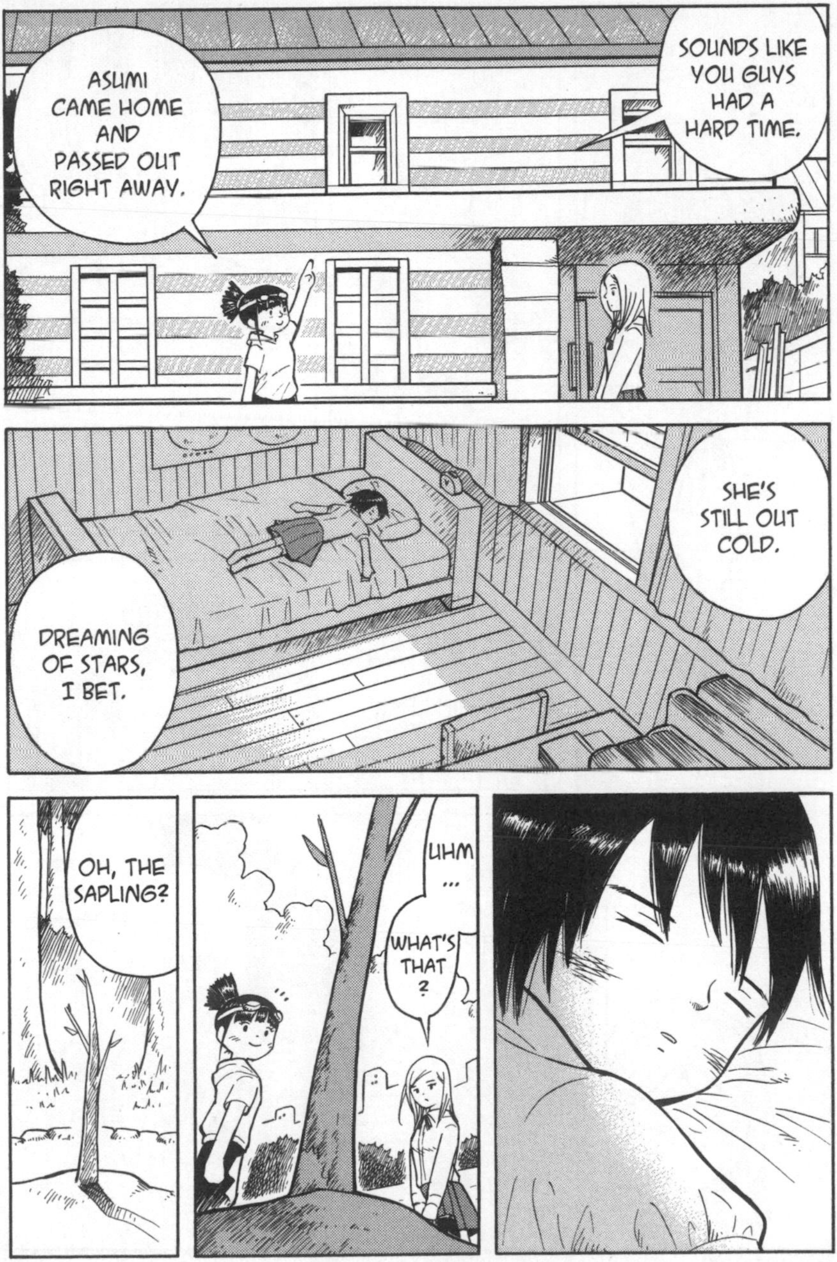
SOUNDS LIKE YOU GUYS HAD A HARD TIME.
ASUMI CAME HOME AND PASSED OUT RIGHT AWAY.
SHE'S STILL OUT COLD.
DREAMING OF STARS, I BET.
UHM ...
WHAT'S THAT ?
OH, THE SAPLING?

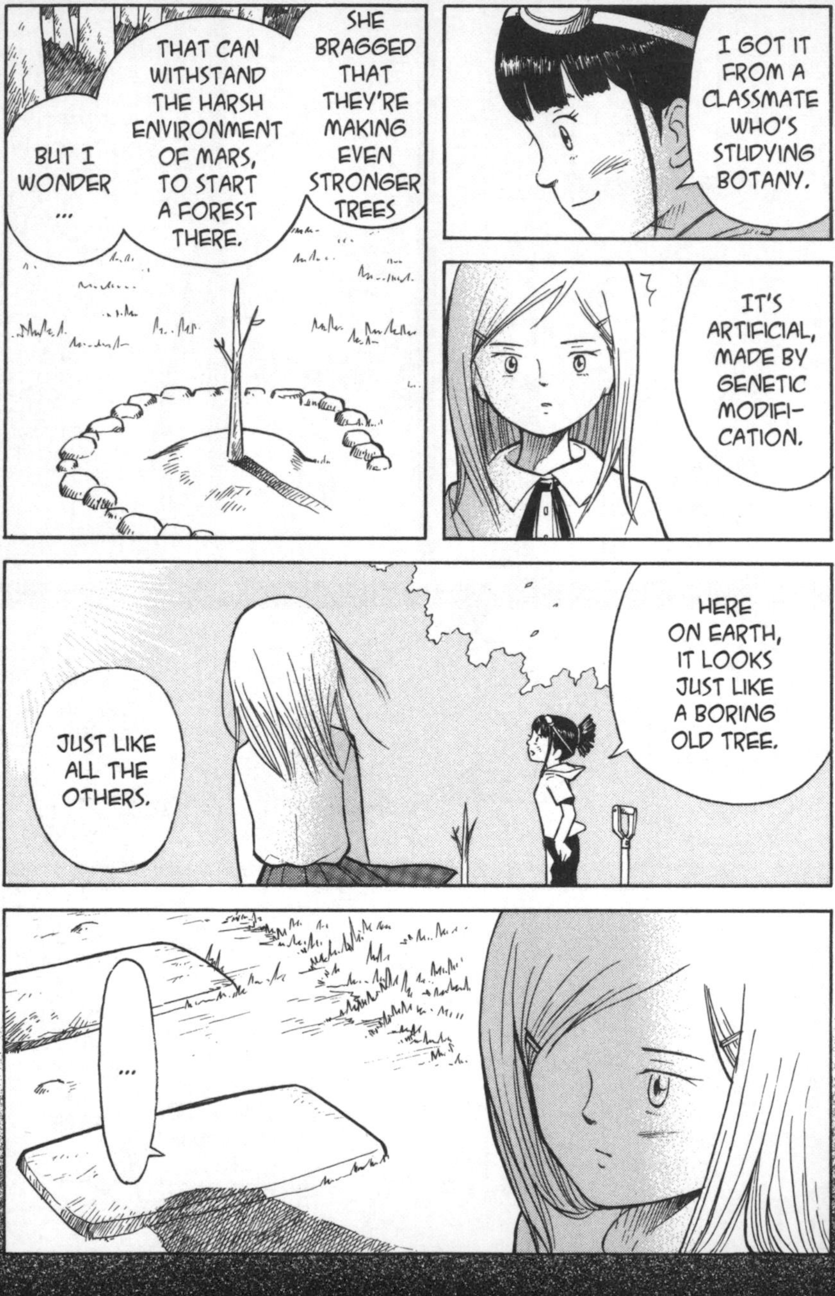
I GOT IT FROM A CLASSMATE WHO'S STUDYING BOTANY.
IT'S ARTIFICIAL, MADE BY GENETIC MODIFICATION.
SHE BRAGGED THAT THEY'RE MAKING EVEN STRONGER TREES
THAT CAN WITHSTAND THE HARSH ENVIRONMENT OF MARS, TO START A FOREST THERE.
BUT I WONDER ...
HERE ON EARTH, IT LOOKS JUST LIKE A BORING OLD TREE.
JUST LIKE ALL THE OTHERS.
...

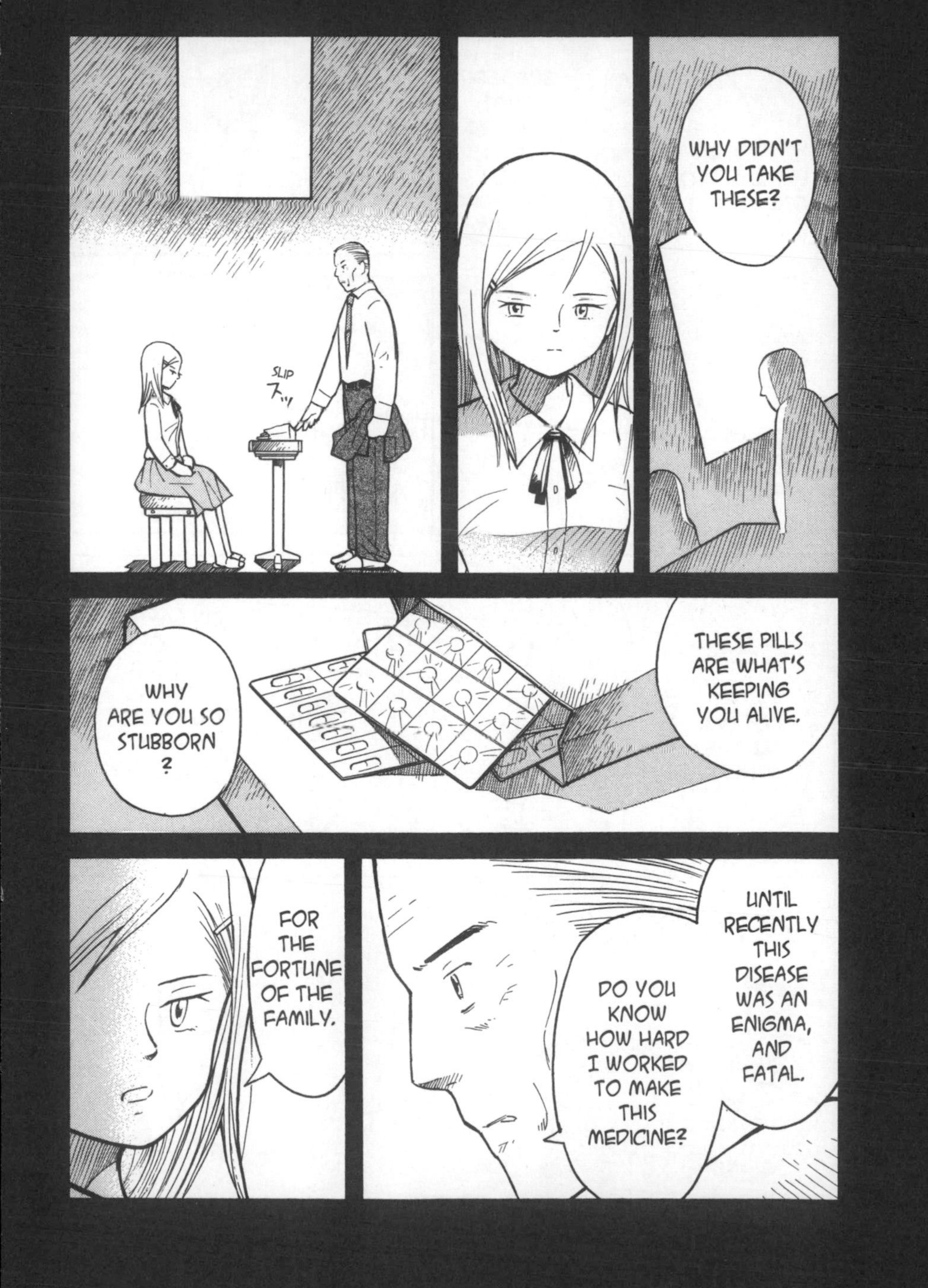
WHY DIDN'T YOU TAKE THESE?
SLIP
スッ
THESE PILLS ARE WHAT'S KEEPING YOU ALIVE.
WHY ARE YOU SO STUBBORN?
UNTIL RECENTLY THIS DISEASE WAS AN ENIGMA, AND FATAL.
DO YOU KNOW HOW HARD I WORKED TO MAKE THIS MEDICINE?
FOR THE FORTUNE OF THE FAMILY.

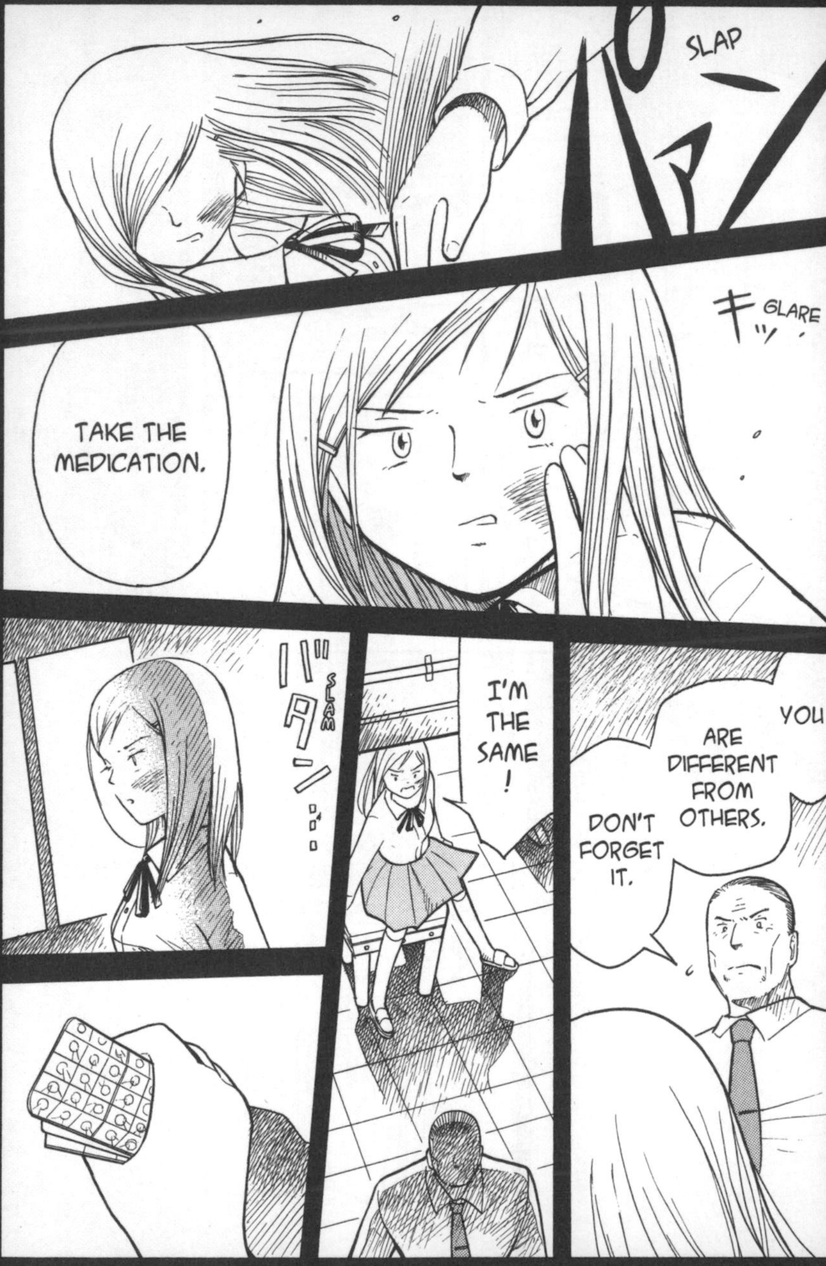
SLAP
キッ GLARE
TAKE THE MEDICATION.
YOU ARE DIFFERENT FROM OTHERS.
DON'T FORGET IT.
I'M THE SAME!
バタン SLAM

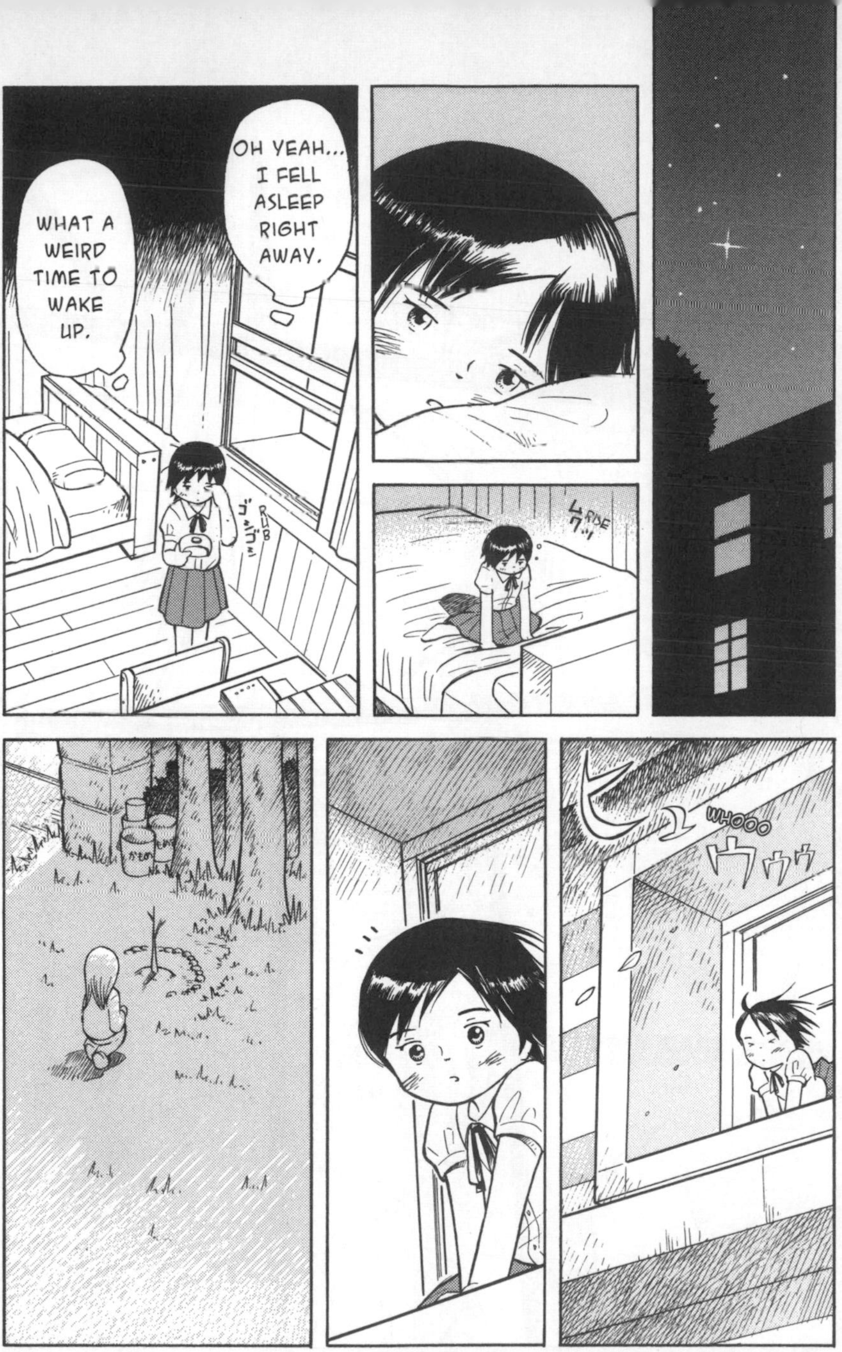
RIDE
OH YEAH... I FELL ASLEEP RIGHT AWAY.
WHAT A WEIRD TIME TO WAKE UP.
RUB
WHOOO

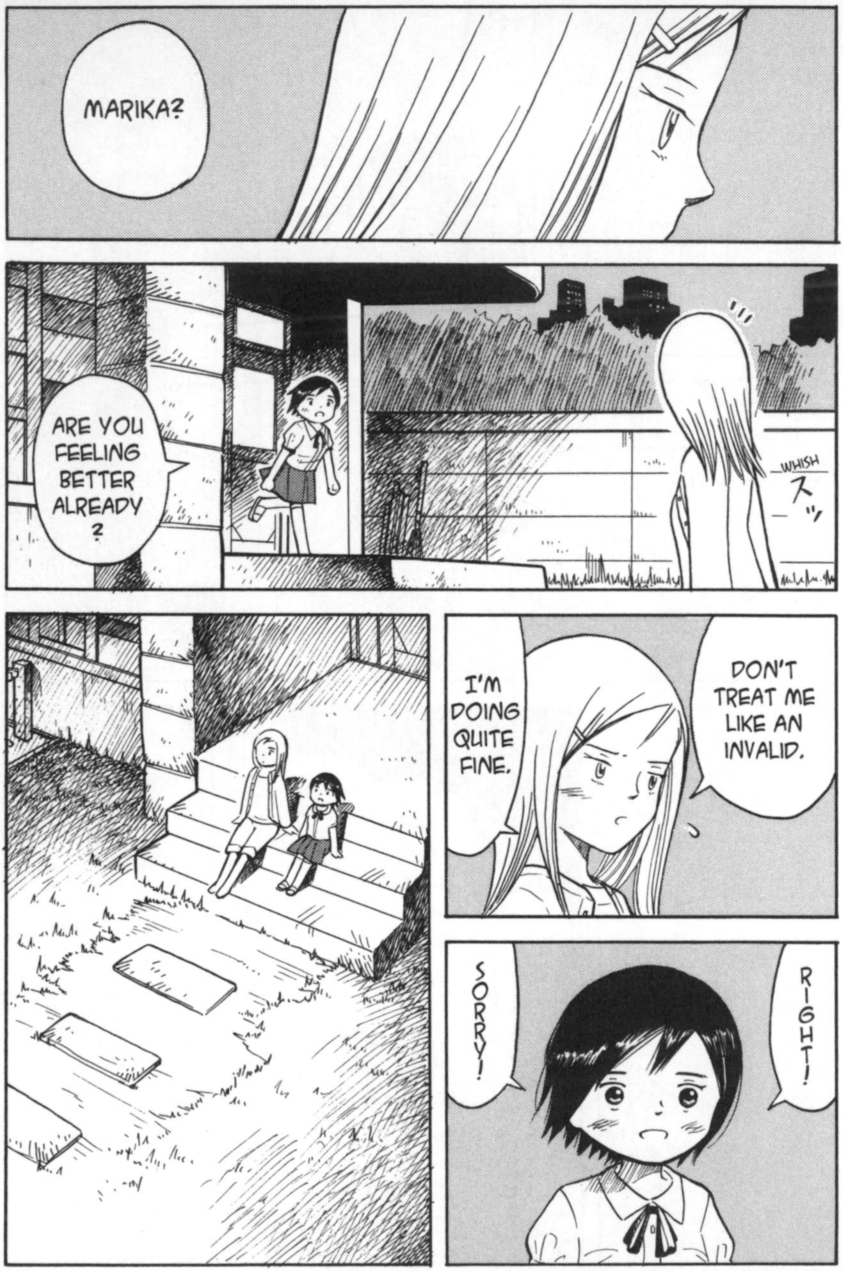

MARIKA?
ARE YOU FEELING BETTER ALREADY?
WHISH
スッ
DON'T TREAT ME LIKE AN INVALID.
I'M DOING QUITE FINE.
RIGHT!
SORRY!

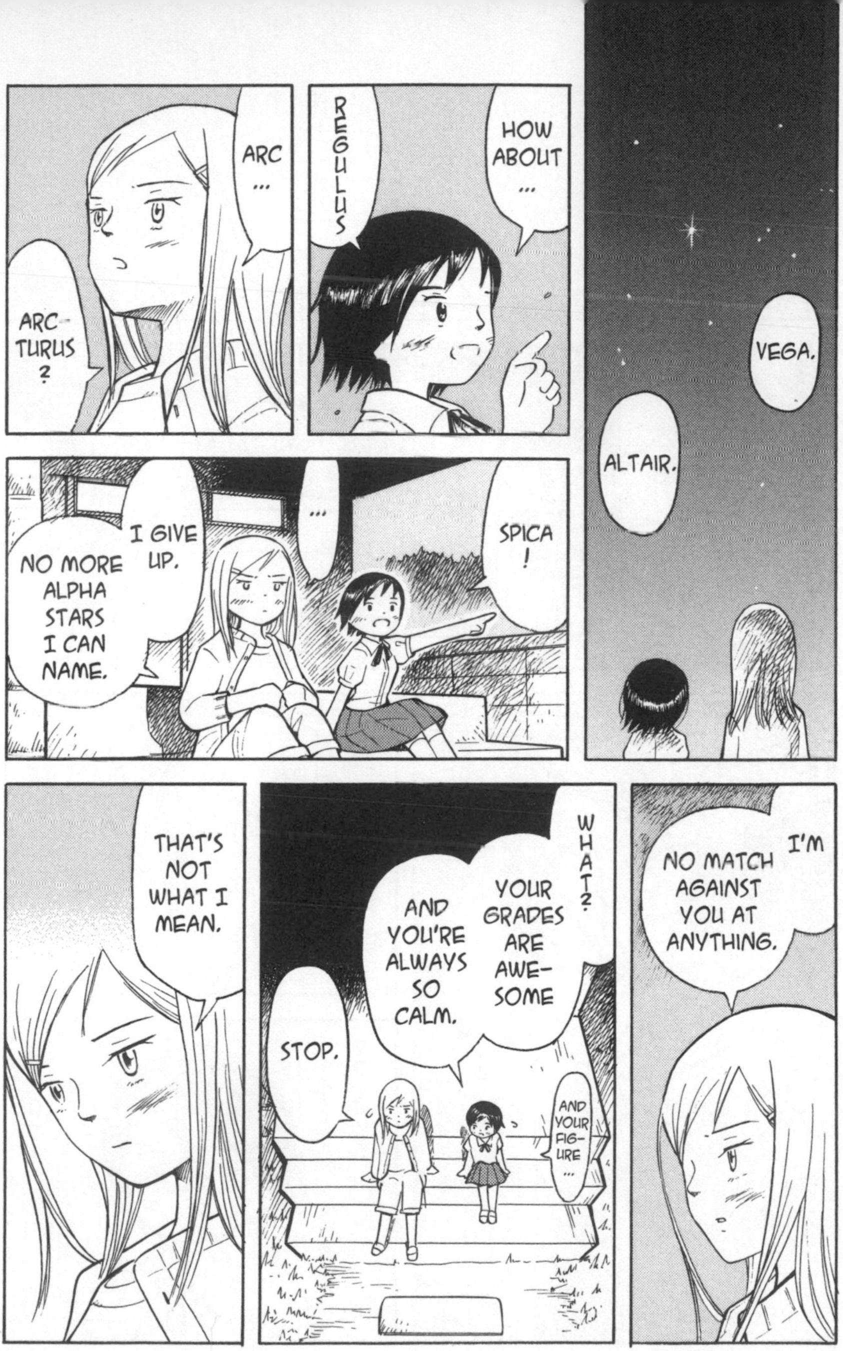
VEGA.
ALTAIR.
HOW ABOUT ...
REGULUS
ARC ...
ARC-TURUS?
SPICA!
...
I GIVE UP.
NO MORE ALPHA STARS I CAN NAME.
I'M NO MATCH AGAINST YOU AT ANYTHING.
WHAT?
YOUR GRADES ARE AWE-SOME
AND YOU'RE ALWAYS SO CALM.
AND YOUR FIG-URE ...
STOP.
THAT'S NOT WHAT I MEAN.

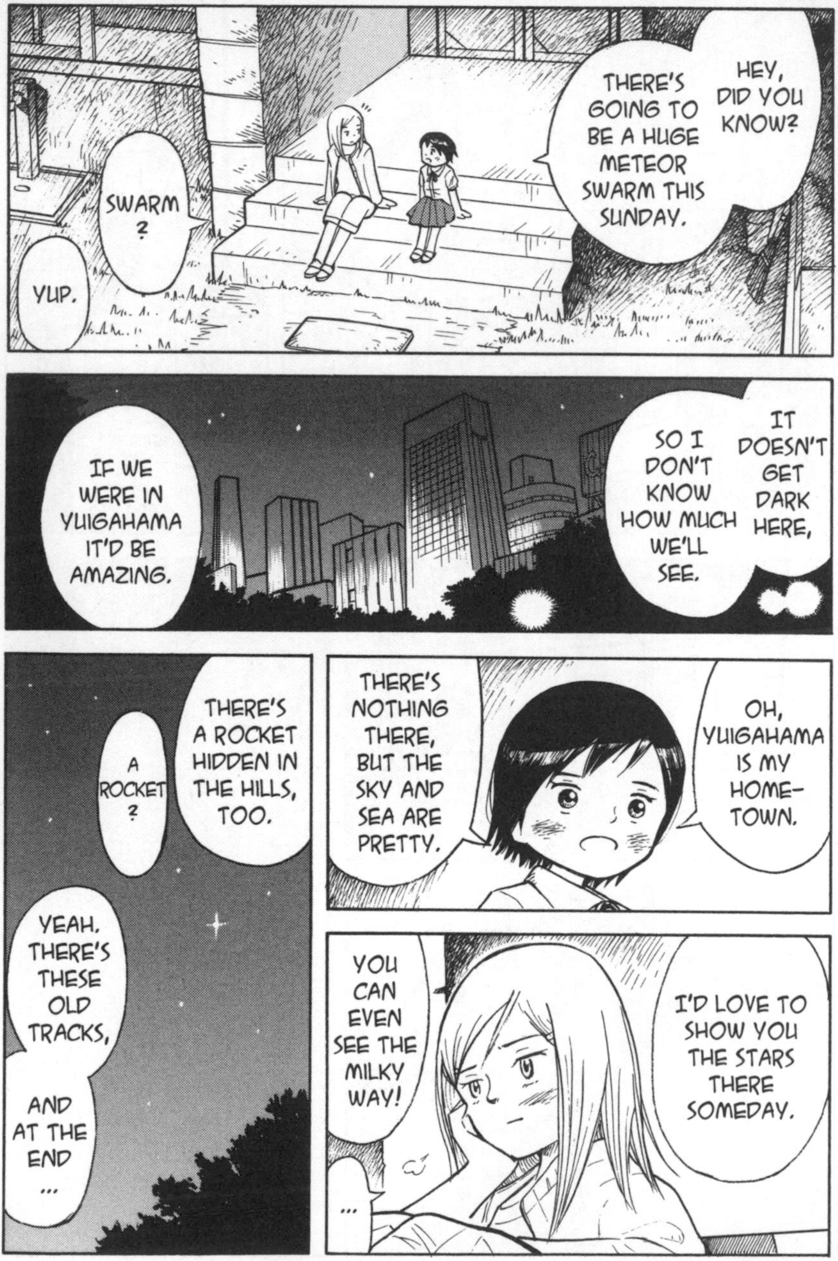
HEY, DID YOU KNOW?
THERE'S GOING TO BE A HUGE METEOR SWARM THIS SUNDAY.
SWARM?
YUP.
IT DOESN'T GET DARK HERE,
SO I DON'T KNOW HOW MUCH WE'LL SEE.
IF WE WERE IN YUIGAHAMA IT'D BE AMAZING.
OH, YUIGAHAMA IS MY HOME-TOWN.
THERE'S NOTHING THERE, BUT THE SKY AND SEA ARE PRETTY.
I'D LOVE TO SHOW YOU THE STARS THERE SOMEDAY.
YOU CAN EVEN SEE THE MILKY WAY!
...
THERE'S A ROCKET HIDDEN IN THE HILLS, TOO.
A ROCKET?
YEAH. THERE'S THESE OLD TRACKS,
AND AT THE END ...

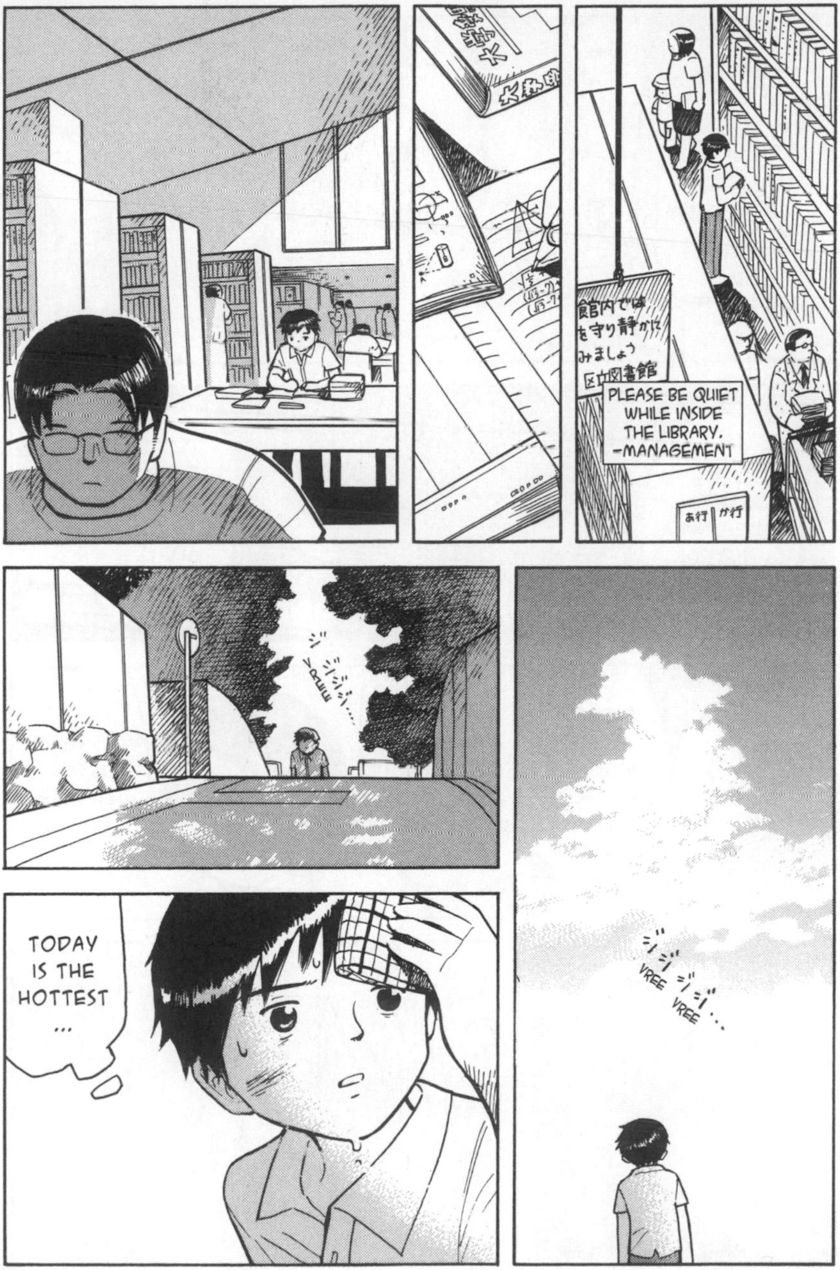
館内では
を守り静かに
みましょう
区立図書館
PLEASE BE QUIET WHILE INSIDE THE LIBRARY. -MANAGEMENT
あ行 か行
ジジ ジジ
VREE VREE
ジジ ジジジ…
VRUUU
TODAY IS THE HOTTEST …

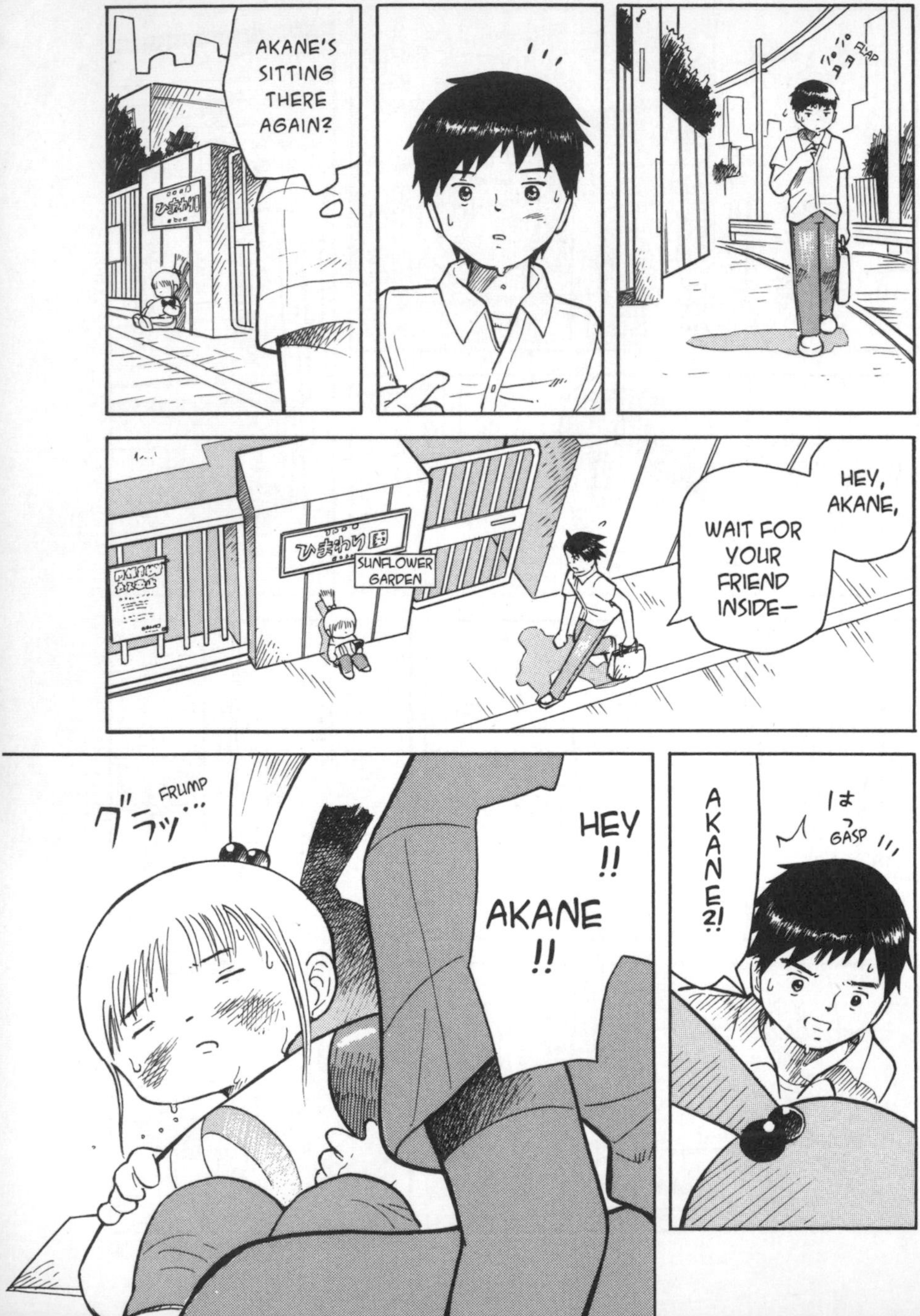

パタ パタ FLAP
AKANE'S SITTING THERE AGAIN?
ひまわり園
SUNFLOWER GARDEN
HEY, AKANE,
WAIT FOR YOUR FRIEND INSIDE—
AKANE?!
はっ GASP
HEY!! AKANE!!
グラッ… FRUMP

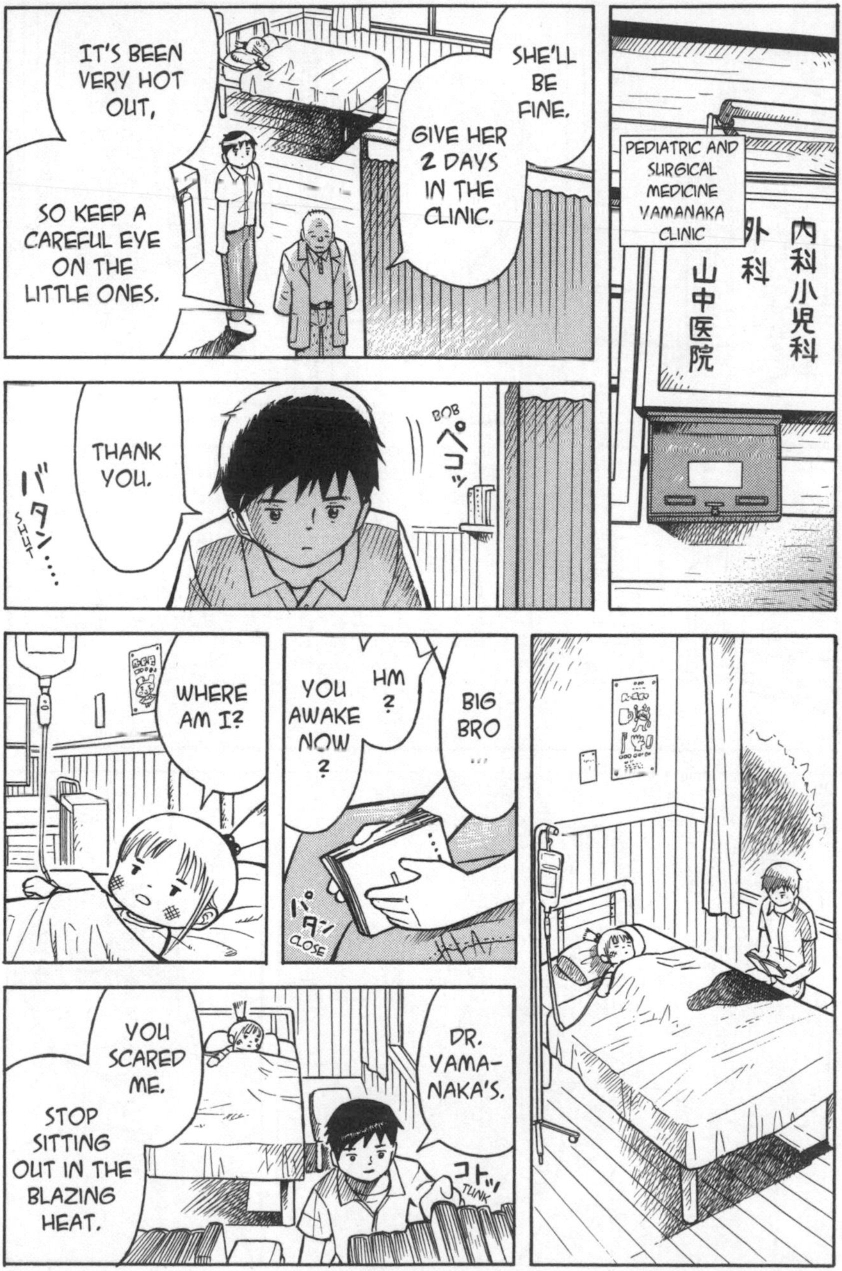
PEDIATRIC AND SURGICAL MEDICINE YAMANAKA CLINIC
内科小児科
外科
山中医院
SHE'LL BE FINE.
GIVE HER 2 DAYS IN THE CLINIC.
IT'S BEEN VERY HOT OUT,
SO KEEP A CAREFUL EYE ON THE LITTLE ONES.
ペコッ
BOB
THANK YOU.
バタン…
SHUT
BIG BRO...
HM?
YOU AWAKE NOW?
パタン
CLOSE
WHERE AM I?
DR. YAMANAKA'S.
コトッ
TUNK
YOU SCARED ME.
STOP SITTING OUT IN THE BLAZING HEAT.

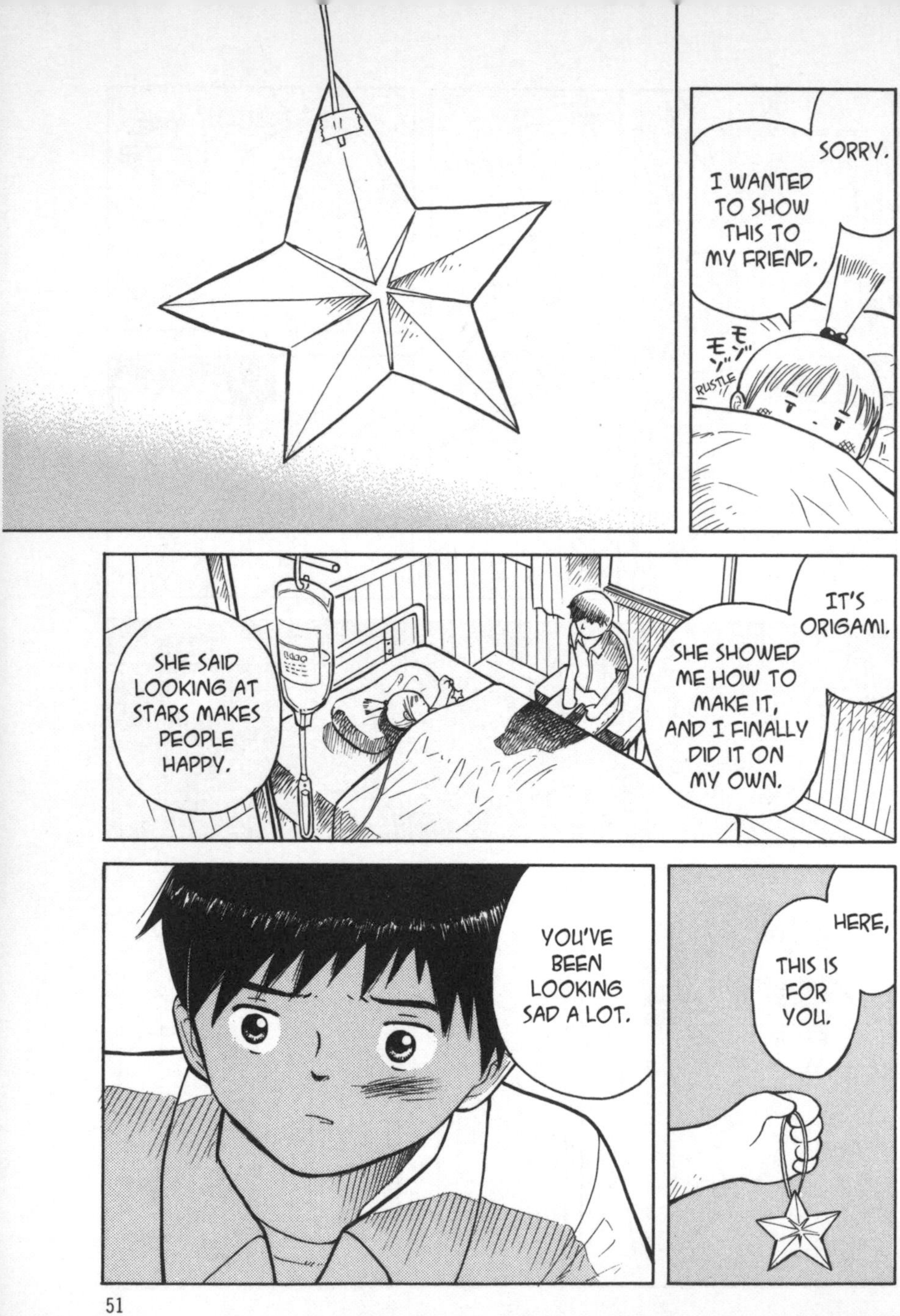
SORRY.
I WANTED TO SHOW THIS TO MY FRIEND.
モゾ モゾ
RUSTLE
IT'S ORIGAMI.
SHE SHOWED ME HOW TO MAKE IT, AND I FINALLY DID IT ON MY OWN.
SHE SAID LOOKING AT STARS MAKES PEOPLE HAPPY.
HERE,
THIS IS FOR YOU.
YOU'VE BEEN LOOKING SAD A LOT.

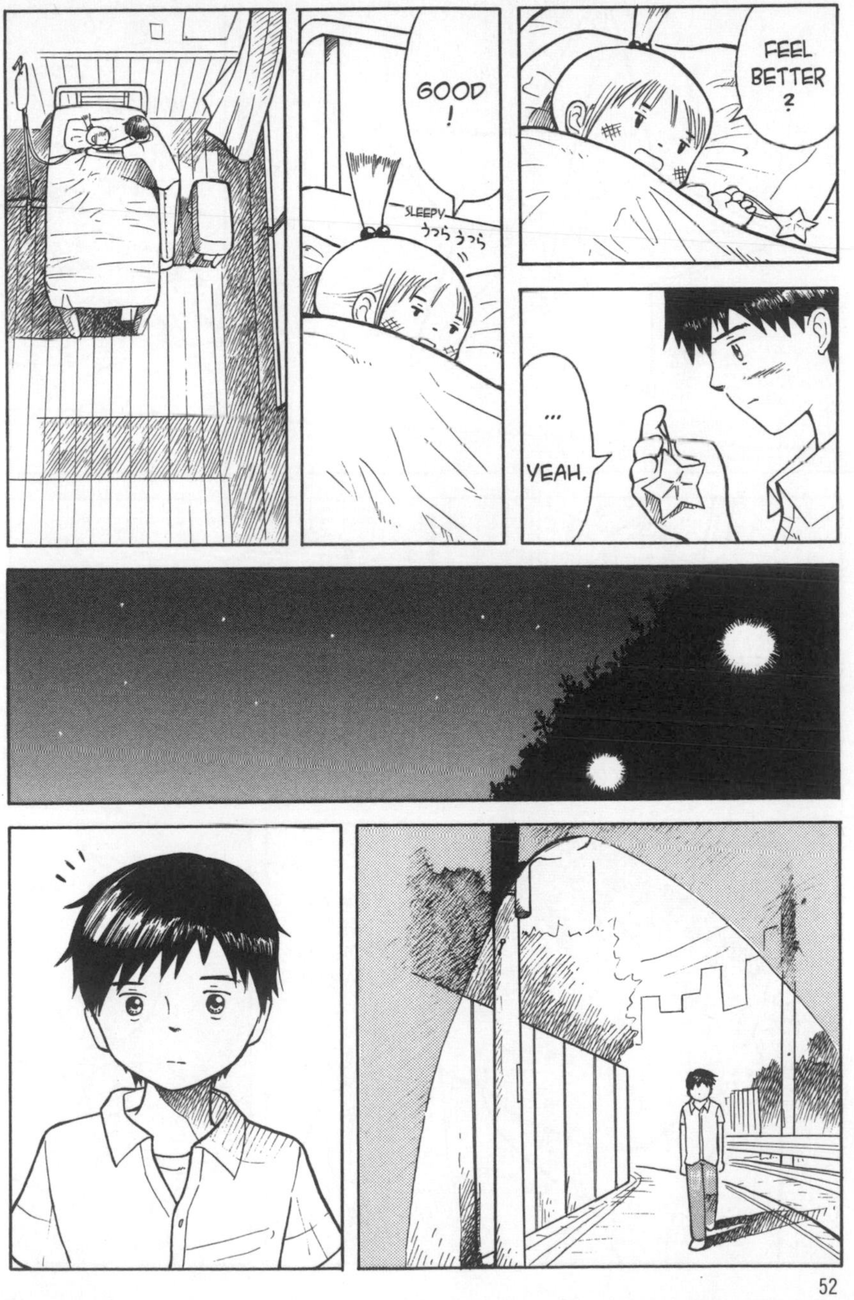

FEEL BETTER ?
...
YEAH.
GOOD !
SLEEPY
うつら うつら

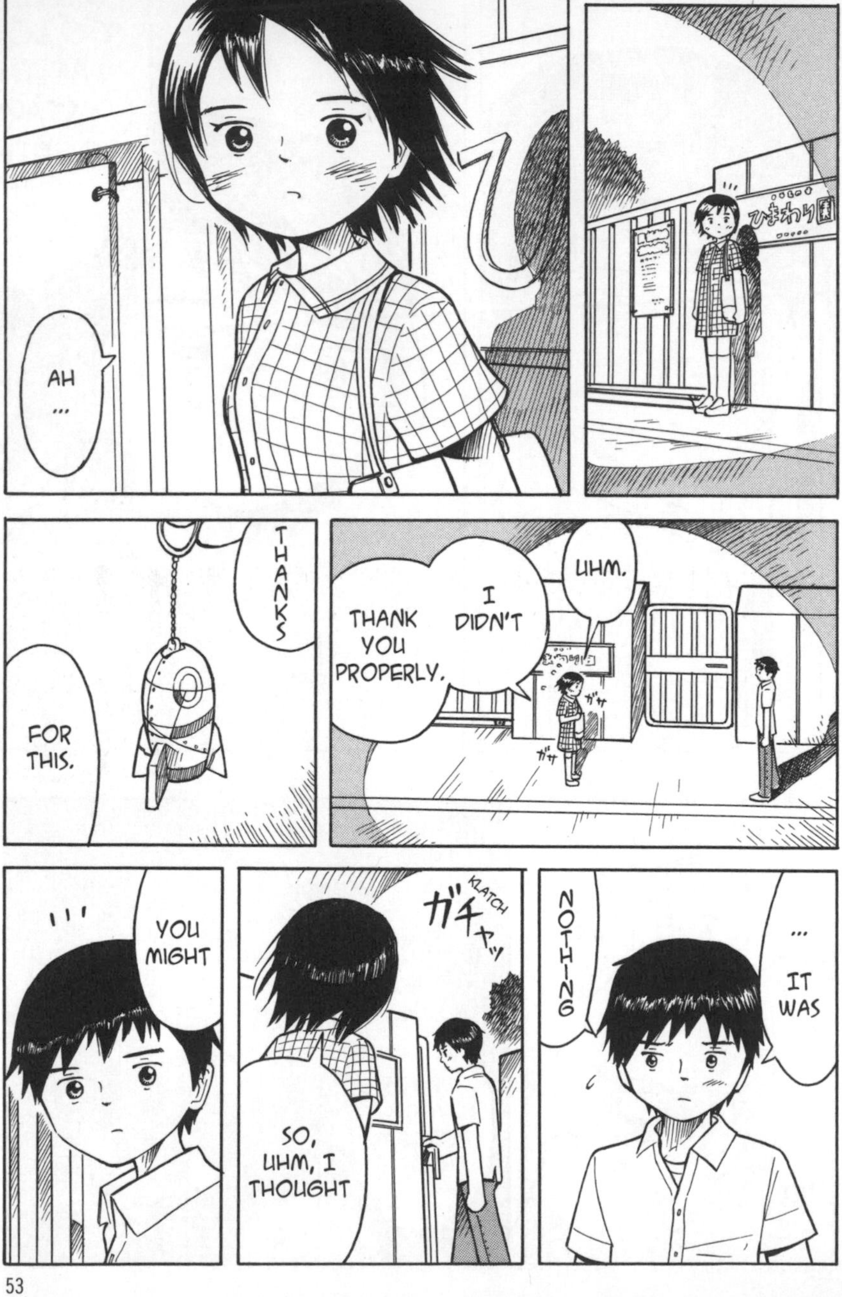
ひまわり園
AH ...
UHM.
I DIDN'T
THANK YOU PROPERLY.
ガサ
ガサ
THANKS
FOR THIS.
... IT WAS
NOTHING
ガチャッ KLATCH
SO, UHM, I THOUGHT
YOU MIGHT

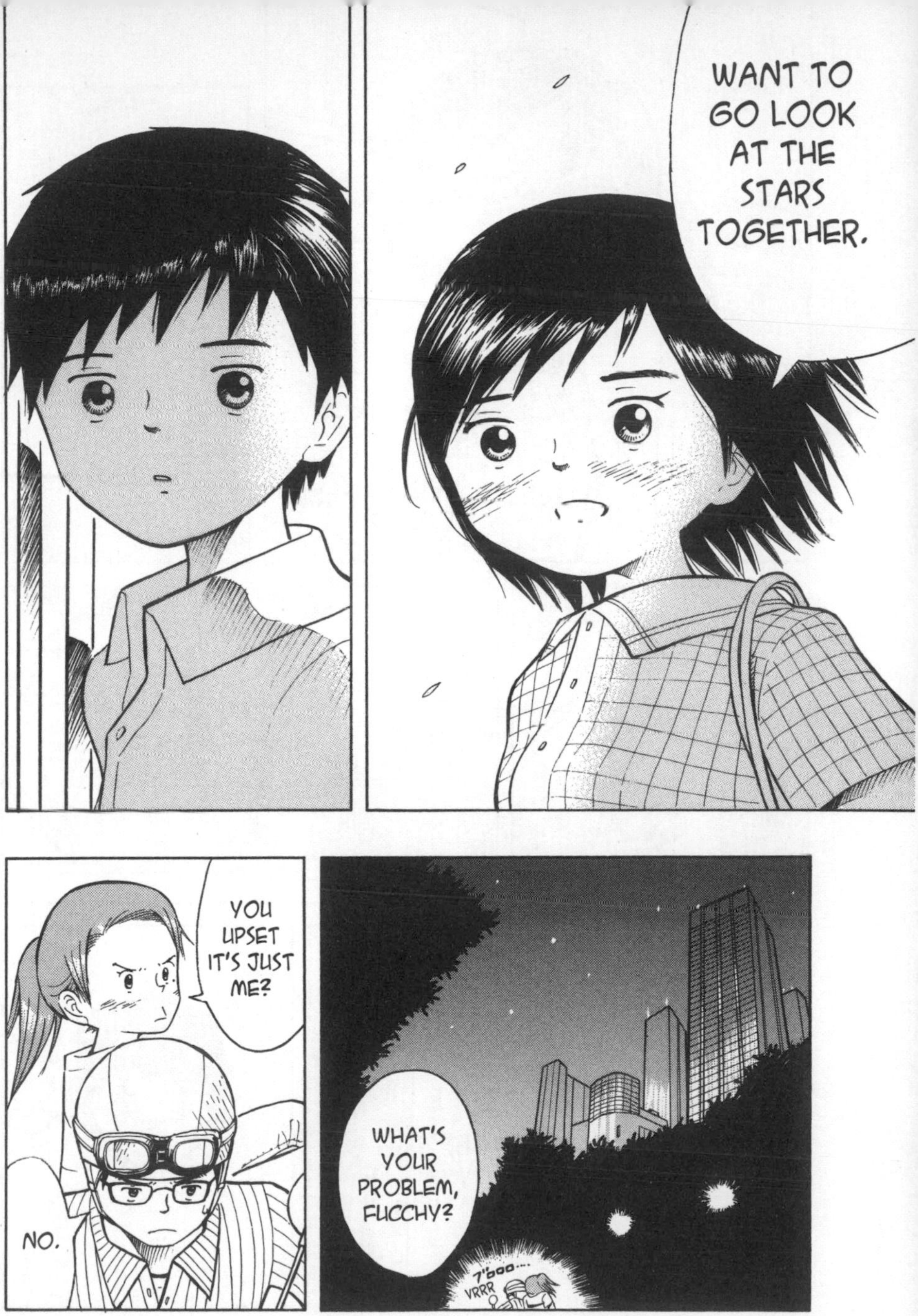
WANT TO GO LOOK AT THE STARS TOGETHER.
WHAT'S YOUR PROBLEM, FUCCHY?
VRRR
YOU UPSET IT'S JUST ME?
NO.

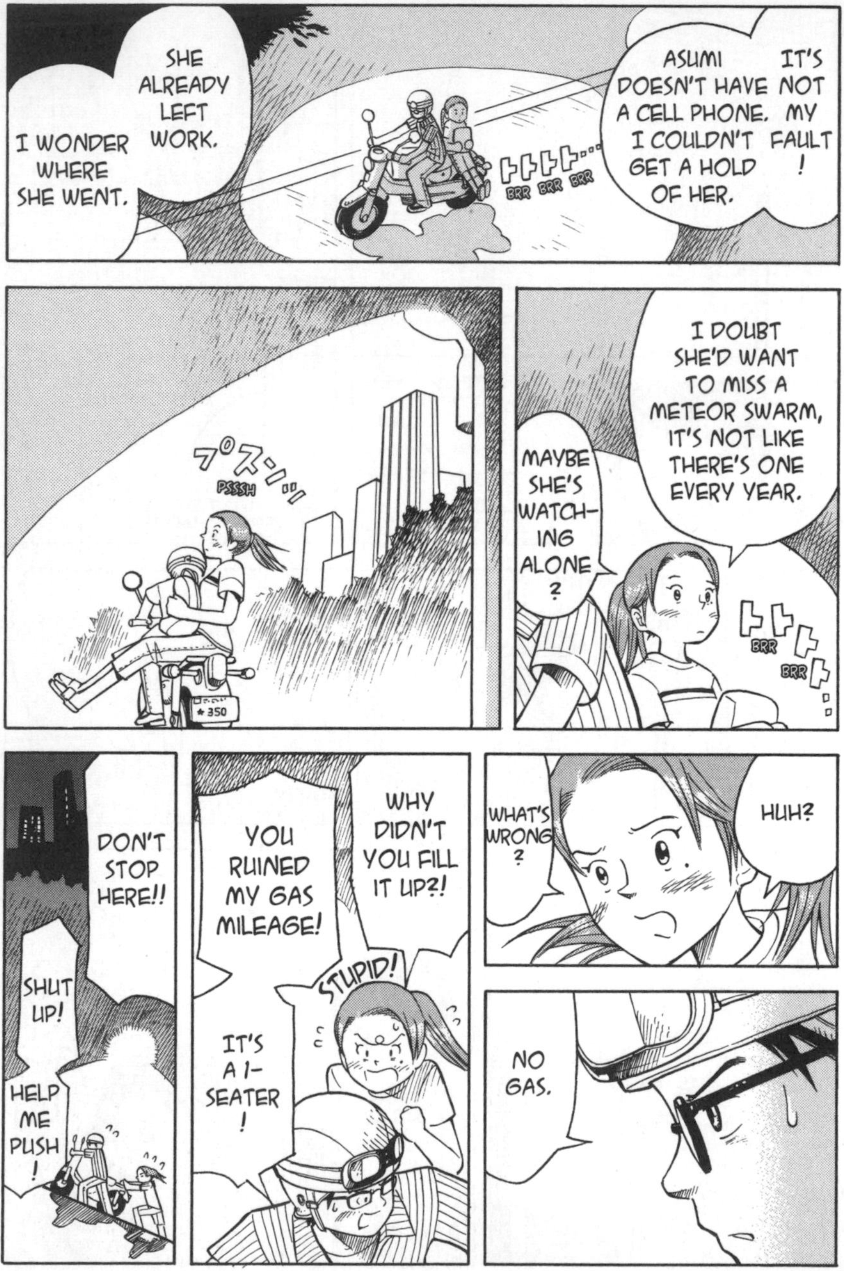
IT'S NOT MY FAULT!
ASUMI DOESN'T HAVE A CELL PHONE. I COULDN'T GET A HOLD OF HER.
トトトト‥
BRR BRR BRR
SHE ALREADY LEFT WORK.
I WONDER WHERE SHE WENT.
I DOUBT SHE'D WANT TO MISS A METEOR SWARM, IT'S NOT LIKE THERE'S ONE EVERY YEAR.
MAYBE SHE'S WATCH-ING ALONE?
トトトト。。
BRR BRR
プスンッ
PSSSH
HUH?
WHAT'S WRONG?
NO GAS.
WHY DIDN'T YOU FILL IT UP?!
YOU RUINED MY GAS MILEAGE!
STUPID!
IT'S A 1-SEATER!
DON'T STOP HERE!!
SHUT UP!
HELP ME PUSH!

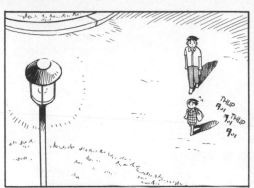

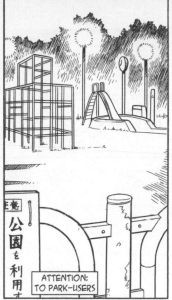

公園を利用す
ATTENTION: TO PARK-USERS
THUP
タッ
THUP
タッ
タッ
CAN WE SEE STARS IN SUCH A BRIGHT PLACE?
WHAT'S SHE DOING?
パカ
KLAK
UH ...
THIS IS IT.
WE SHOULDN'T DO THIS, BUT TODAY'S SPECIAL.
FRET
アセアセ
?
IF WHAT MR. LION SAID IS TRUE,
PULLING THIS LEVER SHOULD TURN OFF ALL THE LIGHTS.

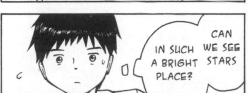

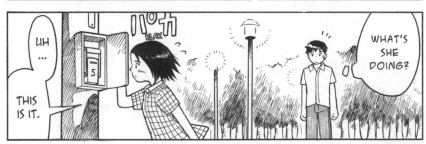

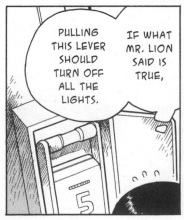

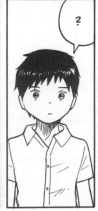

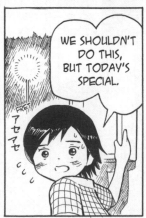

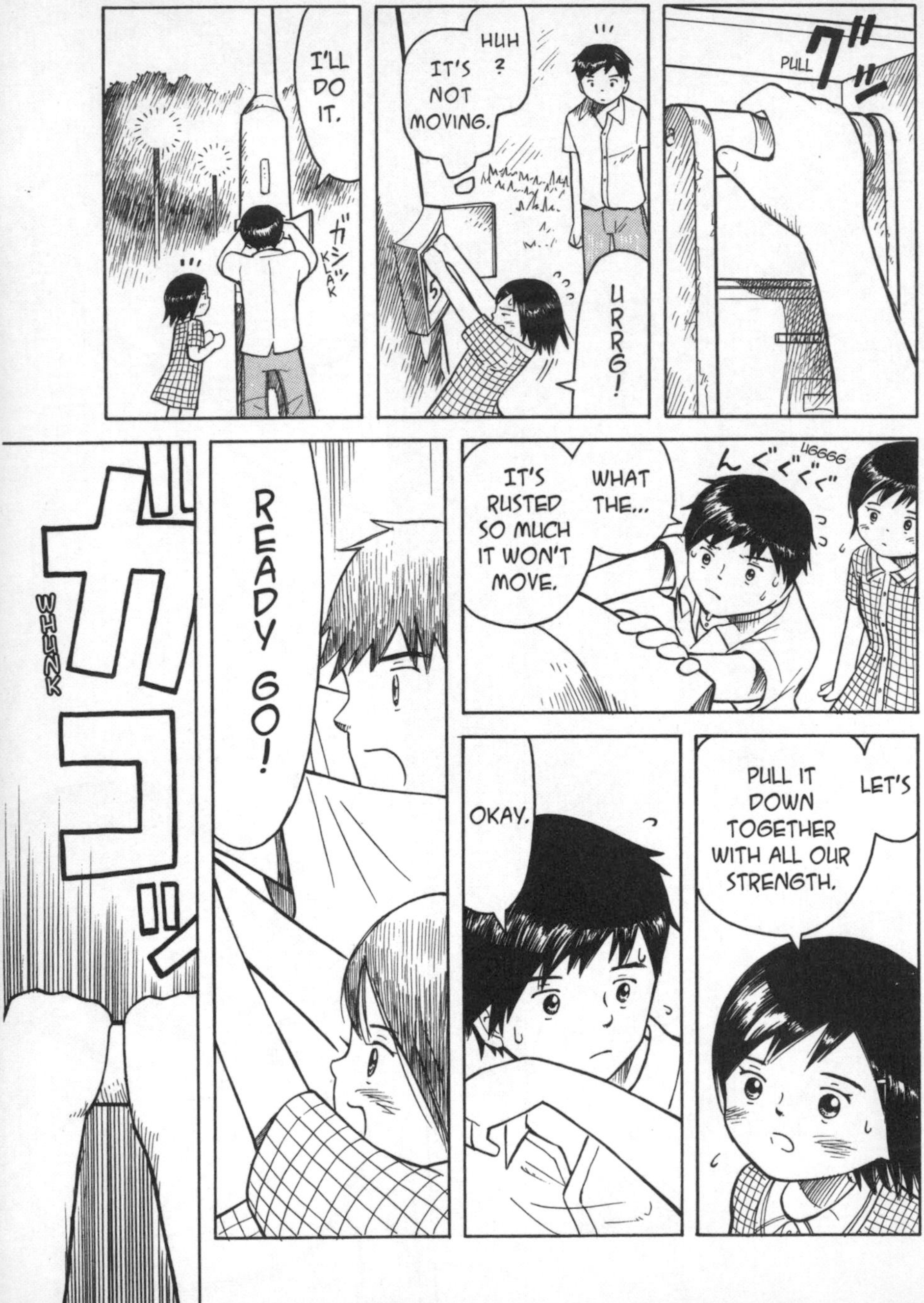
PULL
グ
HUH?
IT'S NOT MOVING.
URRG!
I'LL DO IT.
ガシ
KLAK
んぐぐぐ
UGGGG
WHAT THE...
IT'S RUSTED SO MUCH IT WON'T MOVE.
LET'S PULL IT DOWN TOGETHER WITH ALL OUR STRENGTH.
OKAY.
READY GO!
カコッ
WHUNK

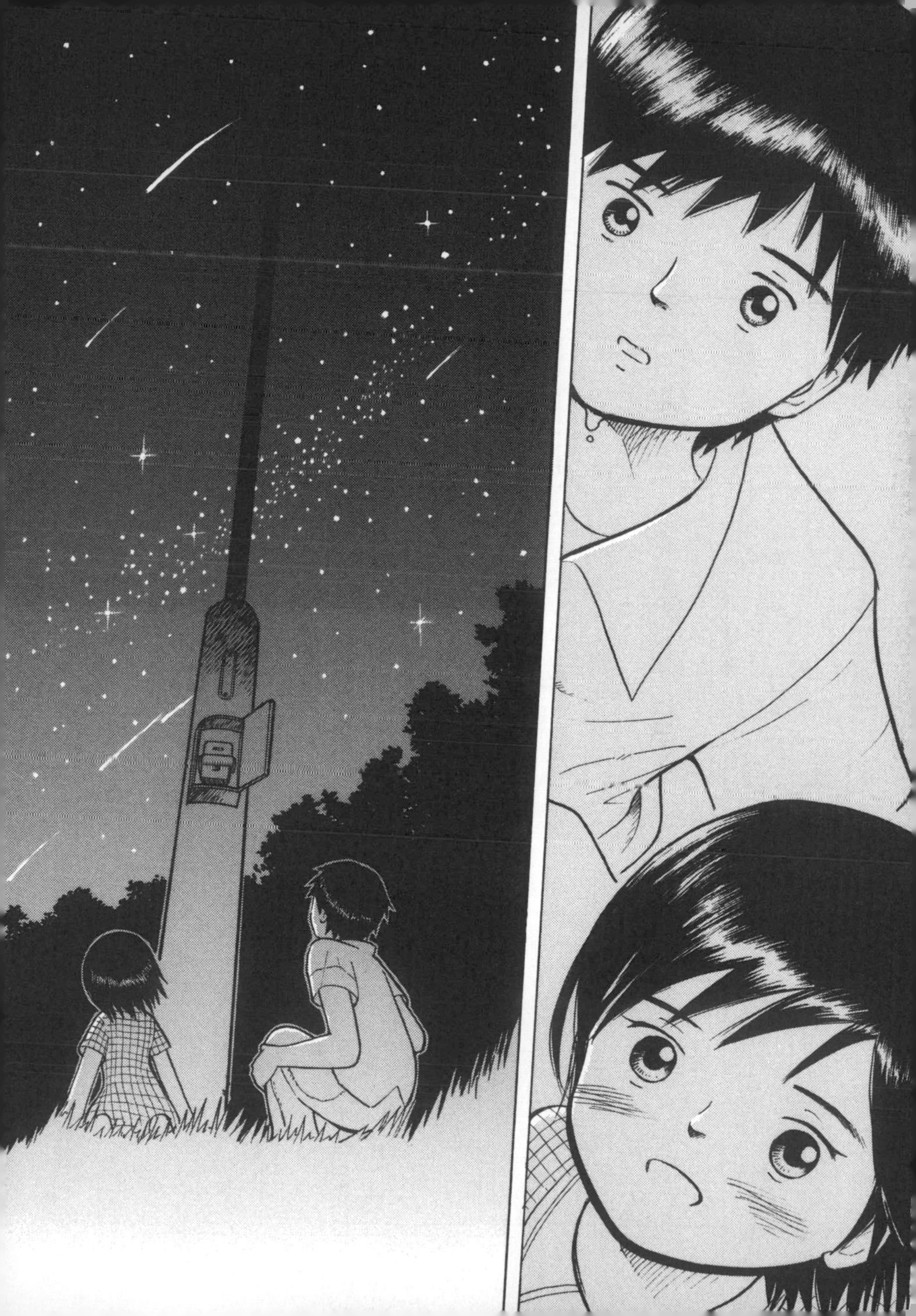

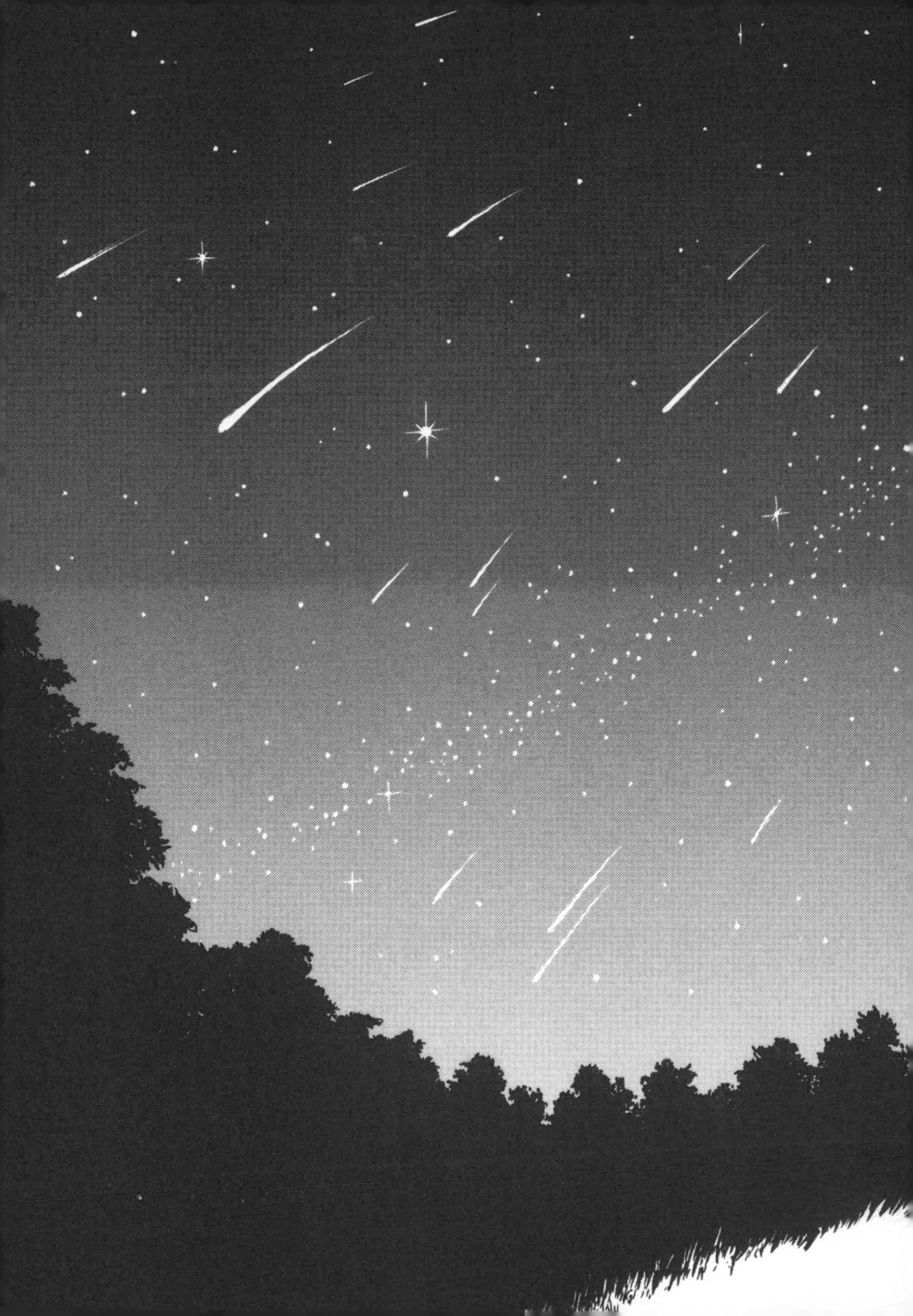

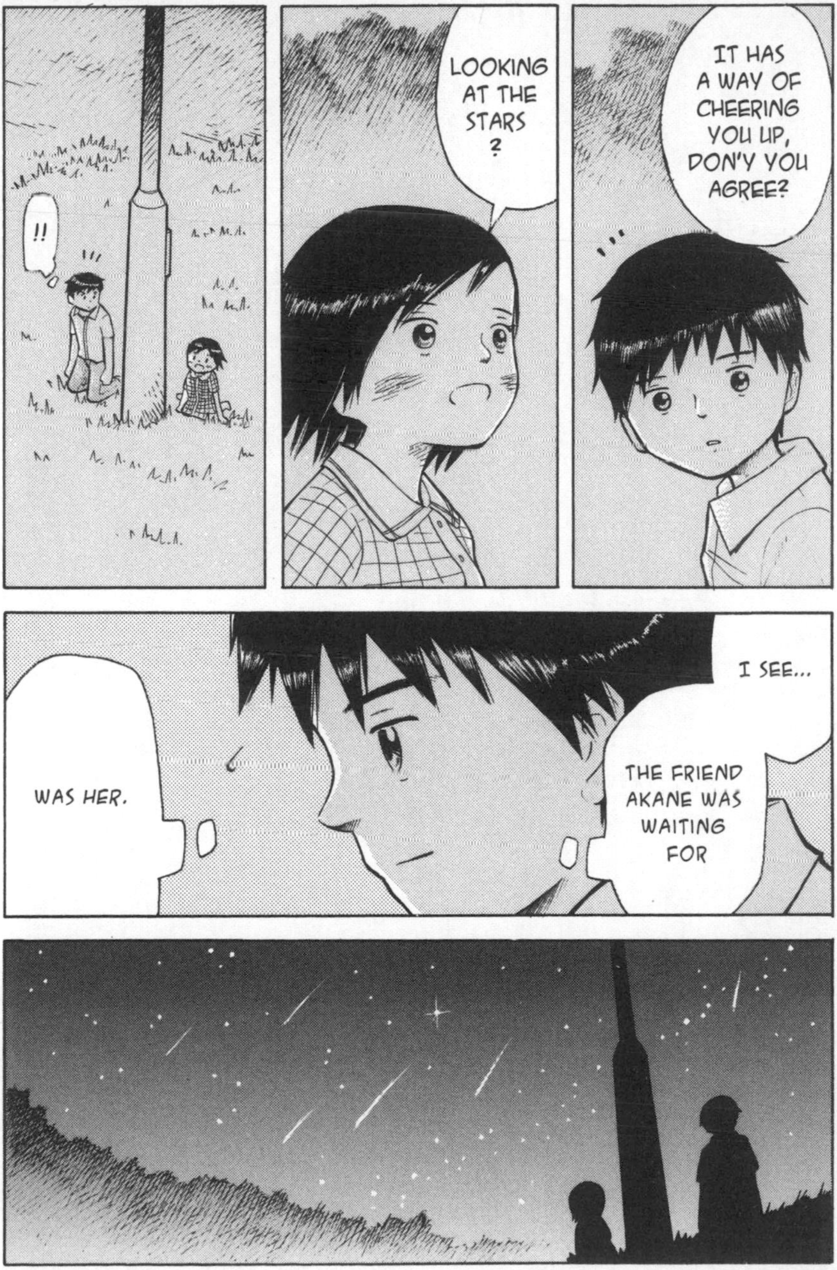
IT HAS A WAY OF CHEERING YOU UP, DON'Y YOU AGREE?
LOOKING AT THE STARS ?
!!
I SEE...
THE FRIEND AKANE WAS WAITING FOR
WAS HER.

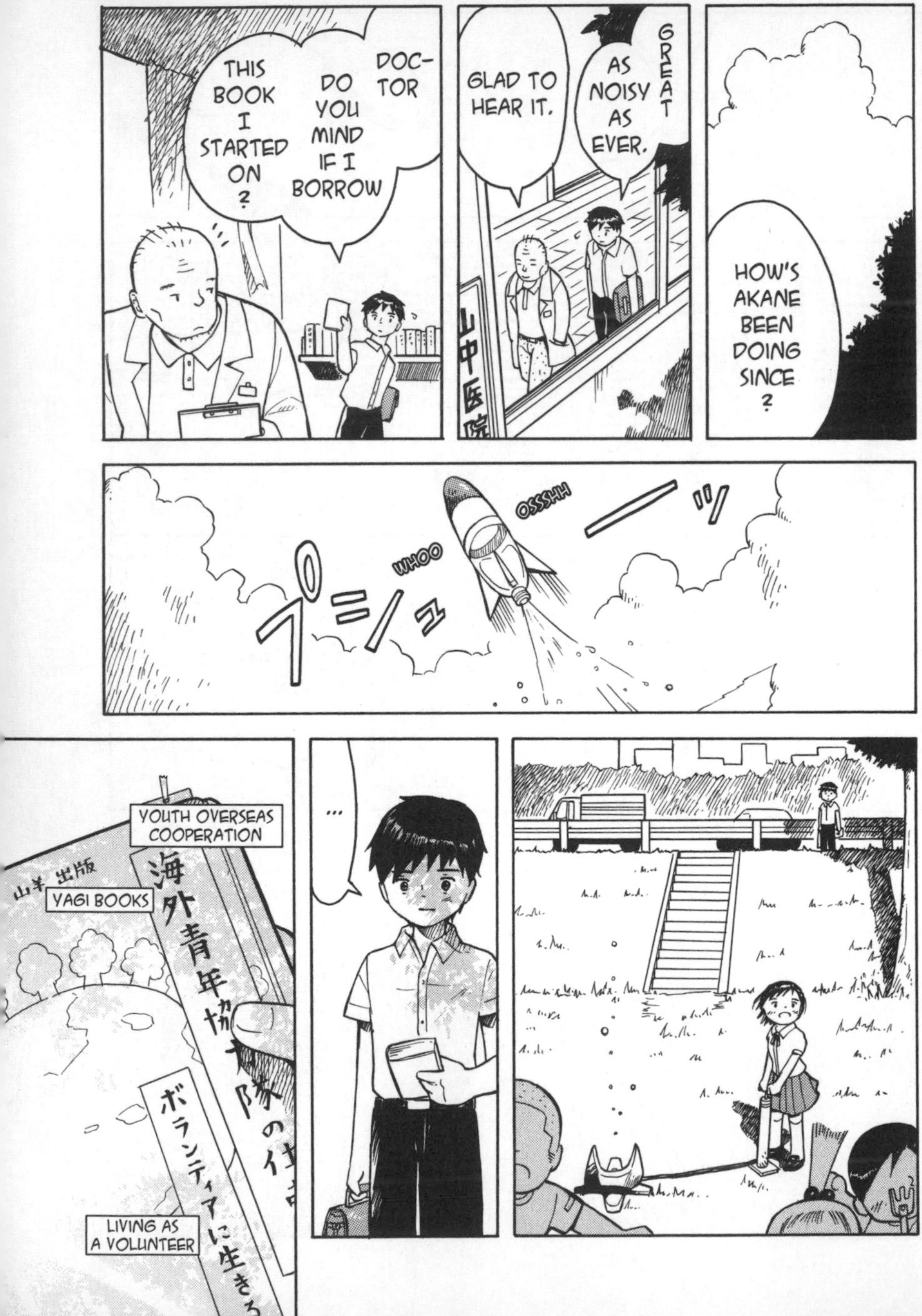

HOW'S AKANE BEEN DOING SINCE?
GREAT
AS NOISY AS EVER.
GLAD TO HEAR IT.
山中医院
DOCTOR DO YOU MIND IF I BORROW THIS BOOK I STARTED ON?
ーッ
OSSSHH
WHOO
プシュ
...
YOUTH OVERSEAS COOPERATION
山羊 出版
YAGI BOOKS
ボランティアに生きる
LIVING AS A VOLUNTEER

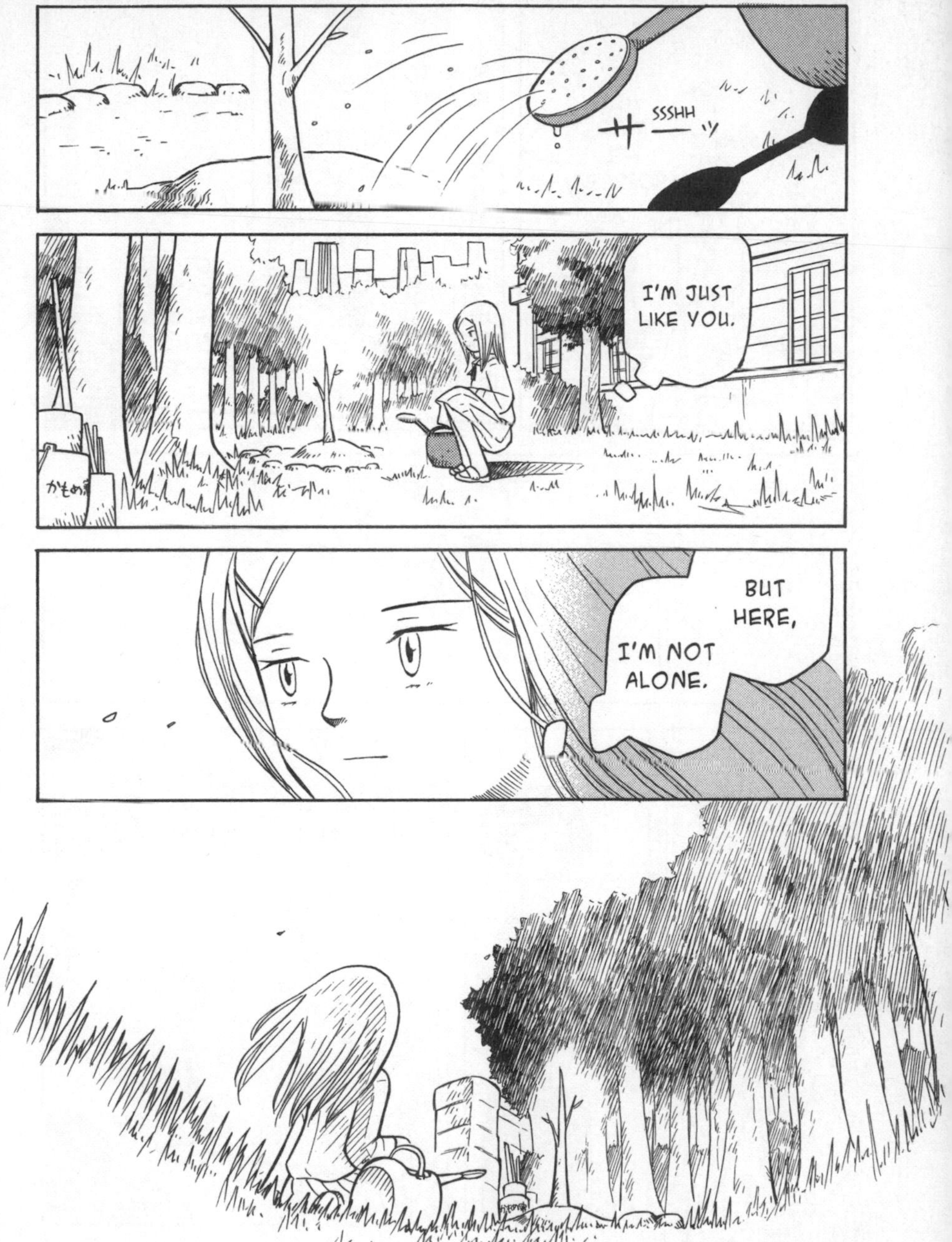
サーッ
SSSHH
I'M JUST LIKE YOU.
BUT HERE,
I'M NOT ALONE.

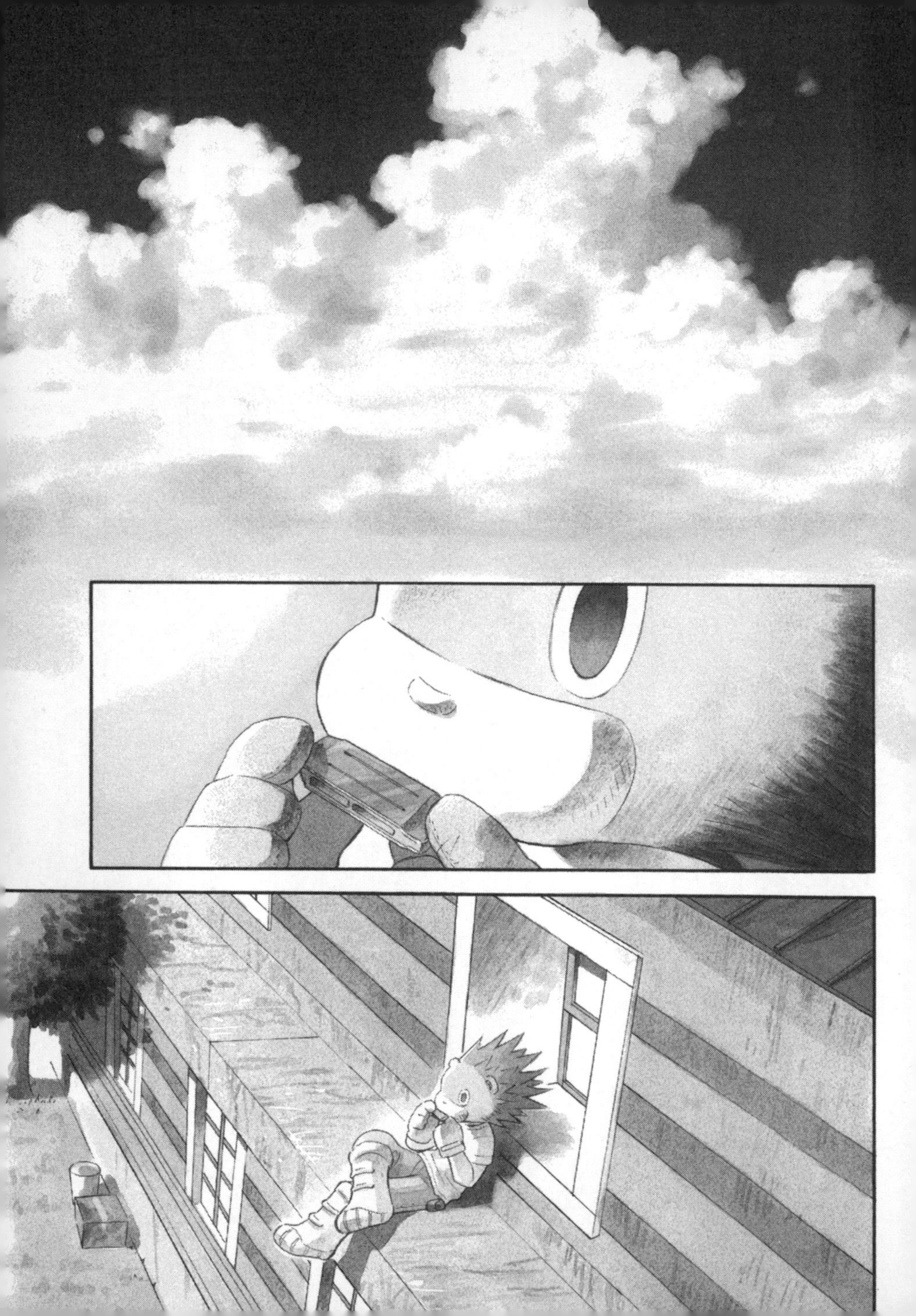

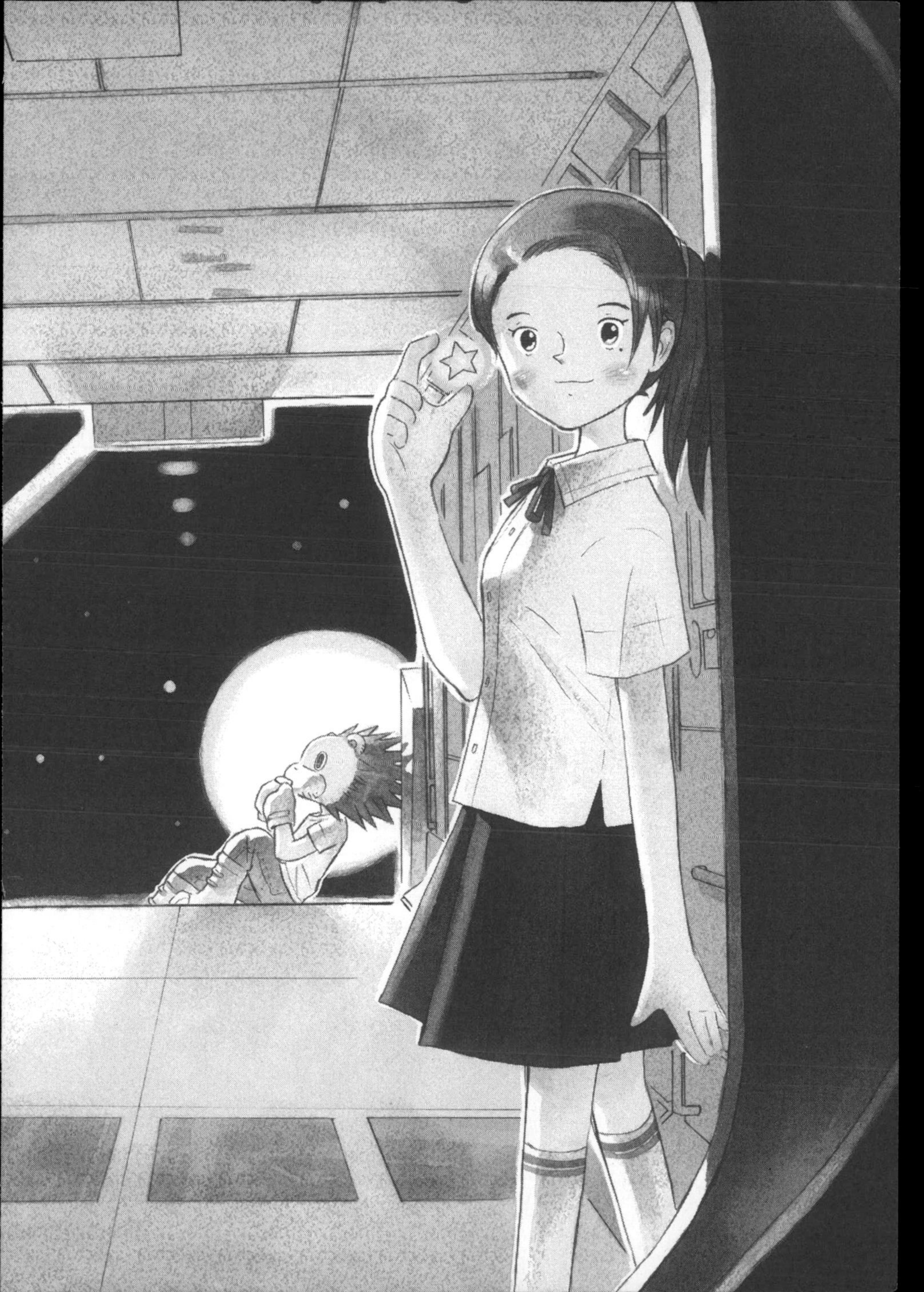

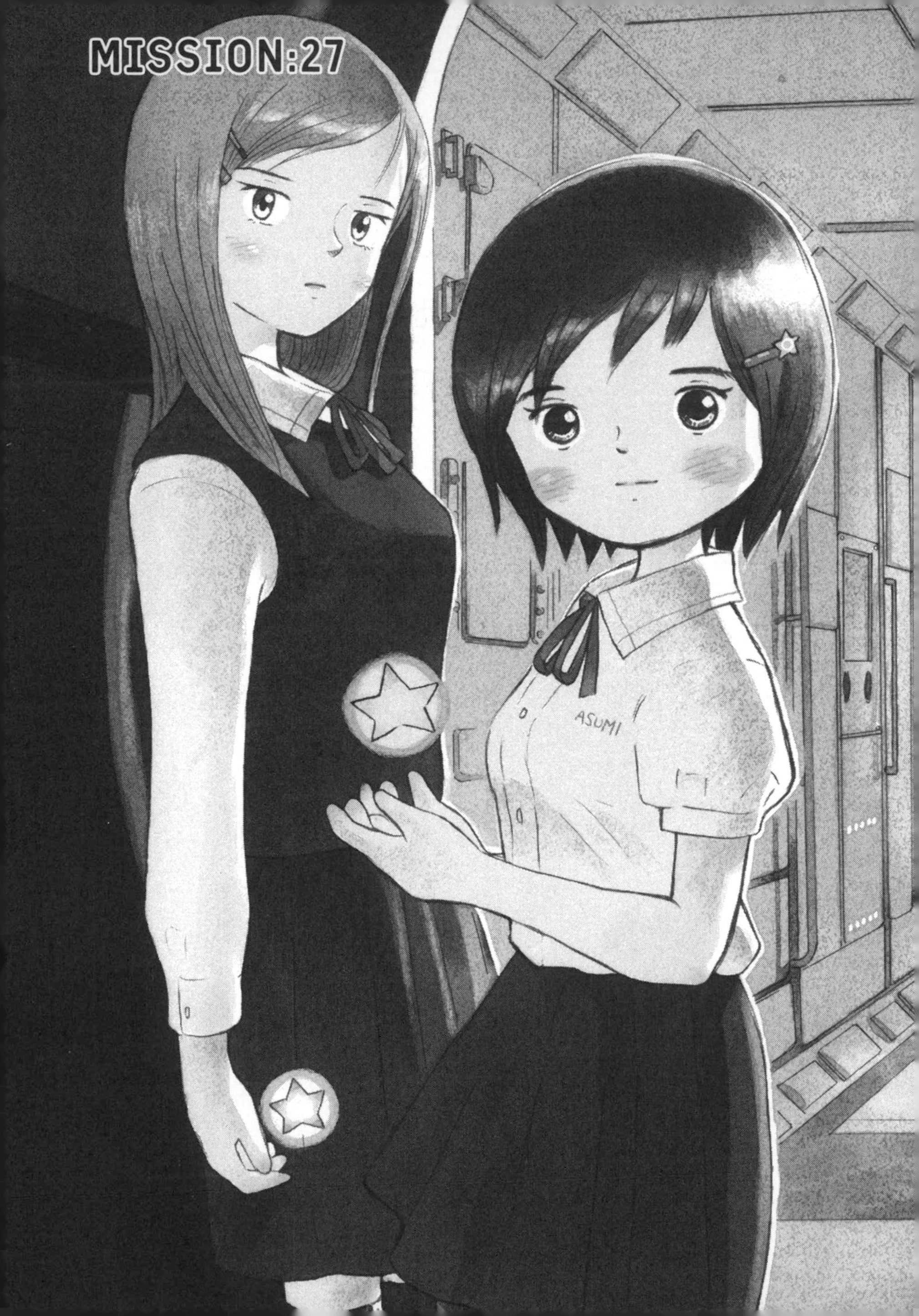
MISSION:27
ASUMI

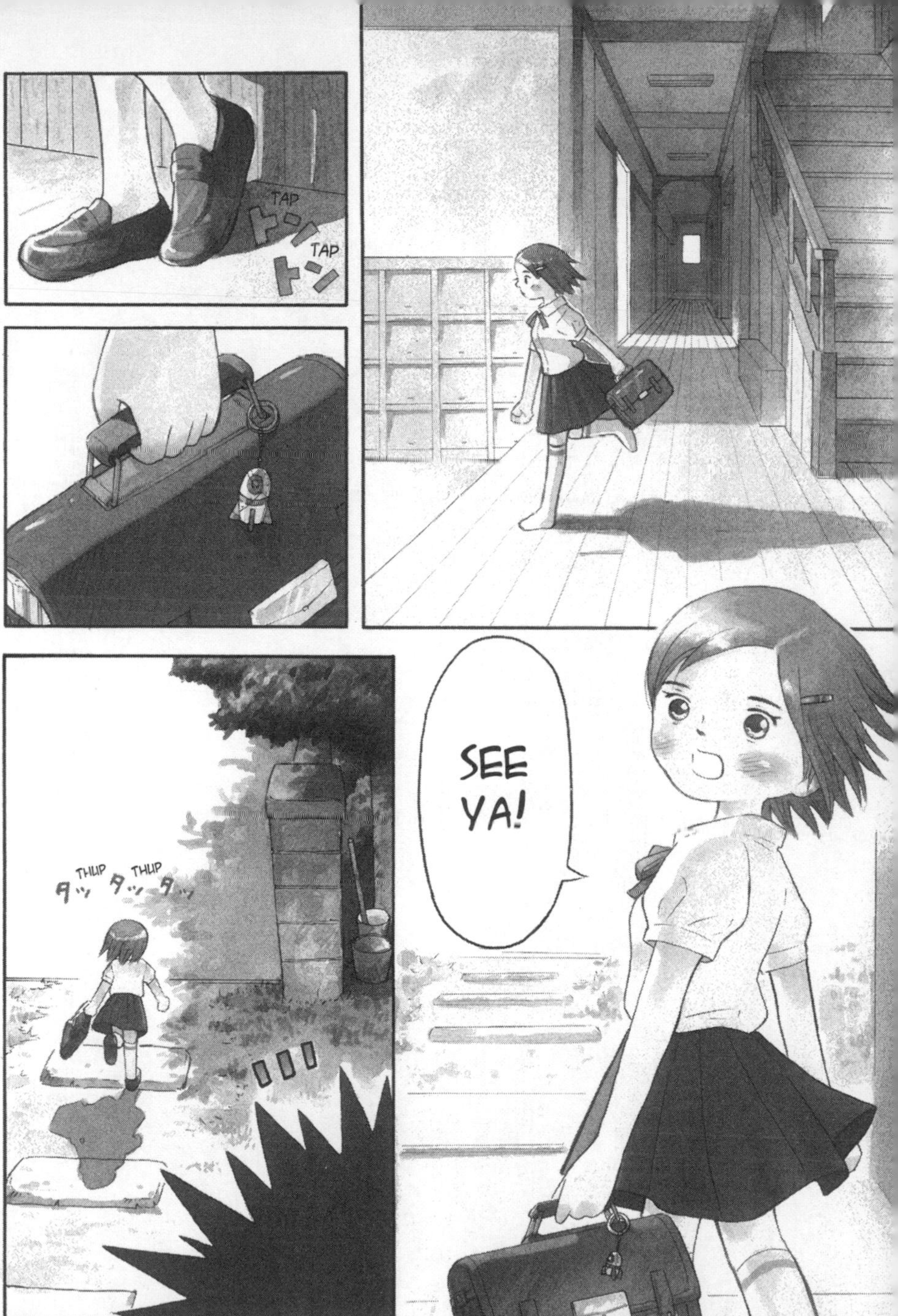
TAP
TAP
SEE YA!
THUP THUP

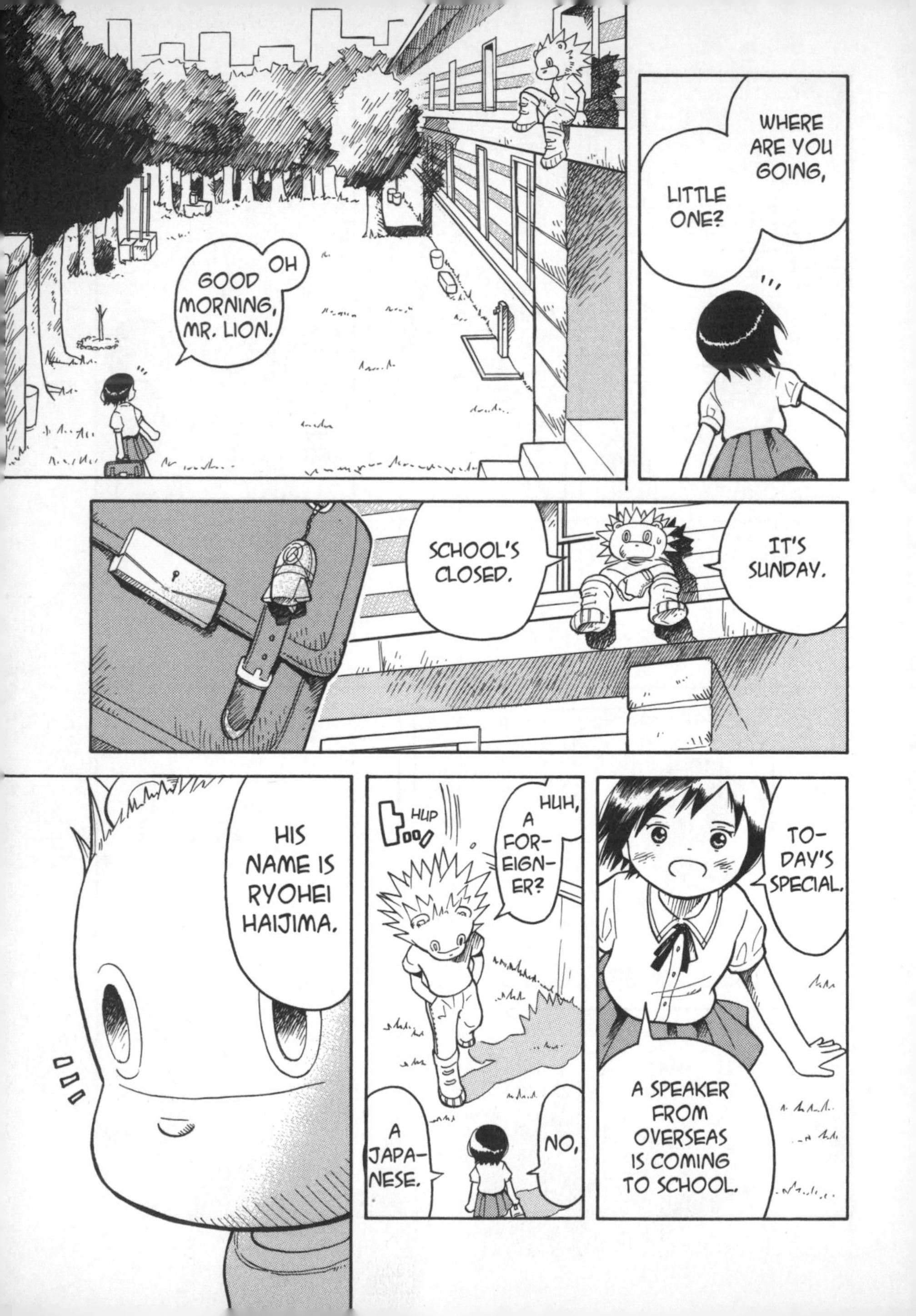
WHERE ARE YOU GOING, LITTLE ONE?
OH GOOD MORNING, MR. LION.
IT'S SUNDAY.
SCHOOL'S CLOSED.
TO-DAY'S SPECIAL.
A SPEAKER FROM OVERSEAS IS COMING TO SCHOOL.
HUP
HUH, A FOR-EIGNER?
NO,
A JAPA-NESE.
HIS NAME IS RYOHEI HAIJIMA.

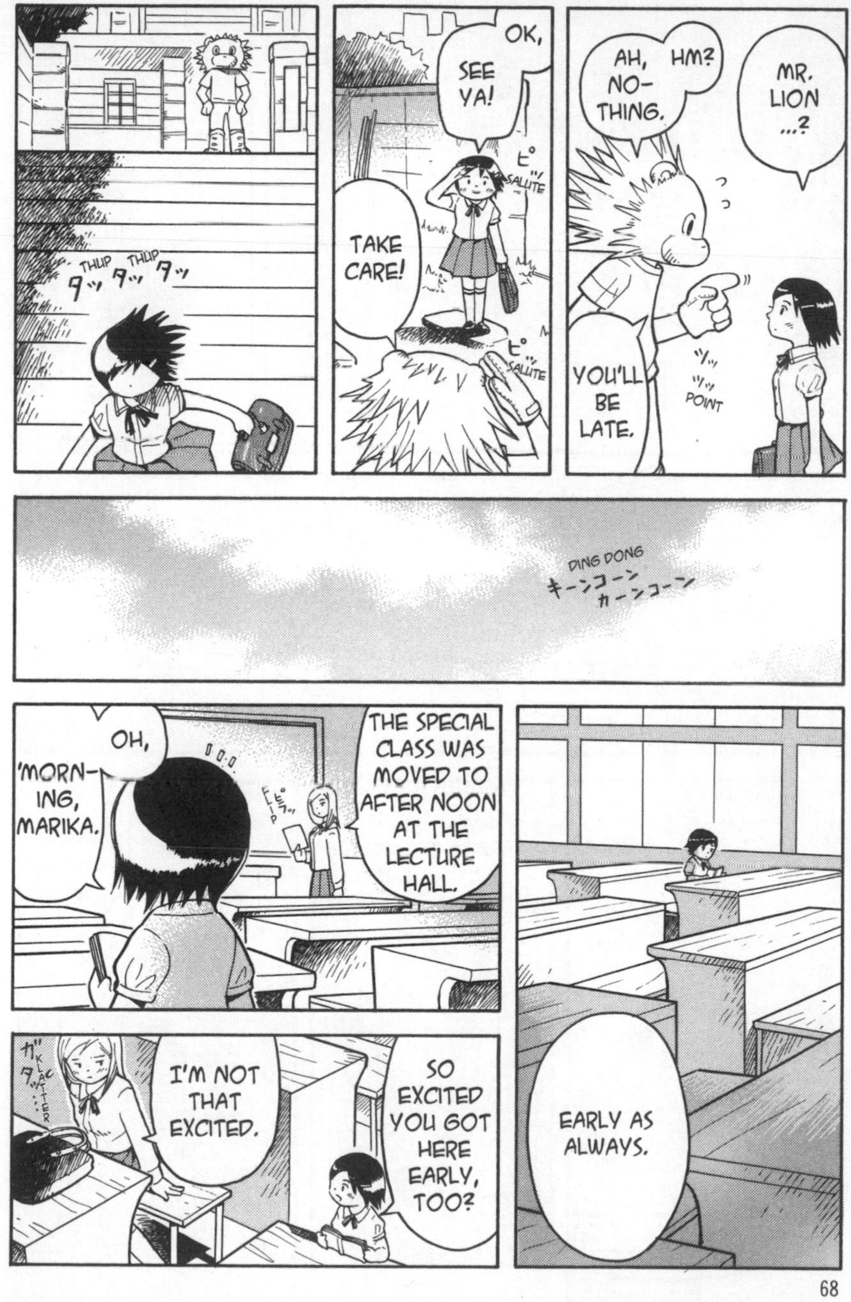

MR. LION ...?
HM?
AH, NO-THING.
ツッ POINT
YOU'LL BE LATE.
OK, SEE YA!
ピッ SALUTE
ピッ SALUTE
TAKE CARE!
THUP THUP タッ タッ タッ
DING DONG キーンコーン カーンコーン
EARLY AS ALWAYS.
THE SPECIAL CLASS WAS MOVED TO AFTER NOON AT THE LECTURE HALL.
FLIP
OH, 'MORN-ING, MARIKA.
SO EXCITED YOU GOT HERE EARLY, TOO?
I'M NOT THAT EXCITED.
ガタッ KLATTER

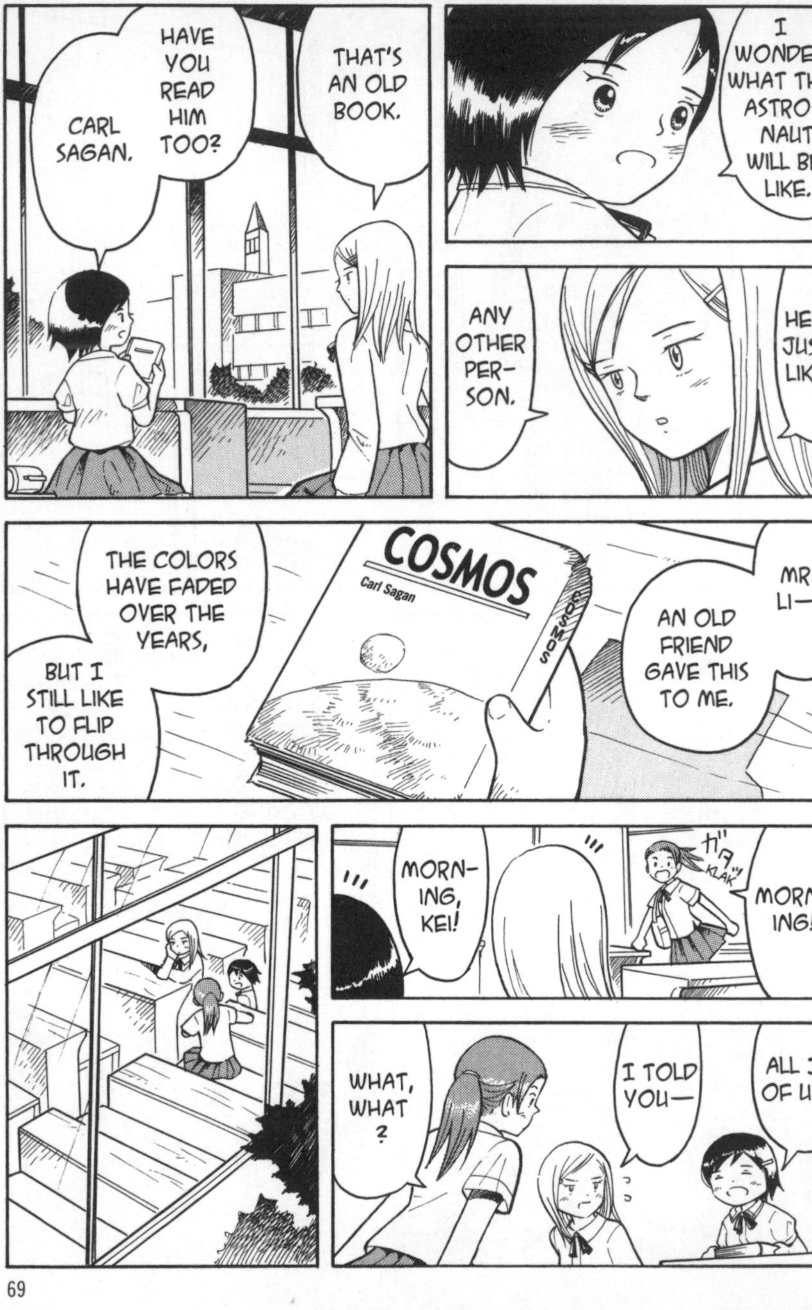
I WONDER WHAT THE ASTRO-NAUT WILL BE LIKE.
HE'S JUST LIKE
ANY OTHER PER-SON.
THAT'S AN OLD BOOK.
HAVE YOU READ HIM TOO?
CARL SAGAN.
MR. LI—
AN OLD FRIEND GAVE THIS TO ME.
COSMOS
Carl Sagan
COSMOS
THE COLORS HAVE FADED OVER THE YEARS,
BUT I STILL LIKE TO FLIP THROUGH IT.
MORN-ING!
ガタ
KLAK
MORN-ING, KEI!
ALL 3 OF US!
I TOLD YOU—
WHAT, WHAT?

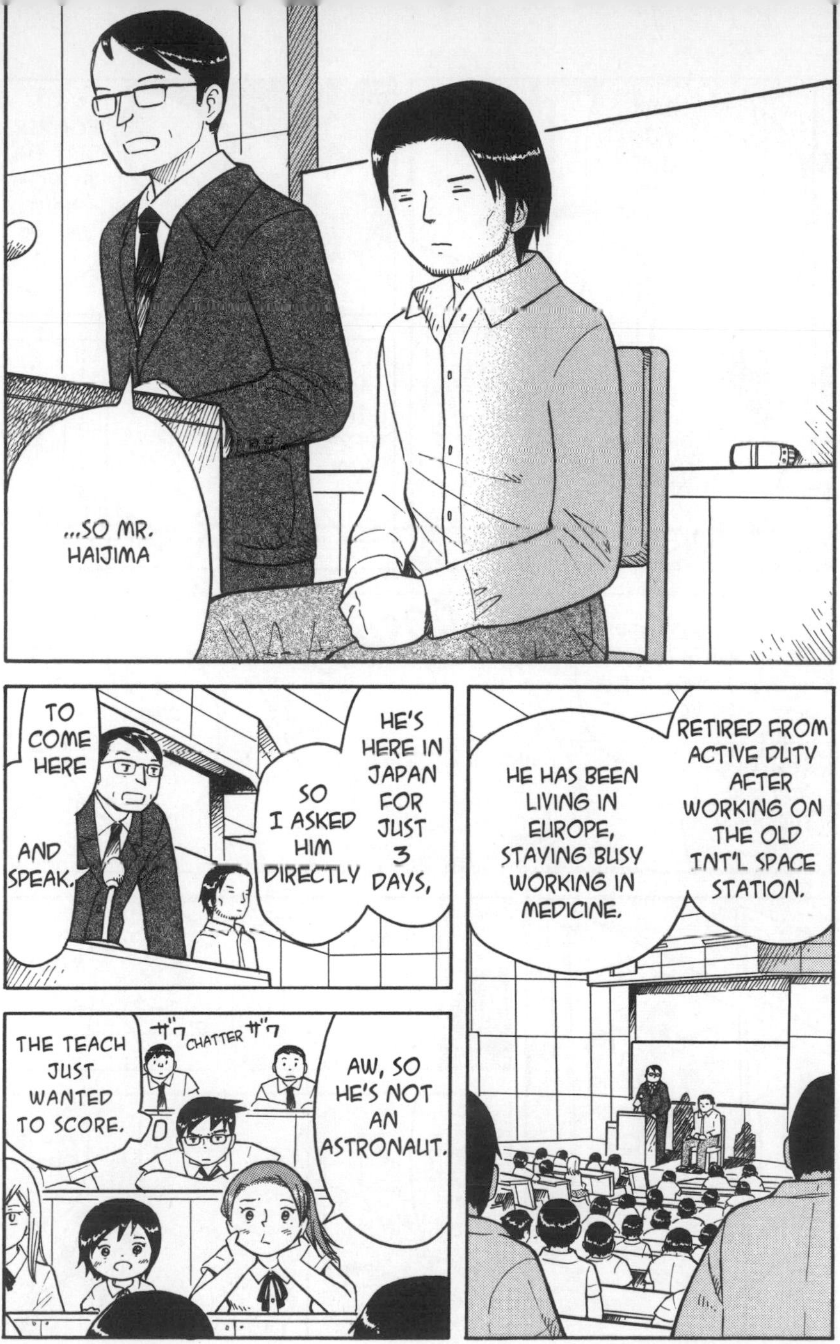
...SO MR. HAIJIMA
RETIRED FROM ACTIVE DUTY AFTER WORKING ON THE OLD INT'L SPACE STATION.
HE HAS BEEN LIVING IN EUROPE, STAYING BUSY WORKING IN MEDICINE.
HE'S HERE IN JAPAN FOR JUST 3 DAYS,
SO I ASKED HIM DIRECTLY
TO COME HERE
AND SPEAK.
AW, SO HE'S NOT AN ASTRONAUT.
ザワ CHATTER ザワ
THE TEACH JUST WANTED TO SCORE.

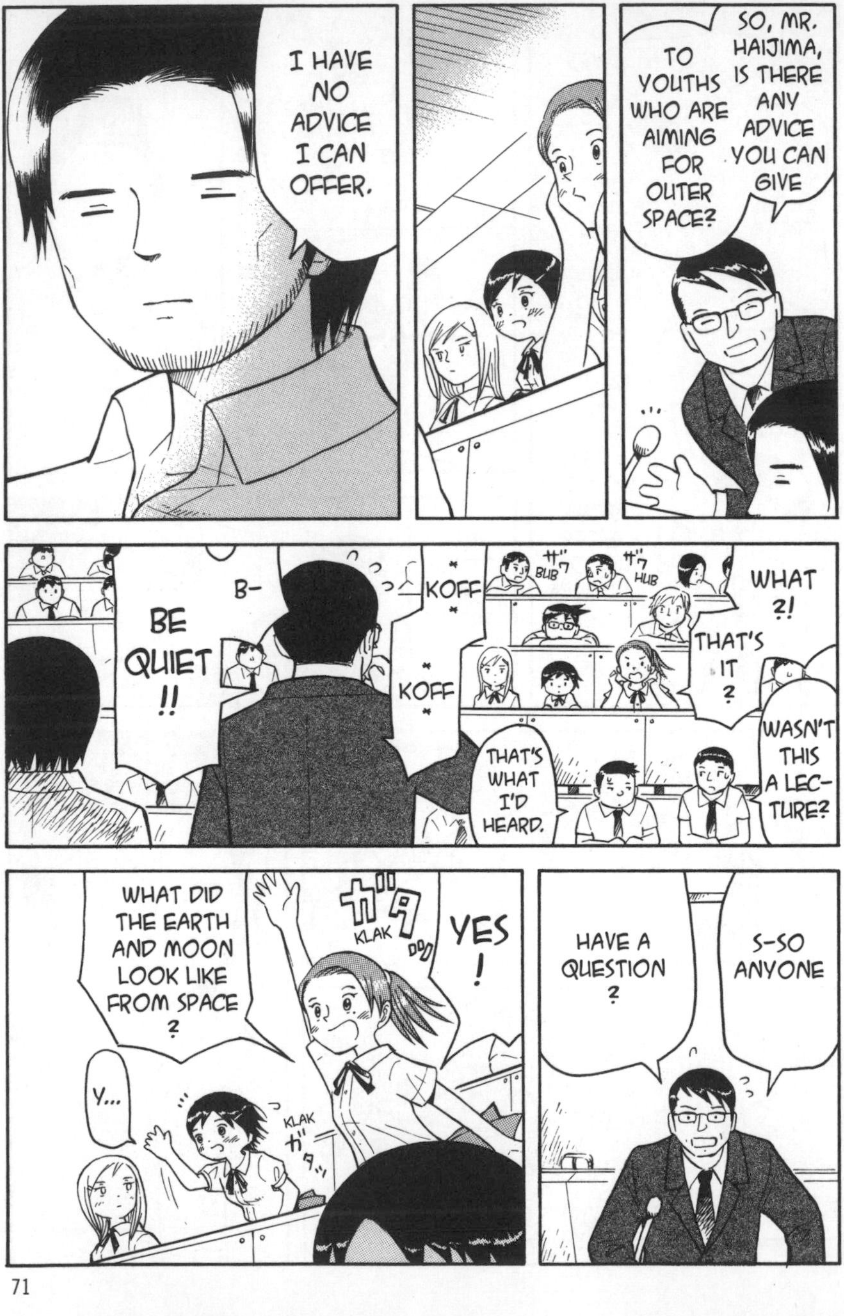
SO, MR. HAIJIMA, IS THERE ANY ADVICE YOU CAN GIVE
TO YOUTHS WHO ARE AIMING FOR OUTER SPACE?
I HAVE NO ADVICE I CAN OFFER.
WHAT ?!
THAT'S IT ?
WASN'T THIS A LEC-TURE?
ザワ HUB
ザワ BUB
THAT'S WHAT I'D HEARD.
KOFF
KOFF
B-
BE QUIET !!
S-SO ANYONE
HAVE A QUESTION ?
YES !
ガタ KLAK
WHAT DID THE EARTH AND MOON LOOK LIKE FROM SPACE ?
Y...
KLAK ガタッ

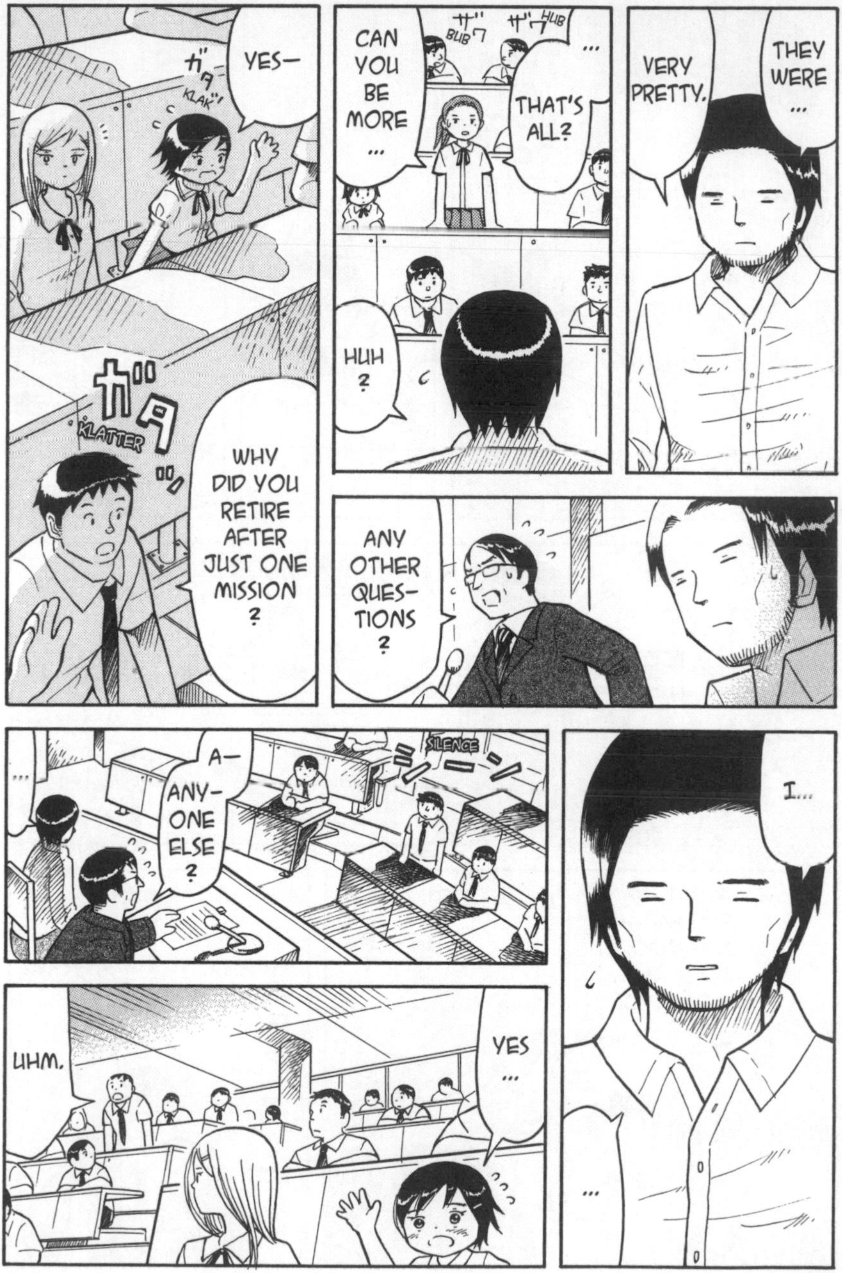
THEY WERE ...
VERY PRETTY.
...
THAT'S ALL?
ザワ HUB
ザワ BUB
CAN YOU BE MORE ...
HUH?
ANY OTHER QUES-TIONS?
YES—
ガタ KLAK
カタ KLATTER
WHY DID YOU RETIRE AFTER JUST ONE MISSION?
I...
...
SILENCE
A— ANYONE ELSE?
...
YES ...
UHM.

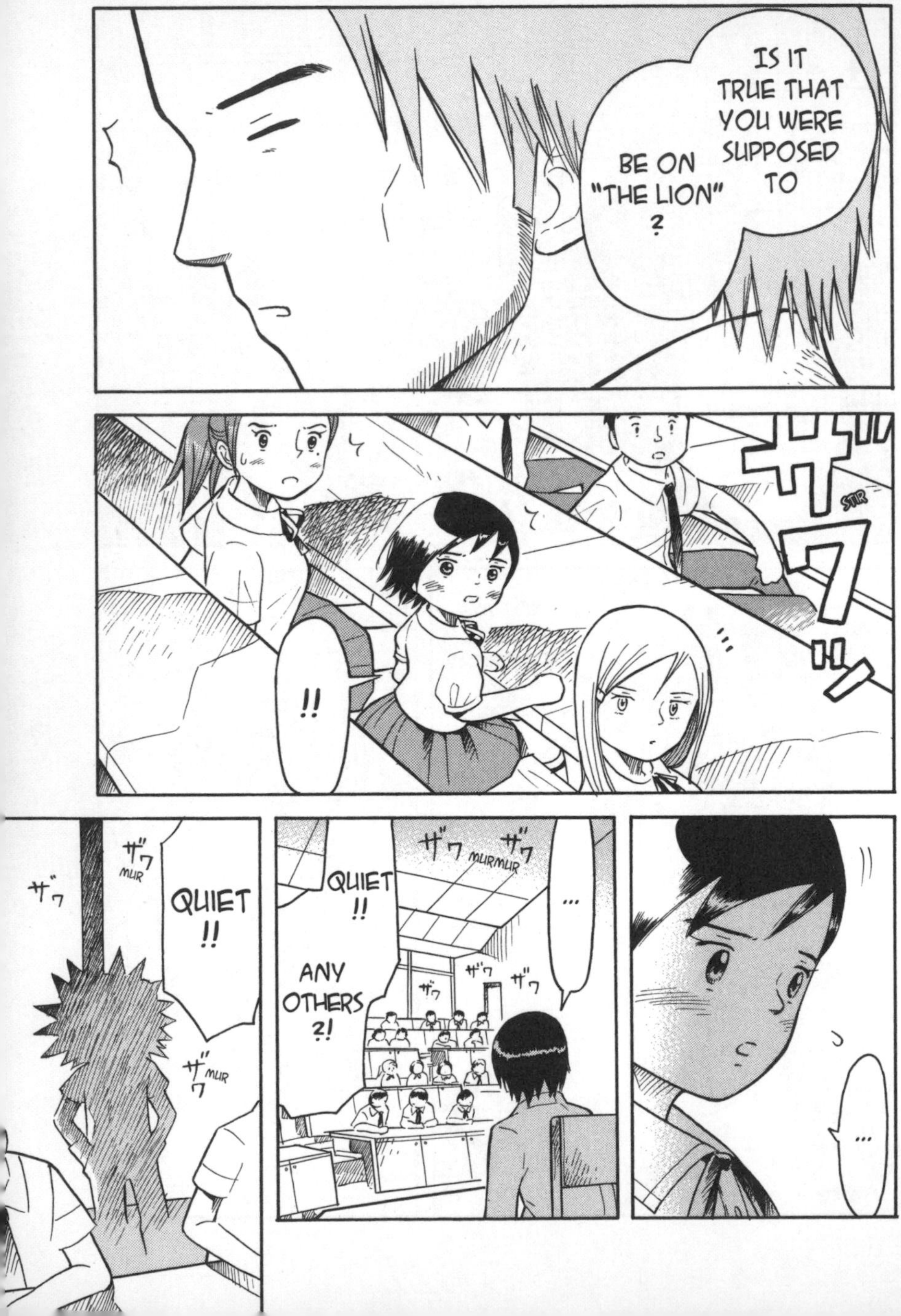
IS IT TRUE THAT YOU WERE SUPPOSED TO
BE ON "THE LION"?
ザワ
STIR
ザワ
!!
...
...
ザワ
MURMUR
ザワ
QUIET!!
ANY OTHERS?!
ザワ
ザワ
ザワ
ザワ
MUR
QUIET!!
ザワ
ザワ
MUR

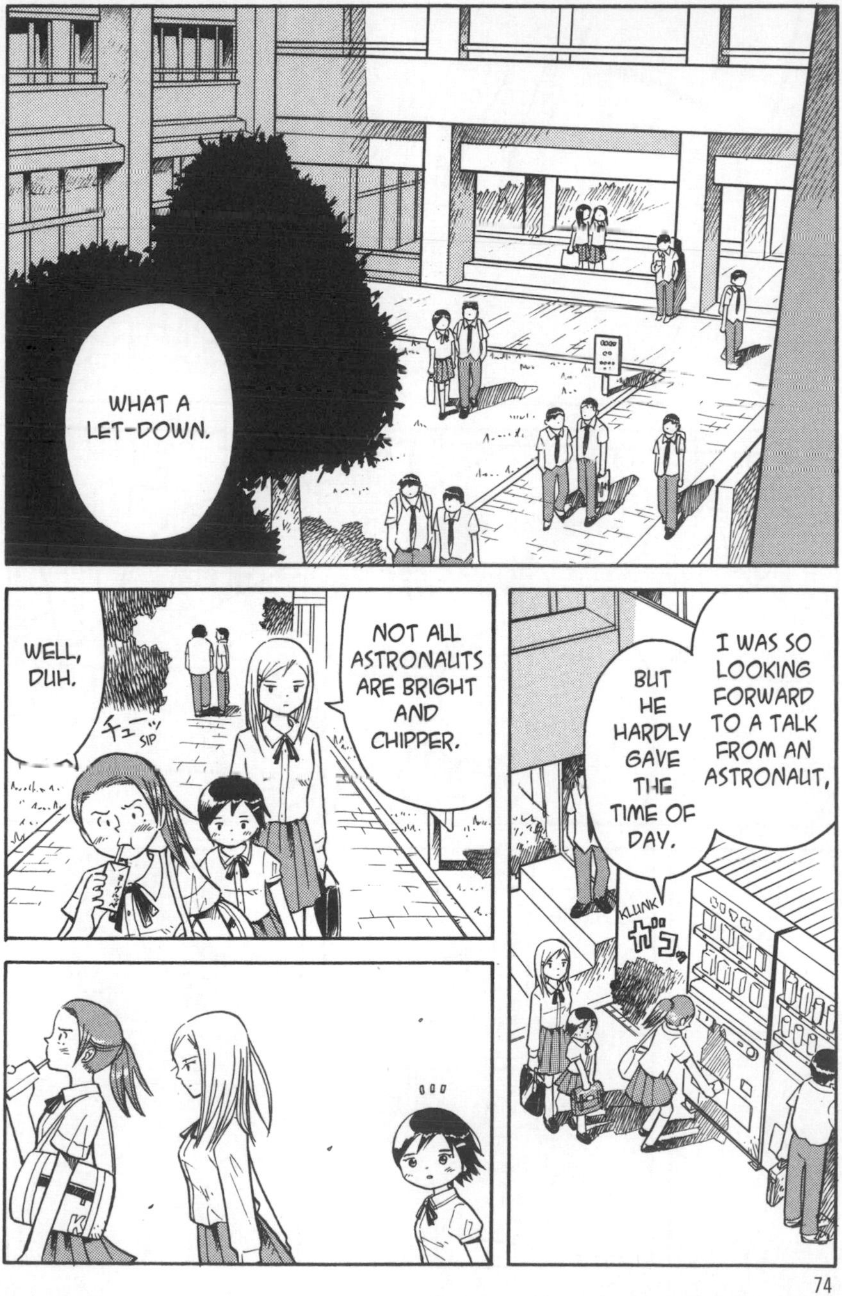
WHAT A LET-DOWN.
I WAS SO LOOKING FORWARD TO A TALK FROM AN ASTRONAUT,
BUT HE HARDLY GAVE THE TIME OF DAY.
KLUNK
ガコ
NOT ALL ASTRONAUTS ARE BRIGHT AND CHIPPER.
WELL, DUH.
チューッ
SIP

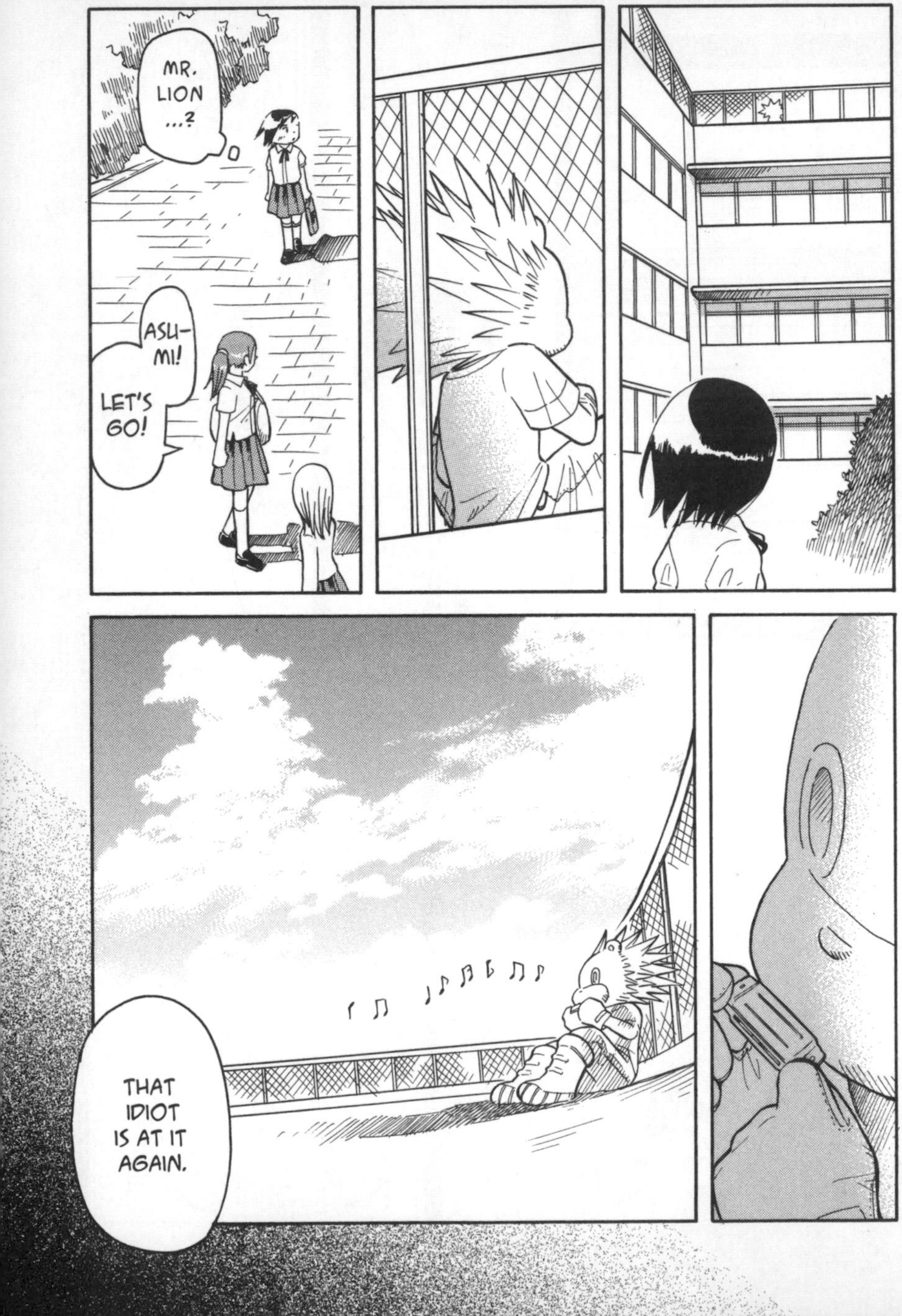
MR. LION ...?
ASUMI!
LET'S GO!
THAT IDIOT IS AT IT AGAIN.

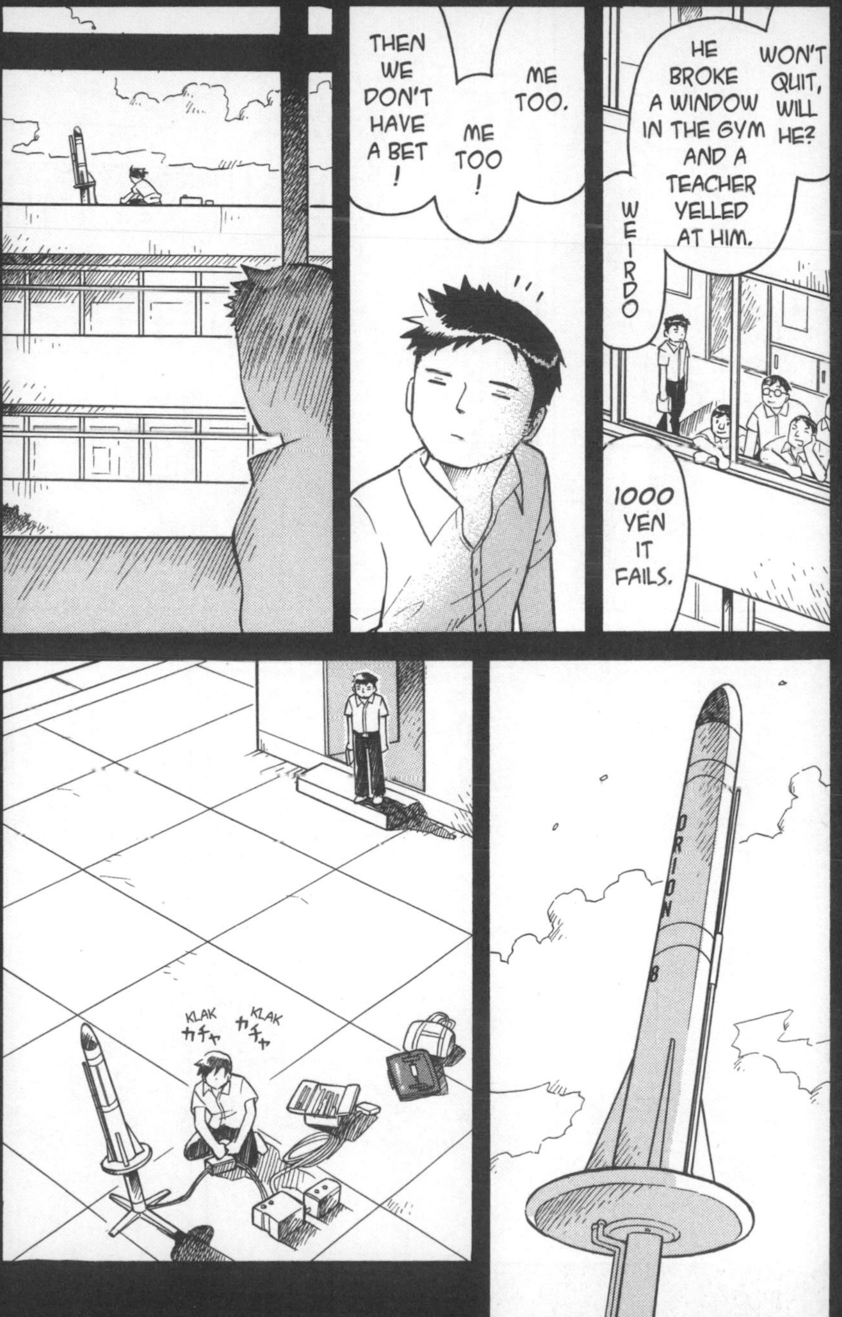
WON'T QUIT, WILL HE?
HE BROKE A WINDOW IN THE GYM AND A TEACHER YELLED AT HIM.
WEIRDO
1000 YEN IT FAILS.
ME TOO.
ME TOO!
THEN WE DON'T HAVE A BET!
ORION
KLAK カチャ
KLAK カチャ

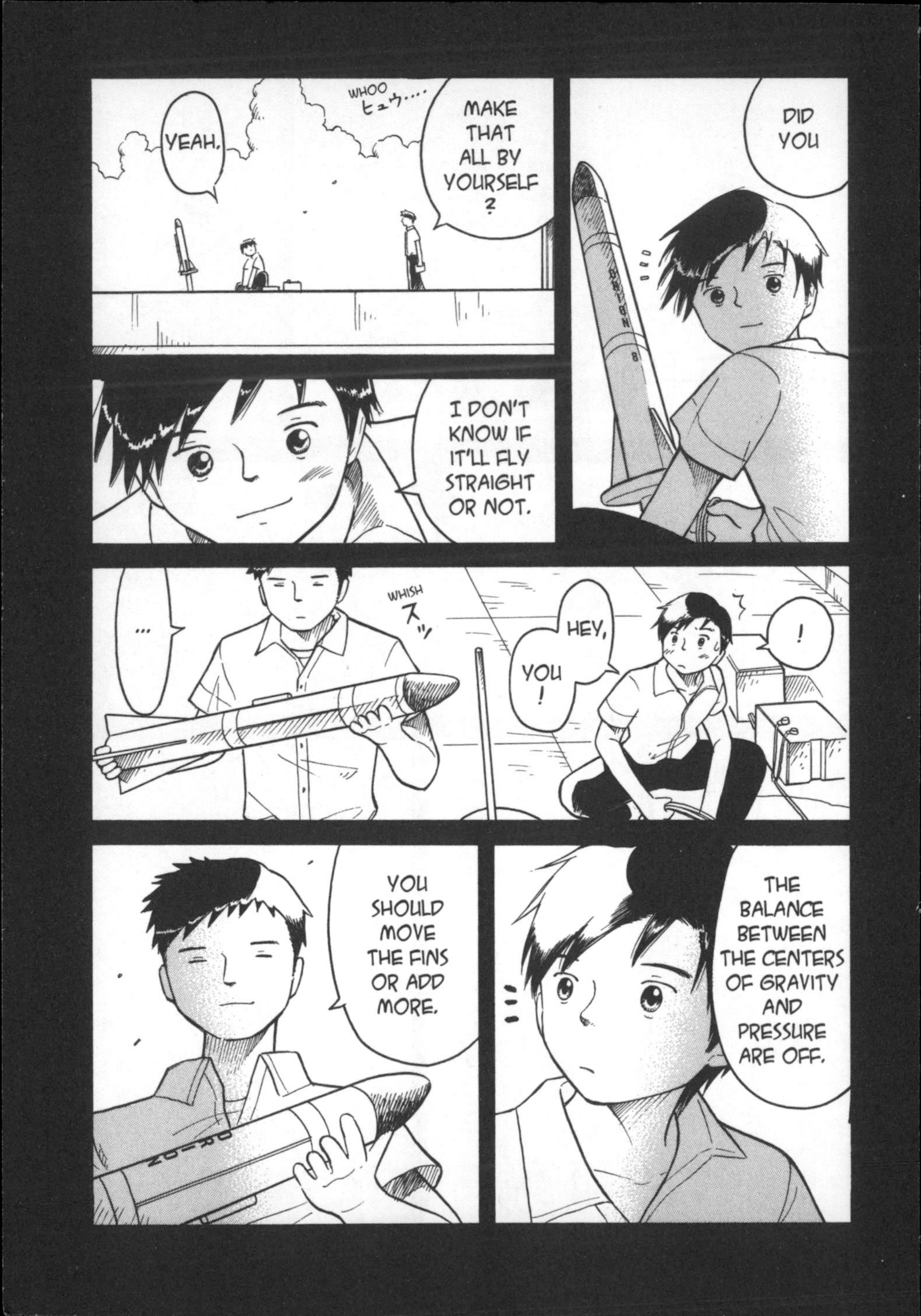
DID YOU
MAKE THAT ALL BY YOURSELF?
WHOO ヒュウ....
YEAH.
I DON'T KNOW IF IT'LL FLY STRAIGHT OR NOT.
!
HEY, YOU!
WHISH スッ
...
THE BALANCE BETWEEN THE CENTERS OF GRAVITY AND PRESSURE ARE OFF.
YOU SHOULD MOVE THE FINS OR ADD MORE.

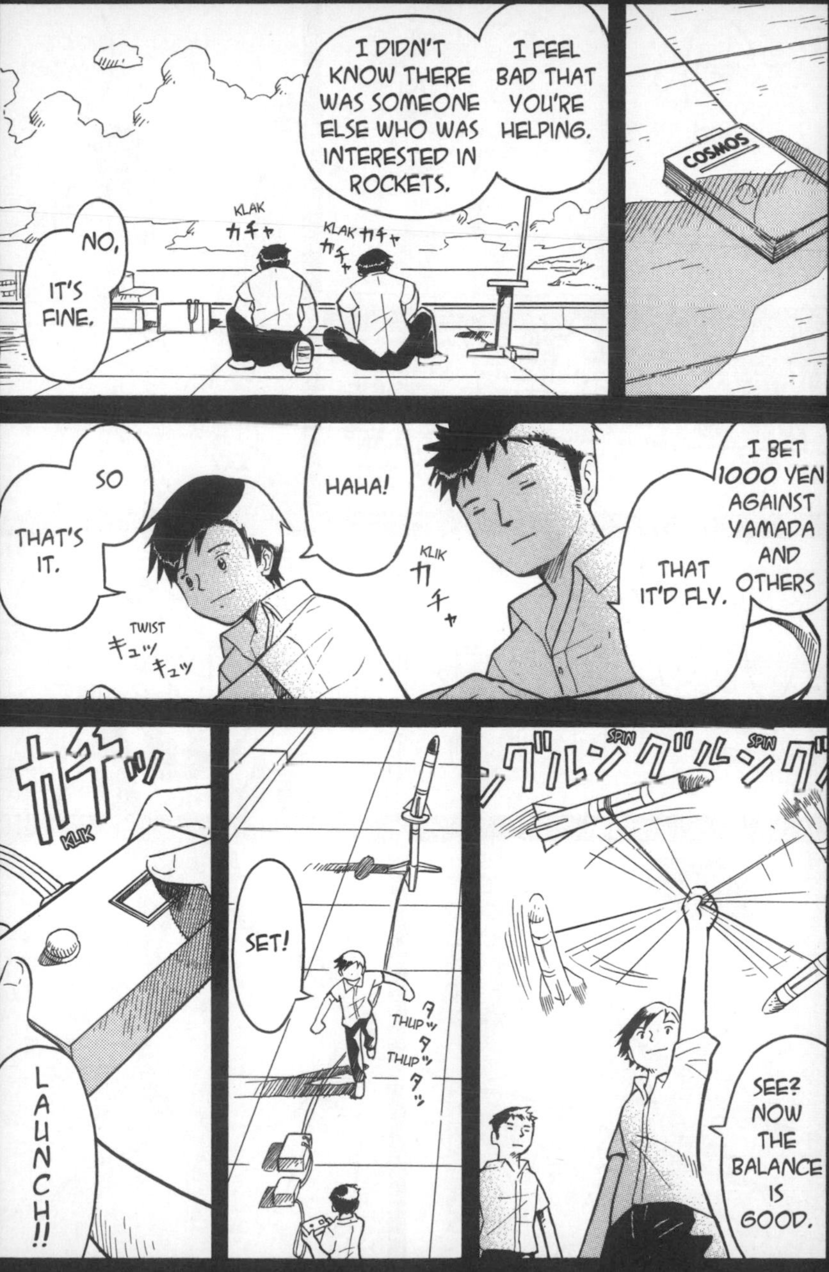

COSMOS
I FEEL BAD THAT YOU'RE HELPING.
I DIDN'T KNOW THERE WAS SOMEONE ELSE WHO WAS INTERESTED IN ROCKETS.
KLAK カチャ
KLAK カチャ カチャ
NO,
IT'S FINE.
I BET 1000 YEN AGAINST YAMADA AND OTHERS
THAT IT'D FLY.
KLIK カチャ
HAHA!
SO
THAT'S IT.
TWIST キュッ キュッ
SPIN グルン
SPIN グルン
SEE? NOW THE BALANCE IS GOOD.
SET!
THUP タッ
THUP タッ
タッ
カチッ
KLIK
LAUNCH!!

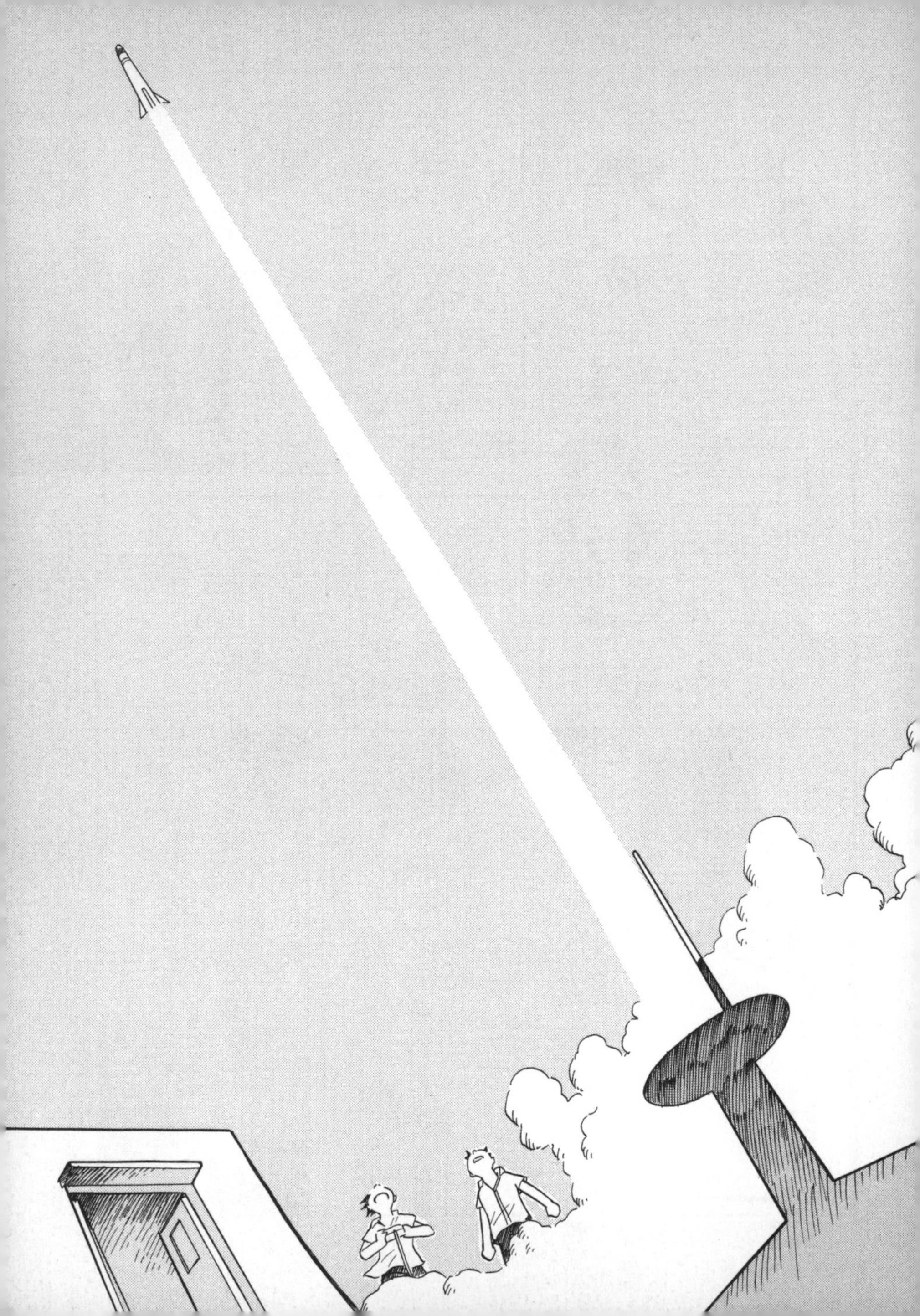

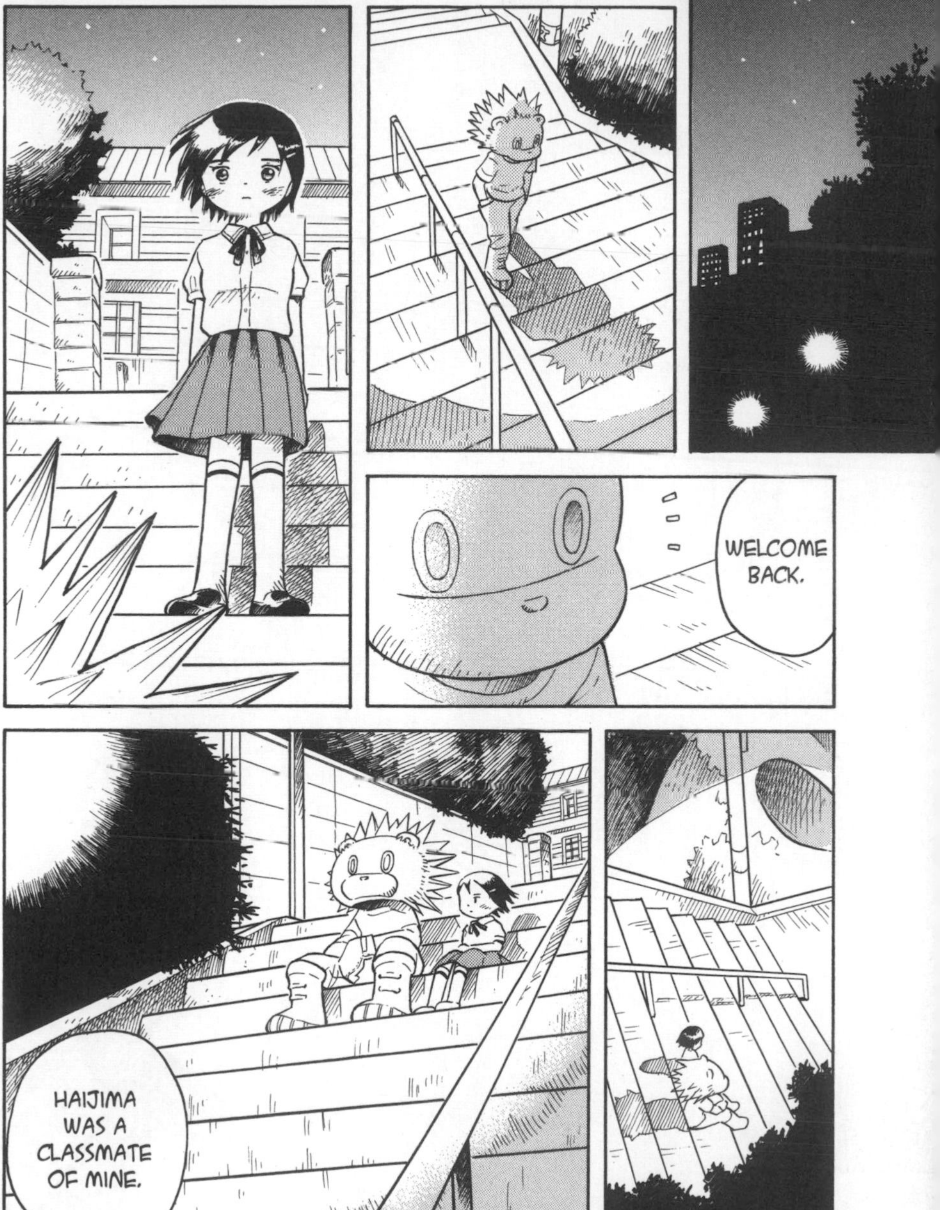
WELCOME BACK.
HAIJIMA WAS A CLASSMATE OF MINE.

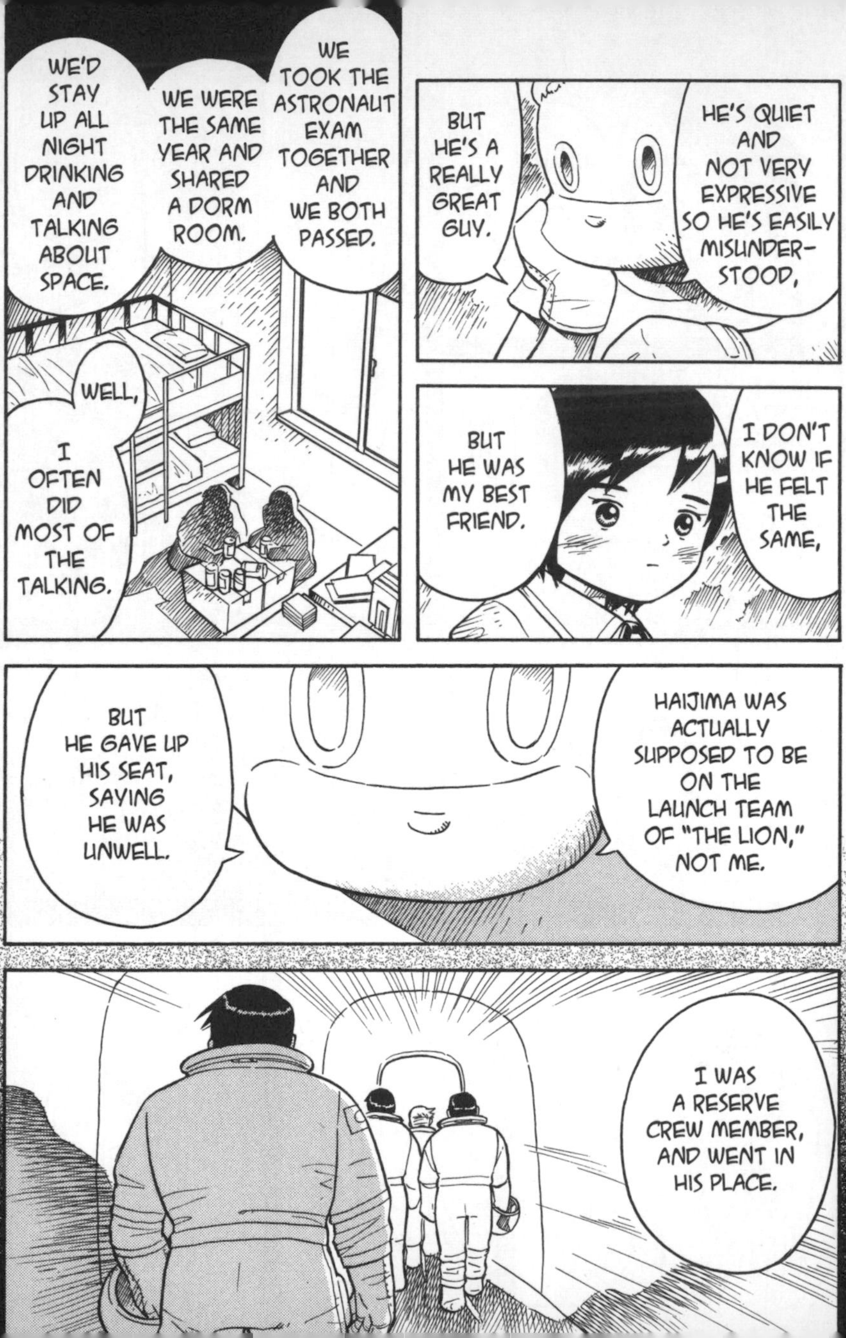
HE'S QUIET AND NOT VERY EXPRESSIVE SO HE'S EASILY MISUNDER-STOOD,
BUT HE'S A REALLY GREAT GUY.
I DON'T KNOW IF HE FELT THE SAME,
BUT HE WAS MY BEST FRIEND.
WE TOOK THE ASTRONAUT EXAM TOGETHER AND WE BOTH PASSED.
WE WERE THE SAME YEAR AND SHARED A DORM ROOM.
WE'D STAY UP ALL NIGHT DRINKING AND TALKING ABOUT SPACE.
WELL, I OFTEN DID MOST OF THE TALKING.
HAIJIMA WAS ACTUALLY SUPPOSED TO BE ON THE LAUNCH TEAM OF "THE LION," NOT ME.
BUT HE GAVE UP HIS SEAT, SAYING HE WAS UNWELL.
I WAS A RESERVE CREW MEMBER, AND WENT IN HIS PLACE.

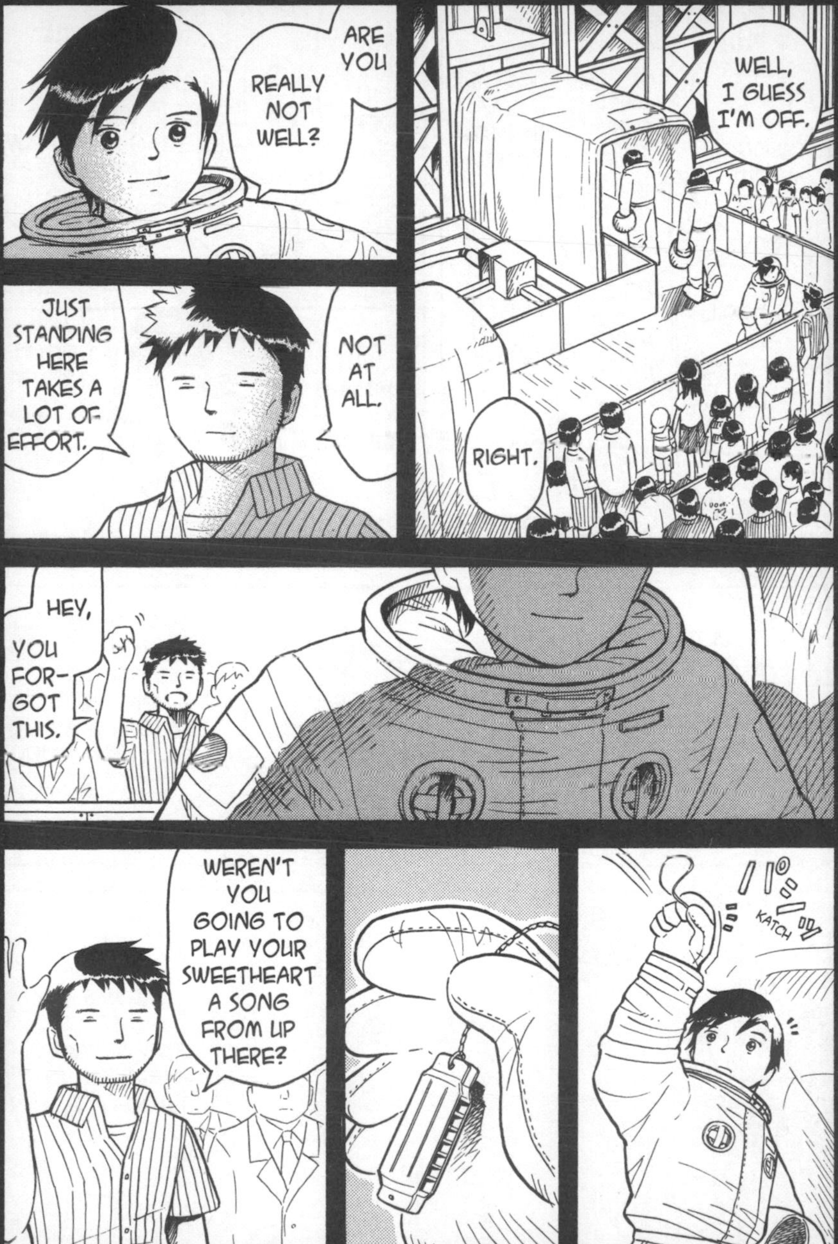
WELL, I GUESS I'M OFF.
RIGHT.
ARE YOU REALLY NOT WELL?
NOT AT ALL.
JUST STANDING HERE TAKES A LOT OF EFFORT.
HEY, YOU FOR-GOT THIS.
KATCH
WEREN'T YOU GOING TO PLAY YOUR SWEETHEART A SONG FROM UP THERE?

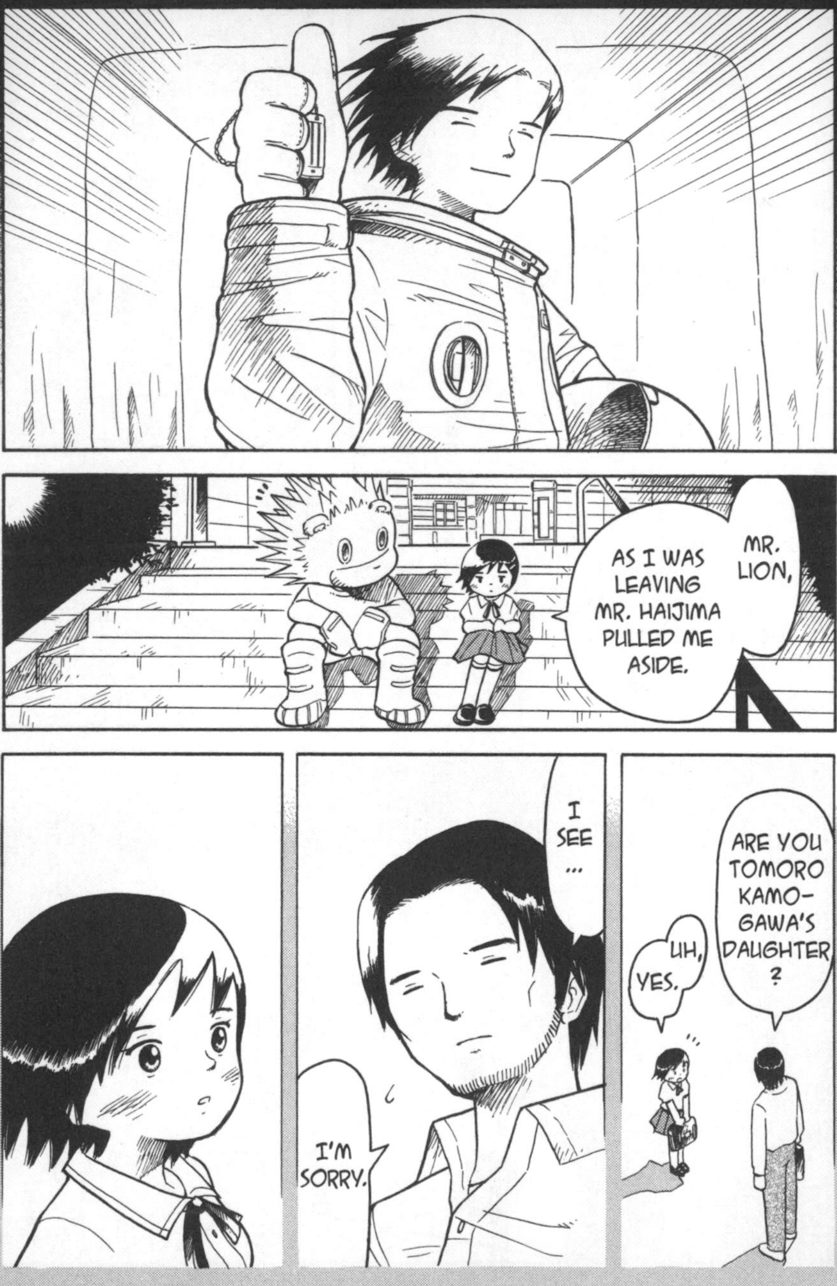
MR. LION,
AS I WAS LEAVING MR. HAIJIMA PULLED ME ASIDE.
ARE YOU TOMORO KAMO-GAWA'S DAUGHTER?
UH, YES.
I SEE ...
I'M SORRY.

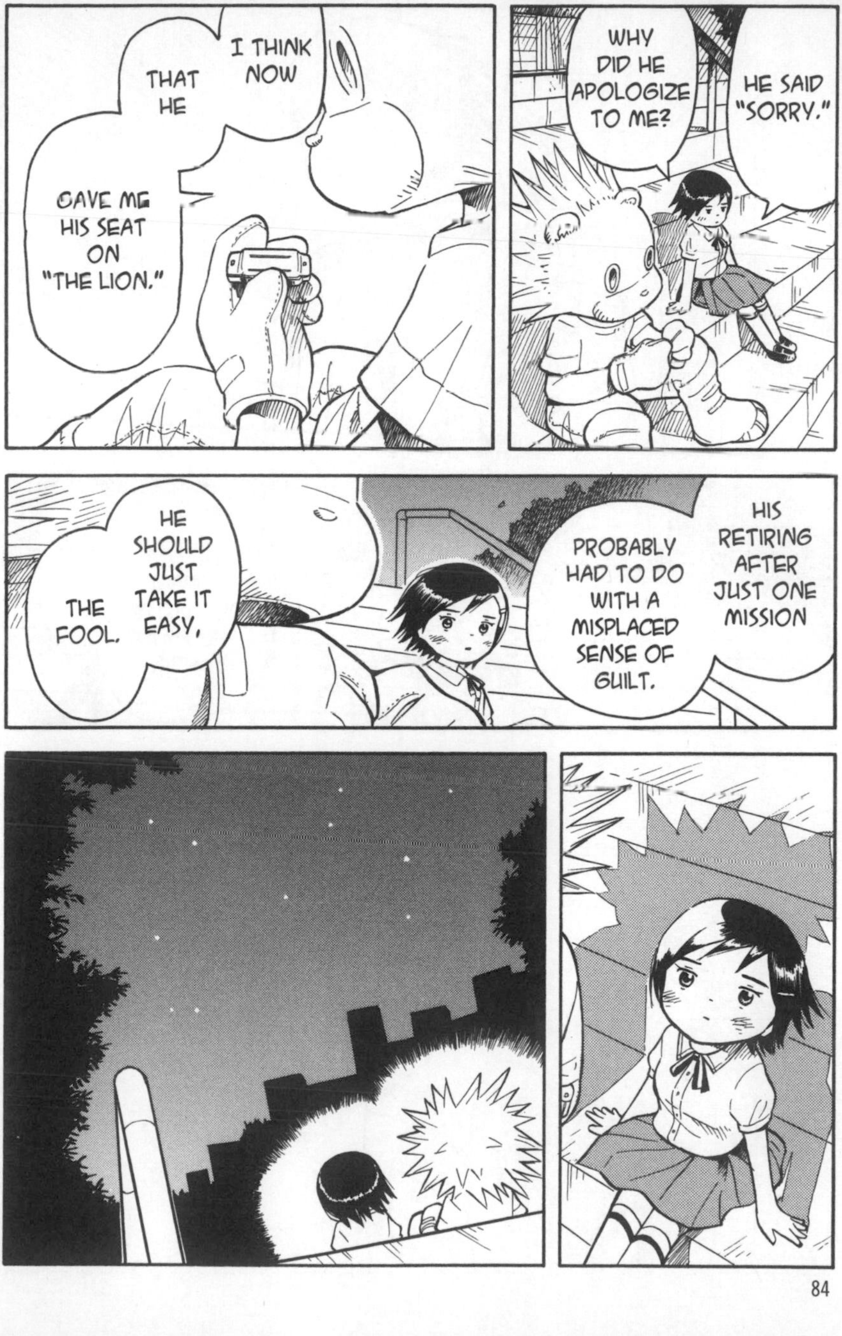
HE SAID "SORRY."
WHY DID HE APOLOGIZE TO ME?
I THINK NOW THAT HE GAVE ME HIS SEAT ON "THE LION."
HIS RETIRING AFTER JUST ONE MISSION PROBABLY HAD TO DO WITH A MISPLACED SENSE OF GUILT.
HE SHOULD JUST TAKE IT EASY, THE FOOL.

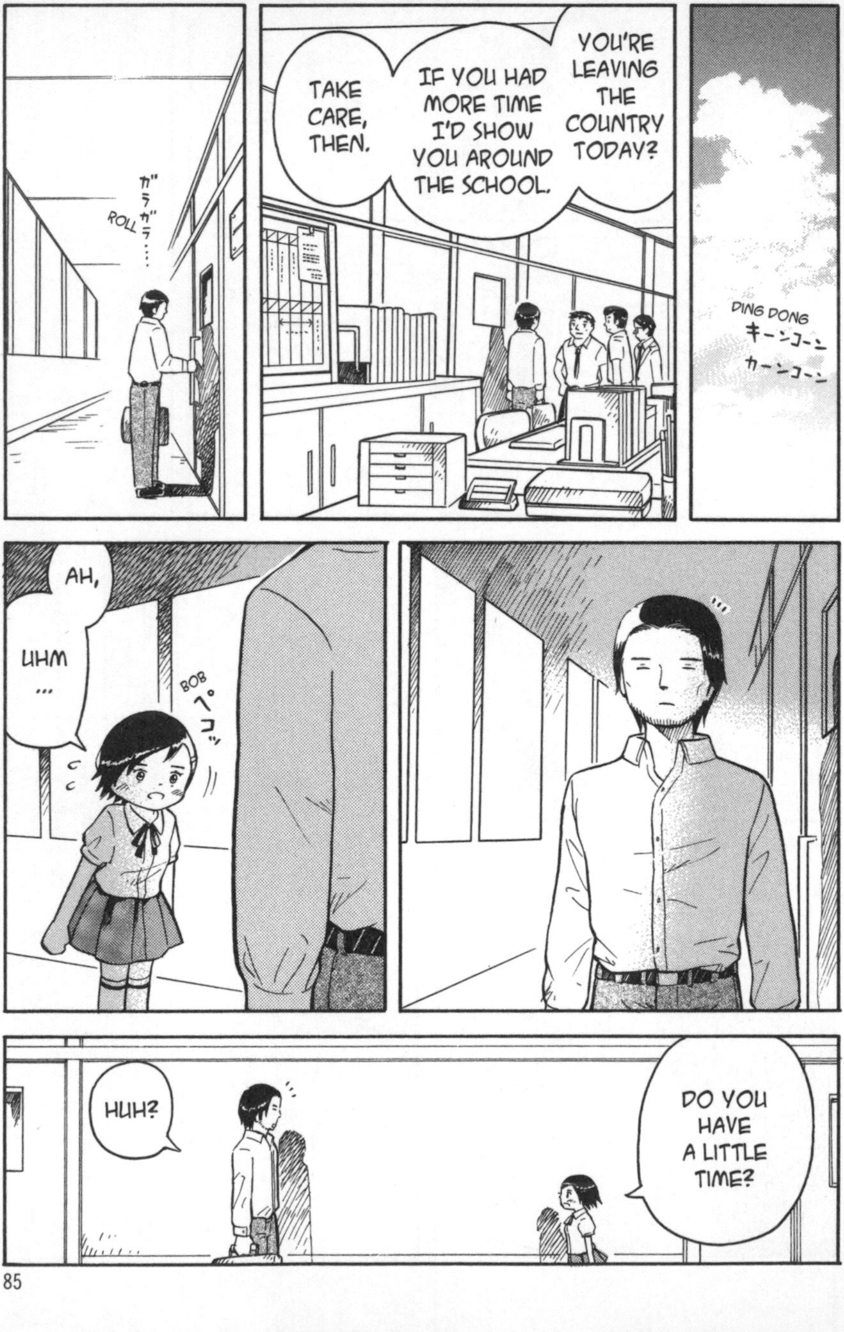
DING DONG
キーンコーン
カーンコーン
YOU'RE LEAVING THE COUNTRY TODAY?
IF YOU HAD MORE TIME I'D SHOW YOU AROUND THE SCHOOL.
TAKE CARE, THEN.
ガラガラ....
ROLL
AH,
UHM ...
BOB
ペコッ
DO YOU HAVE A LITTLE TIME?
HUH?

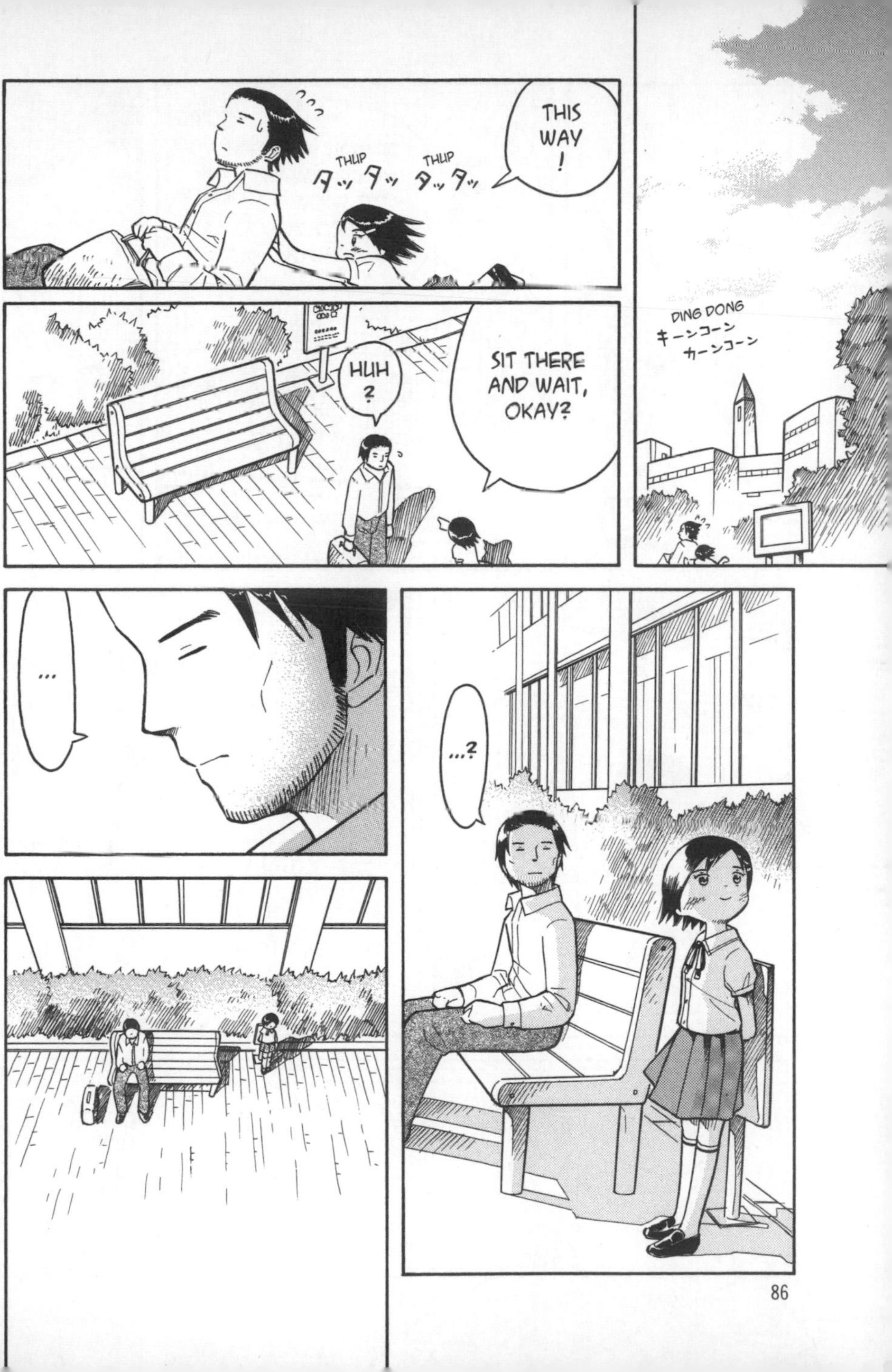
DING DONG
キーンコーン
カーンコーン
THIS WAY!
THUP
タッタッ
THUP
タッタッ
SIT THERE AND WAIT, OKAY?
HUH?
...?
...

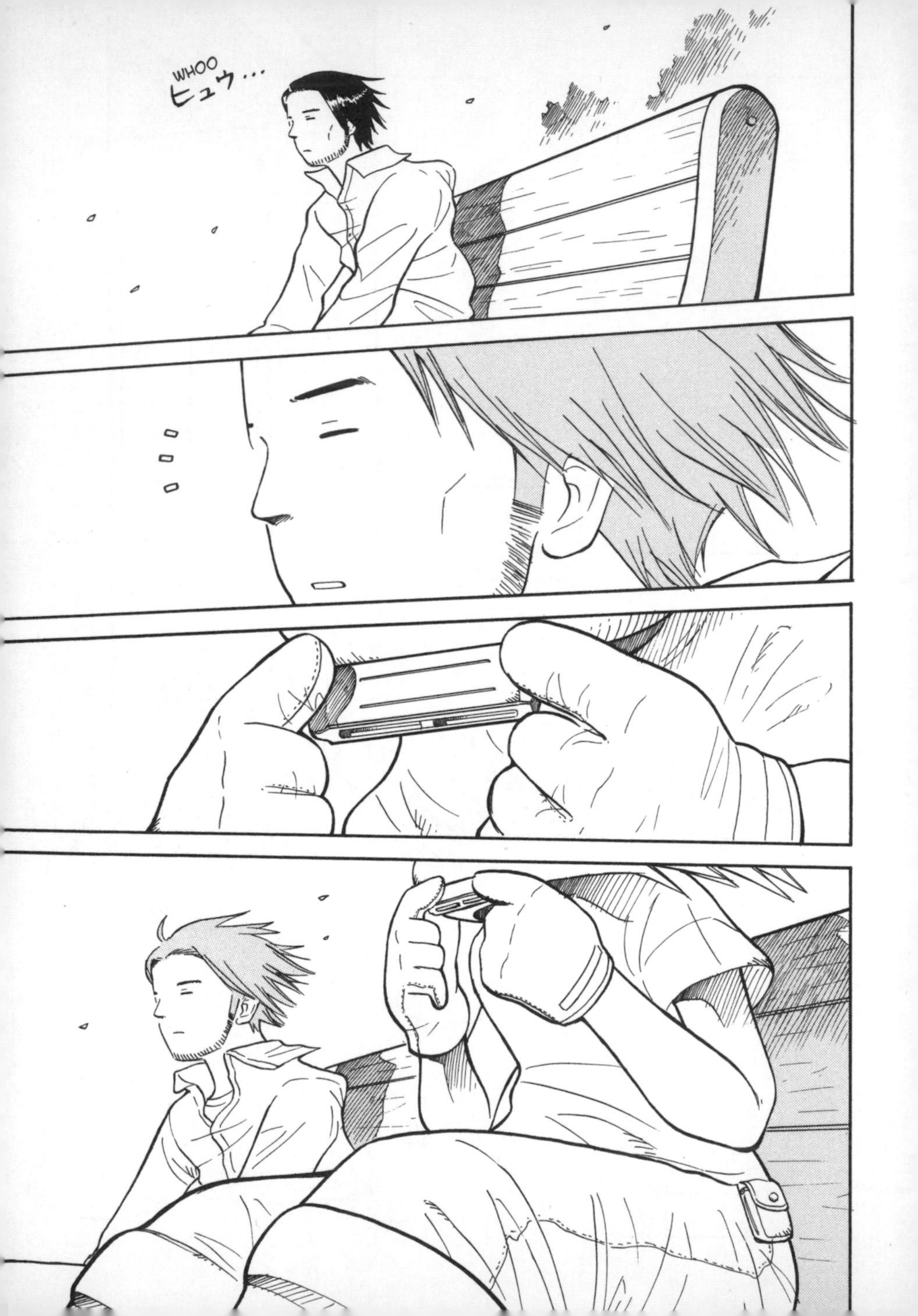
WHOO
ヒュウ…

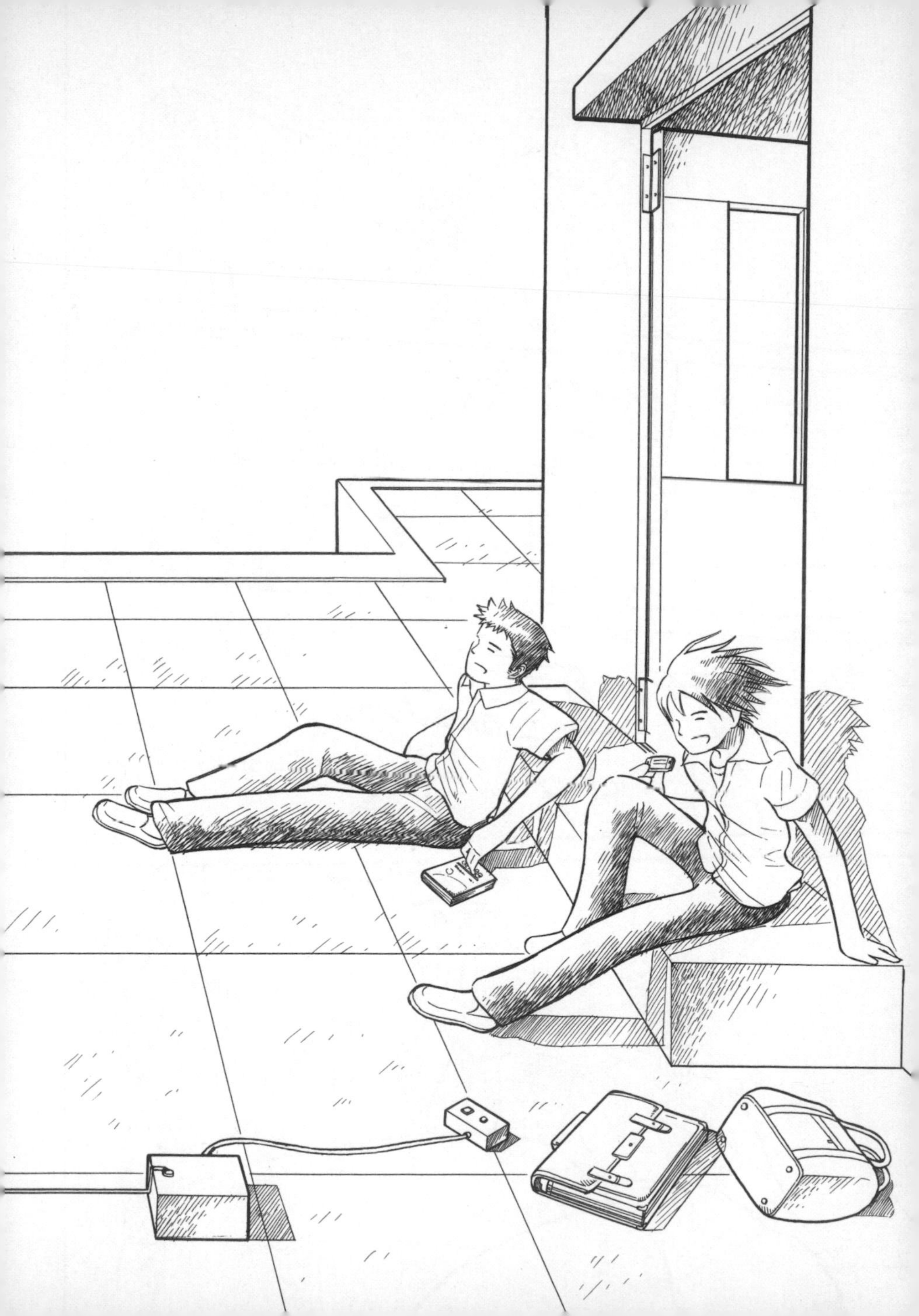

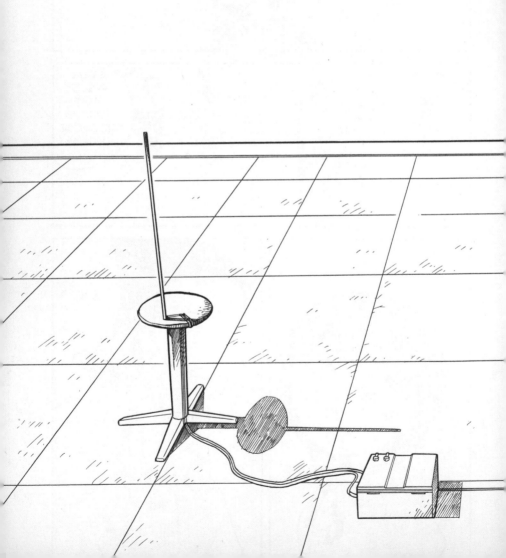

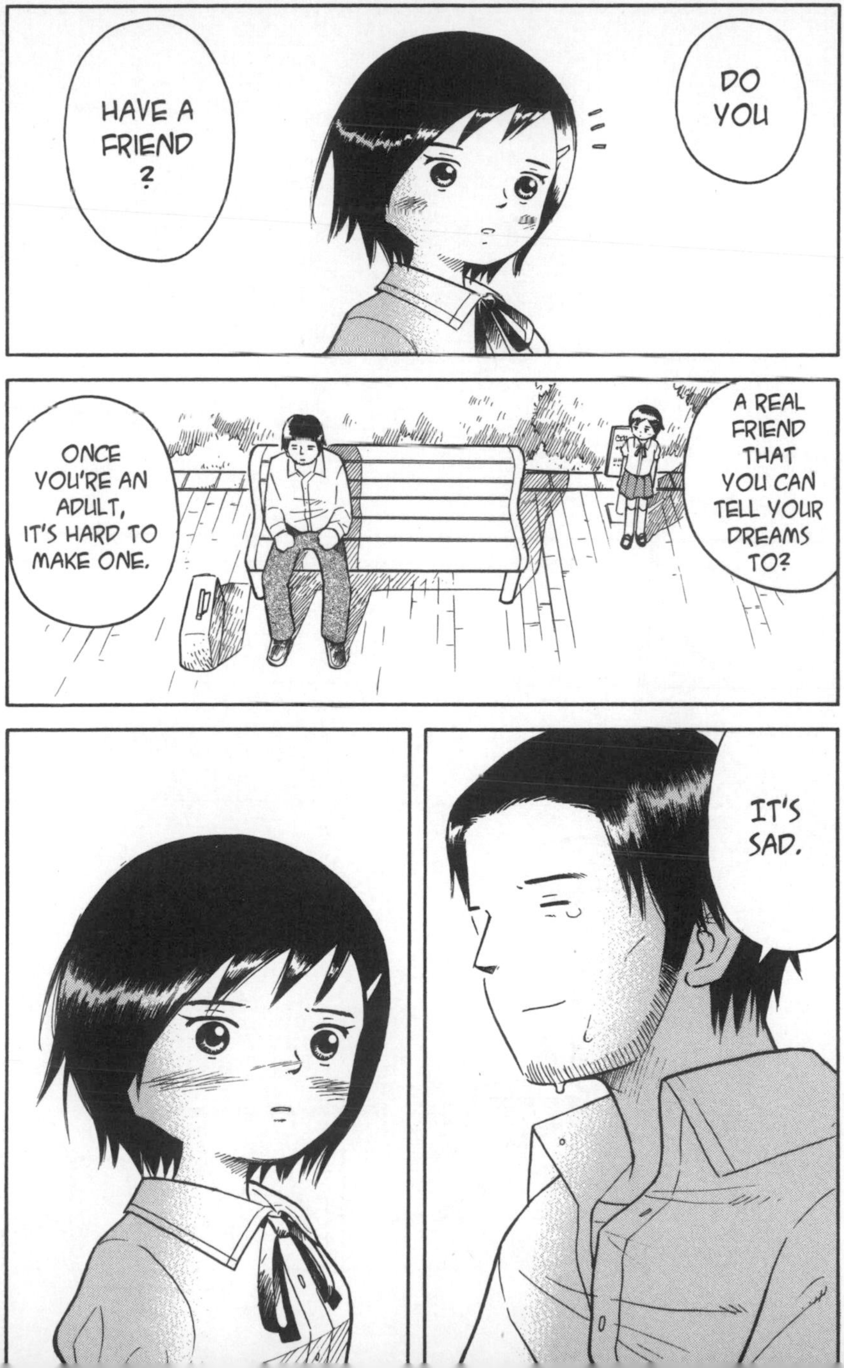
DO YOU
HAVE A FRIEND ?
A REAL FRIEND THAT YOU CAN TELL YOUR DREAMS TO?
ONCE YOU'RE AN ADULT, IT'S HARD TO MAKE ONE.
IT'S SAD.

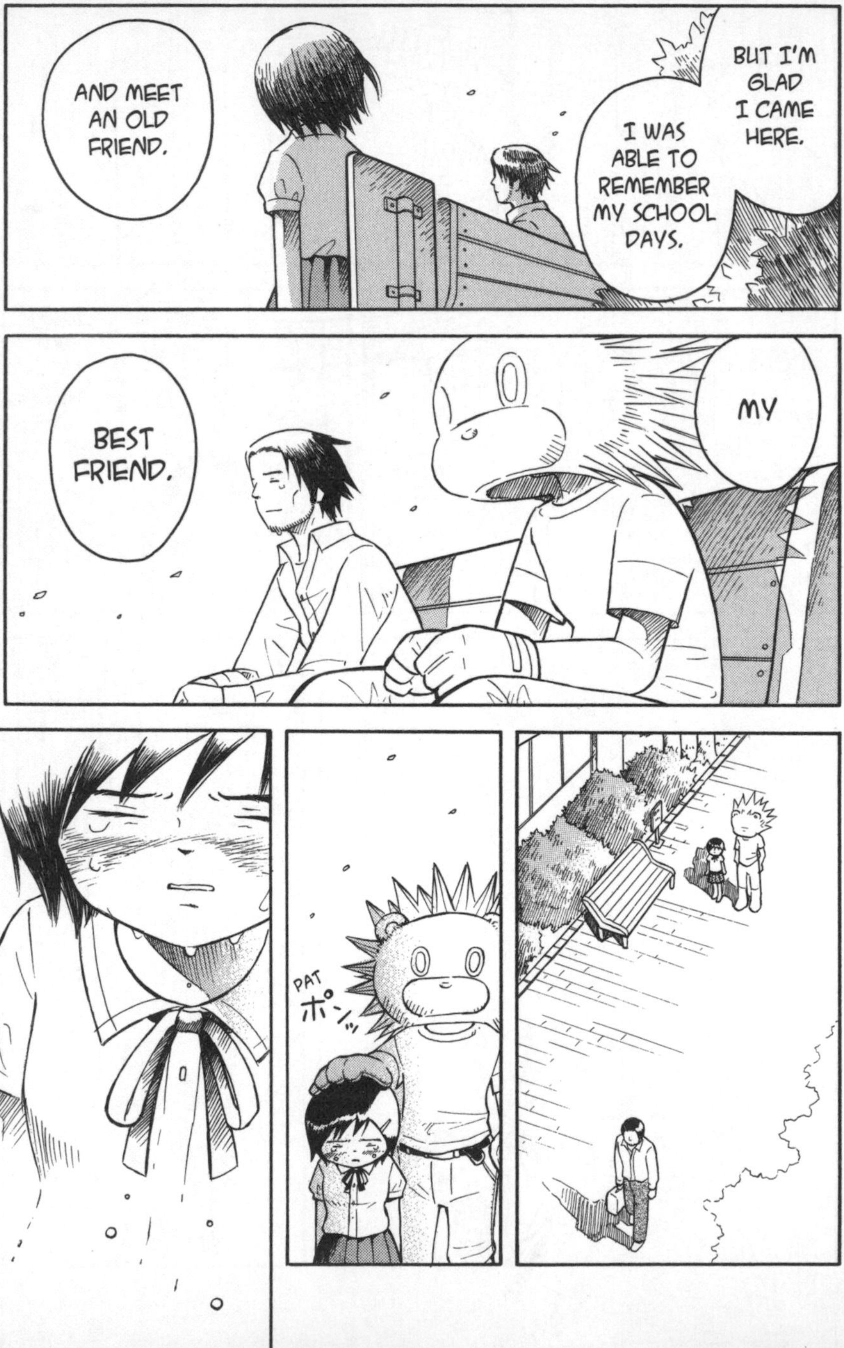
BUT I'M GLAD I CAME HERE.
I WAS ABLE TO REMEMBER MY SCHOOL DAYS.
AND MEET AN OLD FRIEND.
MY
BEST FRIEND.
PAT
ポンッ

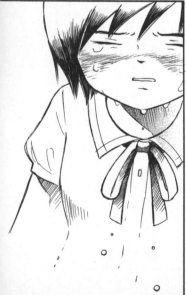

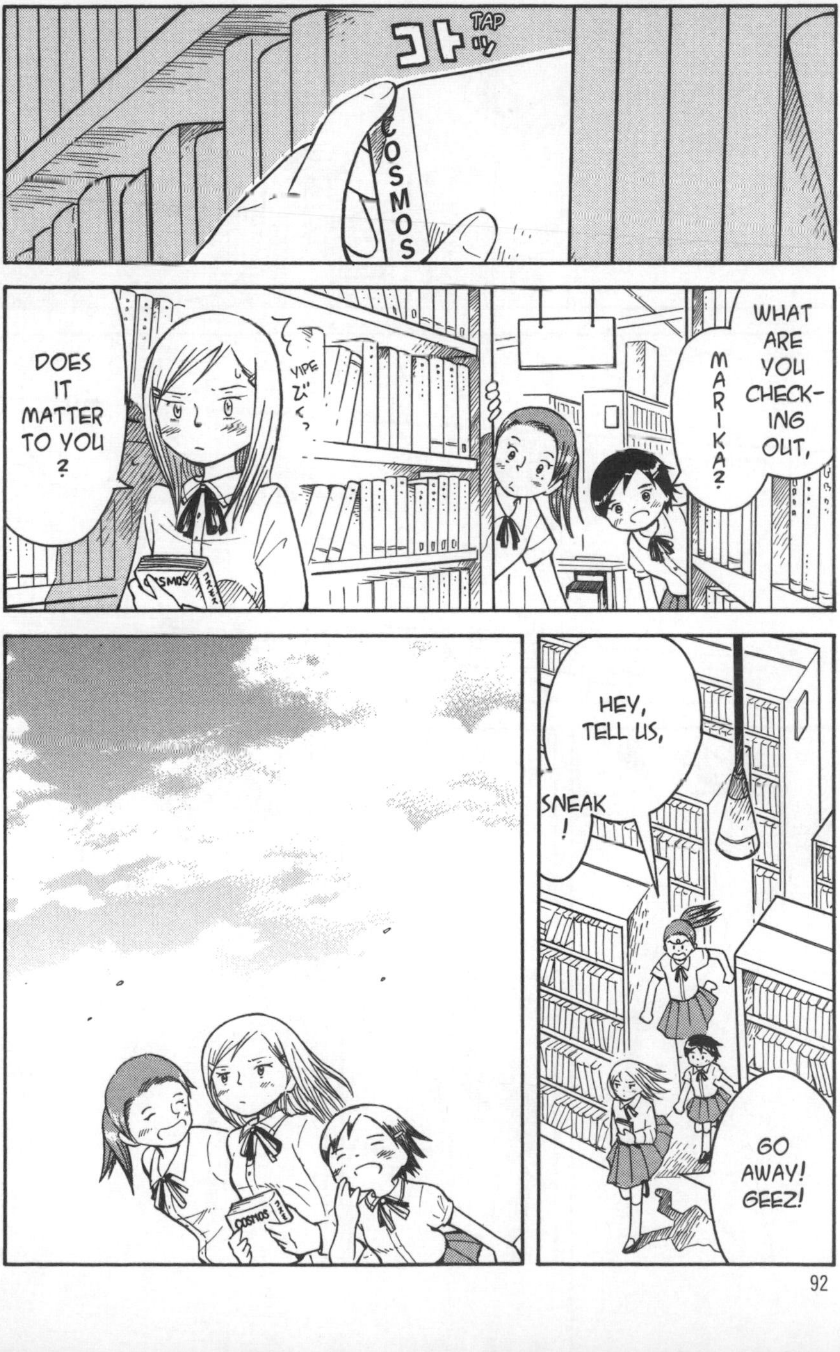

コトッ
TAP
COSMOS
WHAT ARE YOU CHECKING OUT,
MARIKA?
YIPE
ビクッ
DOES IT MATTER TO YOU?
COSMOS
HEY, TELL US,
SNEAK!
GO AWAY! GEEZ!
COSMOS

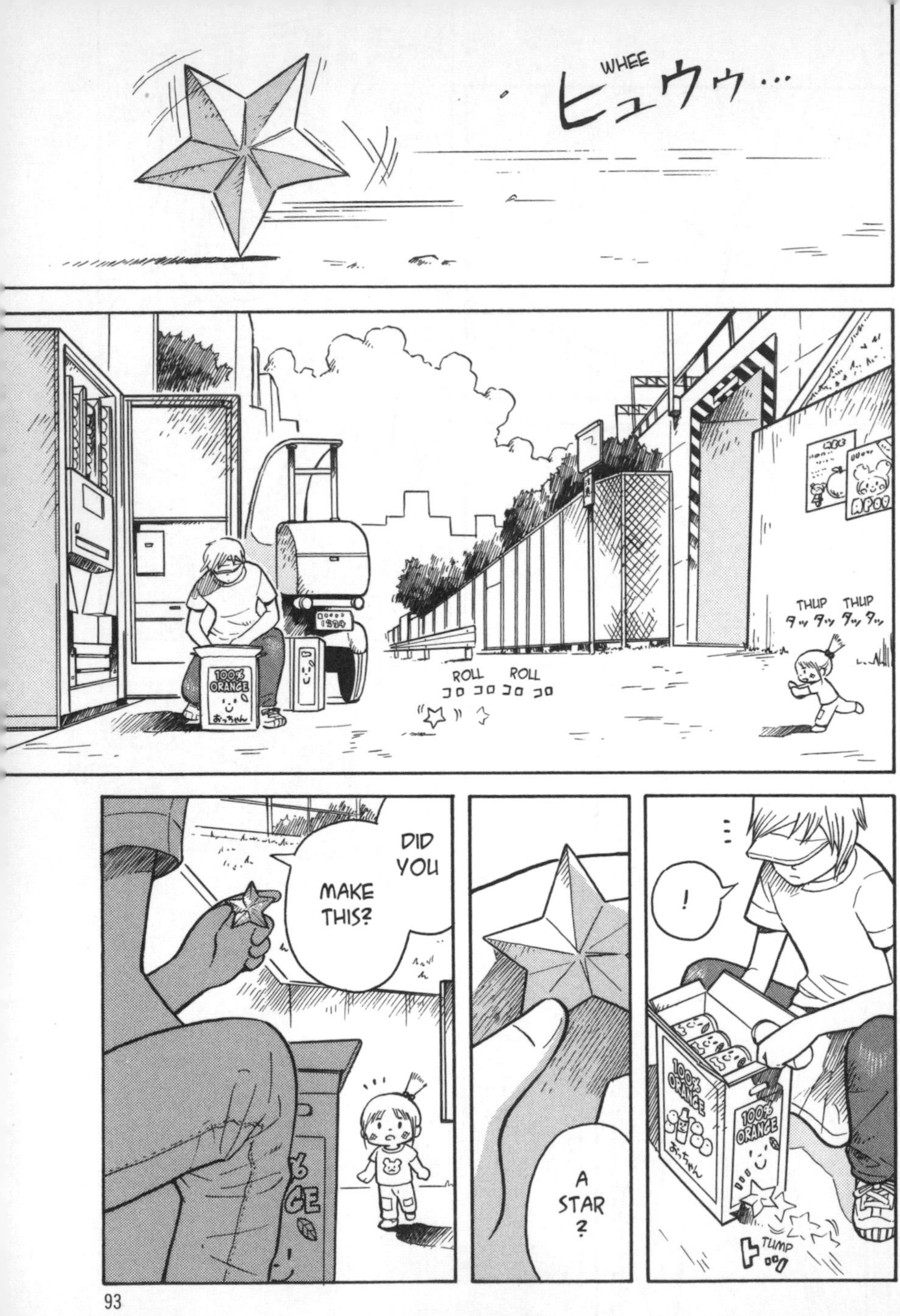
WHEE
ヒュウウ…
THUP THUP
タッタッタッタッ
ROLL ROLL
コロコロコロコロ
…
!
TUMP
トッ
A STAR?
DID YOU MAKE THIS?

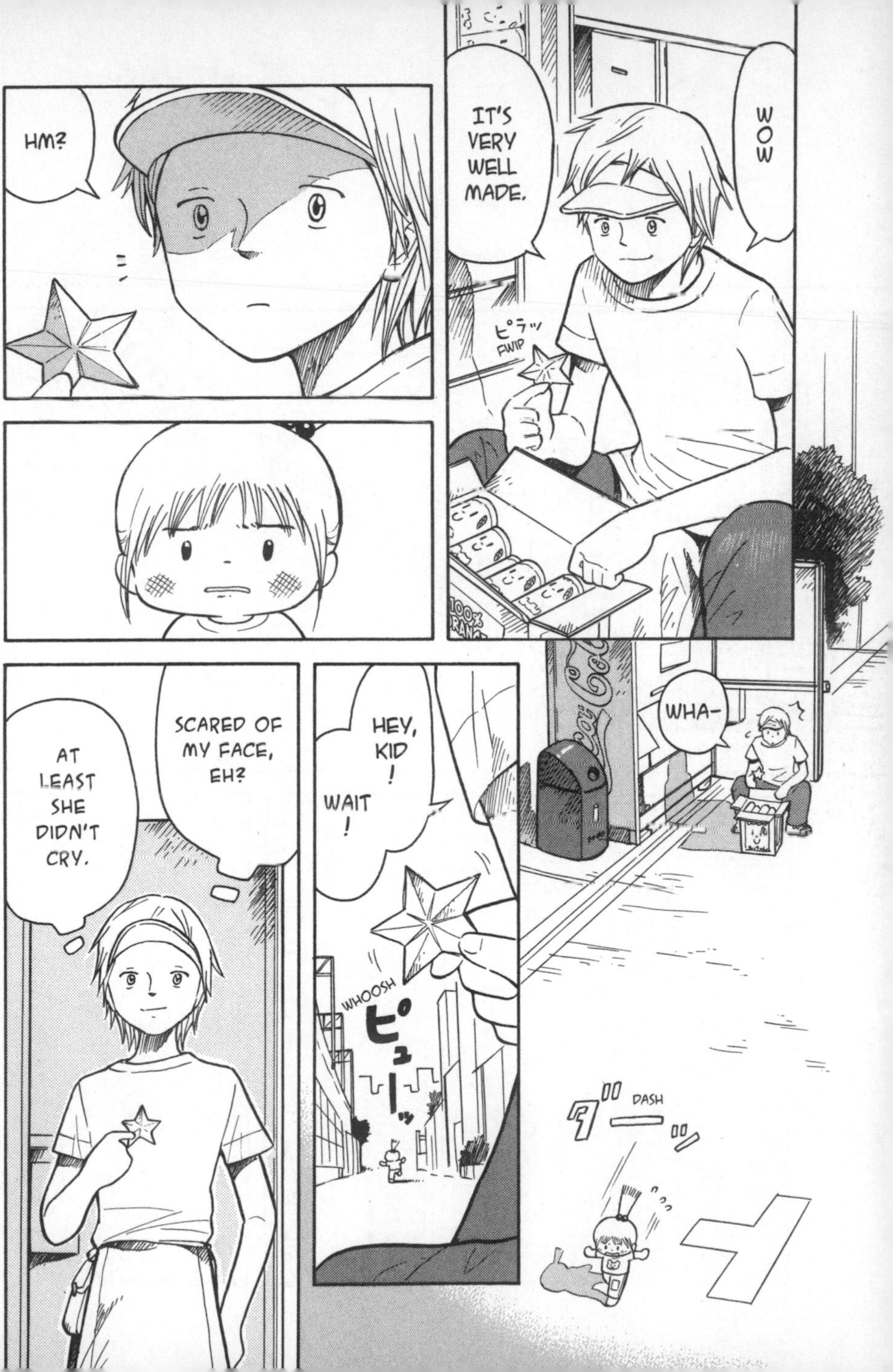

WOW
IT'S VERY WELL MADE.
ピラッ
FWIP
HM?
WHA-
ダーッ
DASH
HEY, KID!
WAIT!
WHOOSH
ピューッ
SCARED OF MY FACE, EH?
AT LEAST SHE DIDN'T CRY.

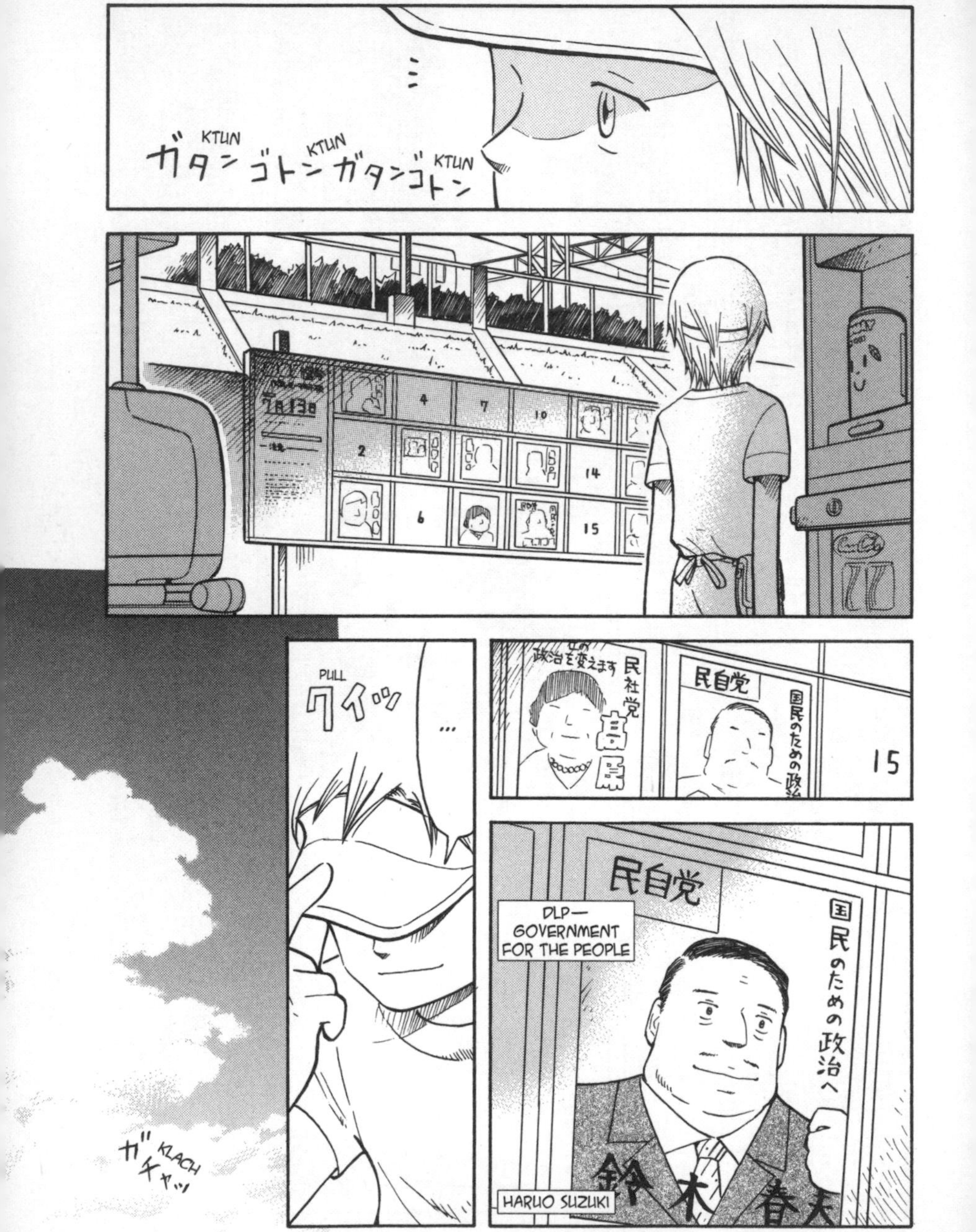

ガタン
KTUN
ゴトン
KTUN
ガタンゴトン
KTUN
民社党
政治を変えます
高原
民自党
国民のための政治
15
民自党
国民のための政治へ
DLP— GOVERNMENT FOR THE PEOPLE
鈴木春夫
HARUO SUZUKI
PULL
クイッ
...
ガチャッ
KLACH

MISSION:28

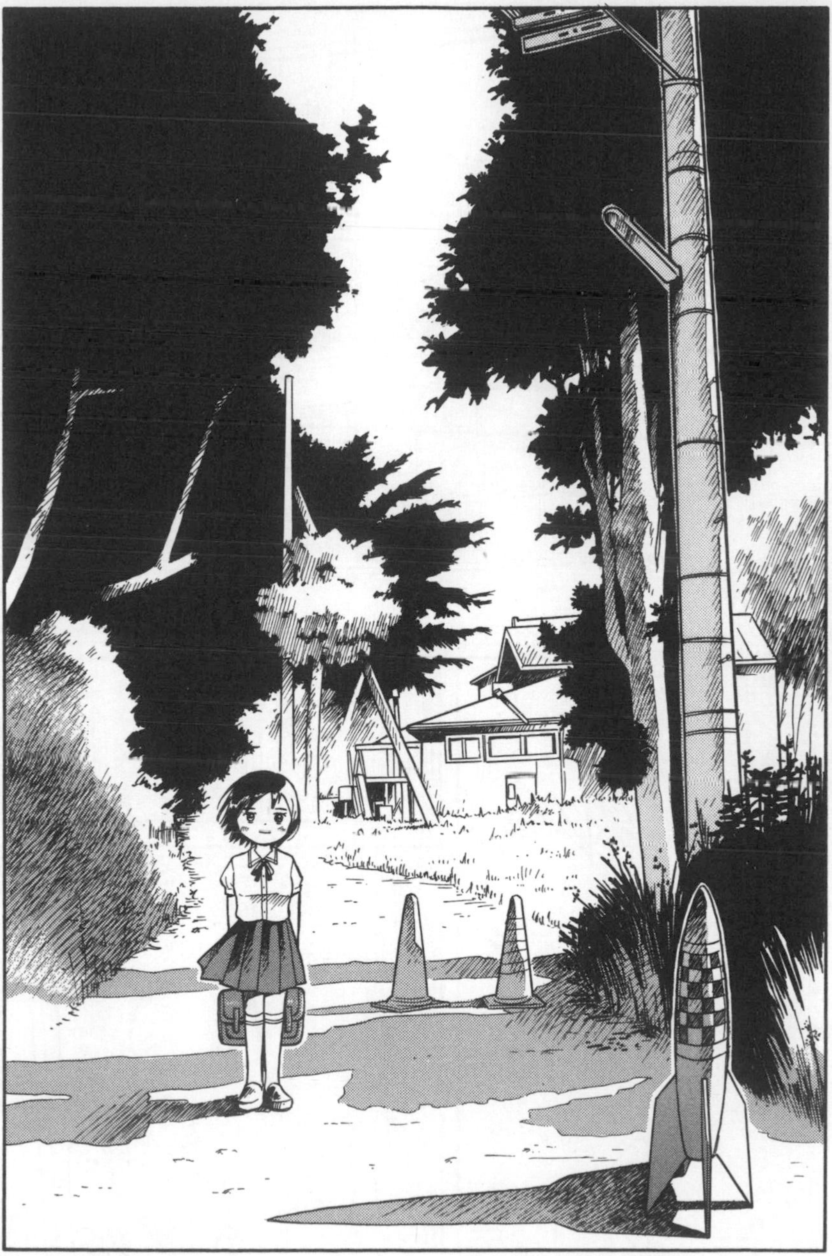

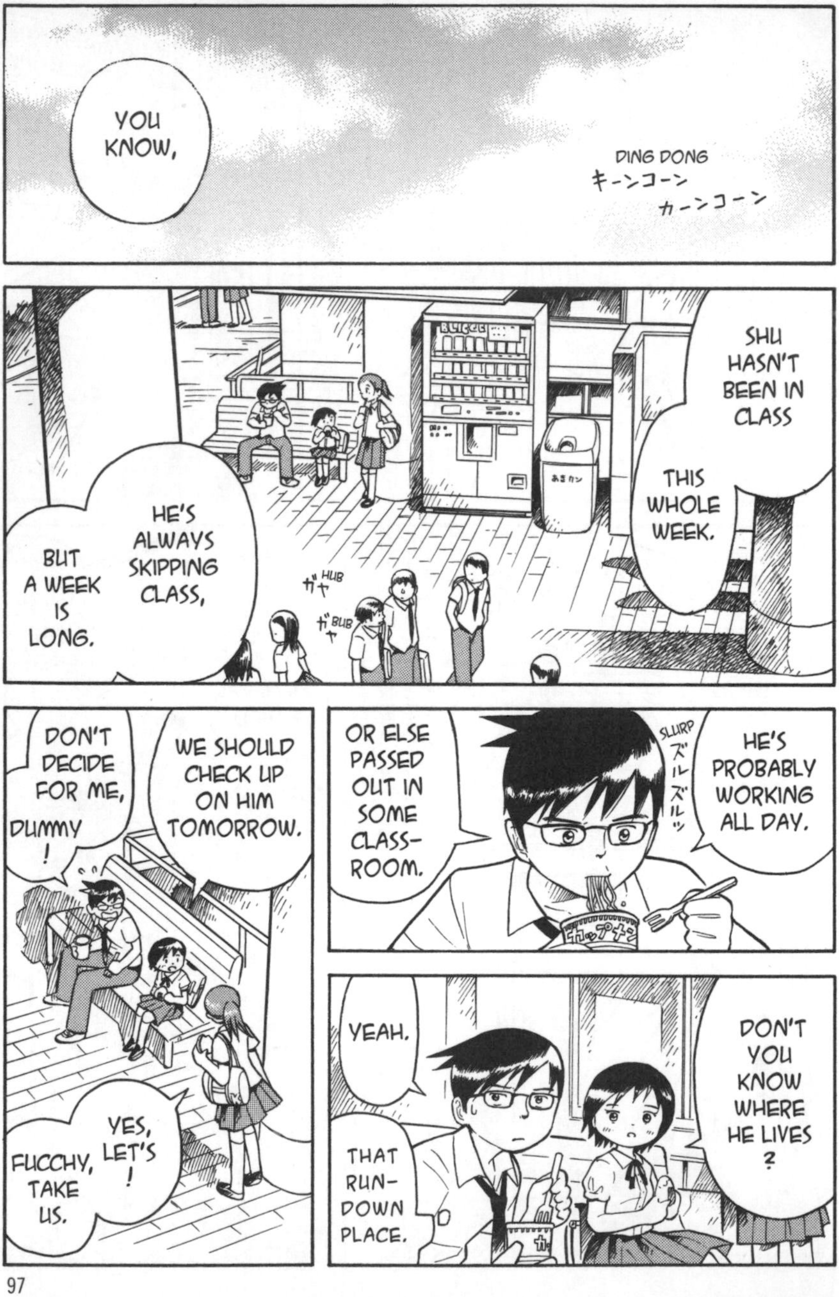
YOU KNOW,
DING DONG
キーンコーン カーンコーン
SHU HASN'T BEEN IN CLASS
THIS WHOLE WEEK.
HE'S ALWAYS SKIPPING CLASS,
BUT A WEEK IS LONG.
HUB BUB
ガヤ ガヤ
あきカン
HE'S PROBABLY WORKING ALL DAY.
SLURP
ズルズルッ
OR ELSE PASSED OUT IN SOME CLASS-ROOM.
DON'T YOU KNOW WHERE HE LIVES?
YEAH.
THAT RUN-DOWN PLACE.
WE SHOULD CHECK UP ON HIM TOMORROW.
DON'T DECIDE FOR ME, DUMMY!
YES, LET'S!
FUCCHY, TAKE US.

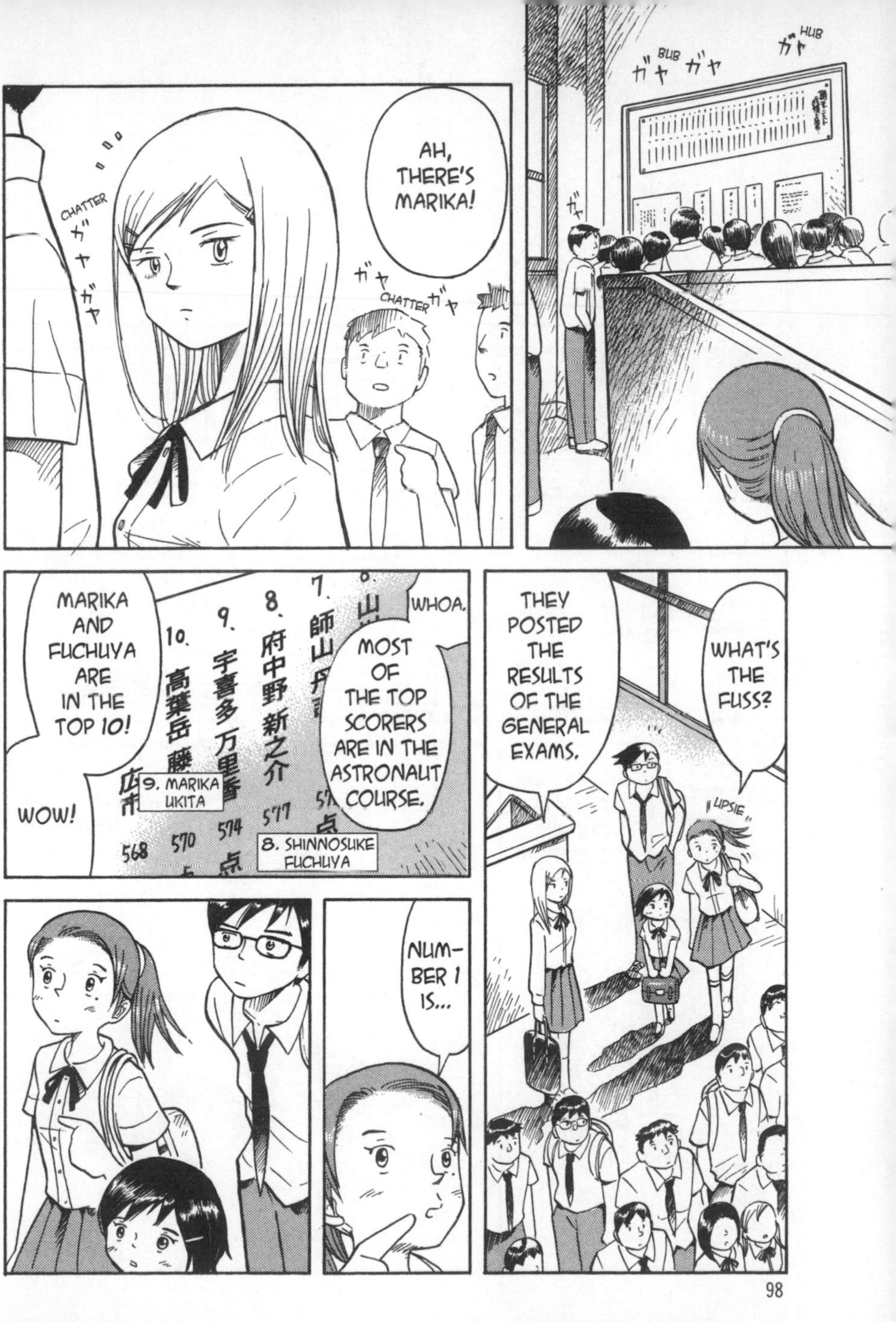
ガヤ BUB ガヤ
ガヤ HUB
ガヤ
AH, THERE'S MARIKA!
CHATTER ガヤガヤ
ガヤ CHATTER ガヤ
WHAT'S THE FUSS?
THEY POSTED THE RESULTS OF THE GENERAL EXAMS.
LIPSIE...
WHOA.
MOST OF THE TOP SCORERS ARE IN THE ASTRONAUT COURSE.
8. 府中野 新之介 577
9. 宇喜多万里香 574
10. 高葉岳 藤
8. SHINNOSUKE FUCHUYA
9. MARIKA UKITA
MARIKA AND FUCHUYA ARE IN THE TOP 10!
WOW!
NUM-BER 1 IS...

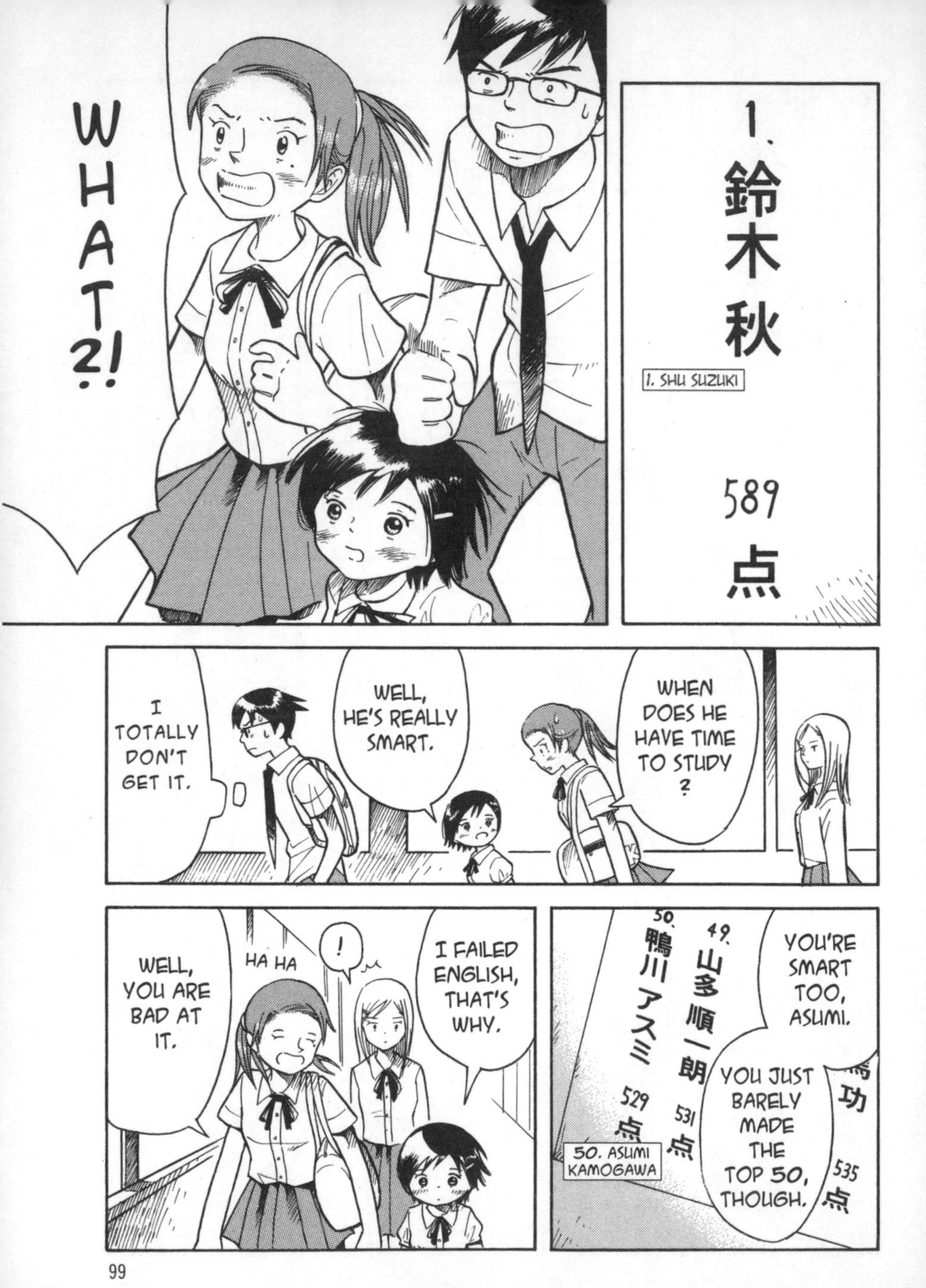
1. 鈴木秋 589点
1. SHU SUZUKI
WHAT?!
WHEN DOES HE HAVE TIME TO STUDY?
WELL, HE'S REALLY SMART.
I TOTALLY DON'T GET IT.
功 535点
YOU'RE SMART TOO, ASUMI.
YOU JUST BARELY MADE THE TOP 50, THOUGH.
49. 山多順一朗 531点
50. 鴨川アスミ 529点
50. ASUMI KAMOGAWA
I FAILED ENGLISH, THAT'S WHY.
!
HA HA
WELL, YOU ARE BAD AT IT.

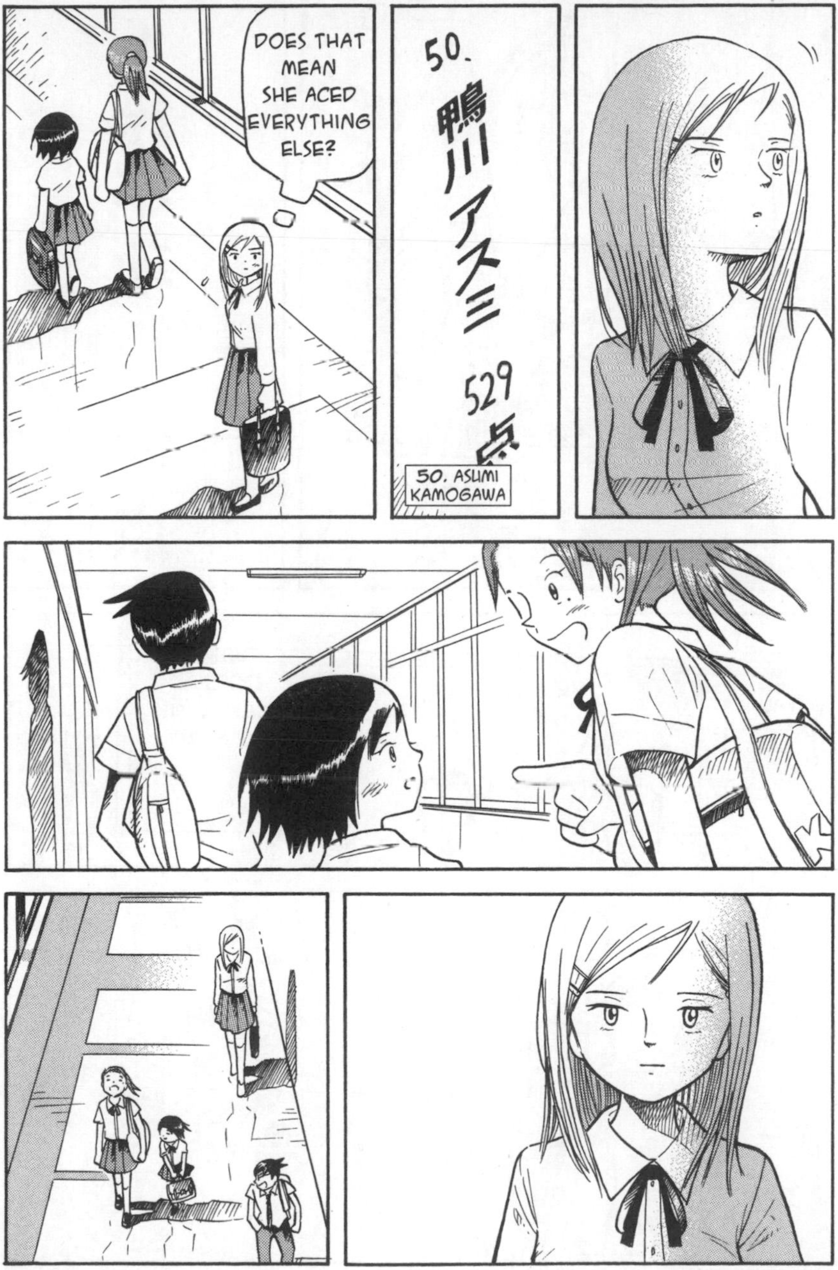
50. 鴨川アスミ 529点
50. ASUMI KAMOGAWA
DOES THAT MEAN SHE ACED EVERYTHING ELSE?

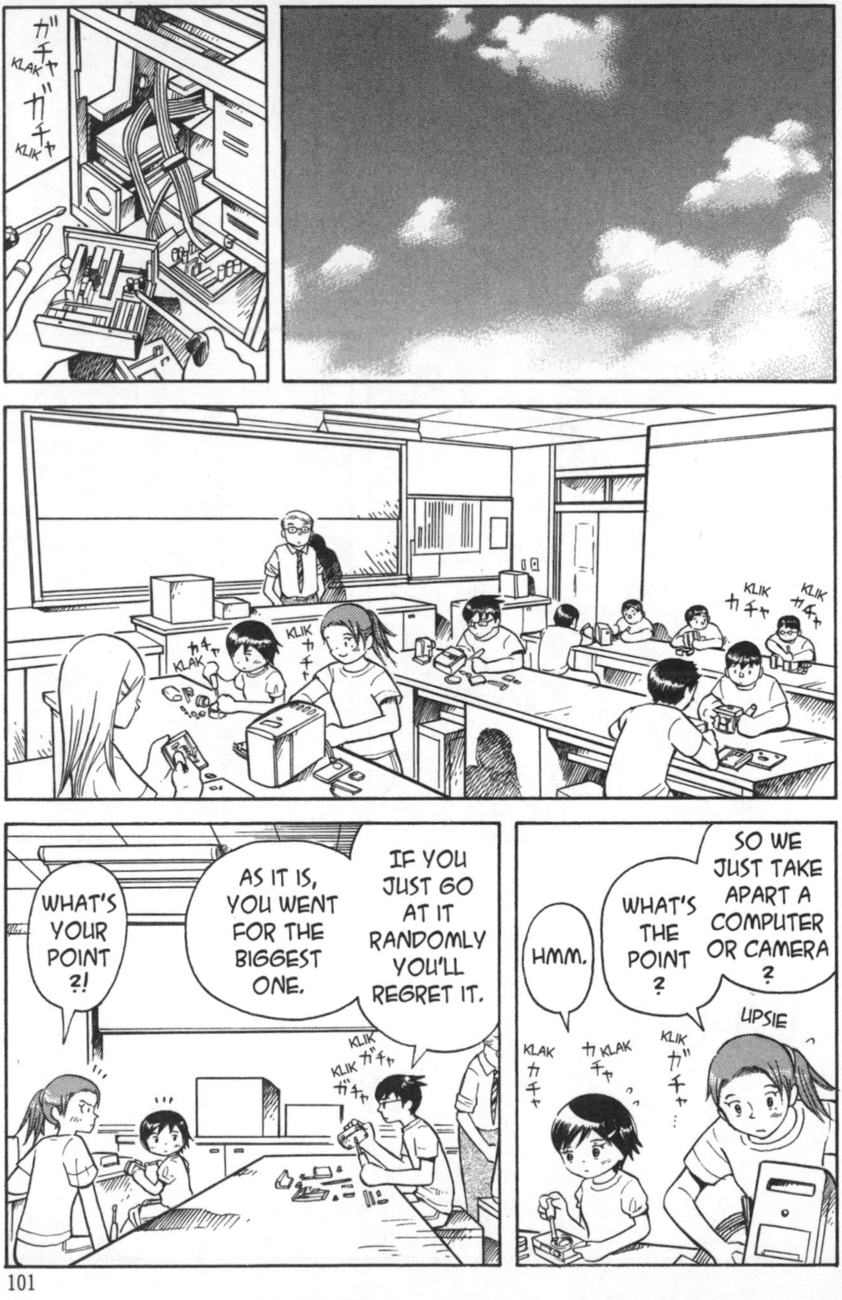
ガチャ KLAK
ガチャ KLIK
KLIK カチャ
KLIK カチャ
KLIK カチャ
カチャ KLAK
SO WE JUST TAKE APART A COMPUTER OR CAMERA?
WHAT'S THE POINT?
HMM.
UPSIE
KLIK ガチャ…
KLAK カチャ
KLAK カチャ
IF YOU JUST GO AT IT RANDOMLY YOU'LL REGRET IT.
AS IT IS, YOU WENT FOR THE BIGGEST ONE.
WHAT'S YOUR POINT?!
KLIK ガチャ
KLIK ガチャ

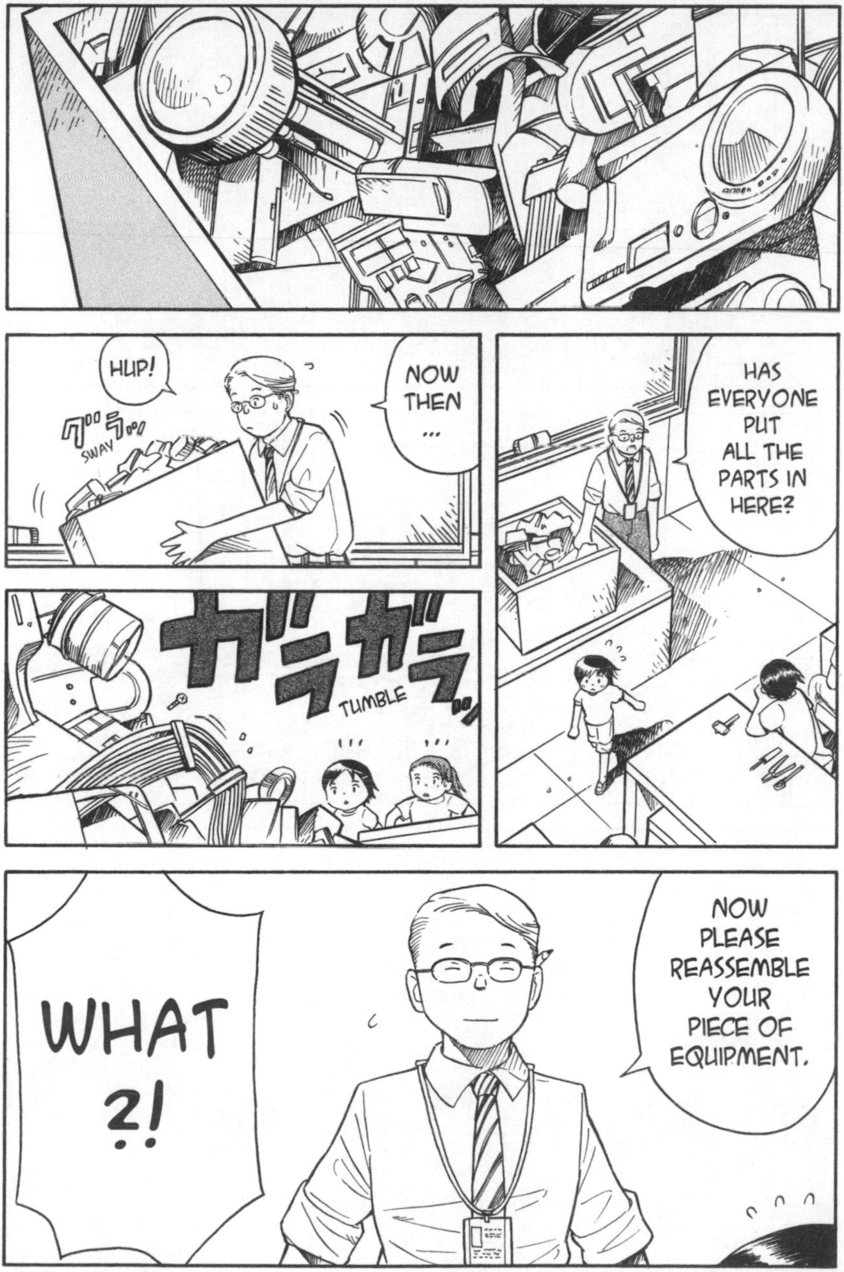
HAS EVERYONE PUT ALL THE PARTS IN HERE?
NOW THEN ...
HUP!
SWAY
TUMBLE
NOW PLEASE REASSEMBLE YOUR PIECE OF EQUIPMENT.
WHAT ?!

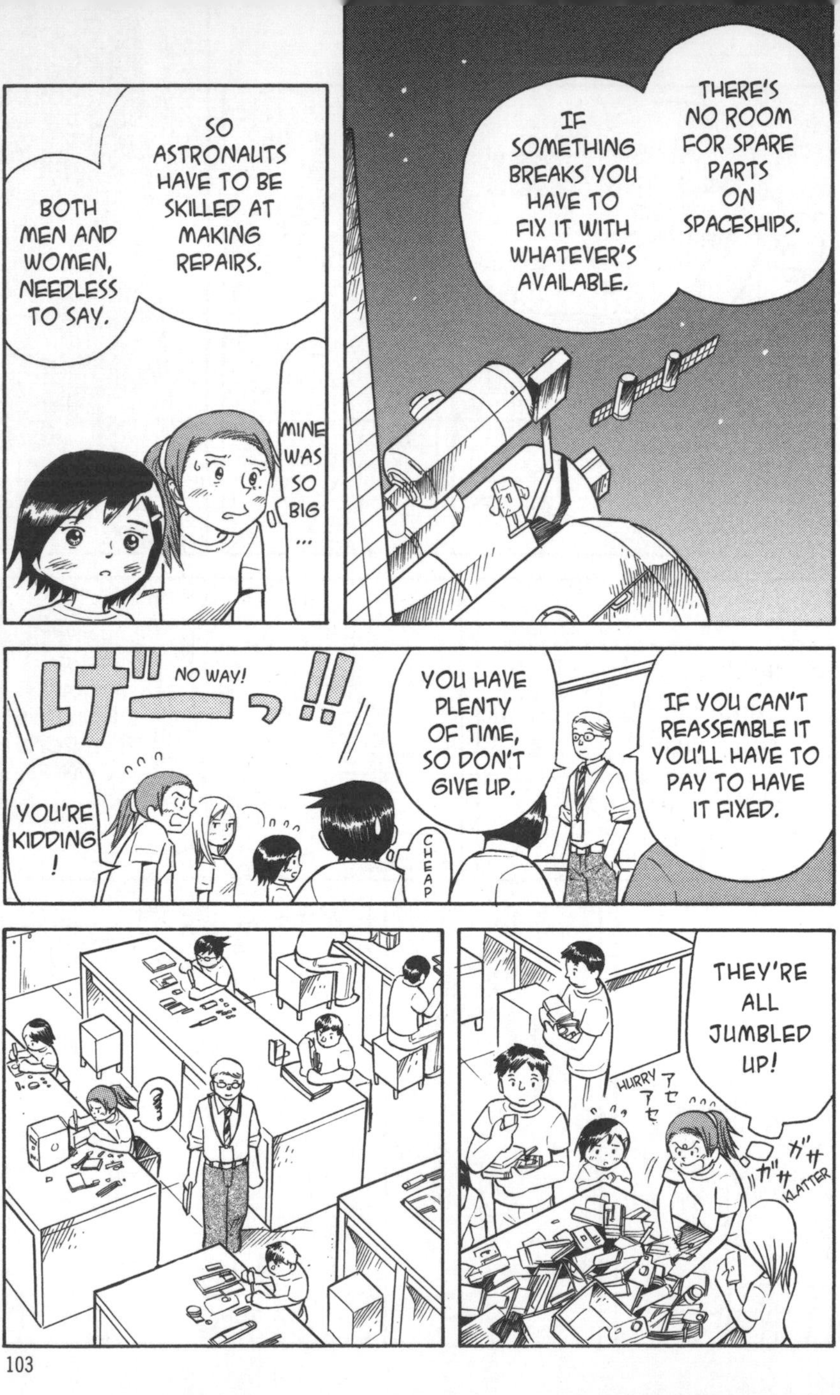
THERE'S NO ROOM FOR SPARE PARTS ON SPACESHIPS.
IF SOMETHING BREAKS YOU HAVE TO FIX IT WITH WHATEVER'S AVAILABLE.
SO ASTRONAUTS HAVE TO BE SKILLED AT MAKING REPAIRS.
BOTH MEN AND WOMEN, NEEDLESS TO SAY.
MINE WAS SO BIG ...
IF YOU CAN'T REASSEMBLE IT YOU'LL HAVE TO PAY TO HAVE IT FIXED.
YOU HAVE PLENTY OF TIME, SO DON'T GIVE UP.
CHEAP
ゲーッ!!
NO WAY!
YOU'RE KIDDING!
THEY'RE ALL JUMBLED UP!
HURRY アセアセ
ガサガサ KLATTER

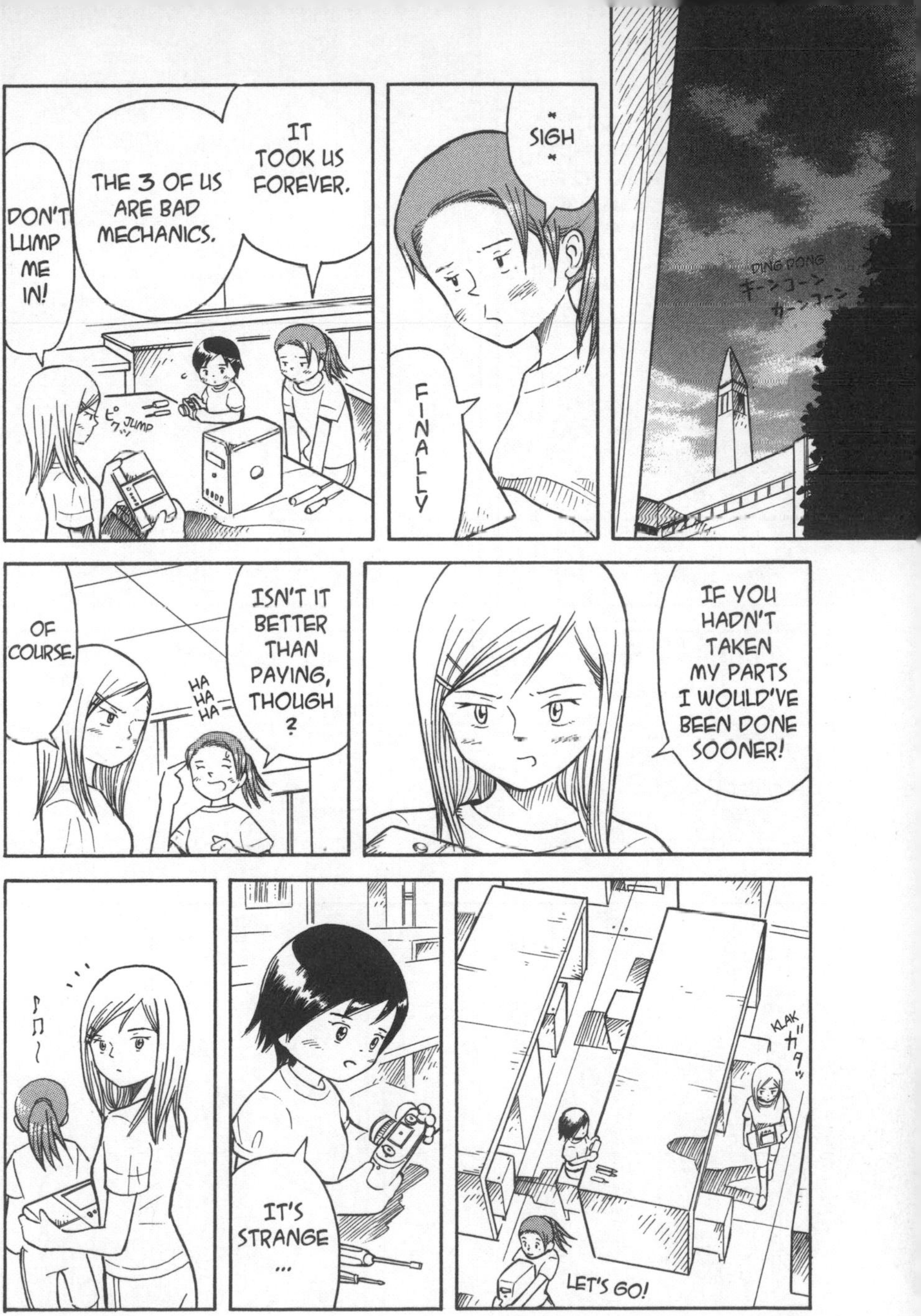
DING DONG
キーンコーン
カーンコーン
* SIGH *
FINALLY
IT TOOK US FOREVER.
THE 3 OF US ARE BAD MECHANICS.
DON'T LUMP ME IN!
ピクッ JUMP
IF YOU HADN'T TAKEN MY PARTS I WOULD'VE BEEN DONE SOONER!
ISN'T IT BETTER THAN PAYING, THOUGH?
HA HA HA
OF COURSE.
KLAK ガタッ
LET'S GO!
IT'S STRANGE ...
♪♫~

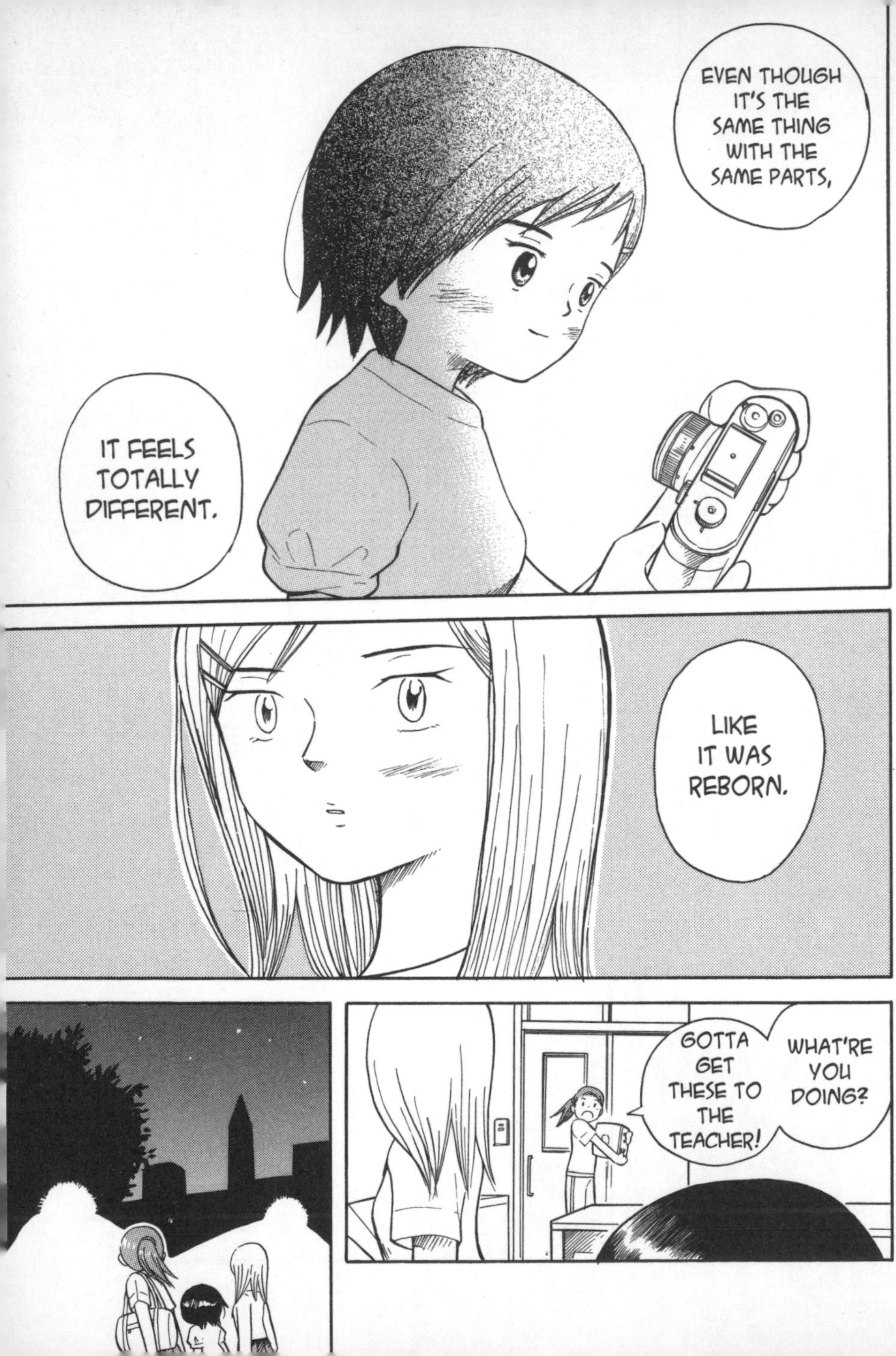
EVEN THOUGH IT'S THE SAME THING WITH THE SAME PARTS,
IT FEELS TOTALLY DIFFERENT.
LIKE IT WAS REBORN.
WHAT'RE YOU DOING?
GOTTA GET THESE TO THE TEACHER!

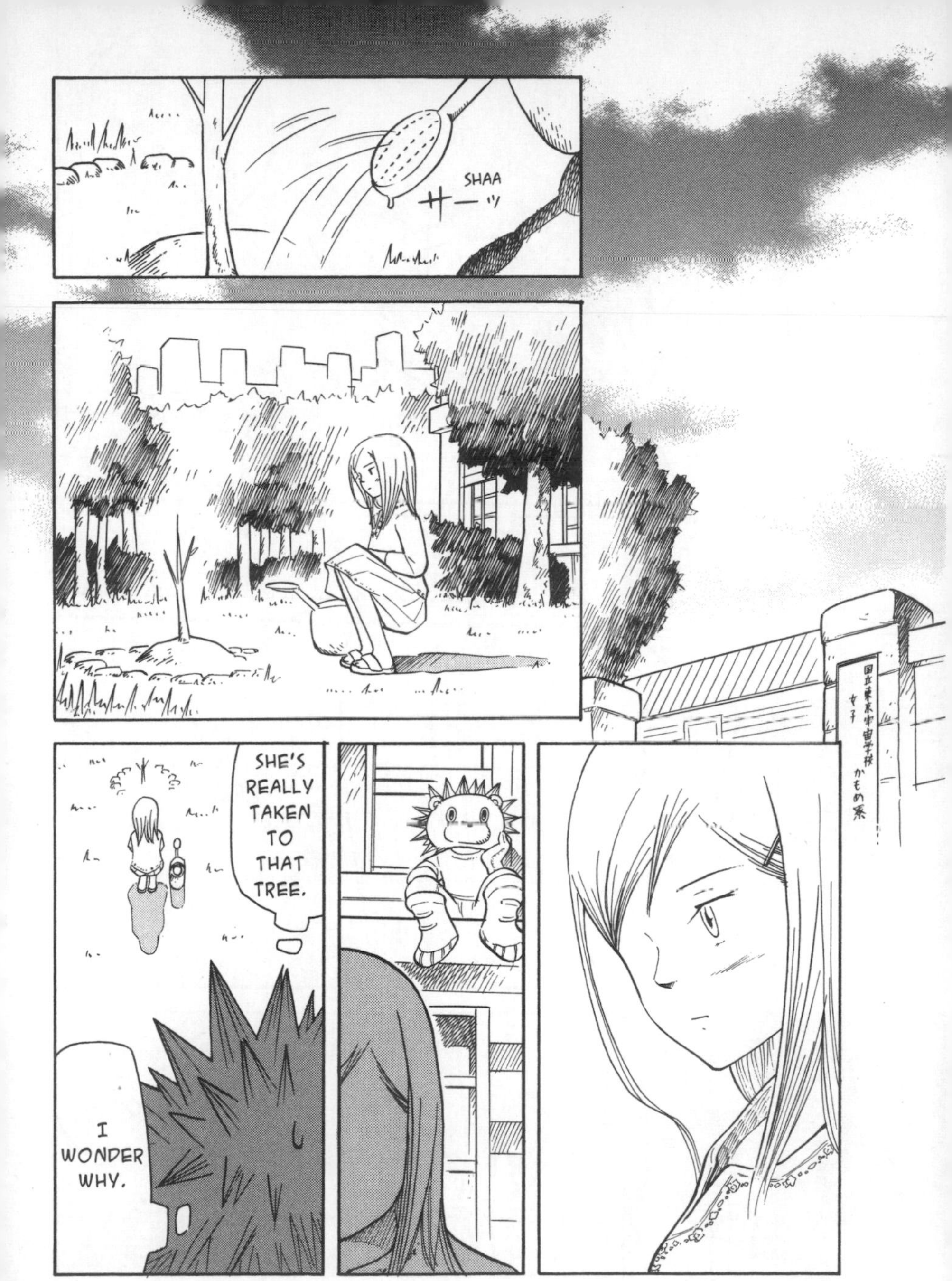
SHAA
サーッ
国立東京宇宙学校
女子かもめ寮
SHE'S REALLY TAKEN TO THAT TREE.
I WONDER WHY.

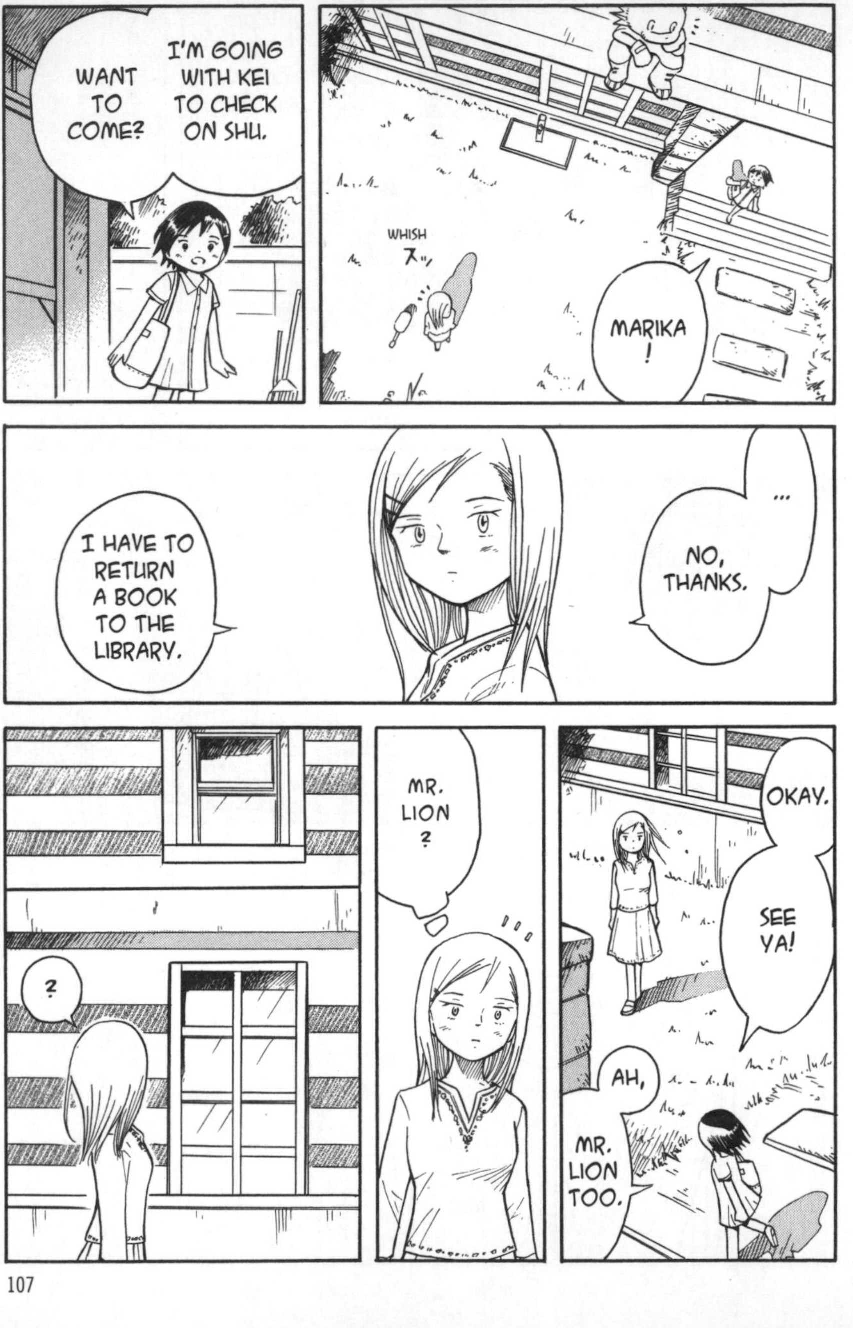
WHISH
スッ
MARIKA!
I'M GOING WITH KEI TO CHECK ON SHU.
WANT TO COME?
... NO, THANKS.
I HAVE TO RETURN A BOOK TO THE LIBRARY.
OKAY.
SEE YA!
AH, MR. LION TOO.
MR. LION?
?

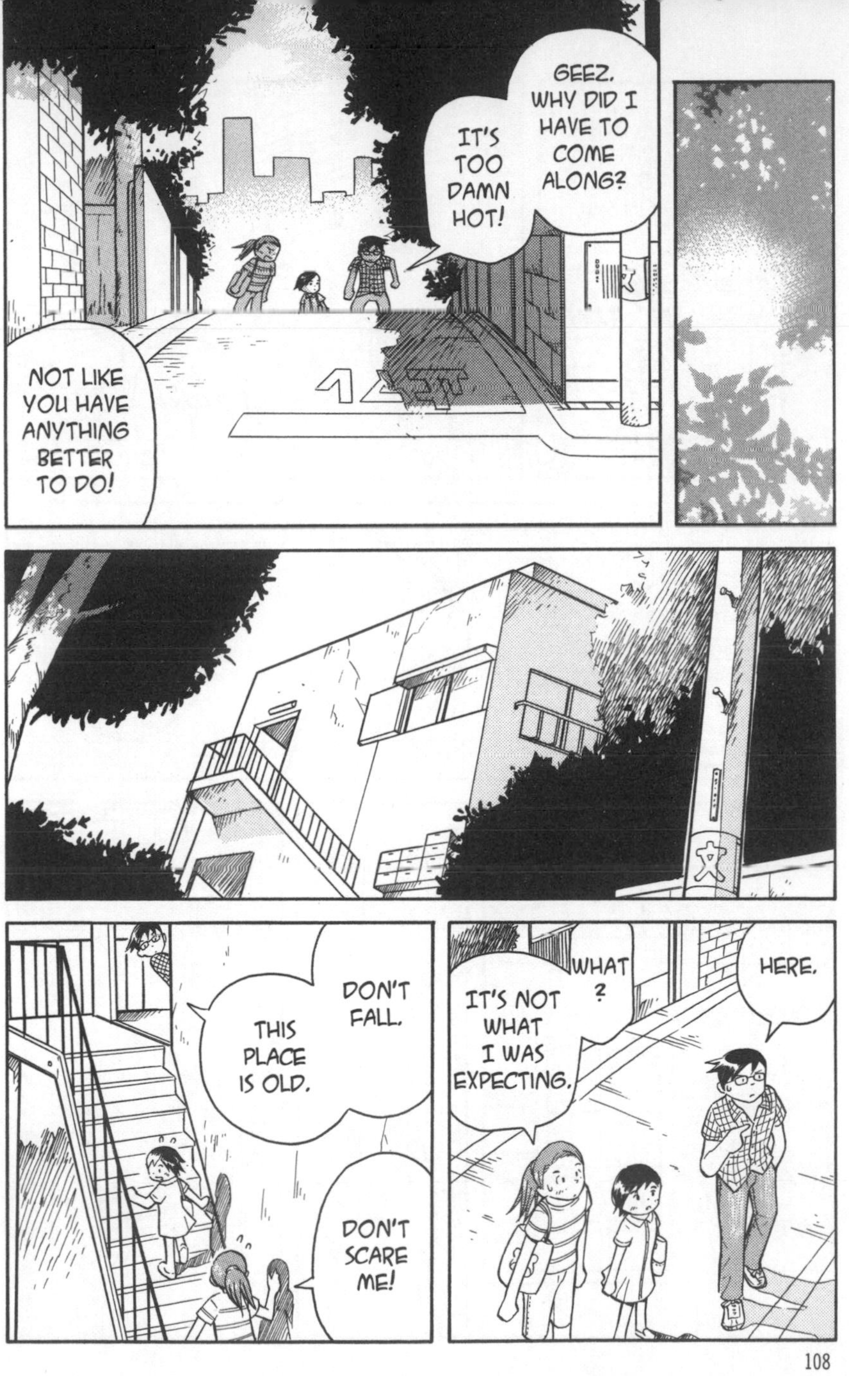
GEEZ. WHY DID I HAVE TO COME ALONG?
IT'S TOO DAMN HOT!
NOT LIKE YOU HAVE ANYTHING BETTER TO DO!
HERE.
WHAT?
IT'S NOT WHAT I WAS EXPECTING.
DON'T FALL.
THIS PLACE IS OLD.
DON'T SCARE ME!

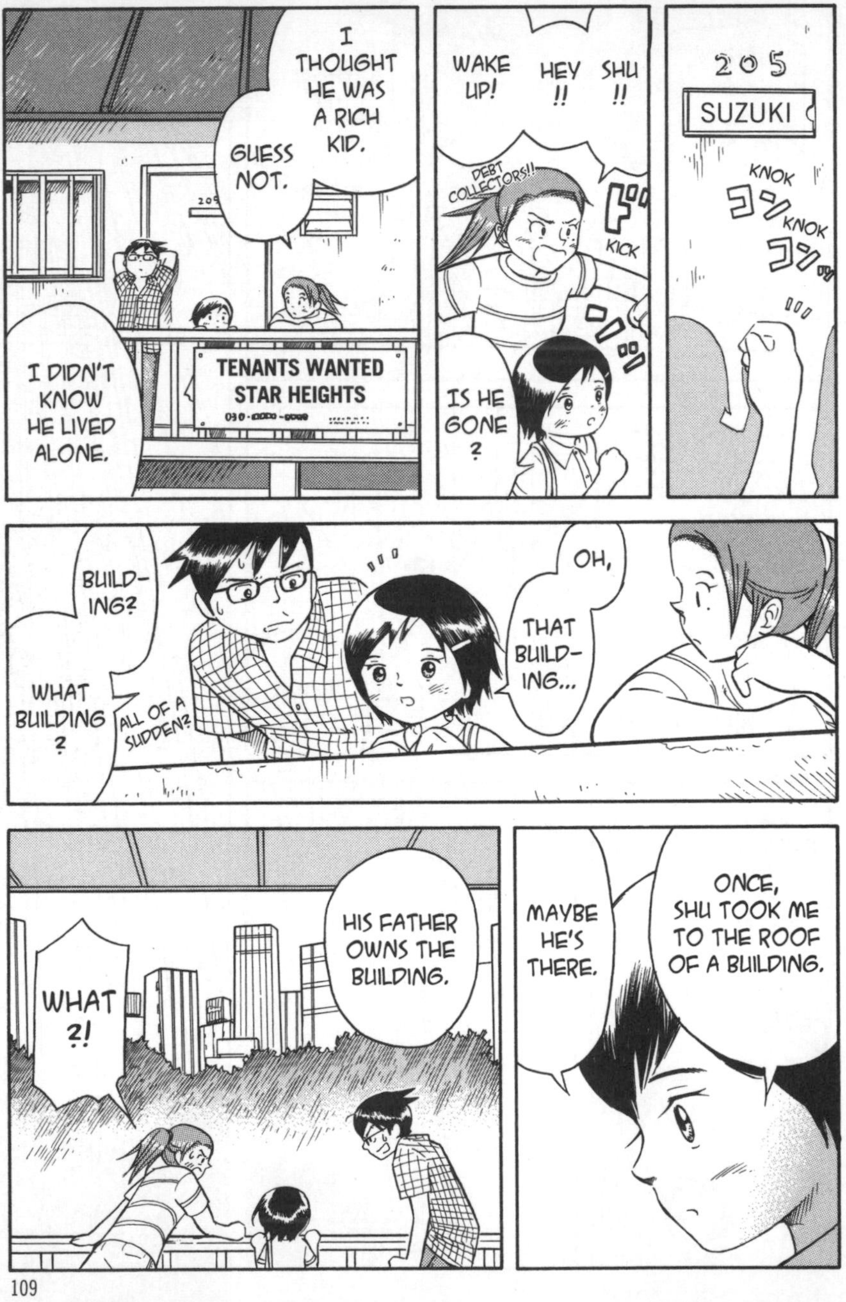
205
SUZUKI
KNOK コン
KNOK コン
WAKE UP! HEY!! SHU!!
DEBT COLLECTORS!!
ド KICK
IS HE GONE?
I THOUGHT HE WAS A RICH KID.
GUESS NOT.
TENANTS WANTED
STAR HEIGHTS
I DIDN'T KNOW HE LIVED ALONE.
OH, THAT BUILDING...
BUILDING?
WHAT BUILDING?
ALL OF A SUDDEN?
ONCE, SHU TOOK ME TO THE ROOF OF A BUILDING.
MAYBE HE'S THERE.
HIS FATHER OWNS THE BUILDING.
WHAT?!

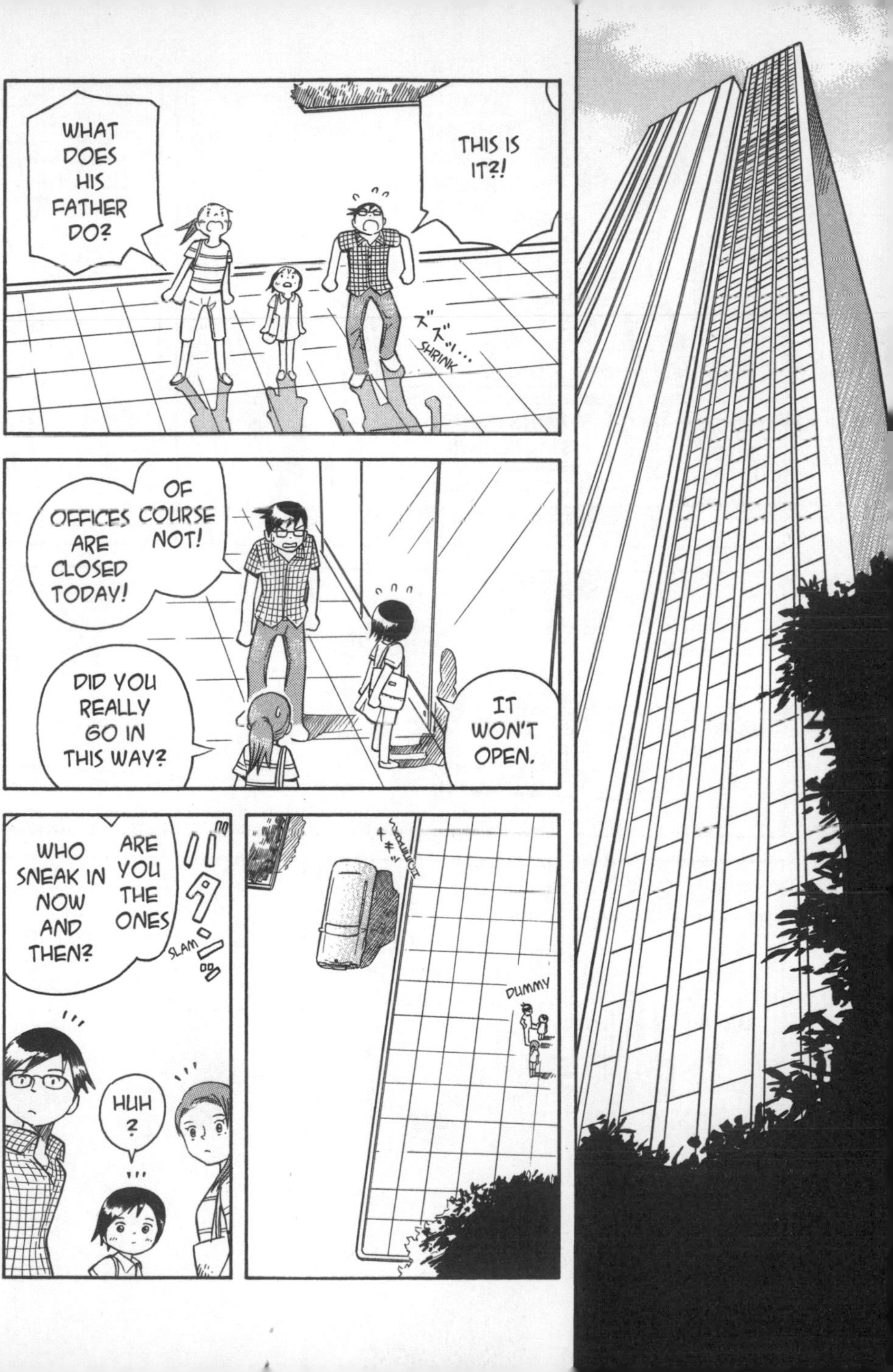
THIS IS IT?!
WHAT DOES HIS FATHER DO?
ズズッ…
SHRINK
OF COURSE NOT! OFFICES ARE CLOSED TODAY!
IT WON'T OPEN.
DID YOU REALLY GO IN THIS WAY?
キキッ
SQUEAK
DUMMY
ARE YOU THE ONES WHO SNEAK IN NOW AND THEN?
SLAM
HUH?

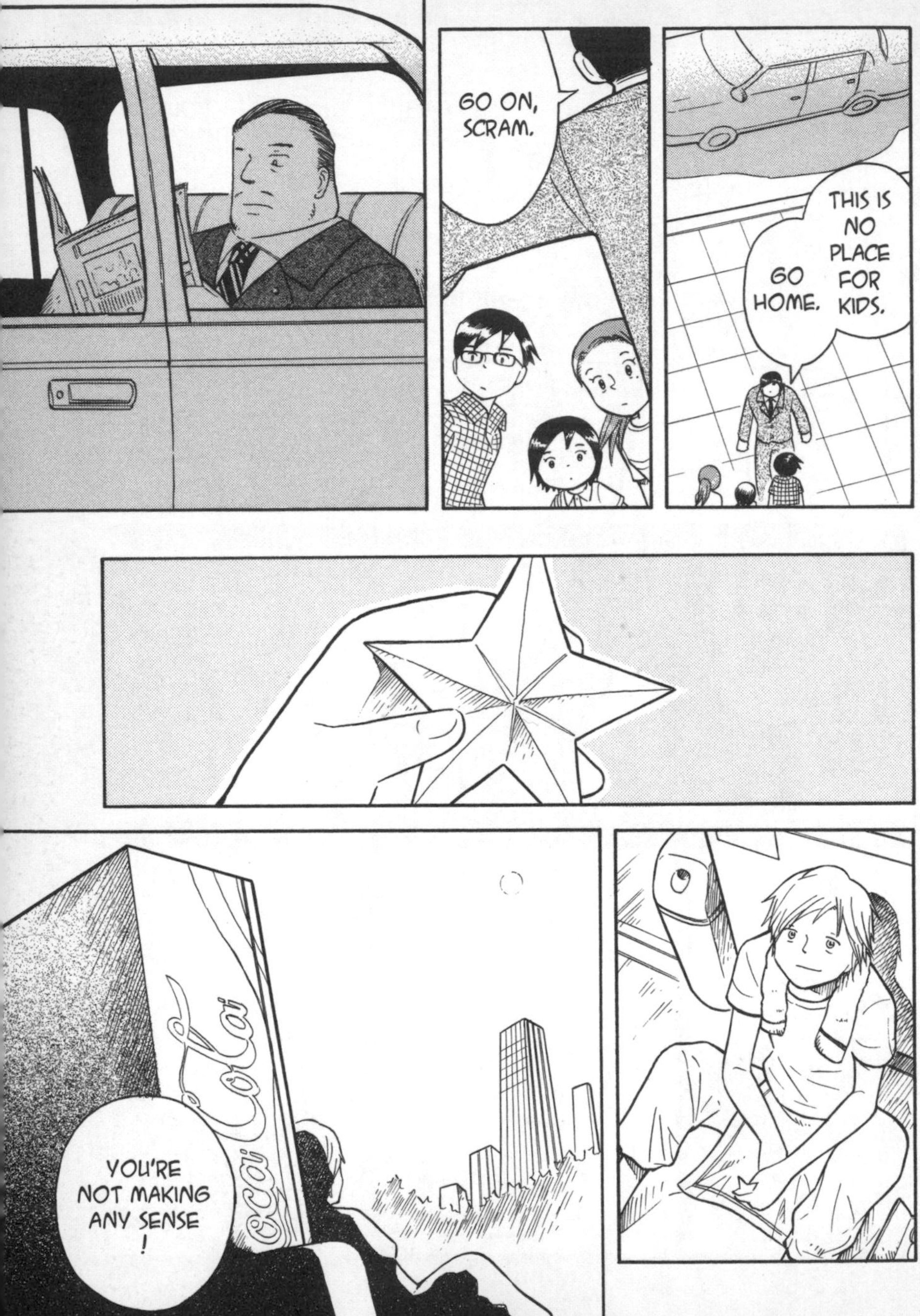
THIS IS NO PLACE FOR KIDS.
GO HOME.
GO ON, SCRAM.
YOU'RE NOT MAKING ANY SENSE!

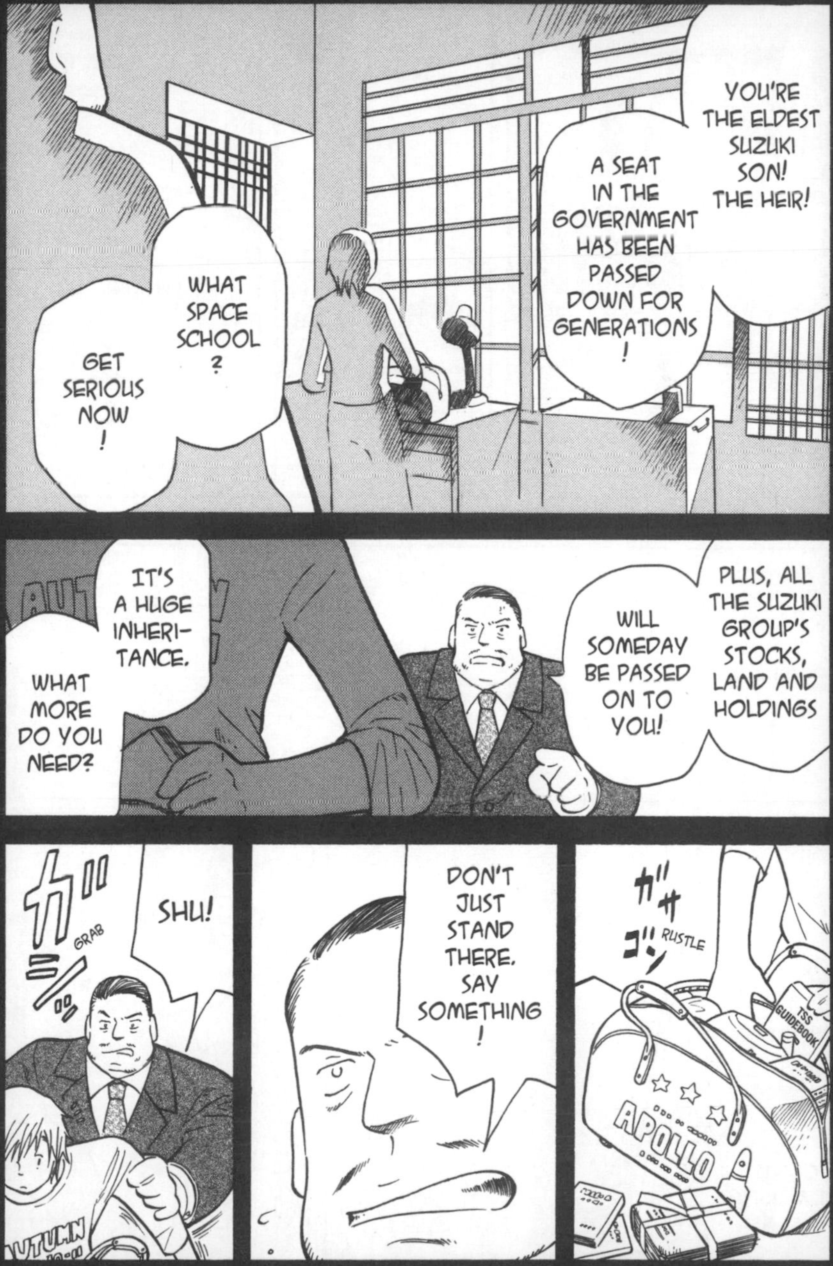
YOU'RE THE ELDEST SUZUKI SON! THE HEIR!
A SEAT IN THE GOVERNMENT HAS BEEN PASSED DOWN FOR GENERATIONS!
WHAT SPACE SCHOOL?
GET SERIOUS NOW!
PLUS, ALL THE SUZUKI GROUP'S STOCKS, LAND AND HOLDINGS
WILL SOMEDAY BE PASSED ON TO YOU!
IT'S A HUGE INHERITANCE.
WHAT MORE DO YOU NEED?
ガサ ゴソ RUSTLE
TSS GUIDEBOOK
APOLLO
DON'T JUST STAND THERE. SAY SOMETHING!
カッ GRAB
SHU!

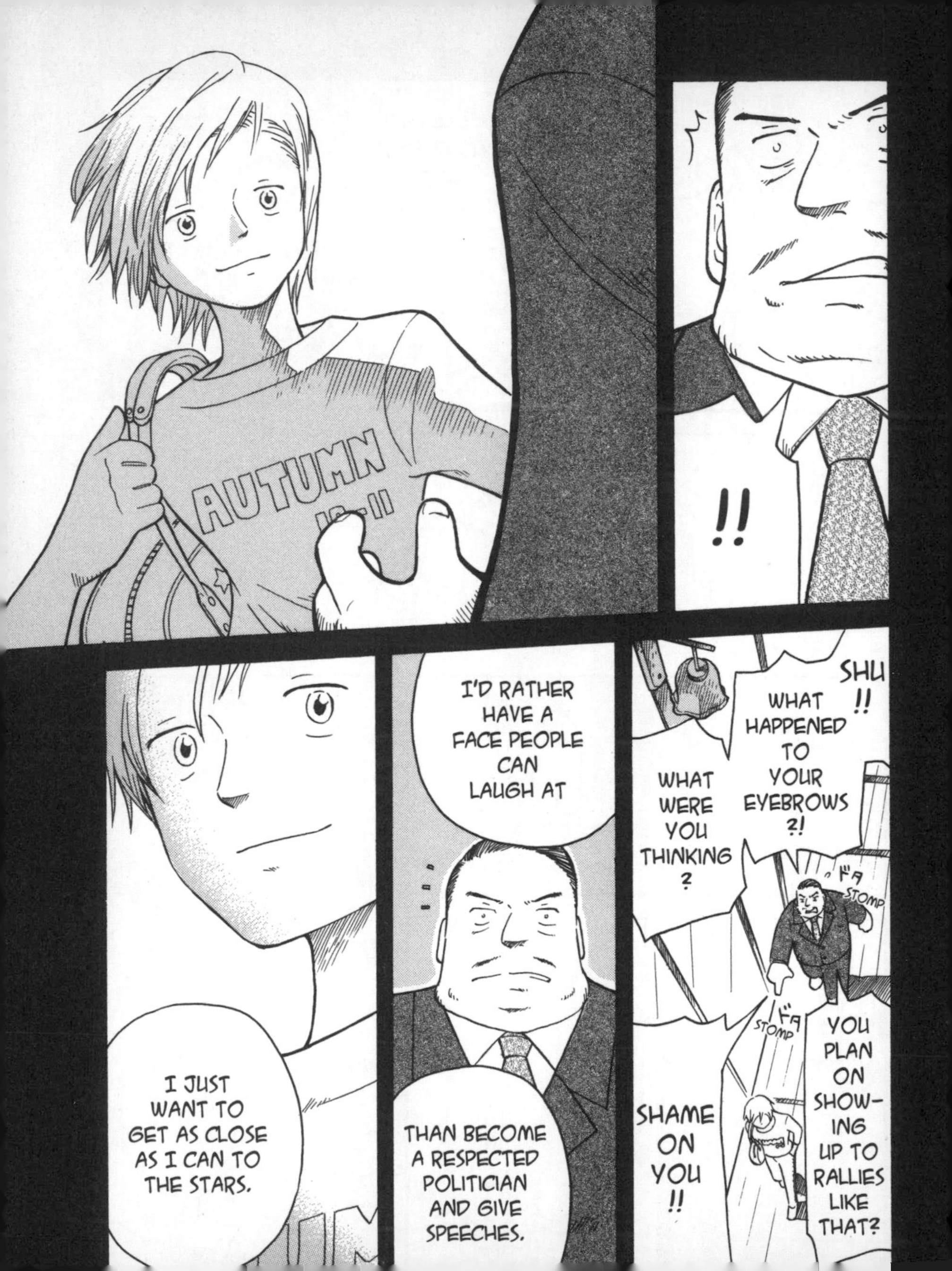
!!
AUTUMN
SHU!!
WHAT HAPPENED TO YOUR EYEBROWS?!
WHAT WERE YOU THINKING?
ドタ STOMP
ドタ STOMP
YOU PLAN ON SHOWING UP TO RALLIES LIKE THAT?
SHAME ON YOU!!
I'D RATHER HAVE A FACE PEOPLE CAN LAUGH AT
THAN BECOME A RESPECTED POLITICIAN AND GIVE SPEECHES.
I JUST WANT TO GET AS CLOSE AS I CAN TO THE STARS.

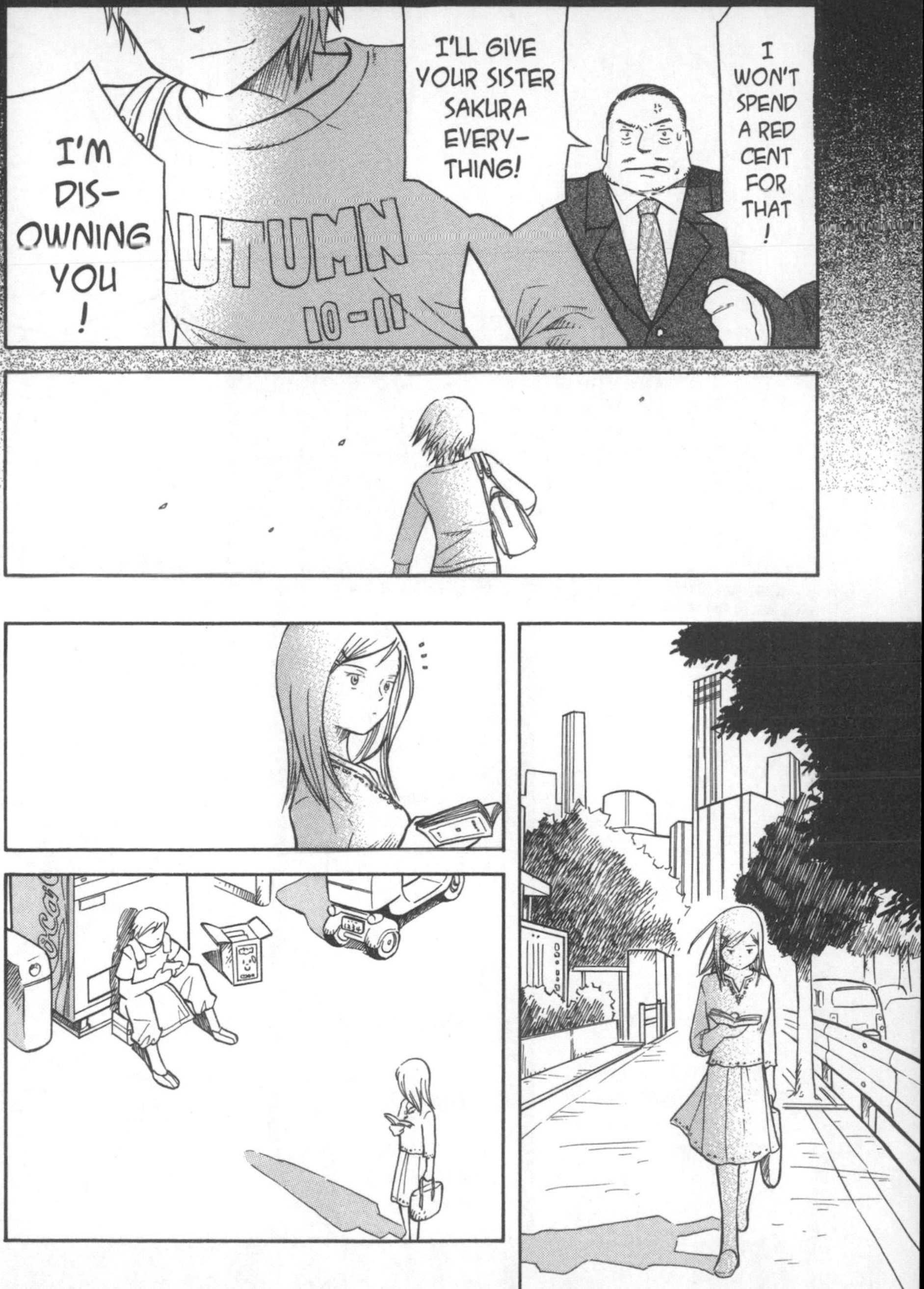
I WON'T SPEND A RED CENT FOR THAT!
I'LL GIVE YOUR SISTER SAKURA EVERYTHING!
I'M DISOWNING YOU!
AUTUMN 10-11

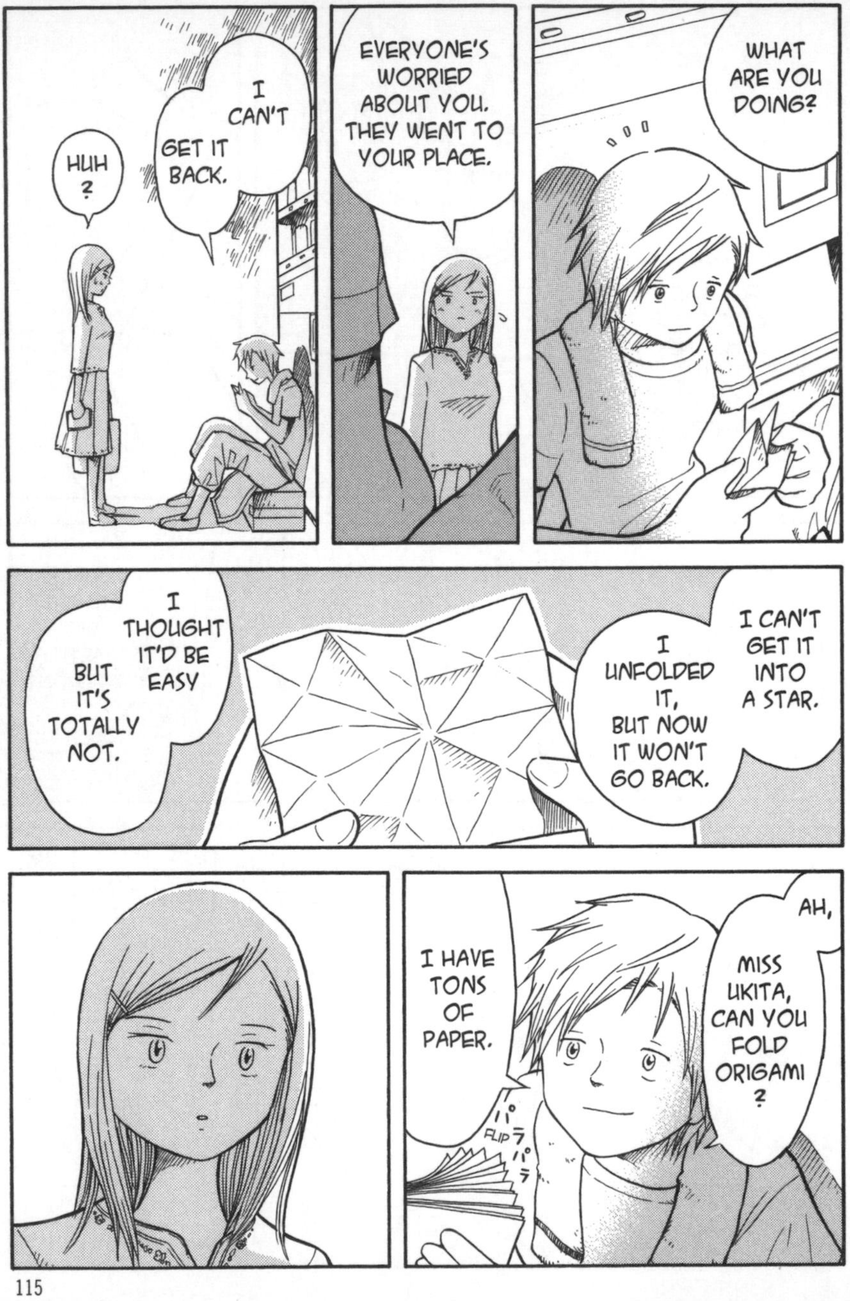
WHAT ARE YOU DOING?
EVERYONE'S WORRIED ABOUT YOU. THEY WENT TO YOUR PLACE.
I CAN'T GET IT BACK.
HUH?
I CAN'T GET IT INTO A STAR.
I UNFOLDED IT, BUT NOW IT WON'T GO BACK.
I THOUGHT IT'D BE EASY BUT IT'S TOTALLY NOT.
AH, MISS UKITA, CAN YOU FOLD ORIGAMI?
I HAVE TONS OF PAPER.
パラパラ
FLIP

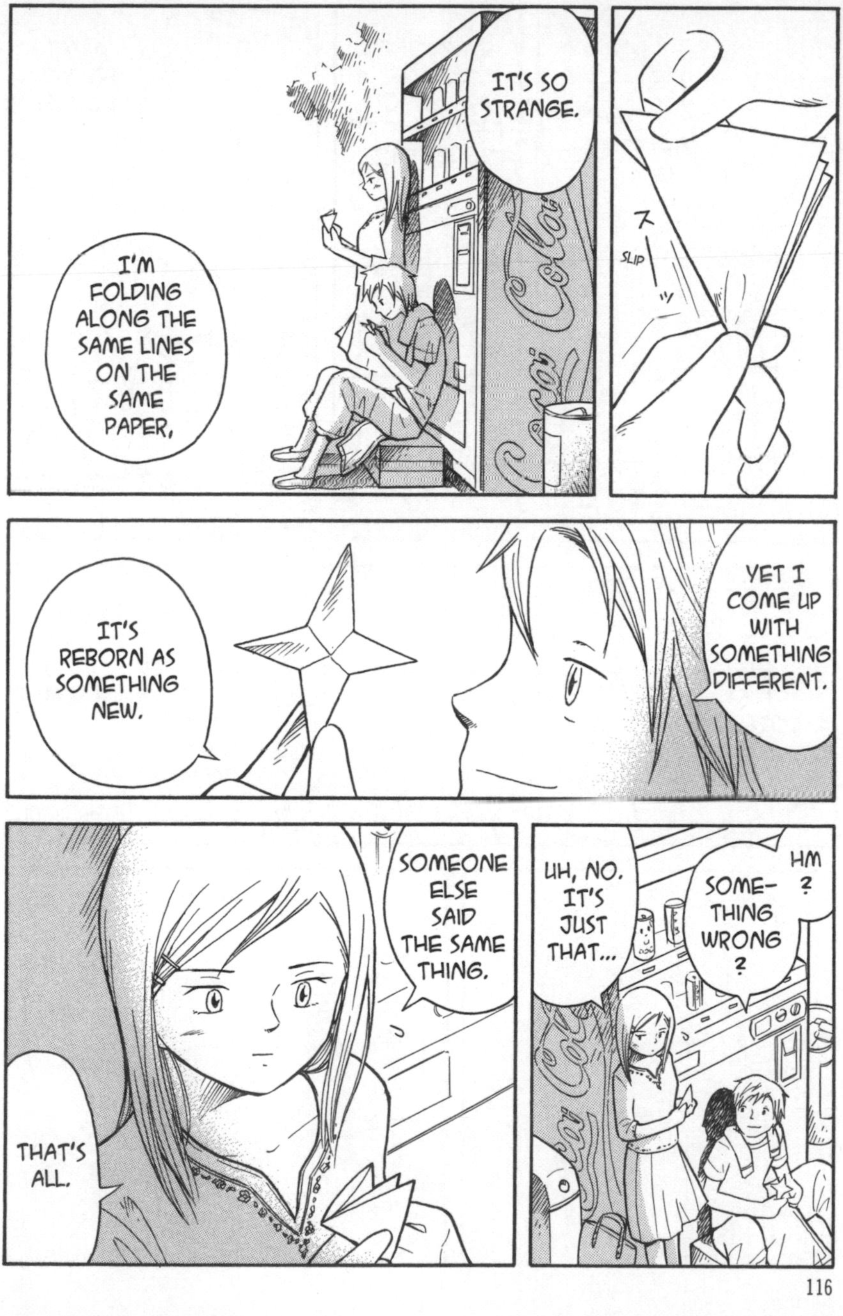
スーッ
SLIP
IT'S SO STRANGE.
I'M FOLDING ALONG THE SAME LINES ON THE SAME PAPER,
YET I COME UP WITH SOMETHING DIFFERENT.
IT'S REBORN AS SOMETHING NEW.
HM?
SOMETHING WRONG?
UH, NO. IT'S JUST THAT...
SOMEONE ELSE SAID THE SAME THING.
THAT'S ALL.

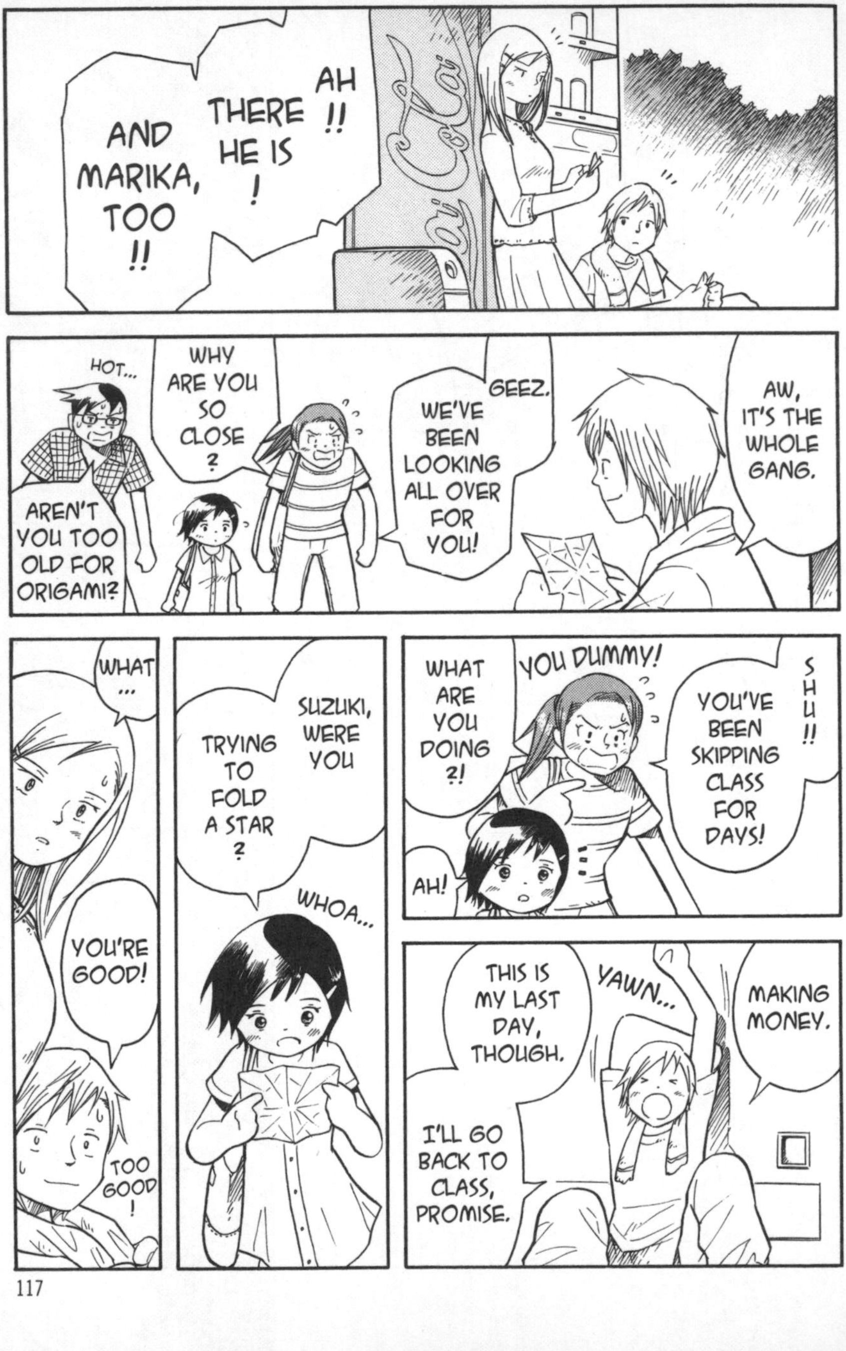
AH !!
THERE HE IS !
AND MARIKA, TOO !!
AW, IT'S THE WHOLE GANG.
GEEZ.
WE'VE BEEN LOOKING ALL OVER FOR YOU!
WHY ARE YOU SO CLOSE?
HOT...
AREN'T YOU TOO OLD FOR ORIGAMI?
SHU!!
YOU'VE BEEN SKIPPING CLASS FOR DAYS!
YOU DUMMY!
WHAT ARE YOU DOING?!
AH!
MAKING MONEY.
YAWN...
THIS IS MY LAST DAY, THOUGH.
I'LL GO BACK TO CLASS, PROMISE.
SUZUKI, WERE YOU
TRYING TO FOLD A STAR?
WHOA...
WHAT...
YOU'RE GOOD!
TOO GOOD!

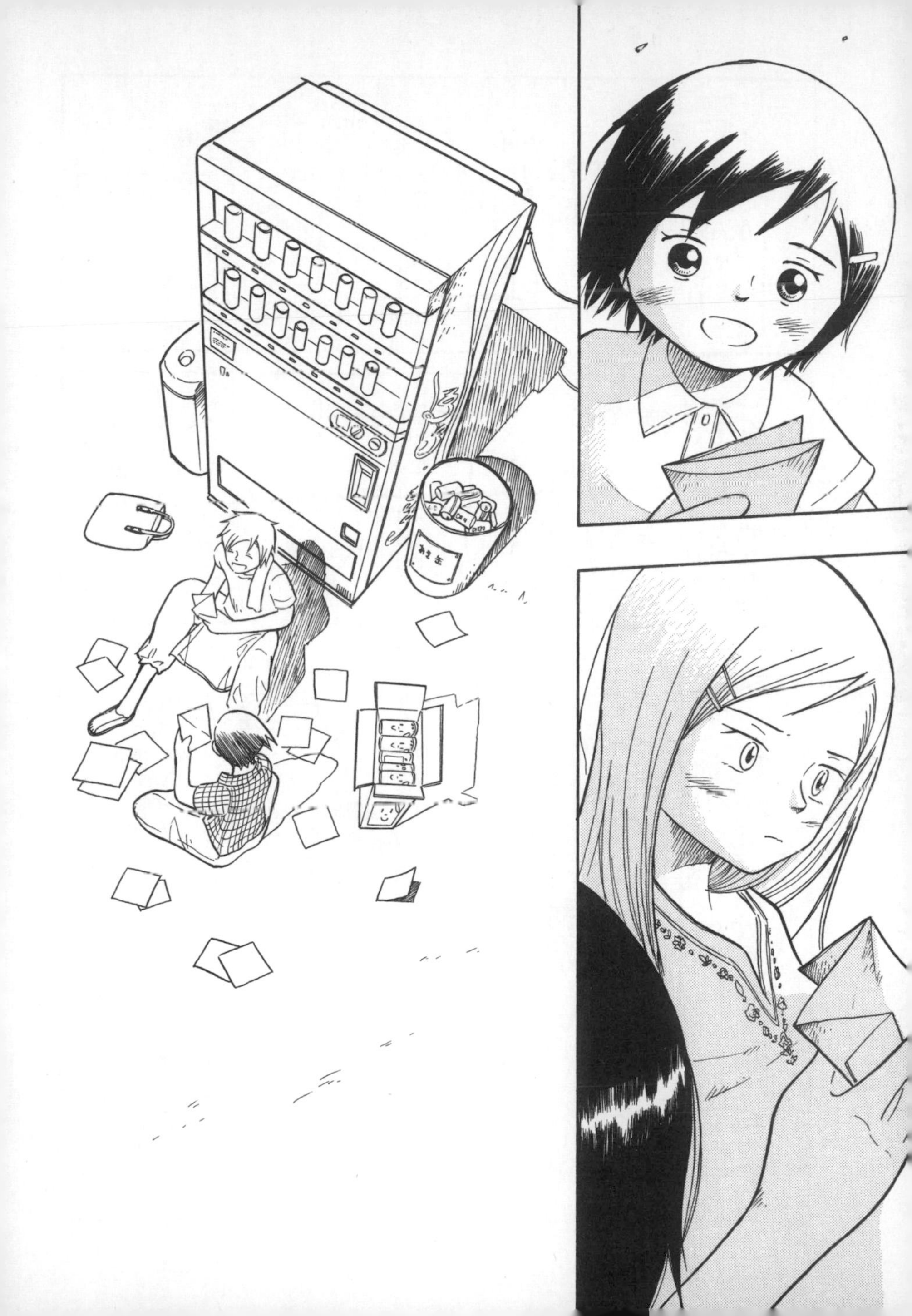
あき缶

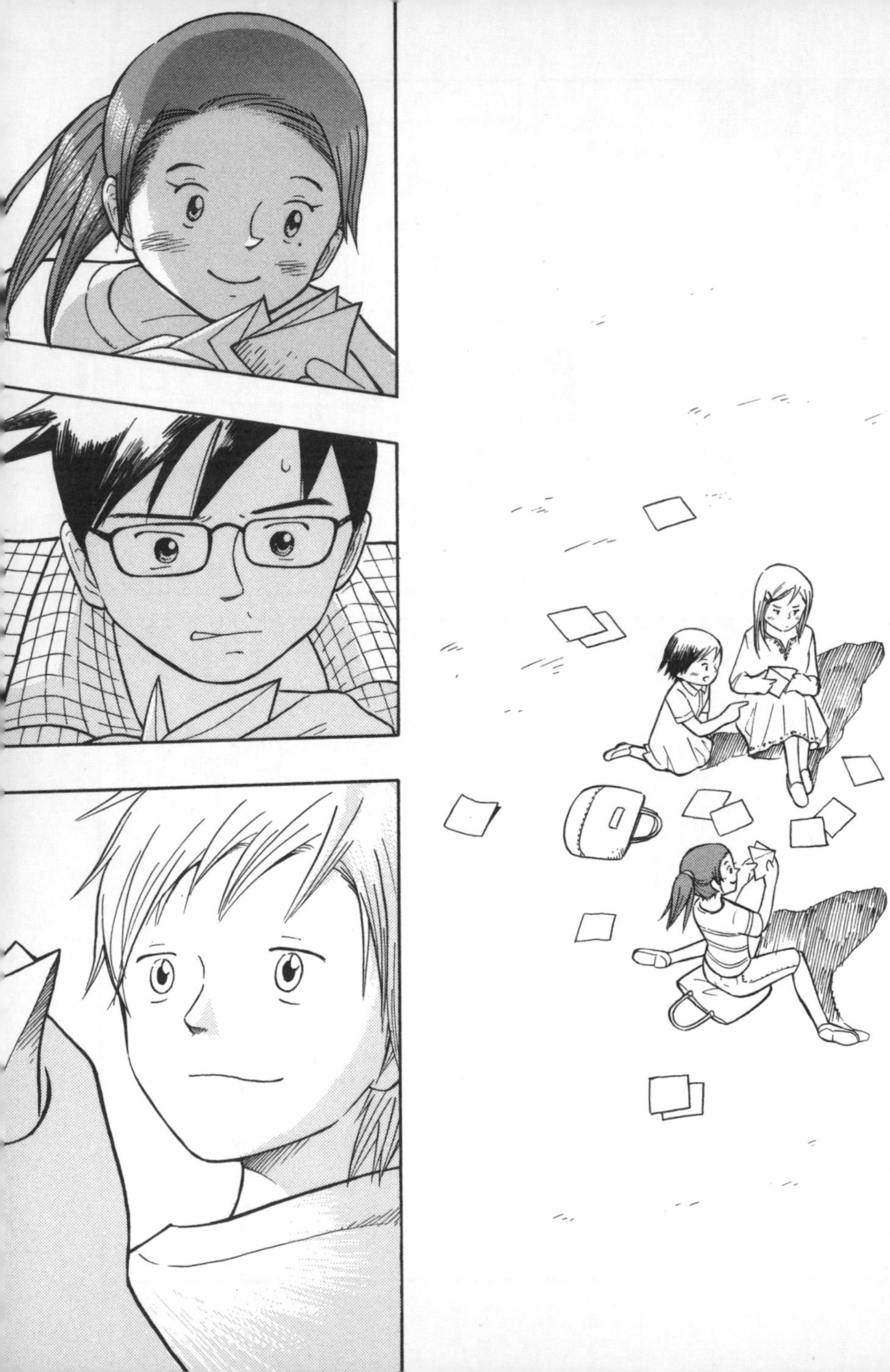

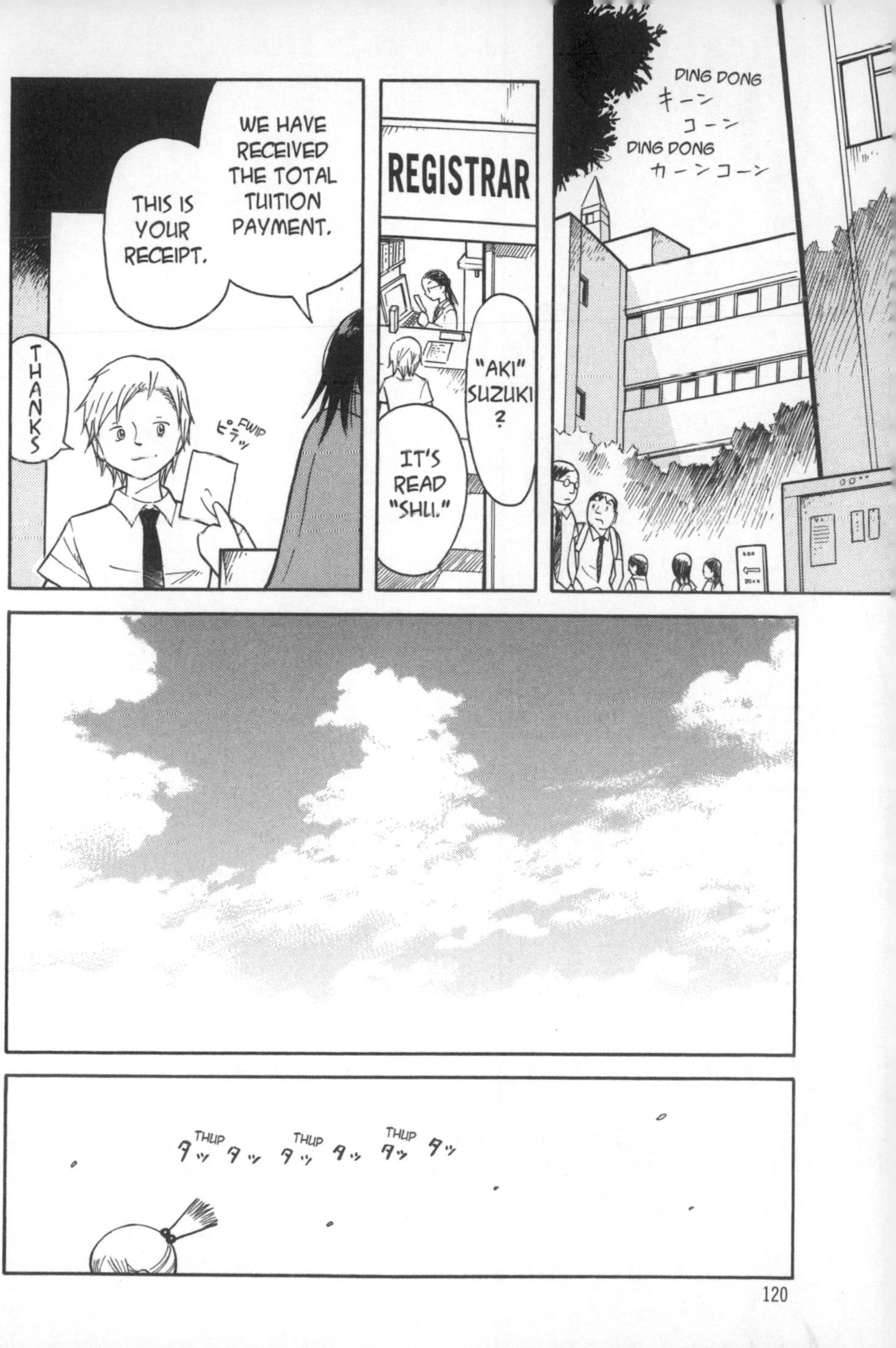
DING DONG
キーン
コーン
DING DONG
カーンコーン
REGISTRAR
"AKI" SUZUKI?
IT'S READ "SHU."
WE HAVE RECEIVED THE TOTAL TUITION PAYMENT.
THIS IS YOUR RECEIPT.
FWIP
ピラッ
THANKS
THUP THUP THUP
タッ タッ タッ タッ タッ タッ

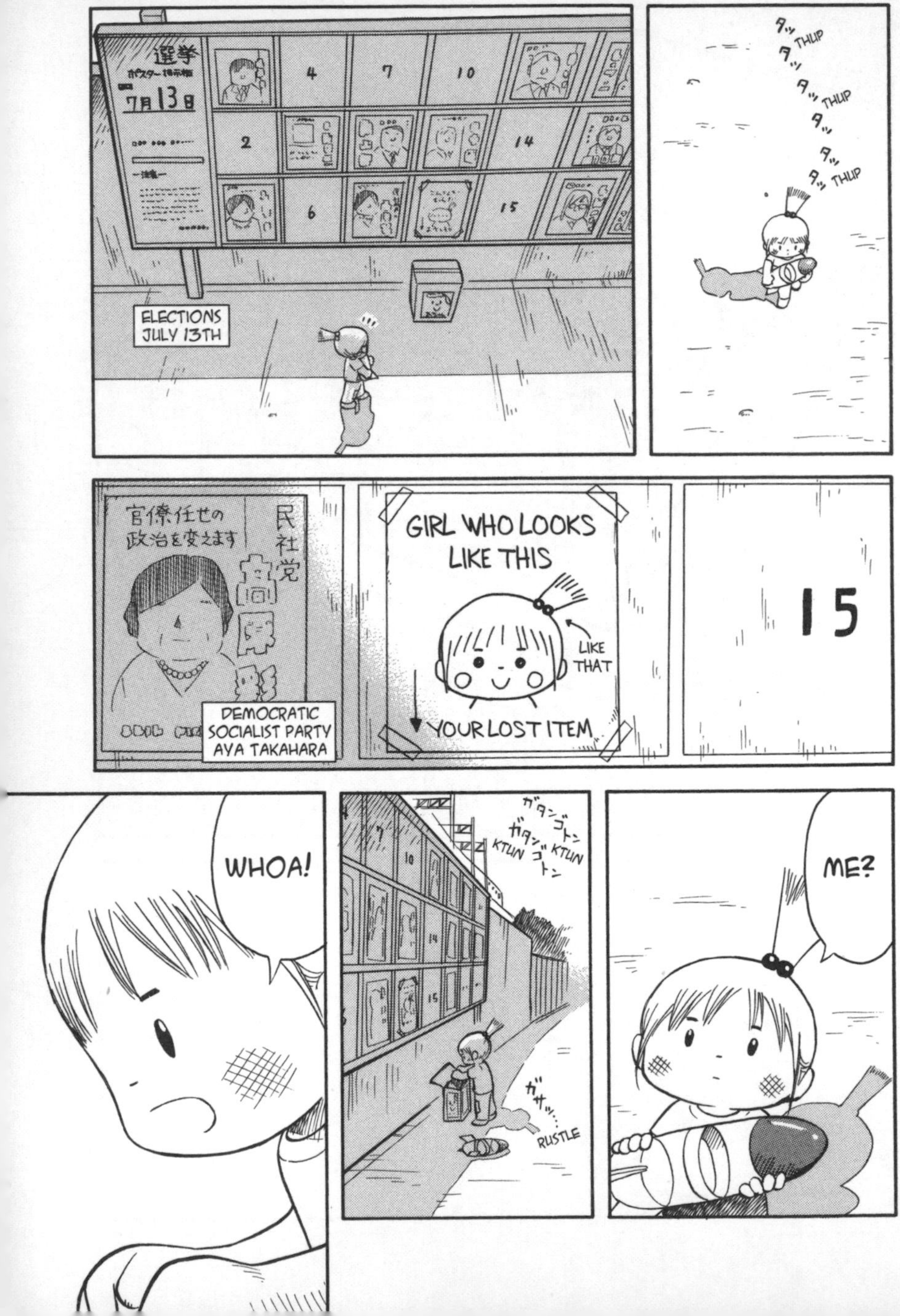

タッ THUP
タッ
タッ THUP
タッ
タッ
タッ THUP
選挙
7月13日
ELECTIONS JULY 13TH
15
GIRL WHO LOOKS LIKE THIS
LIKE THAT
YOUR LOST ITEM
官僚任せの政治を変えます
民社党
DEMOCRATIC SOCIALIST PARTY AYA TAKAHARA
ME?
ガタン ゴトン KTUN
ガタン ゴトン KTUN
ガサッ… RUSTLE
WHOA!

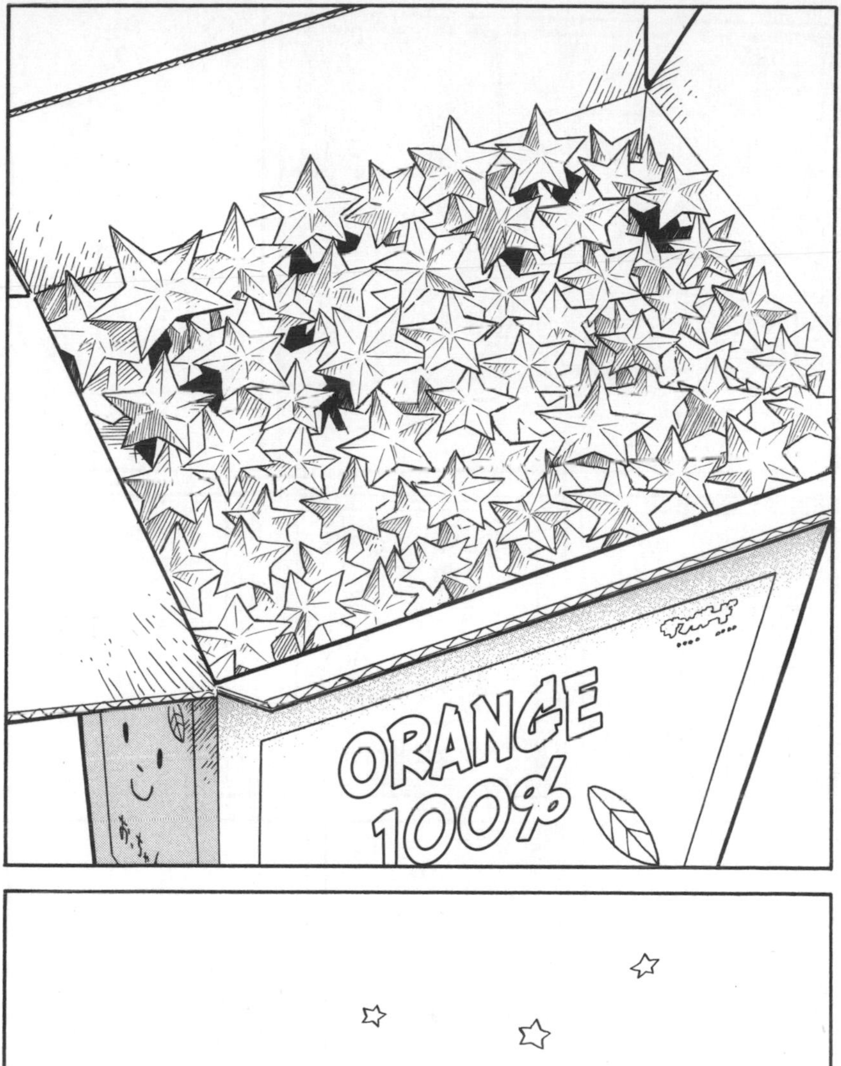
ORANGE
100%
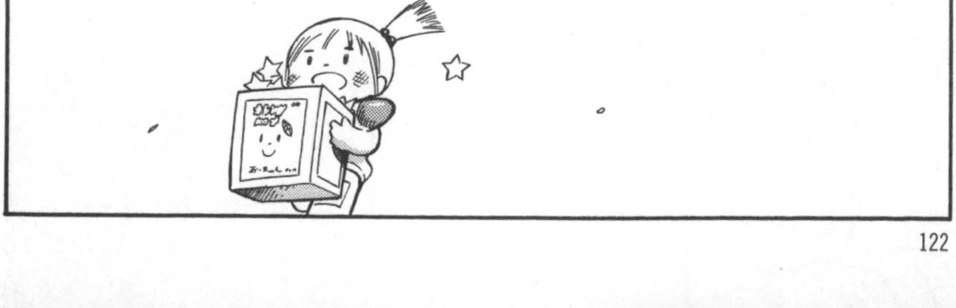

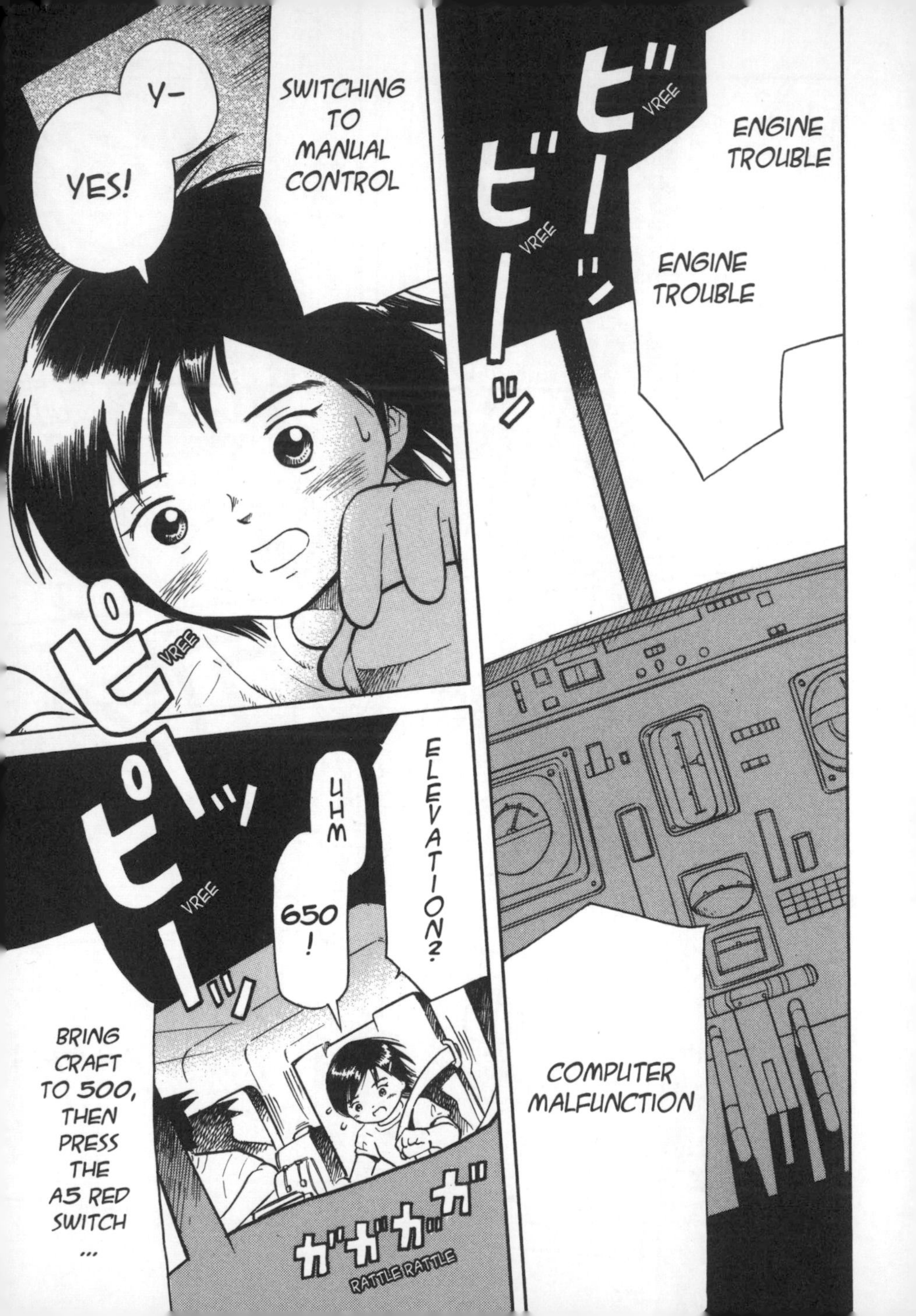
ビーッ
VREE
ENGINE TROUBLE
ビー
VREE
ENGINE TROUBLE
COMPUTER MALFUNCTION
SWITCHING TO MANUAL CONTROL
Y-
YES!
ピー
VREE
ELEVATION?
UHM
650!
ピーッ
ピー
VREE
BRING CRAFT TO 500, THEN PRESS THE A5 RED SWITCH ...
ガガガガ
RATTLE RATTLE

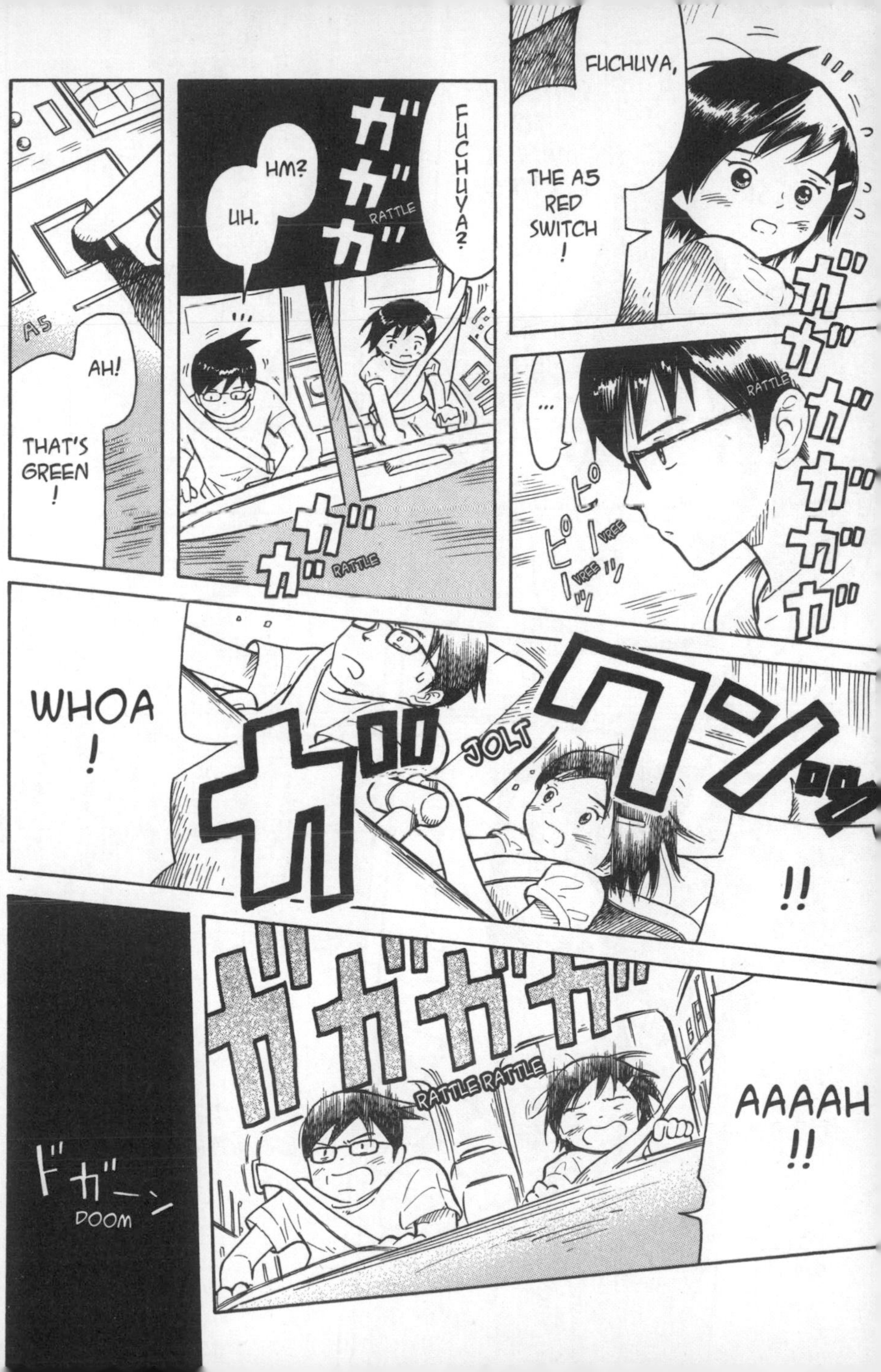
FUCHUYA,
THE A5 RED SWITCH!
...
RATTLE
VREE
VREE
FUCHUYA?
HM?
UH.
RATTLE
RATTLE
A5
AH!
THAT'S GREEN!
JOLT
!!
WHOA!
AAAAH!!
RATTLE RATTLE
DOOM

MISSION:29

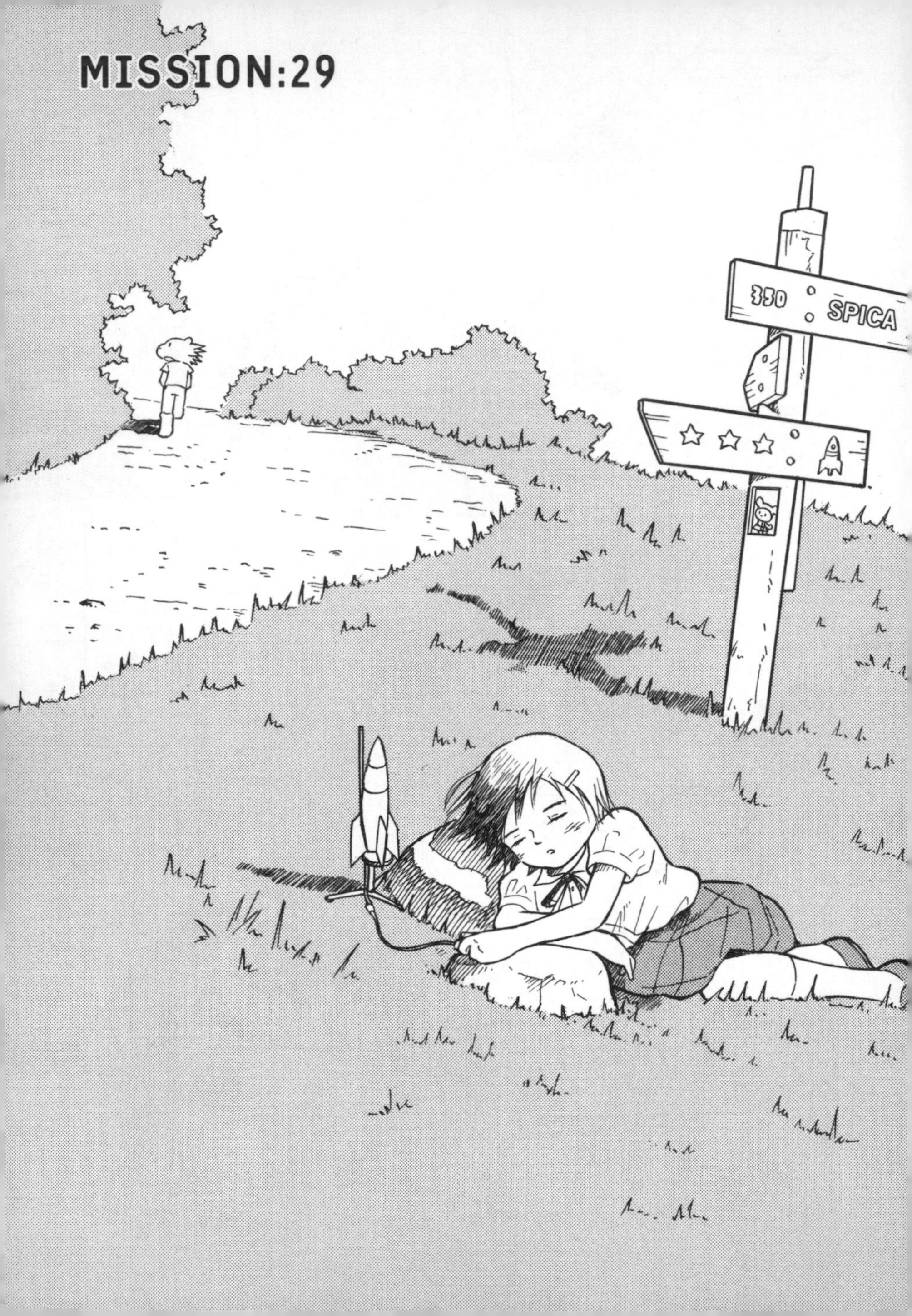
350 SPICA

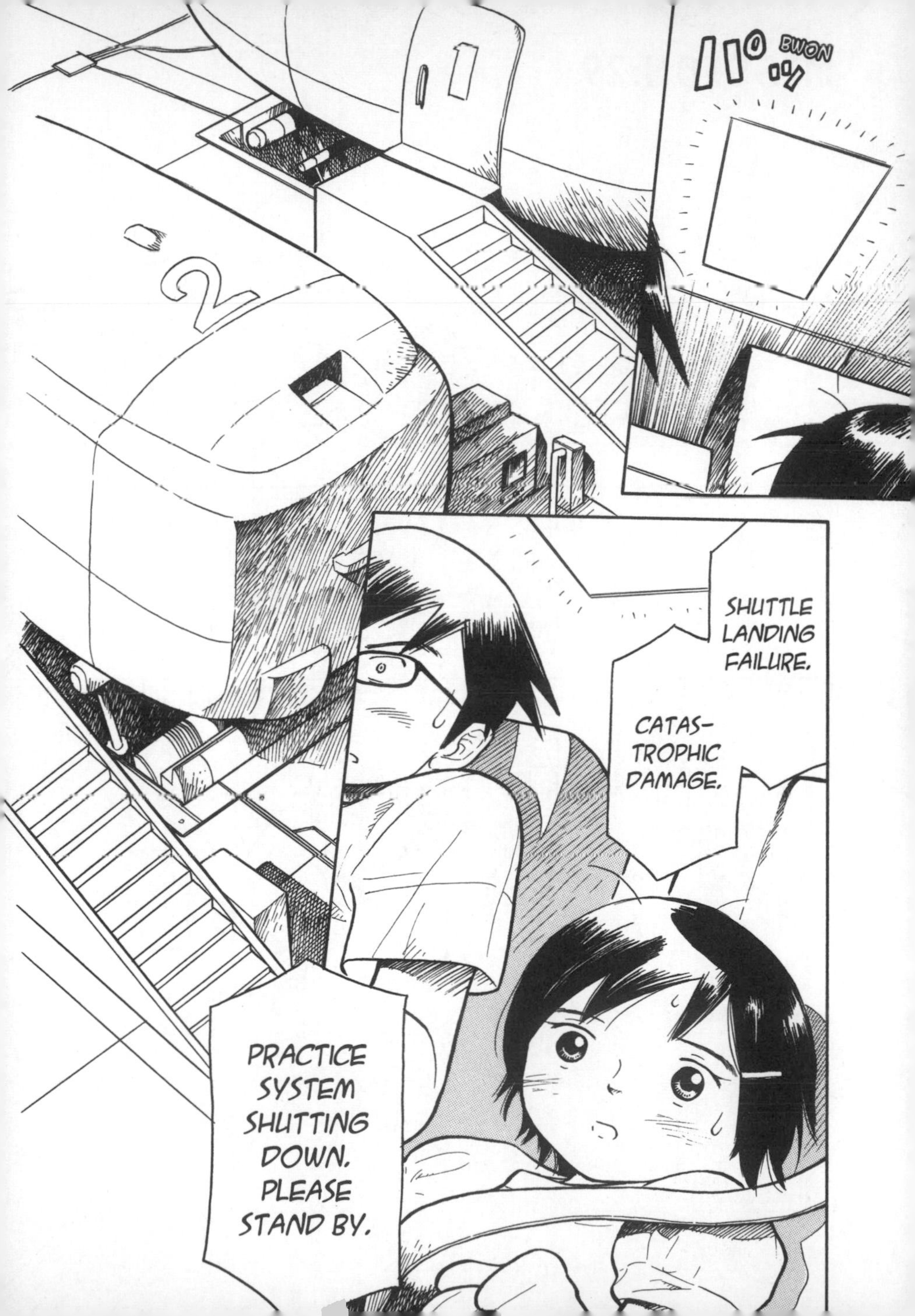
BWON
SHUTTLE LANDING FAILURE.
CATAS-TROPHIC DAMAGE.
PRACTICE SYSTEM SHUTTING DOWN. PLEASE STAND BY.

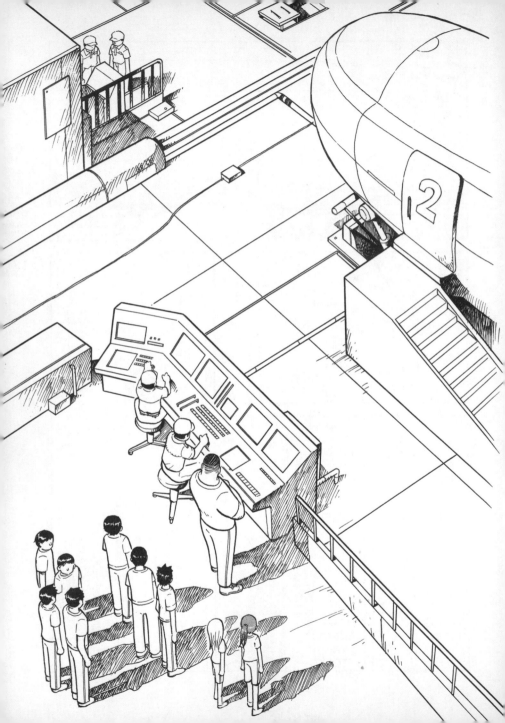

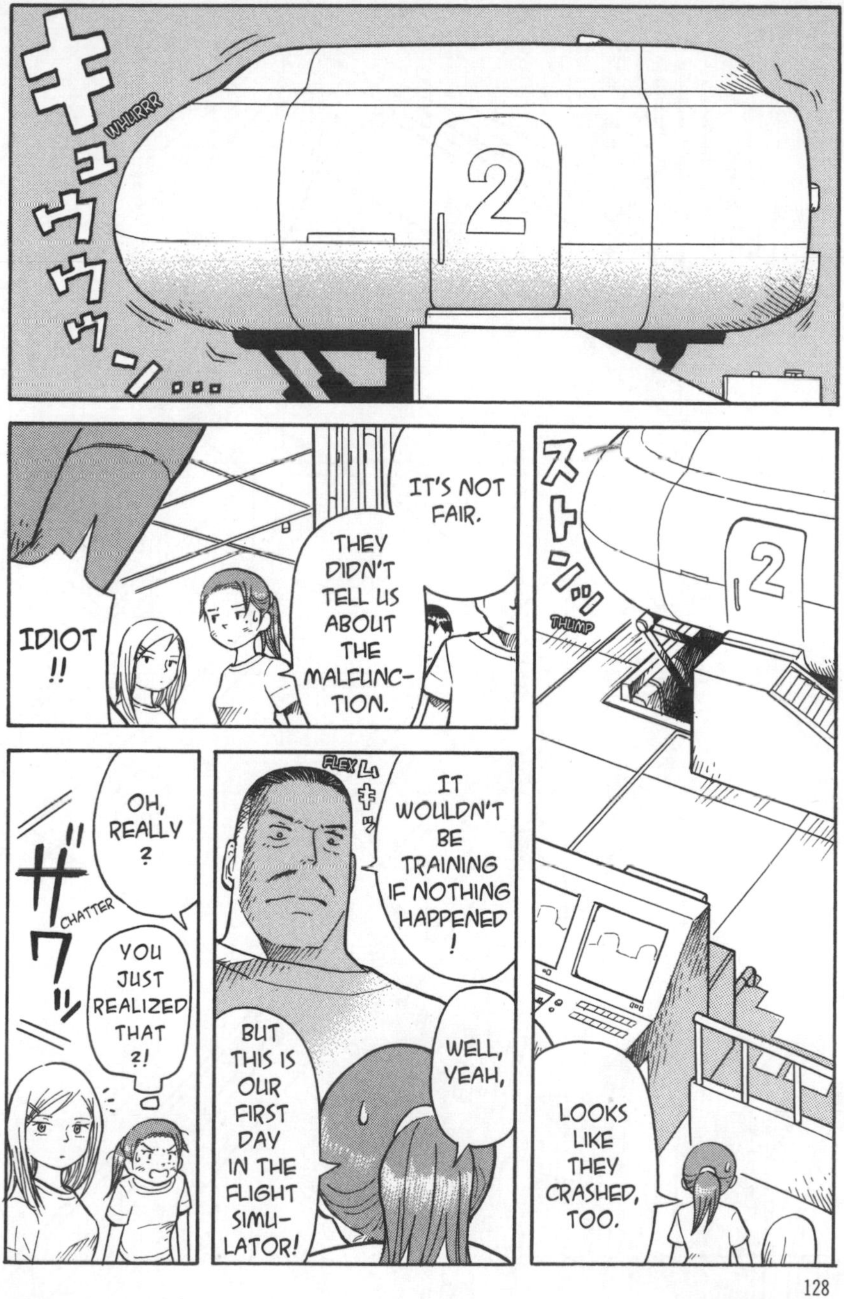

キュウウウーン…
WHURRR
ストンッ
THUMP
LOOKS LIKE THEY CRASHED, TOO.
IT'S NOT FAIR.
THEY DIDN'T TELL US ABOUT THE MALFUNCTION.
IDIOT!!
FLEX
ムキッ
IT WOULDN'T BE TRAINING IF NOTHING HAPPENED!
WELL, YEAH,
BUT THIS IS OUR FIRST DAY IN THE FLIGHT SIMULATOR!
OH, REALLY?
ザワッ
CHATTER
YOU JUST REALIZED THAT?!

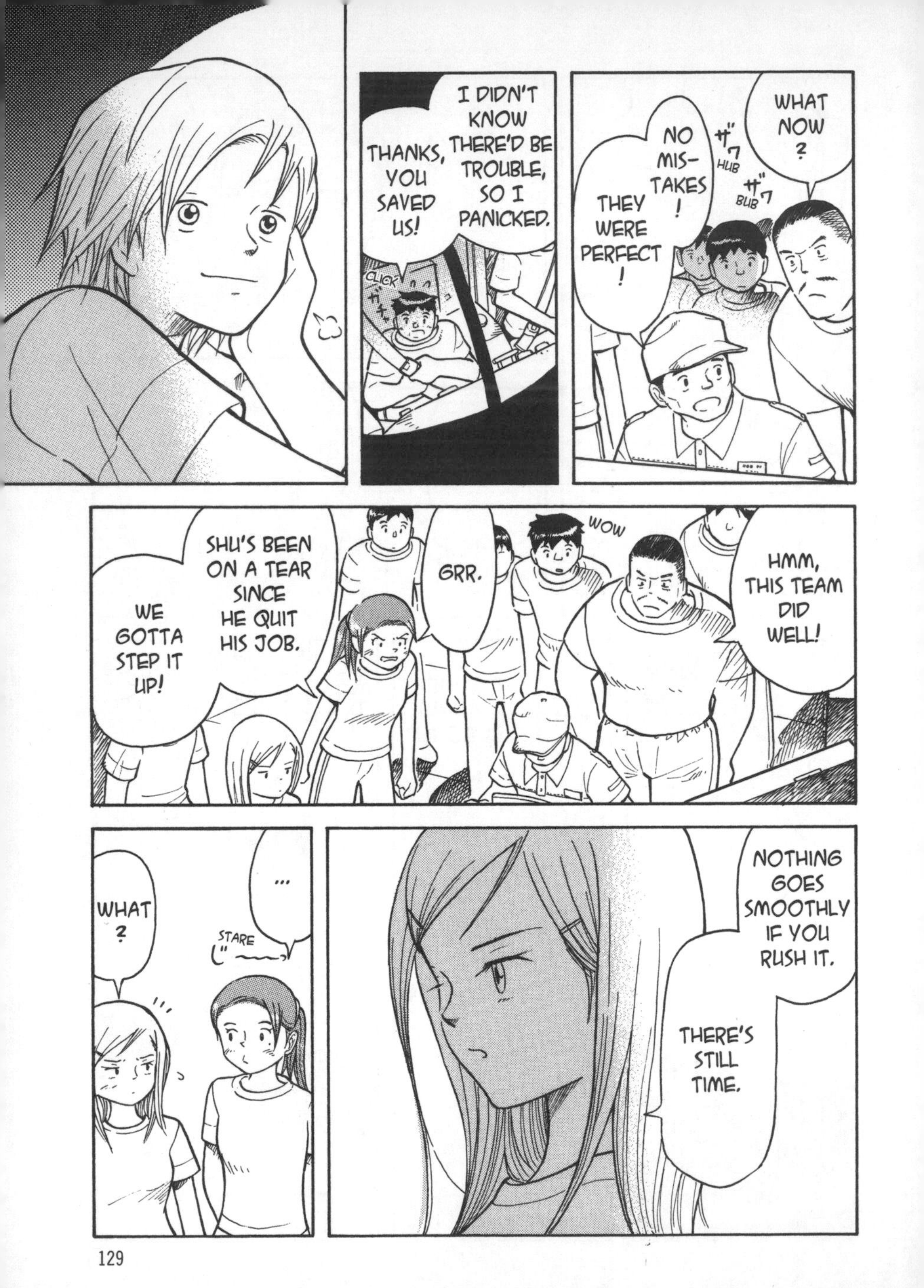
WHAT NOW?
HUB
BUB
NO MIS-TAKES!
THEY WERE PERFECT!
I DIDN'T KNOW THERE'D BE TROUBLE, SO I PANICKED.
THANKS, YOU SAVED US!
CLICK
HMM, THIS TEAM DID WELL!
WOW
GRR.
SHU'S BEEN ON A TEAR SINCE HE QUIT HIS JOB.
WE GOTTA STEP IT UP!
NOTHING GOES SMOOTHLY IF YOU RUSH IT.
THERE'S STILL TIME.
...
STARE
WHAT?

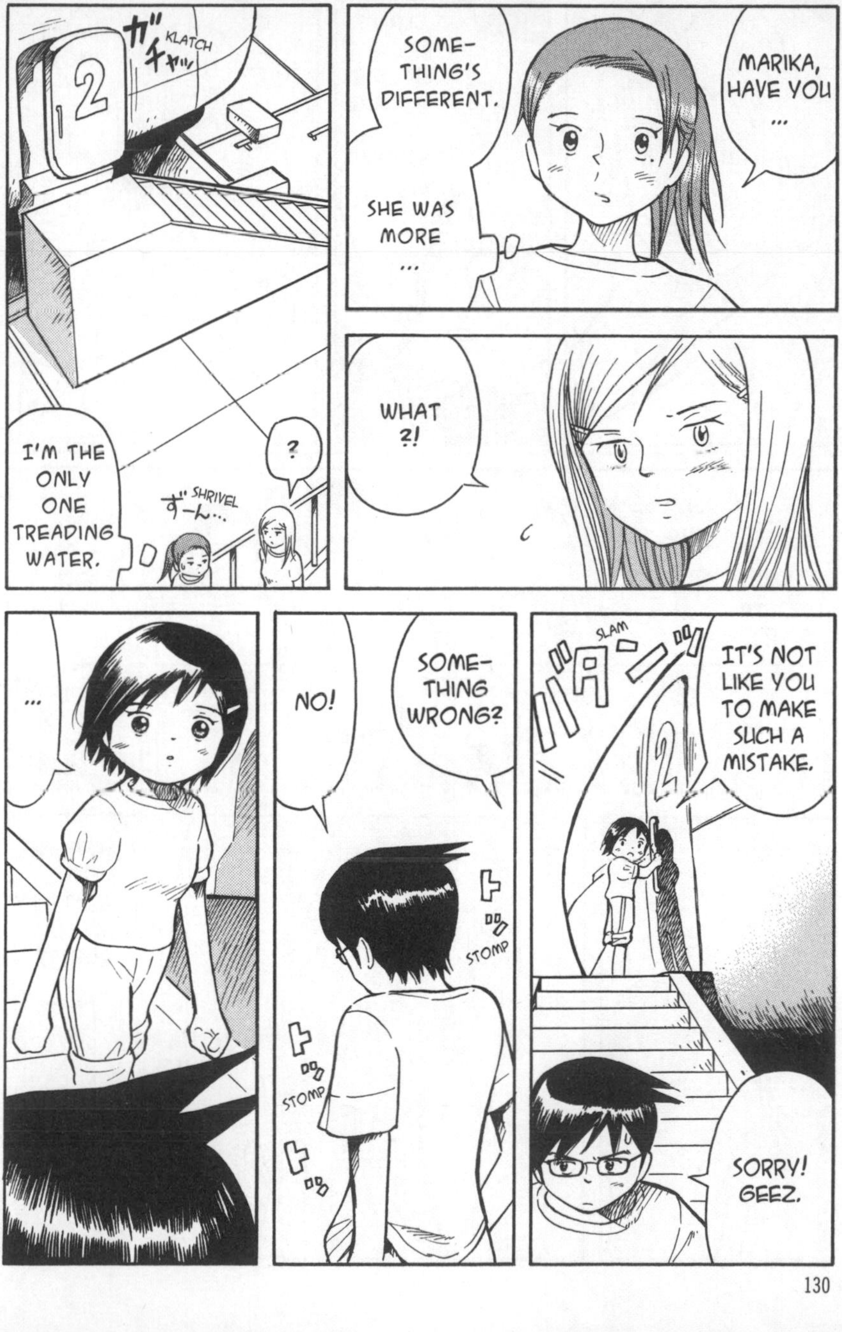

MARIKA, HAVE YOU ...
SOME-THING'S DIFFERENT.
SHE WAS MORE ...
WHAT ?!
ガチャッ
KLATCH
?
ずーん…
SHRIVEL
I'M THE ONLY ONE TREADING WATER.
バターン
SLAM
IT'S NOT LIKE YOU TO MAKE SUCH A MISTAKE.
SORRY! GEEZ.
SOME-THING WRONG?
NO!
トッ
STOMP
トッ
STOMP
トッ
...

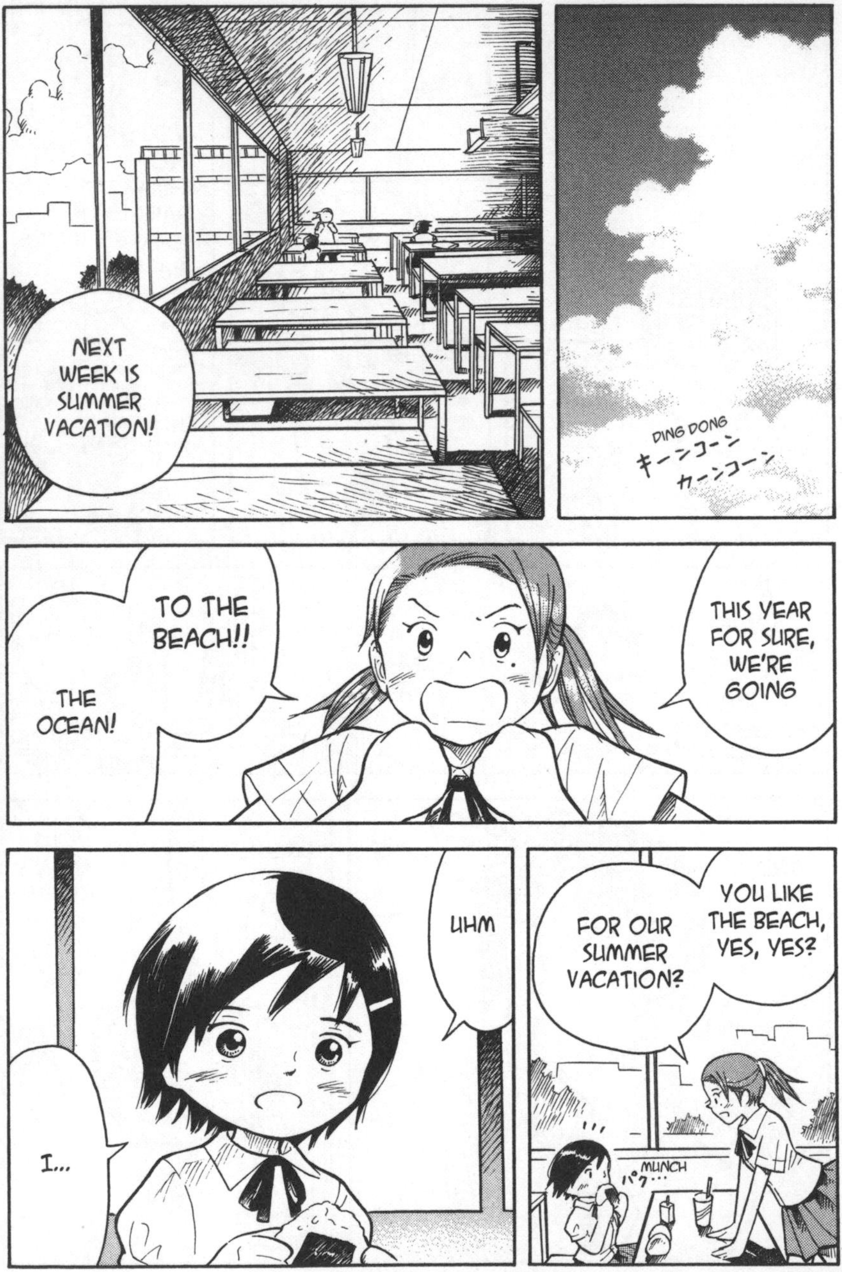
DING DONG
キーンコーン
カーンコーン
NEXT WEEK IS SUMMER VACATION!
THIS YEAR FOR SURE, WE'RE GOING
TO THE BEACH!!
THE OCEAN!
YOU LIKE THE BEACH, YES, YES?
FOR OUR SUMMER VACATION?
MUNCH
パク…
UHM
I...

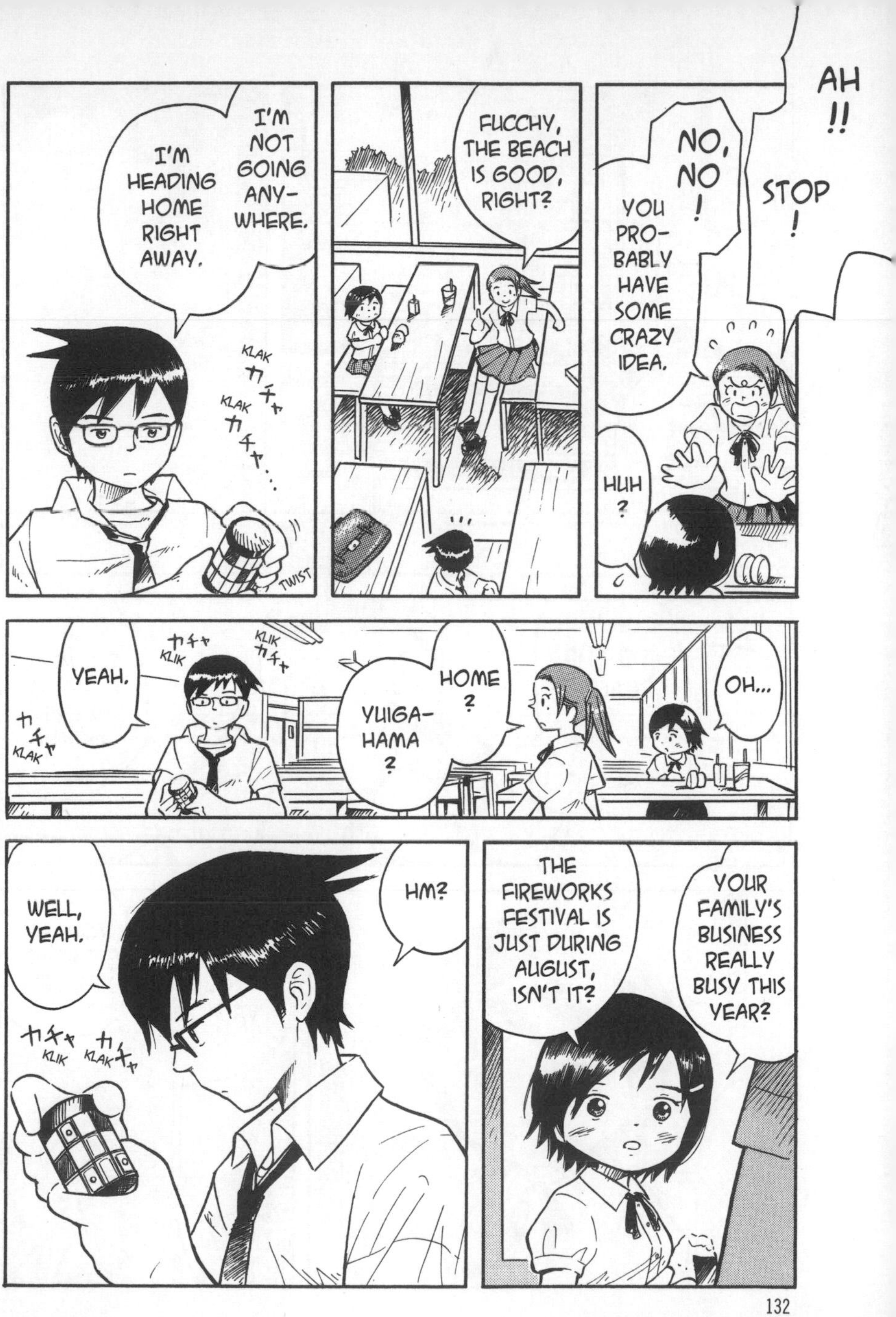
AH!! STOP!
NO, NO!
YOU PROBABLY HAVE SOME CRAZY IDEA.
HUH?
FUCCHY, THE BEACH IS GOOD, RIGHT?
I'M NOT GOING ANYWHERE.
I'M HEADING HOME RIGHT AWAY.
カチャ KLAK
カチャ… KLAK
TWIST
OH...
HOME? YUIGAHAMA?
カチャ KLIK
カチャ KLIK
YEAH.
カチャ KLAK
YOUR FAMILY'S BUSINESS REALLY BUSY THIS YEAR?
THE FIREWORKS FESTIVAL IS JUST DURING AUGUST, ISN'T IT?
HM?
WELL, YEAH.
カチャ KLIK
カチャ KLAK

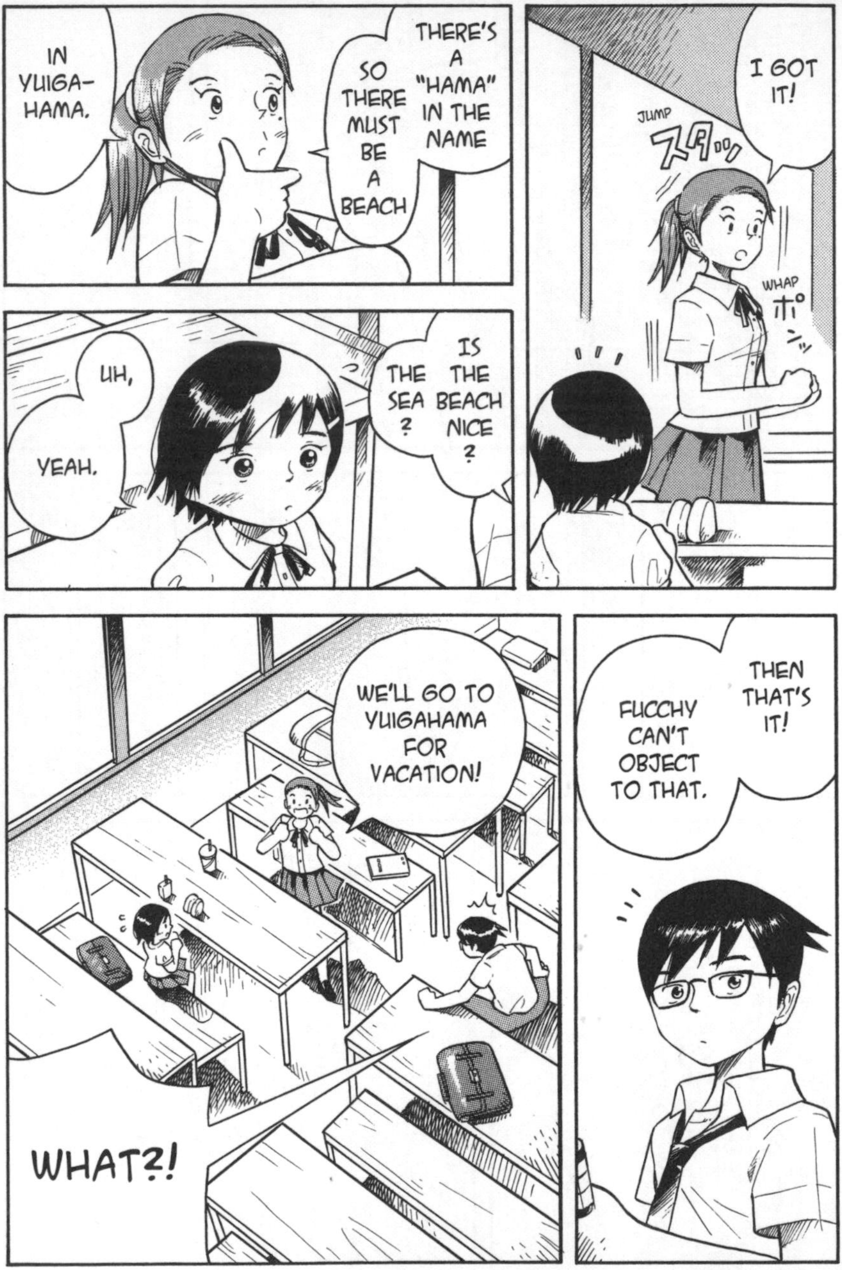
I GOT IT!
JUMP スタッ
WHAP ポンッ
THERE'S A "HAMA" IN THE NAME
SO THERE MUST BE A BEACH
IN YUIGA-HAMA.
IS THE BEACH NICE?
THE SEA?
UH,
YEAH.
THEN THAT'S IT!
FUCCHY CAN'T OBJECT TO THAT.
WE'LL GO TO YUIGAHAMA FOR VACATION!
WHAT?!

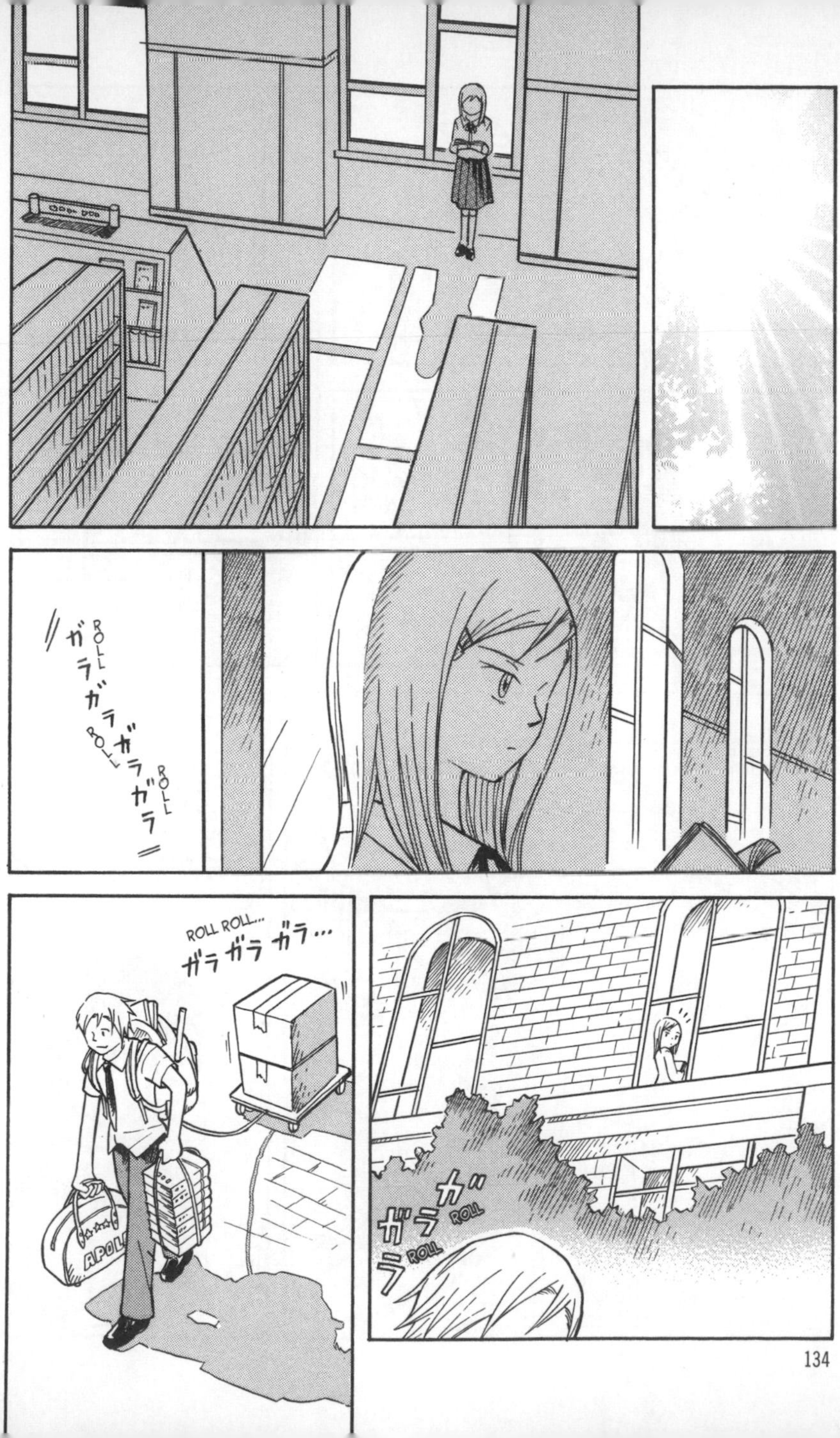

ガラガラ ROLL
ガラガラ ROLL ROLL
ガガラ ROLL
ラ ROLL
ROLL ROLL...
ガラガラ ガラ...

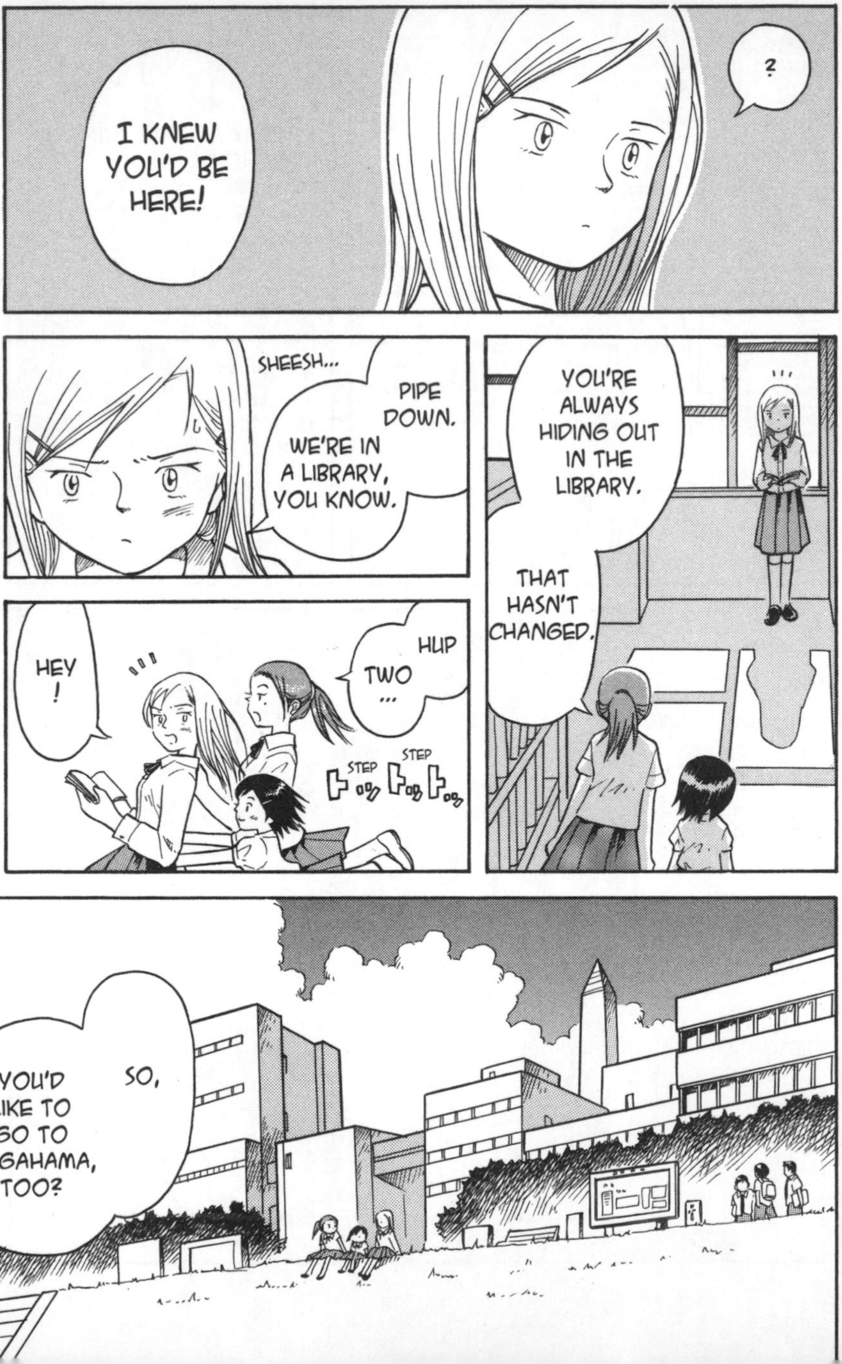
?
I KNEW YOU'D BE HERE!
YOU'RE ALWAYS HIDING OUT IN THE LIBRARY.
THAT HASN'T CHANGED.
SHEESH...
PIPE DOWN.
WE'RE IN A LIBRARY, YOU KNOW.
HUP TWO ...
STEP STEP
HEY !
SO,
YOU'D LIKE TO GO TO YUIGAHAMA, TOO?

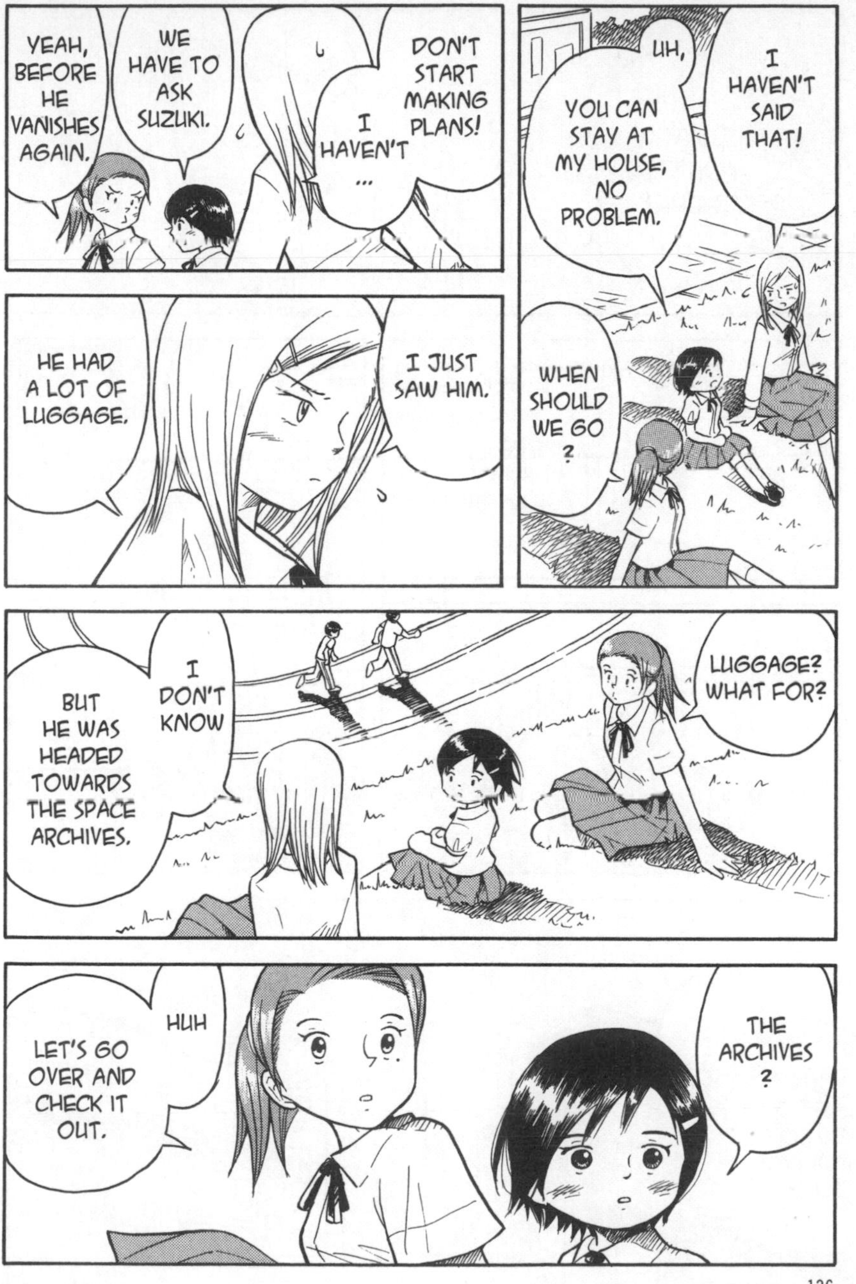
I HAVEN'T SAID THAT!
UH,
YOU CAN STAY AT MY HOUSE, NO PROBLEM.
WHEN SHOULD WE GO ?
DON'T START MAKING PLANS!
I HAVEN'T ...
WE HAVE TO ASK SUZUKI.
YEAH, BEFORE HE VANISHES AGAIN.
I JUST SAW HIM.
HE HAD A LOT OF LUGGAGE.
LUGGAGE? WHAT FOR?
I DON'T KNOW
BUT HE WAS HEADED TOWARDS THE SPACE ARCHIVES.
THE ARCHIVES ?
HUH
LET'S GO OVER AND CHECK IT OUT.

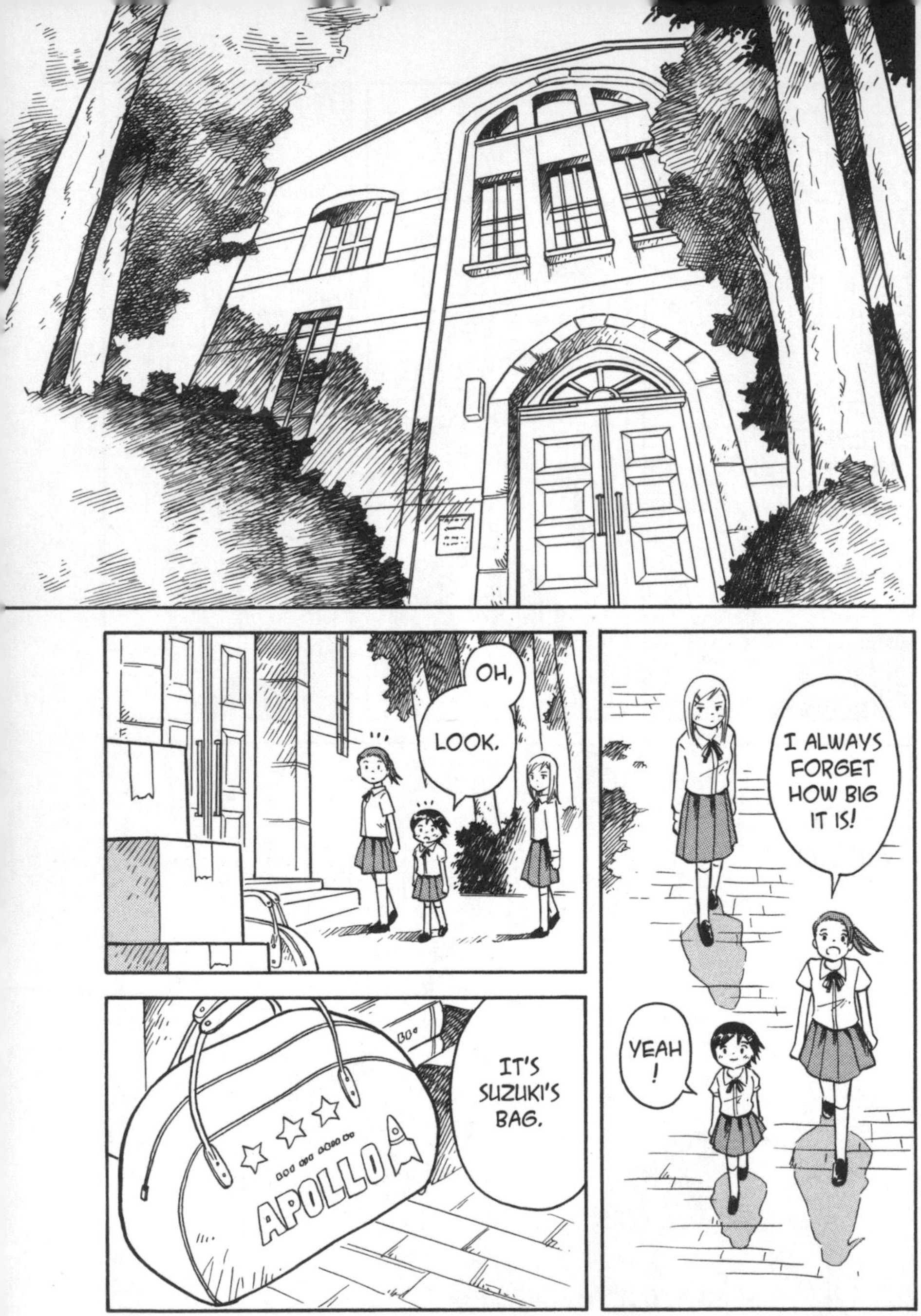
I ALWAYS FORGET HOW BIG IT IS!
YEAH!
OH,
LOOK.
IT'S SUZUKI'S BAG.
APOLLO

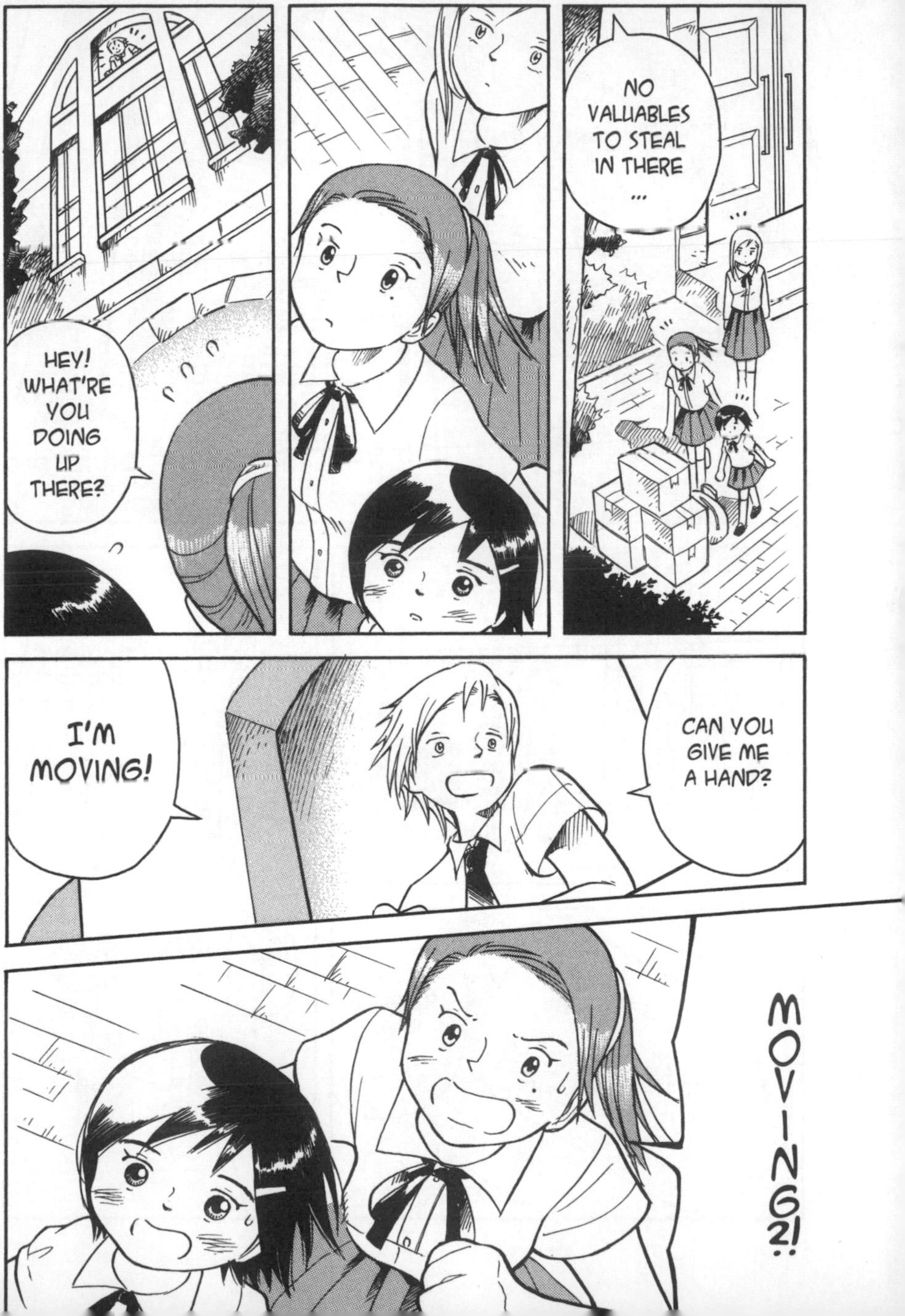
NO VALUABLES TO STEAL IN THERE ...
HEY! WHAT'RE YOU DOING UP THERE?
CAN YOU GIVE ME A HAND?
I'M MOVING!
MOVING?!

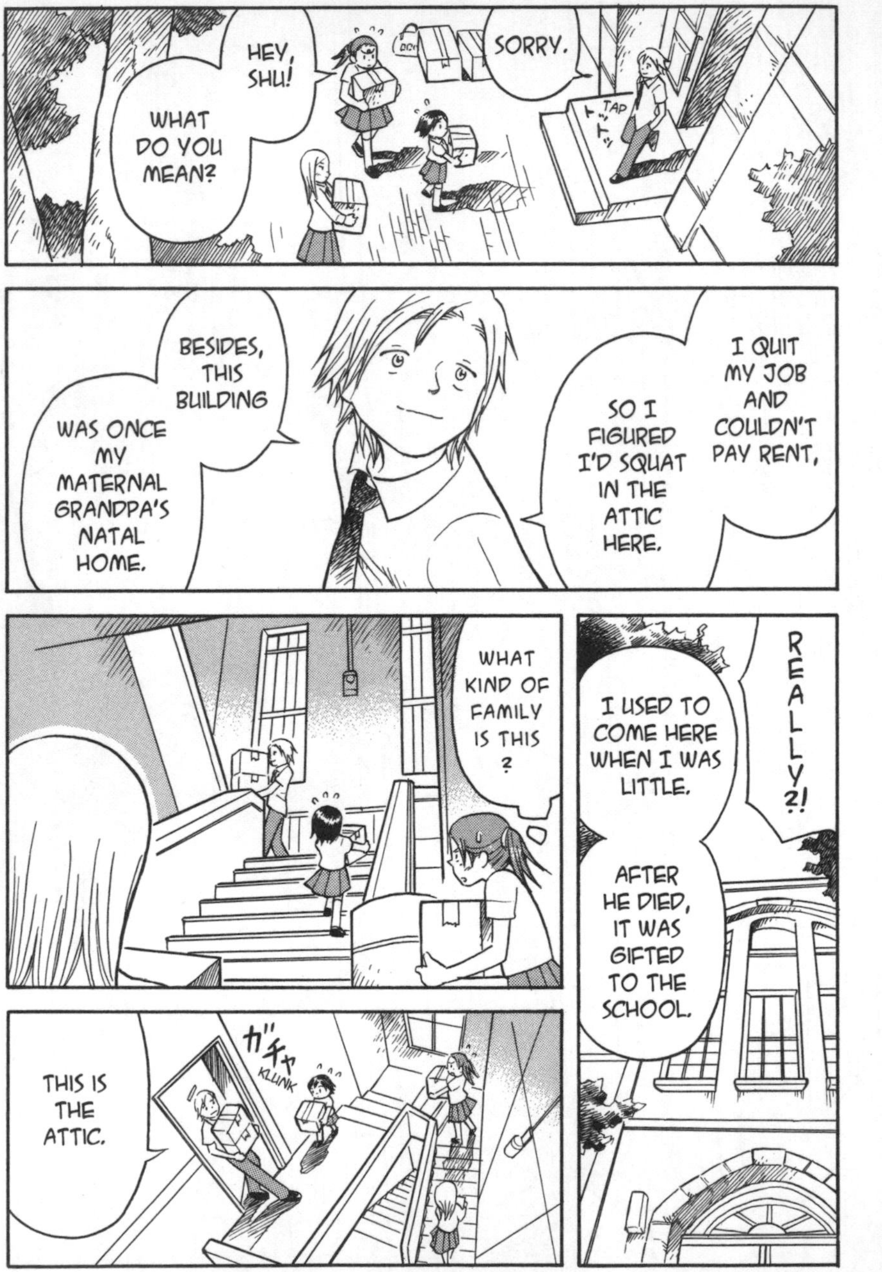
SORRY.
TAP
HEY, SHU!
WHAT DO YOU MEAN?
I QUIT MY JOB AND COULDN'T PAY RENT,
SO I FIGURED I'D SQUAT IN THE ATTIC HERE.
BESIDES, THIS BUILDING
WAS ONCE MY MATERNAL GRANDPA'S NATAL HOME.
REALLY?!
I USED TO COME HERE WHEN I WAS LITTLE.
AFTER HE DIED, IT WAS GIFTED TO THE SCHOOL.
WHAT KIND OF FAMILY IS THIS?
ガチャ KLUNK
THIS IS THE ATTIC.

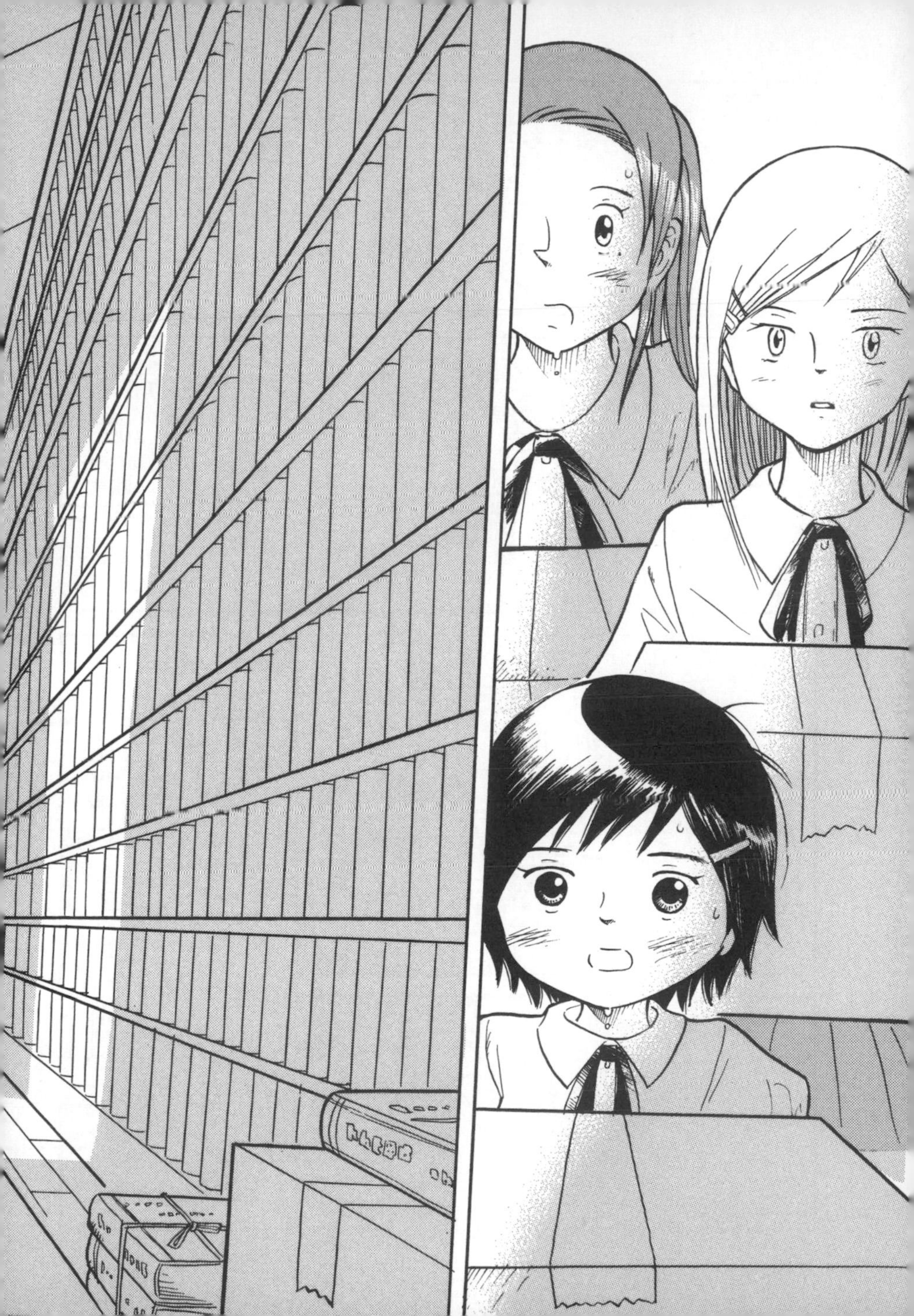

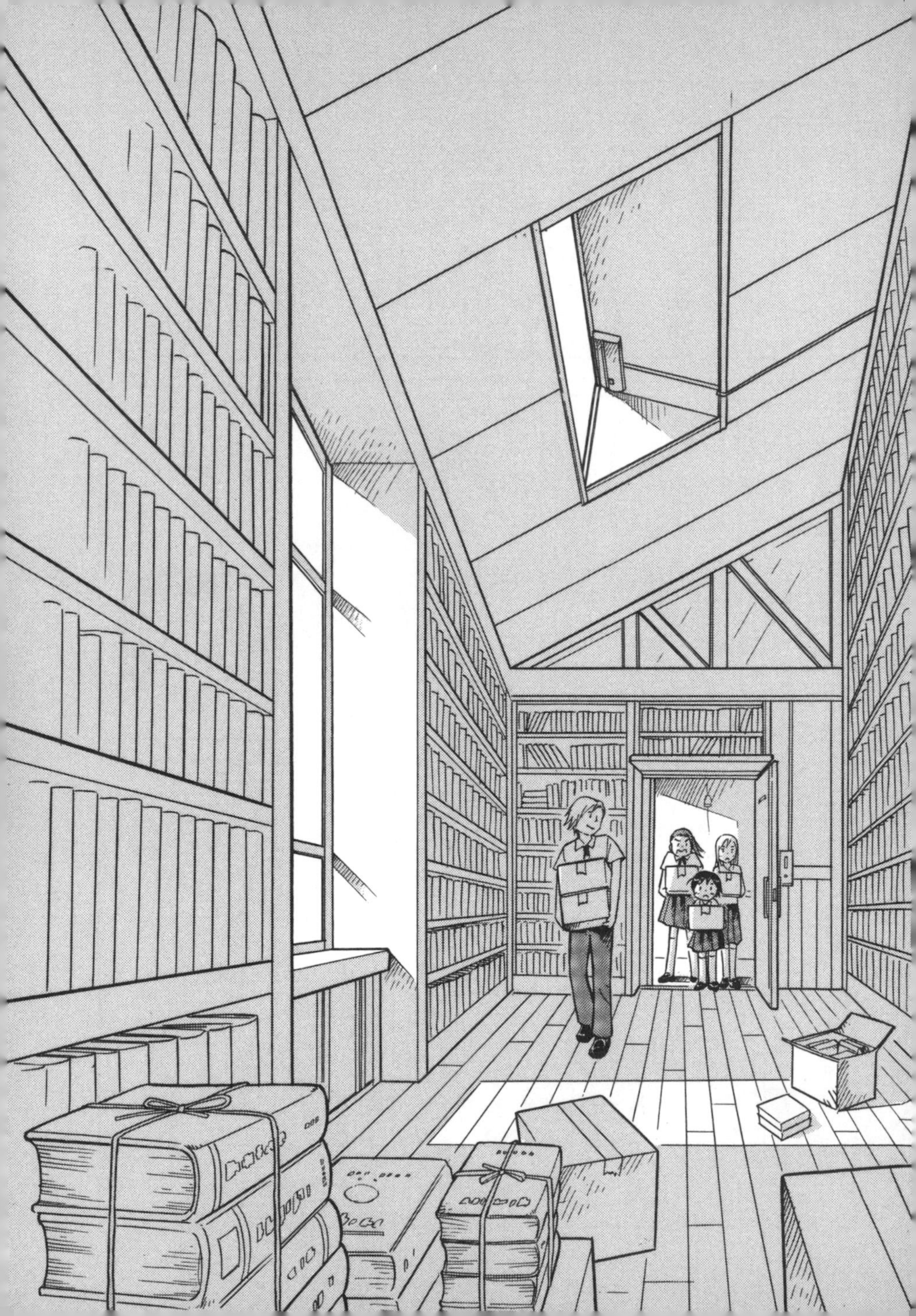

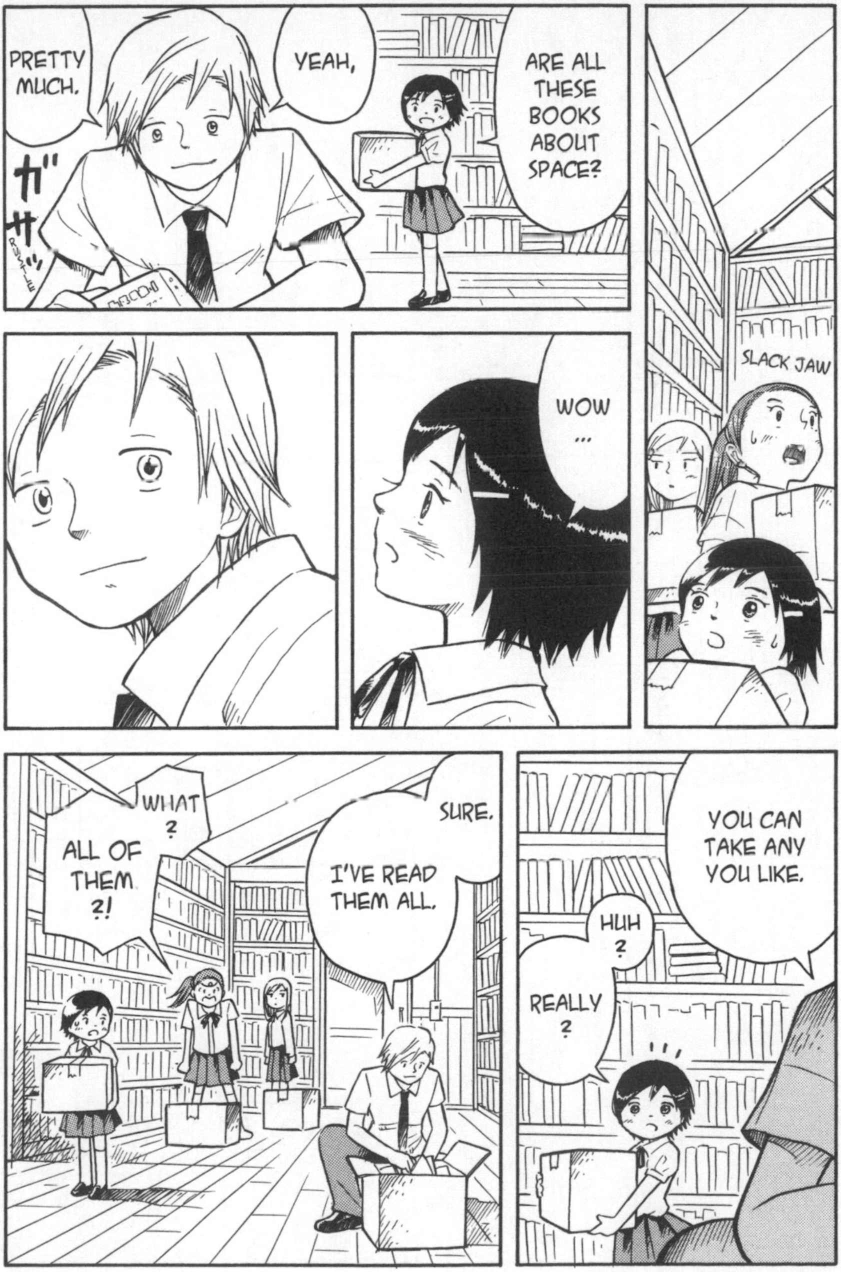
SLACK JAW
ARE ALL THESE BOOKS ABOUT SPACE?
YEAH,
PRETTY MUCH.
ガサッ
RUSTLE
WOW ...
YOU CAN TAKE ANY YOU LIKE.
HUH?
REALLY?
SURE.
I'VE READ THEM ALL.
WHAT?
ALL OF THEM?!

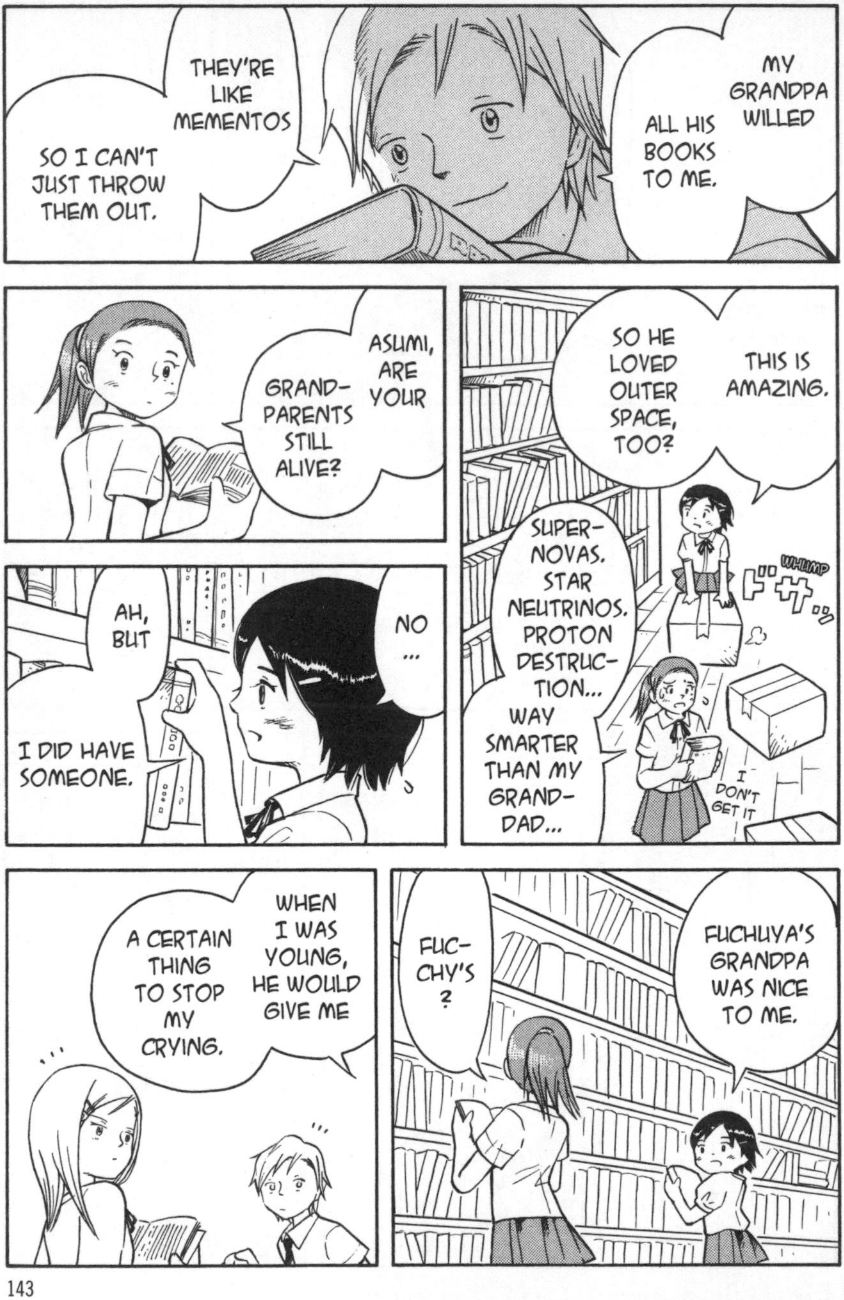
MY GRANDPA WILLED ALL HIS BOOKS TO ME.
THEY'RE LIKE MEMENTOS SO I CAN'T JUST THROW THEM OUT.
THIS IS AMAZING.
SO HE LOVED OUTER SPACE, TOO?
SUPER-NOVAS. STAR NEUTRINOS. PROTON DESTRUC-TION... WAY SMARTER THAN MY GRAND-DAD...
WHUMP
ドサッ
I DON'T GET IT
ASUMI, ARE YOUR GRAND-PARENTS STILL ALIVE?
NO ...
AH, BUT I DID HAVE SOMEONE.
FUCHUYA'S GRANDPA WAS NICE TO ME.
FUC-CHY'S?
WHEN I WAS YOUNG, HE WOULD GIVE ME A CERTAIN THING TO STOP MY CRYING.
...

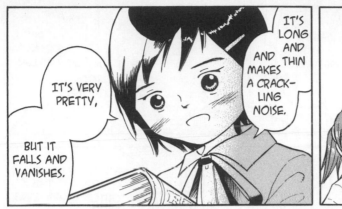

WHAT WAS IT?
IT'S LONG AND THIN
AND MAKES A CRACK-LING NOISE.
IT'S VERY PRETTY,
BUT IT FALLS AND VANISHES.
JUST TELL ME!
WHAT'S THIS THING?
WHEN WE'RE IN YUIGAHAMA I'LL TELL YOU.
I SHOULD GET ONE THIS YEAR.
YUIGA-HAMA?
OH, RIGHT! WE CAME TO TELL YOU
ABOUT OUR SUMMER PLANS.
WE'RE GOING TO YUIGA-HAMA!
!!!
プニッ POINK
プニッ
プニッ POINK
NO CHOICE, EH?
ARE YOU
WITH US OR NOT ?
WITH!
DING DONG
キーンコーン
カーンコーン

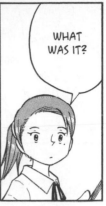

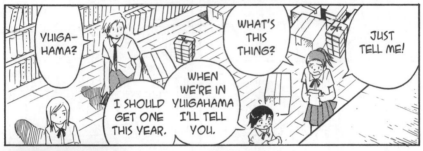

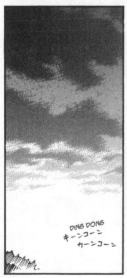

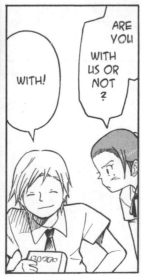

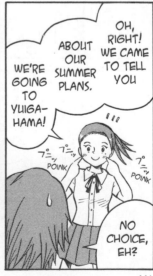

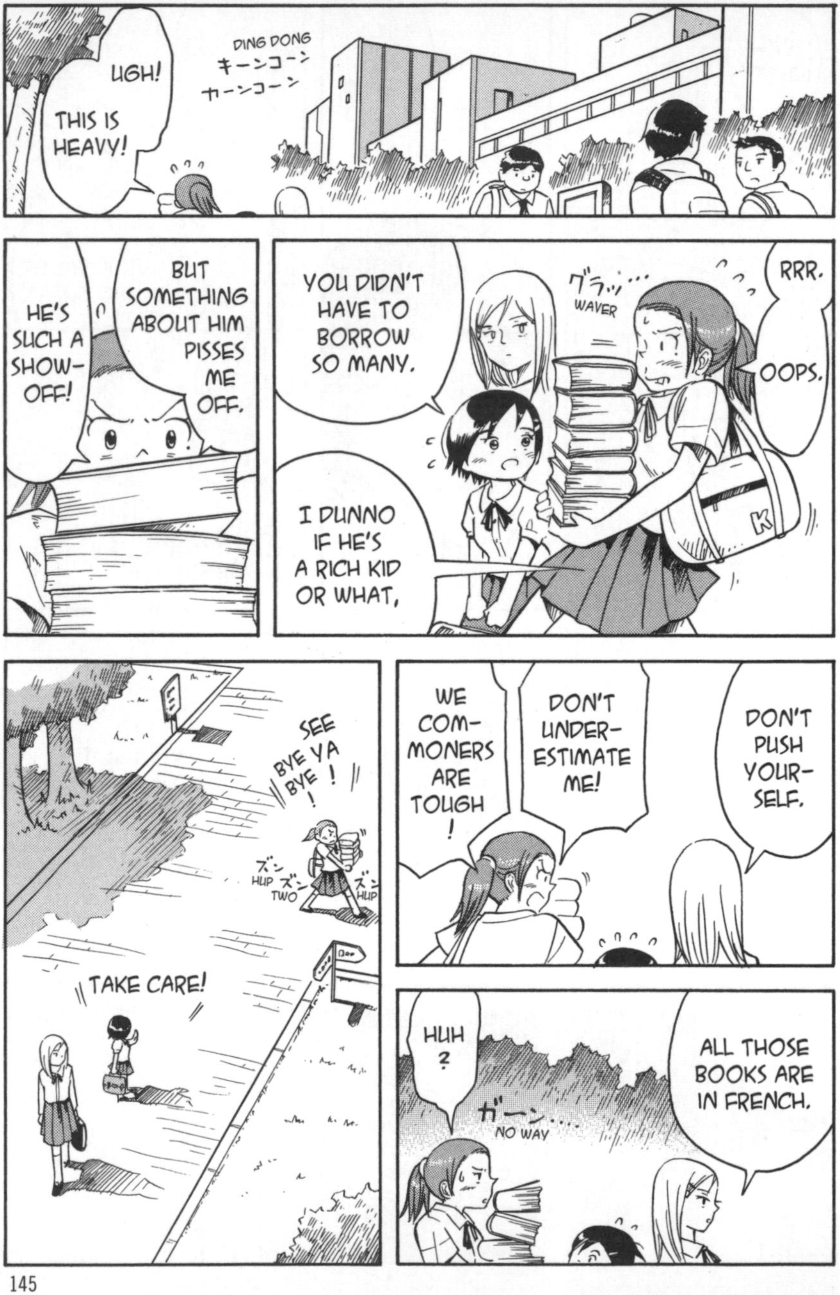
DING DONG
キーンコーン
カーンコーン
UGH!
THIS IS HEAVY!
RRR.
OOPS.
グラッ…
WAVER
YOU DIDN'T HAVE TO BORROW SO MANY.
I DUNNO IF HE'S A RICH KID OR WHAT,
BUT SOMETHING ABOUT HIM PISSES ME OFF.
HE'S SUCH A SHOW-OFF!
DON'T PUSH YOUR-SELF.
DON'T UNDER-ESTIMATE ME!
WE COM-MONERS ARE TOUGH!
ALL THOSE BOOKS ARE IN FRENCH.
HUH?
ガーン…
NO WAY
SEE YA!
BYE BYE!
ズン ズン ズン
HUP TWO HUP
TAKE CARE!

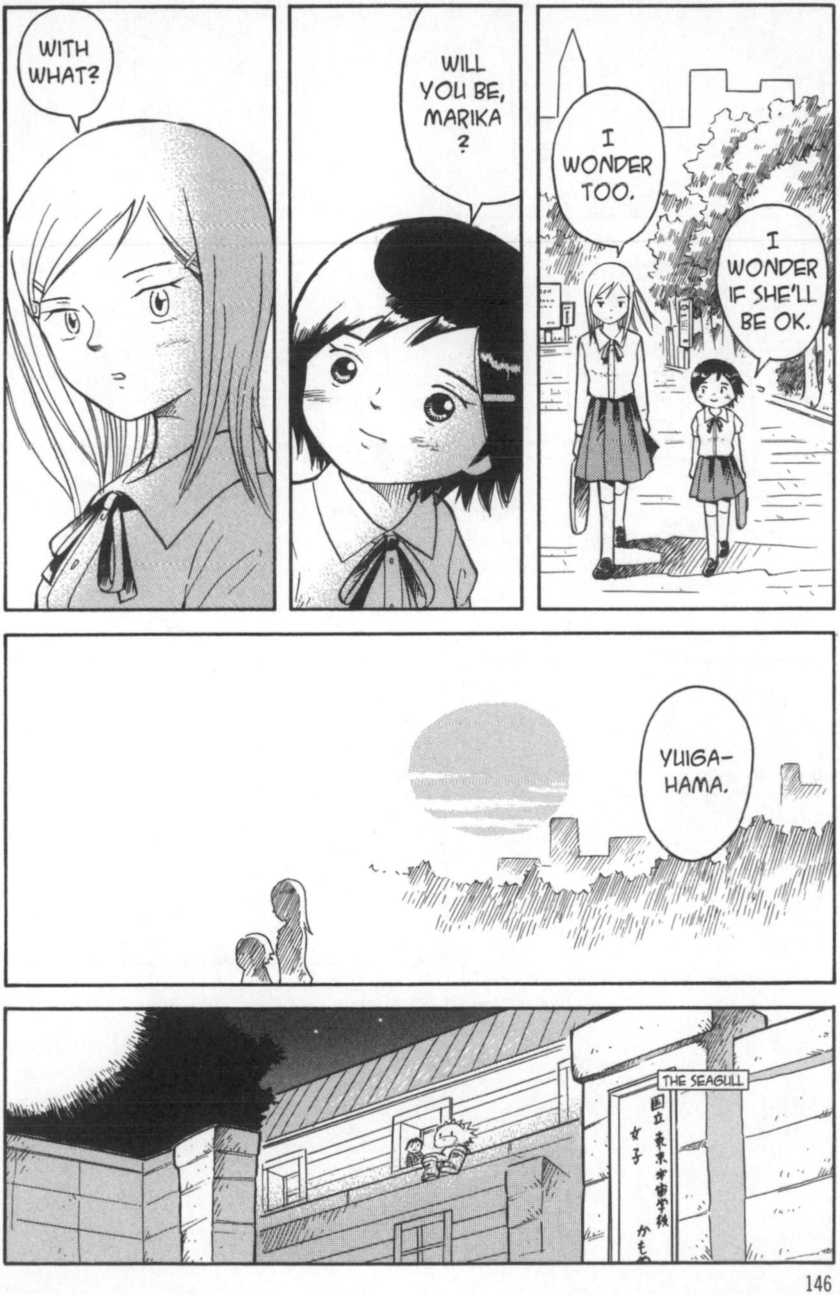
I WONDER IF SHE'LL BE OK.
I WONDER TOO.
WILL YOU BE, MARIKA?
WITH WHAT?
YUIGA-HAMA.
THE SEAGULL
国立 東京宇宙学校
女子
かもめ

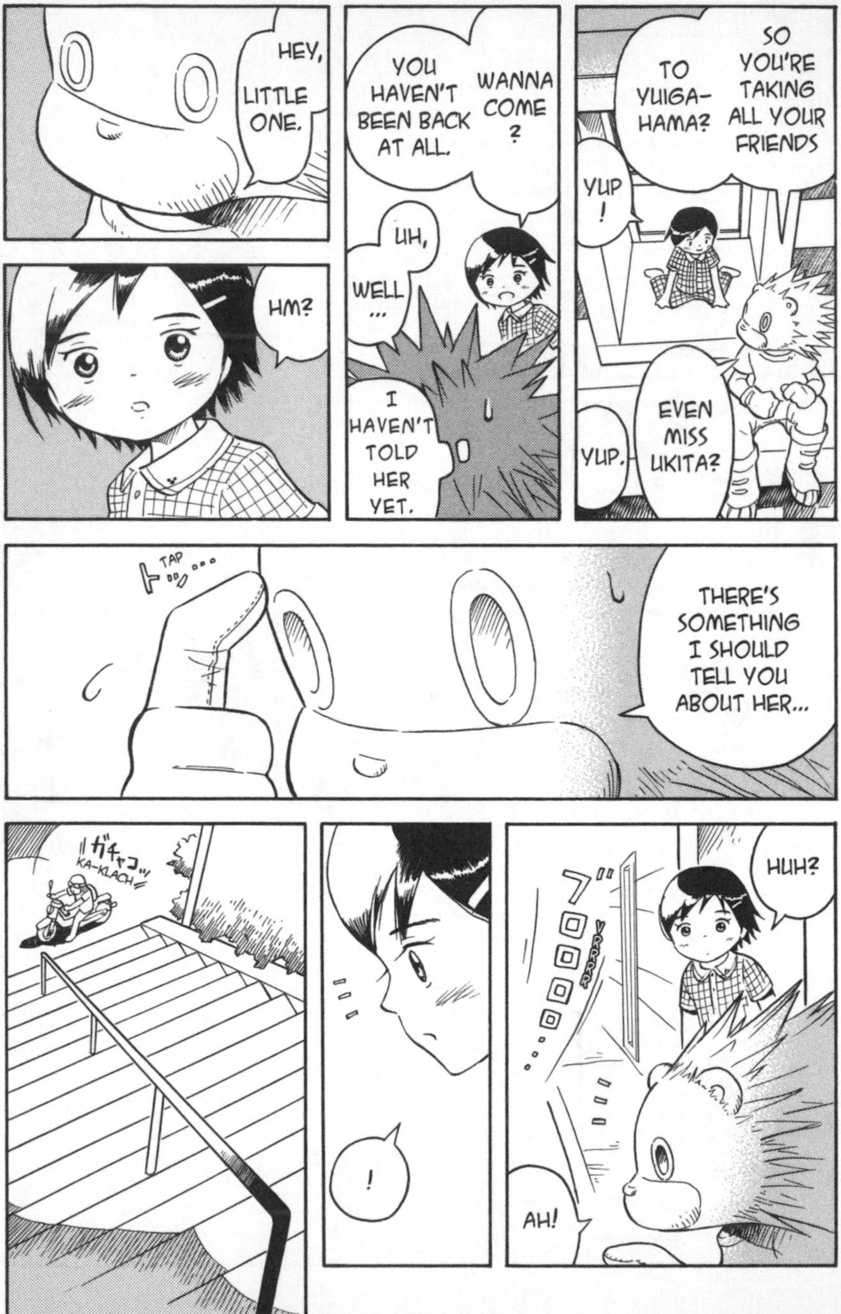
SO YOU'RE TAKING ALL YOUR FRIENDS
TO YUIGA-HAMA?
YUP!
EVEN MISS UKITA?
YUP.
WANNA COME?
YOU HAVEN'T BEEN BACK AT ALL.
UH, WELL...
I HAVEN'T TOLD HER YET.
HEY, LITTLE ONE.
HM?
TAP
THERE'S SOMETHING I SHOULD TELL YOU ABOUT HER...
HUH?
VRRRRR
AH!
!
KA-KLACH

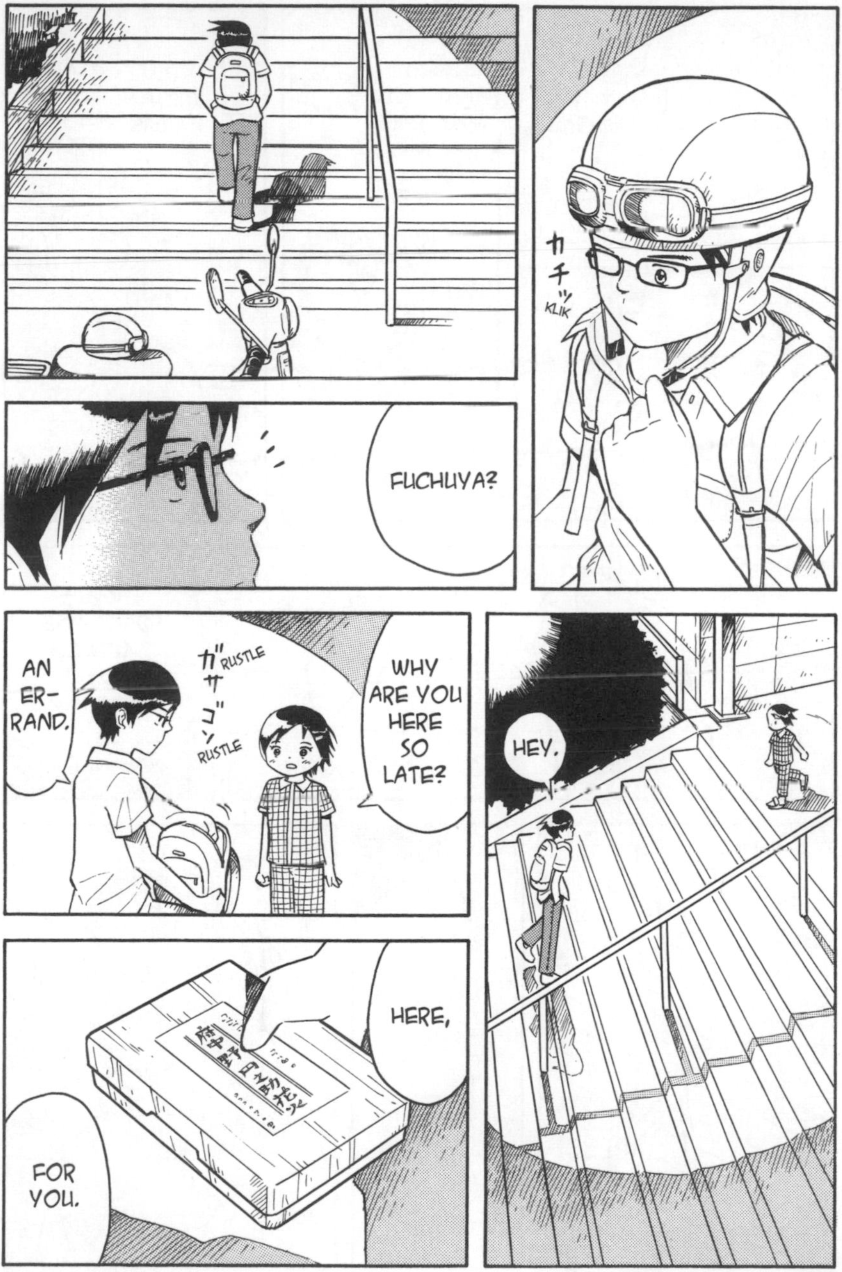

カチッ
KLIK
FUCHUYA?
HEY.
WHY ARE YOU HERE SO LATE?
ガサゴソ
RUSTLE RUSTLE
AN ER-RAND.
HERE,
FOR YOU.

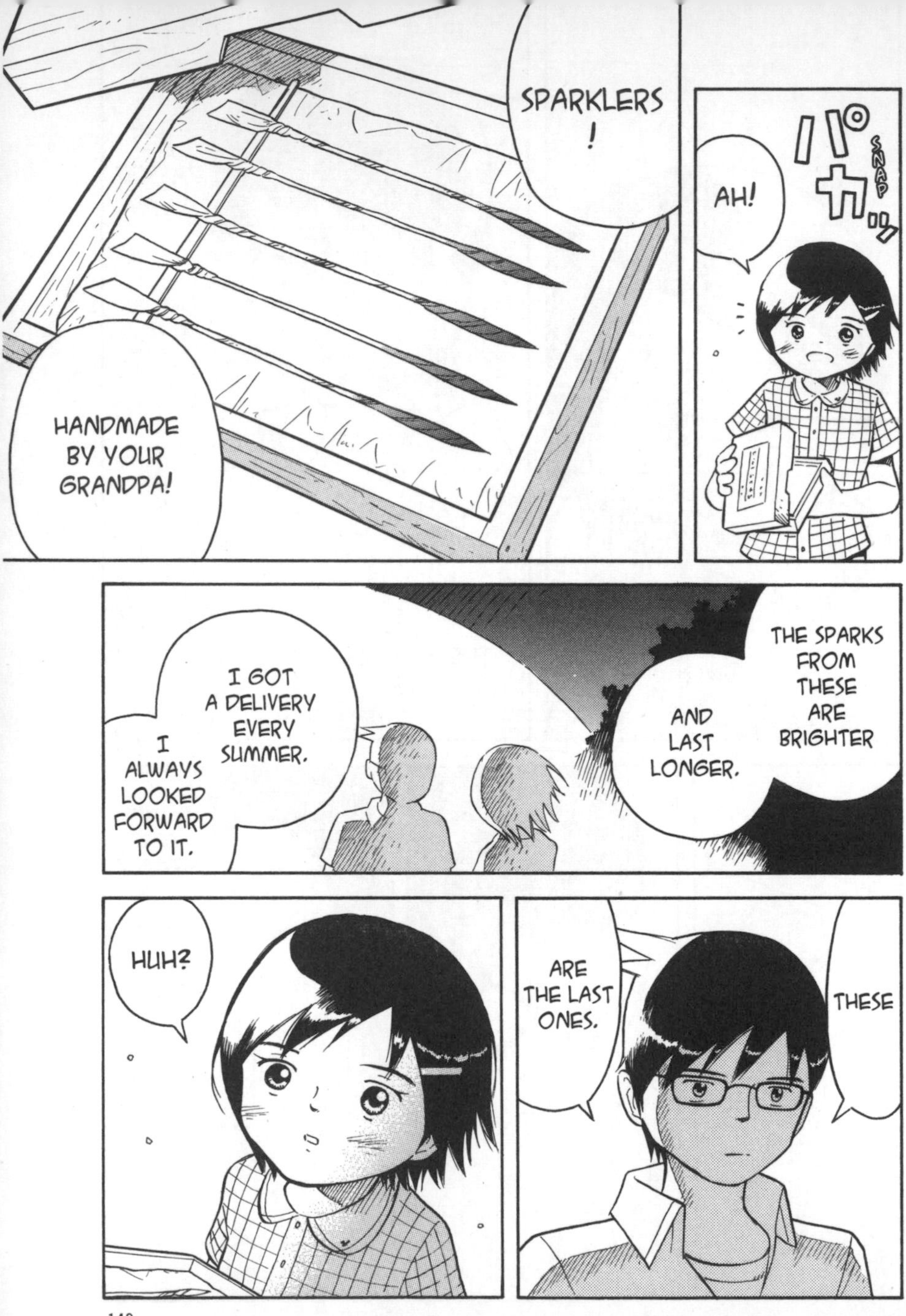
パカッ
SNAP
AH!
SPARKLERS!
HANDMADE BY YOUR GRANDPA!
THE SPARKS FROM THESE ARE BRIGHTER
AND LAST LONGER.
I GOT A DELIVERY EVERY SUMMER.
I ALWAYS LOOKED FORWARD TO IT.
THESE
ARE THE LAST ONES.
HUH?

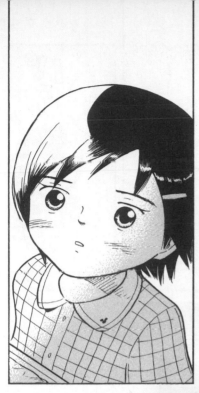

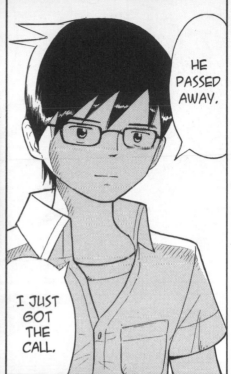

HE PASSED AWAY.

I JUST GOT THE CALL.

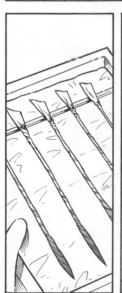

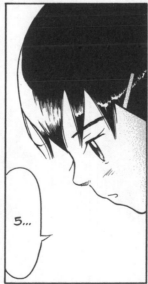

5...

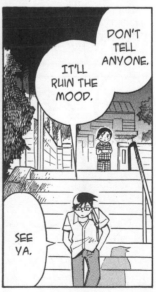

DON'T TELL ANYONE.

IT'LL RUIN THE MOOD.

SEE YA.

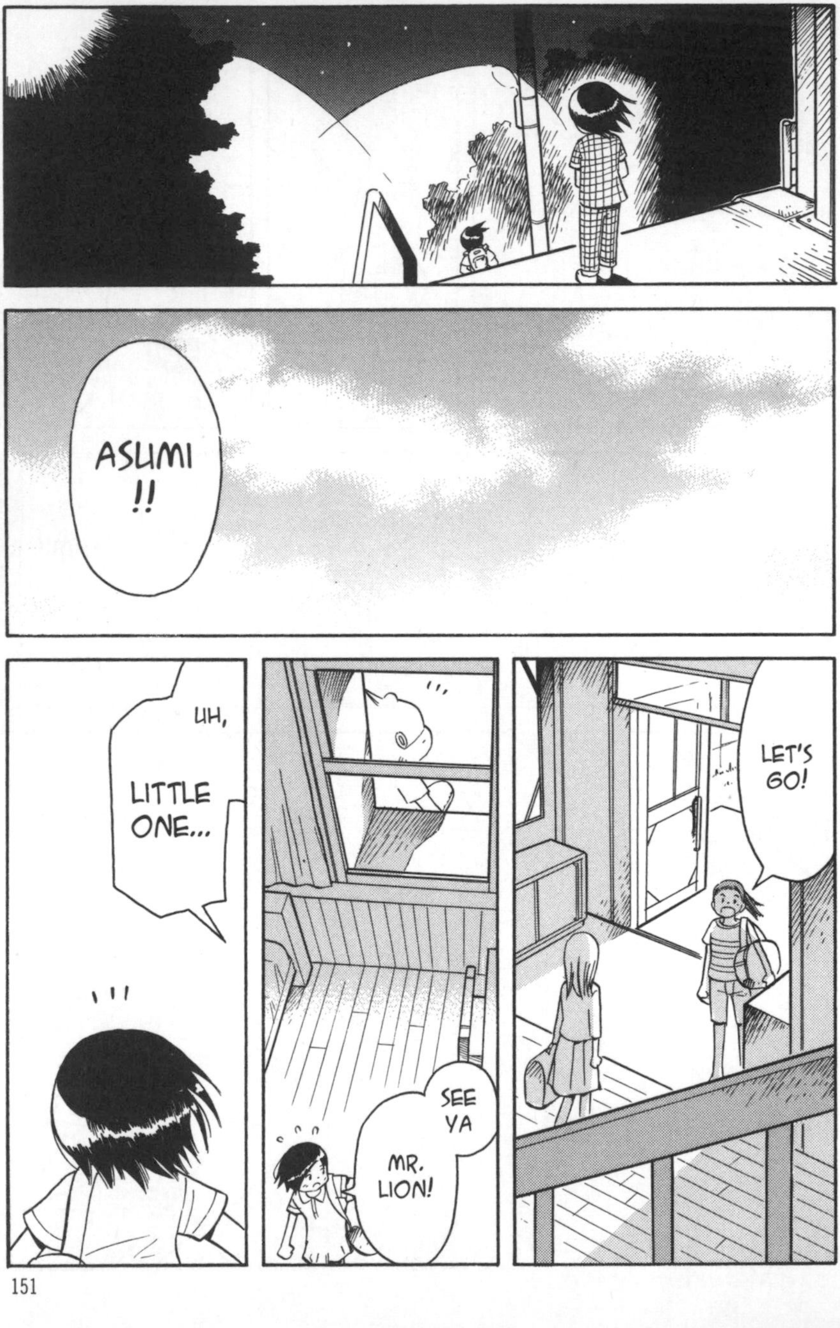
ASUMI !!
LET'S GO!
SEE YA MR. LION!
UH, LITTLE ONE...

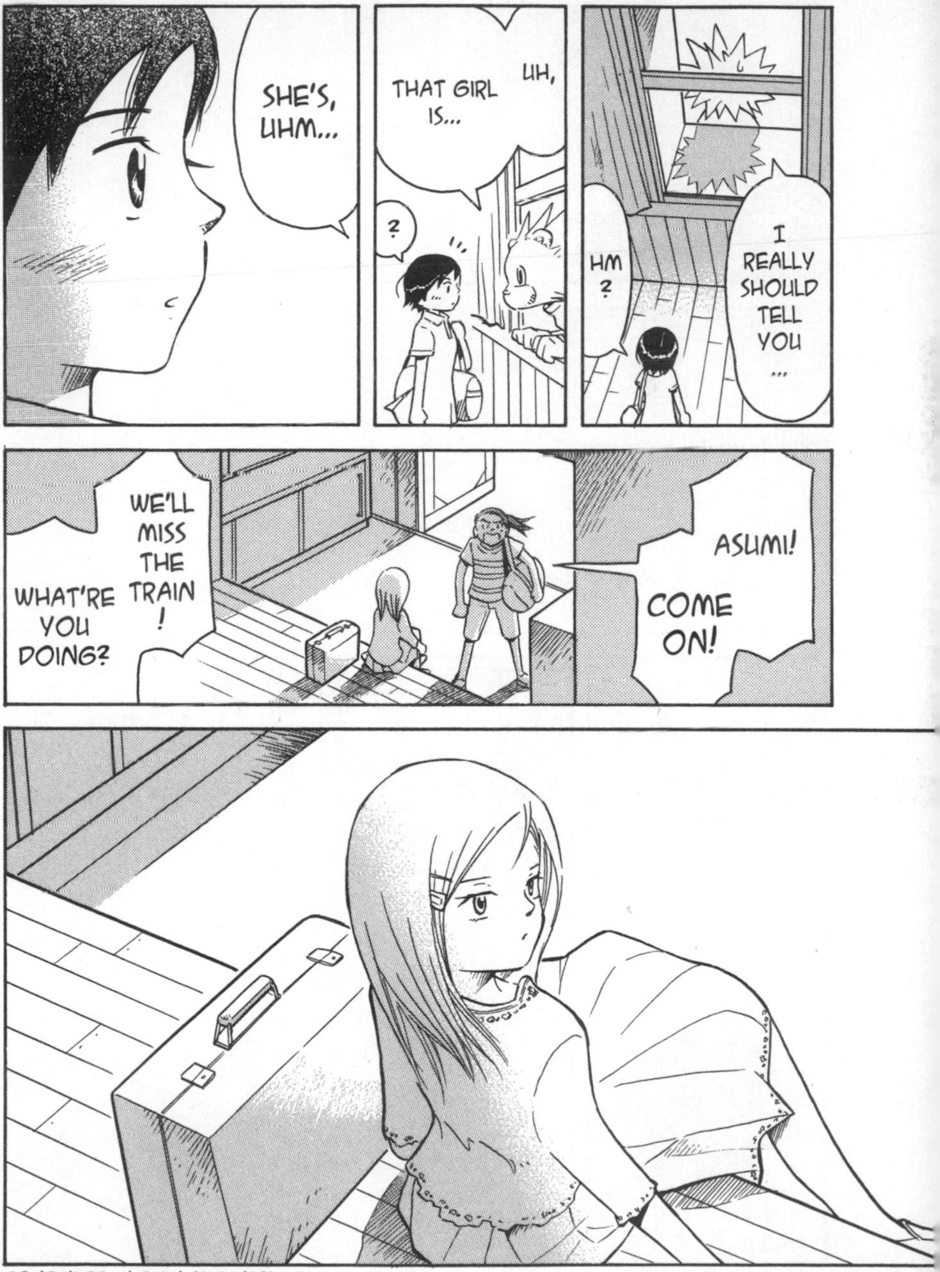
I REALLY SHOULD TELL YOU ...
HM ?
UH, THAT GIRL IS...
?
SHE'S, UHM...
ASUMI! COME ON!
WE'LL MISS THE TRAIN!
WHAT'RE YOU DOING?

CONTINUED IN TWIN SPICA VOL. 7

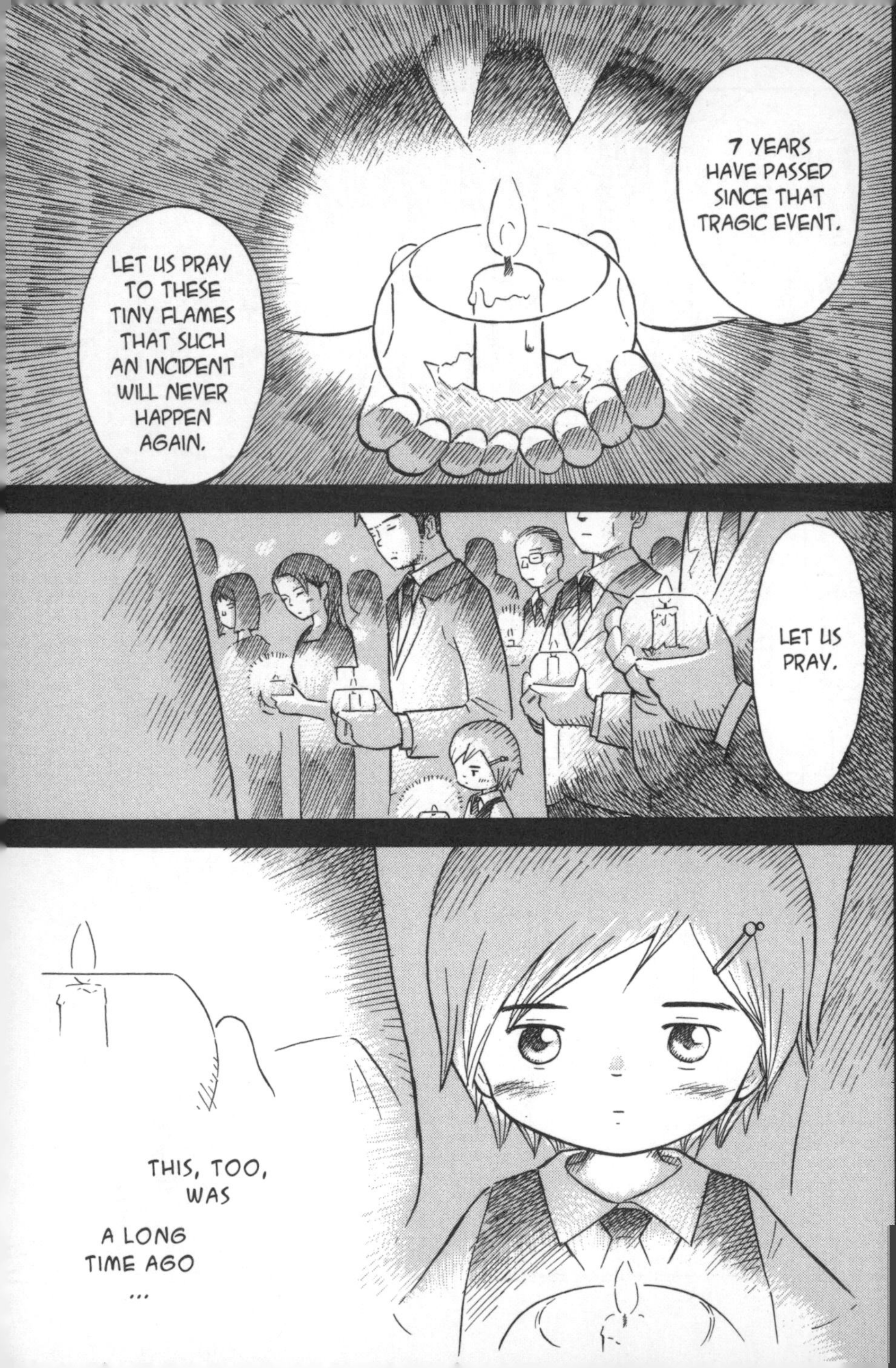
7 YEARS HAVE PASSED SINCE THAT TRAGIC EVENT.
LET US PRAY TO THESE TINY FLAMES THAT SUCH AN INCIDENT WILL NEVER HAPPEN AGAIN.
LET US PRAY.
THIS, TOO, WAS
A LONG TIME AGO ...

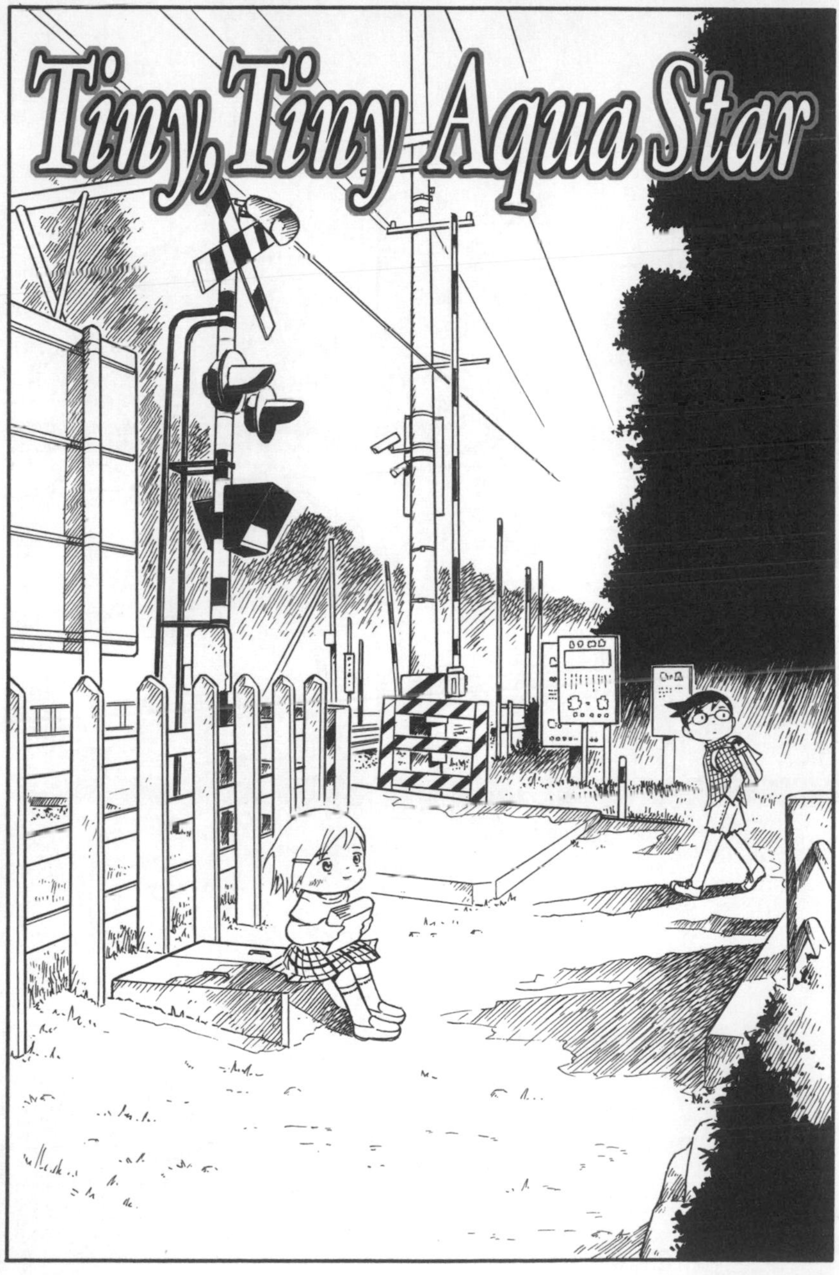
Tiny, Tiny Aqua Star

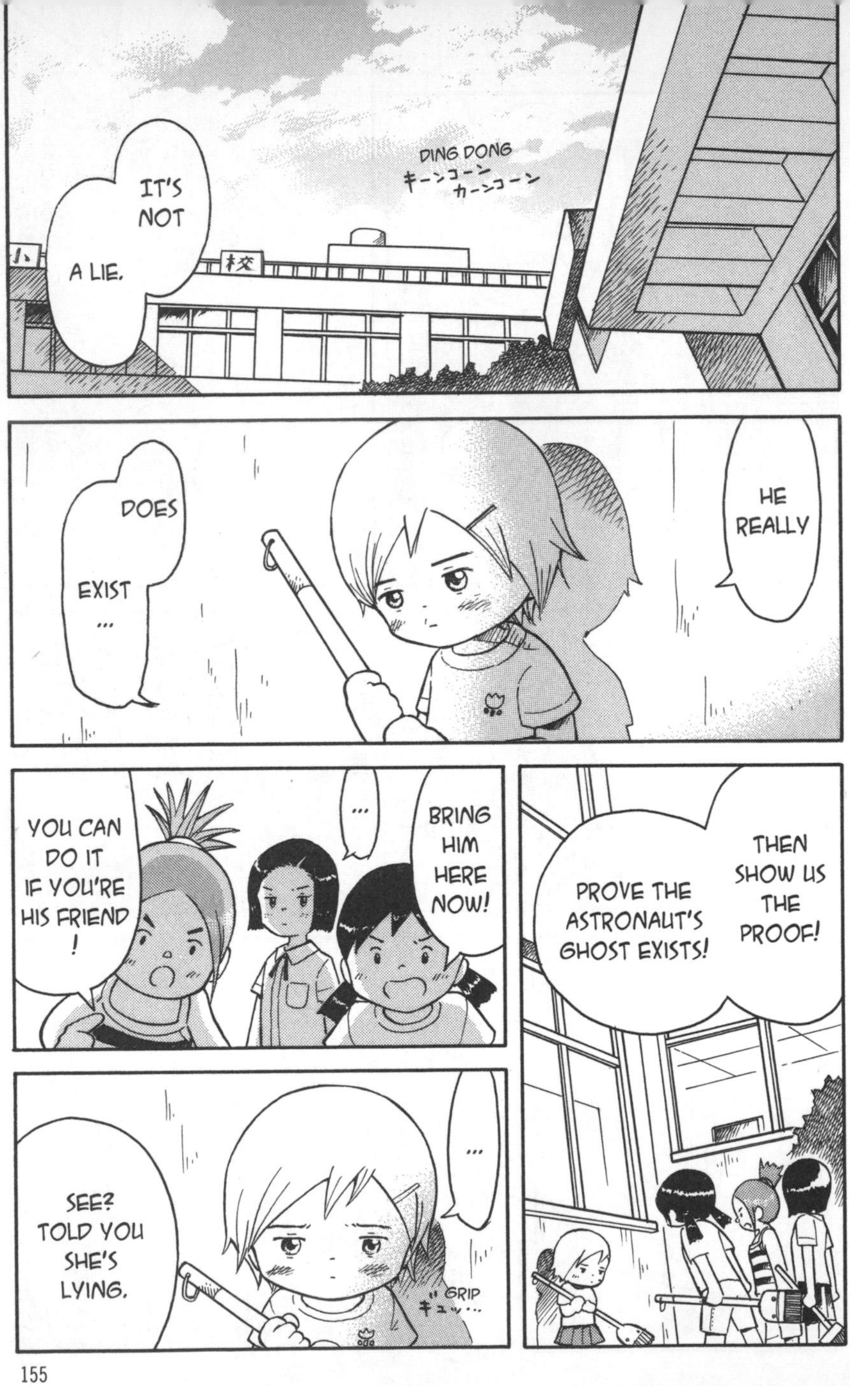
DING DONG
キーンコーン カーンコーン
IT'S NOT A LIE.
HE REALLY
DOES EXIST ...
THEN SHOW US THE PROOF!
PROVE THE ASTRONAUT'S GHOST EXISTS!
BRING HIM HERE NOW!
...
YOU CAN DO IT IF YOU'RE HIS FRIEND!
...
GRIP
ギュッ...
SEE? TOLD YOU SHE'S LYING.

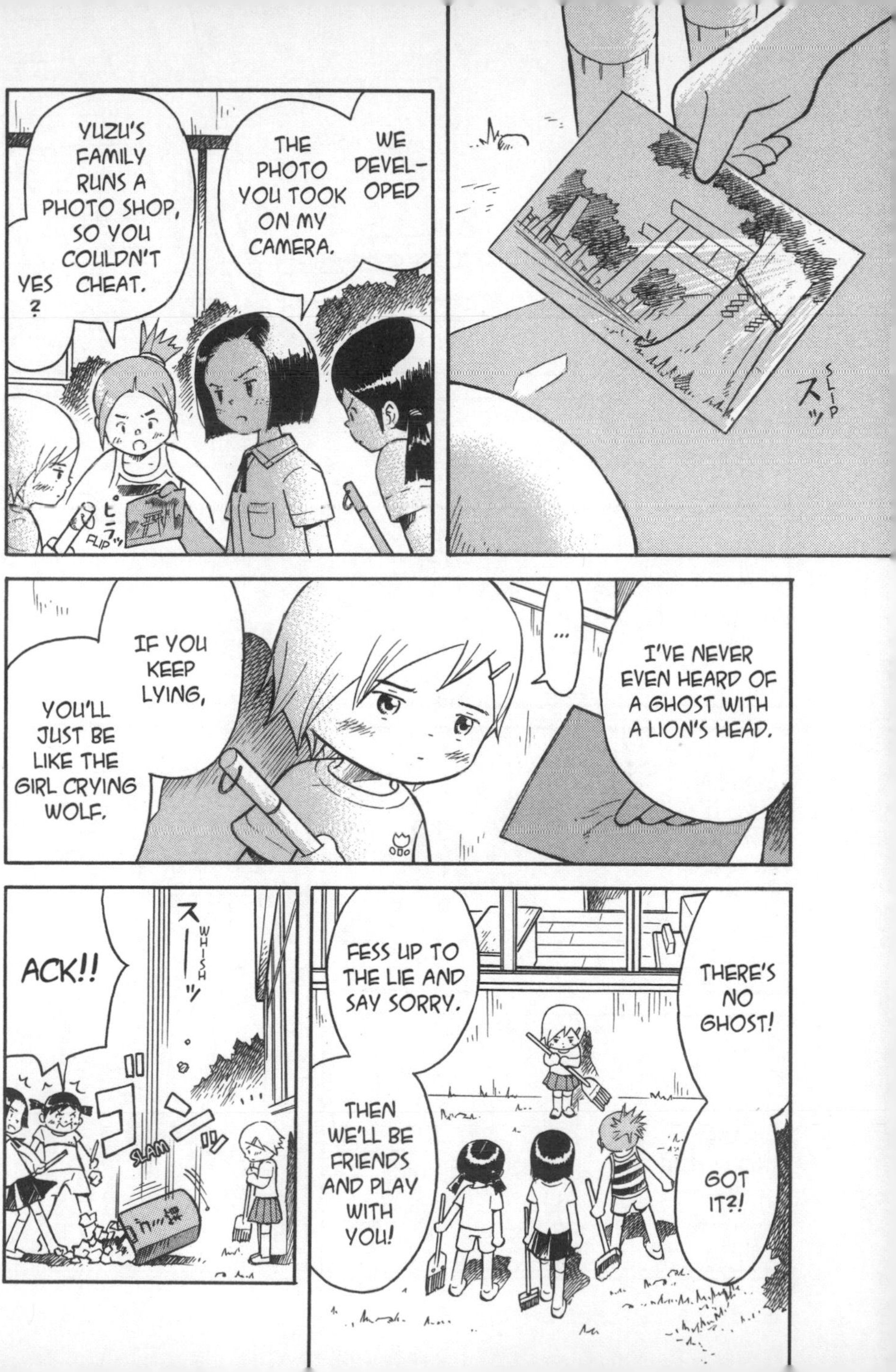

SLIP
WE DEVELOPED
THE PHOTO YOU TOOK ON MY CAMERA.
YUZU'S FAMILY RUNS A PHOTO SHOP, SO YOU COULDN'T CHEAT.
YES?
FLIP
I'VE NEVER EVEN HEARD OF A GHOST WITH A LION'S HEAD.
...
IF YOU KEEP LYING,
YOU'LL JUST BE LIKE THE GIRL CRYING WOLF.
THERE'S NO GHOST!
GOT IT?!
FESS UP TO THE LIE AND SAY SORRY.
THEN WE'LL BE FRIENDS AND PLAY WITH YOU!
WHISH
ACK!!
SLAM

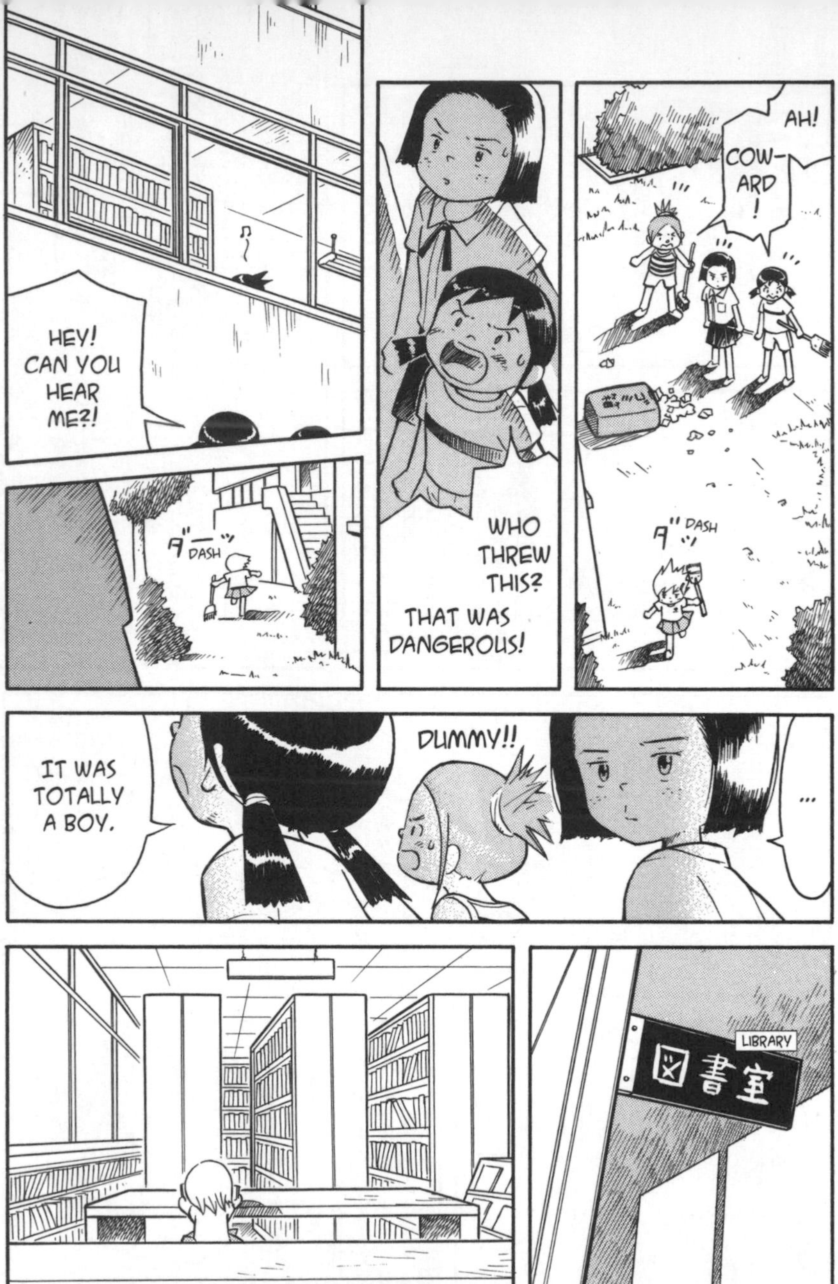

AH!
COWARD!
ダッ
DASH
WHO THREW THIS?
THAT WAS DANGEROUS!
HEY! CAN YOU HEAR ME?!
ダーッ
DASH
...
DUMMY!!
IT WAS TOTALLY A BOY.
LIBRARY
図書室

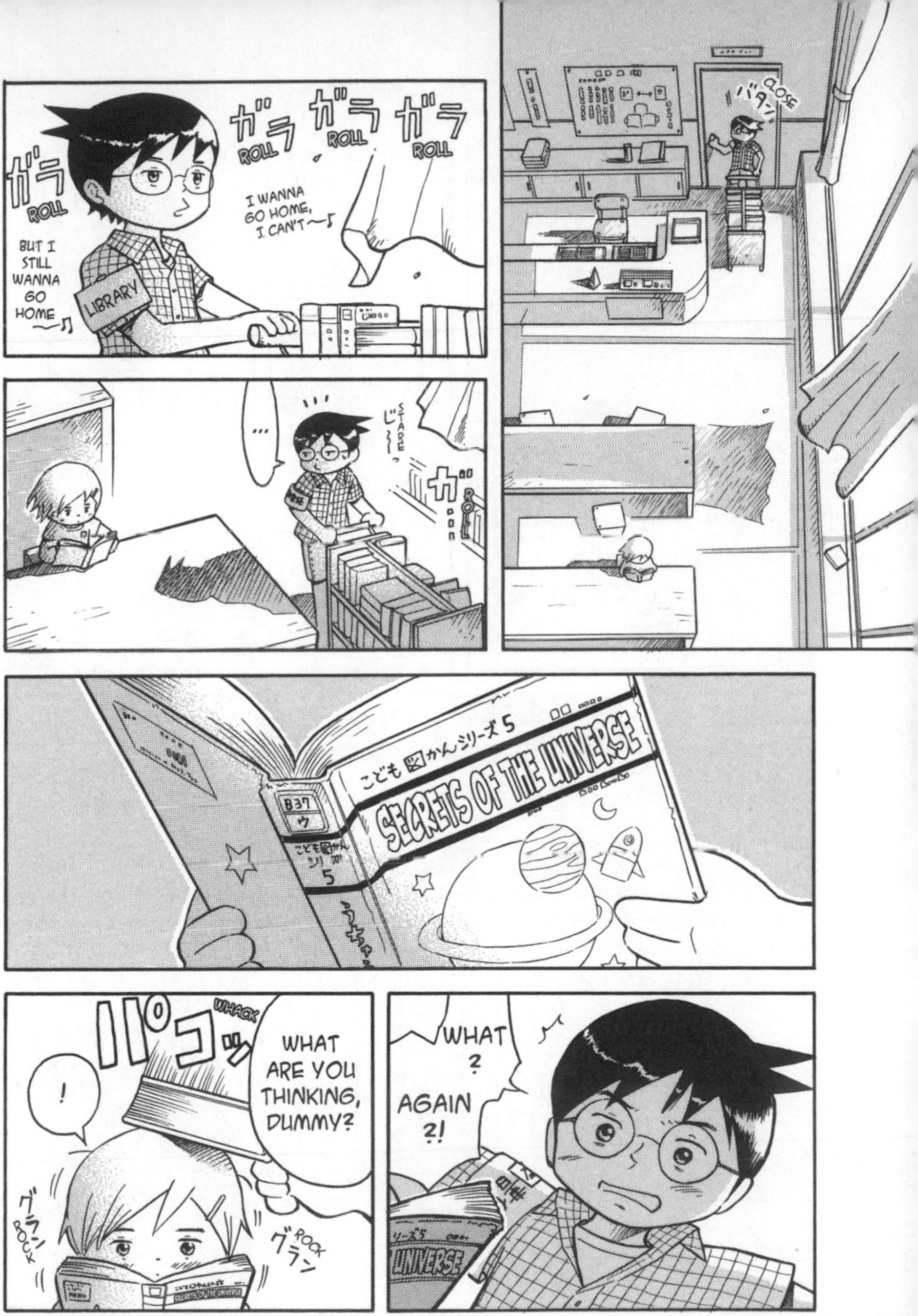
バタン
CLOSE
ガラ ガラ ガラ
ROLL ROLL ROLL
I WANNA GO HOME, I CAN'T~♪
ガラ
ROLL
BUT I STILL WANNA GO HOME~♪
LIBRARY
じ~~っ
STARE
...
ガ
ROLL
こども図かんシリーズ5
SECRETS OF THE UNIVERSE
B37 ウ
こども図かん シリーズ 5
WHAT ?
AGAIN ?!
UNIVERSE
WHAT ARE YOU THINKING, DUMMY?
パコッ
WHACK
!
グラン
ROCK
グラン
ROCK
SECRETS OF THE UNIVERSE

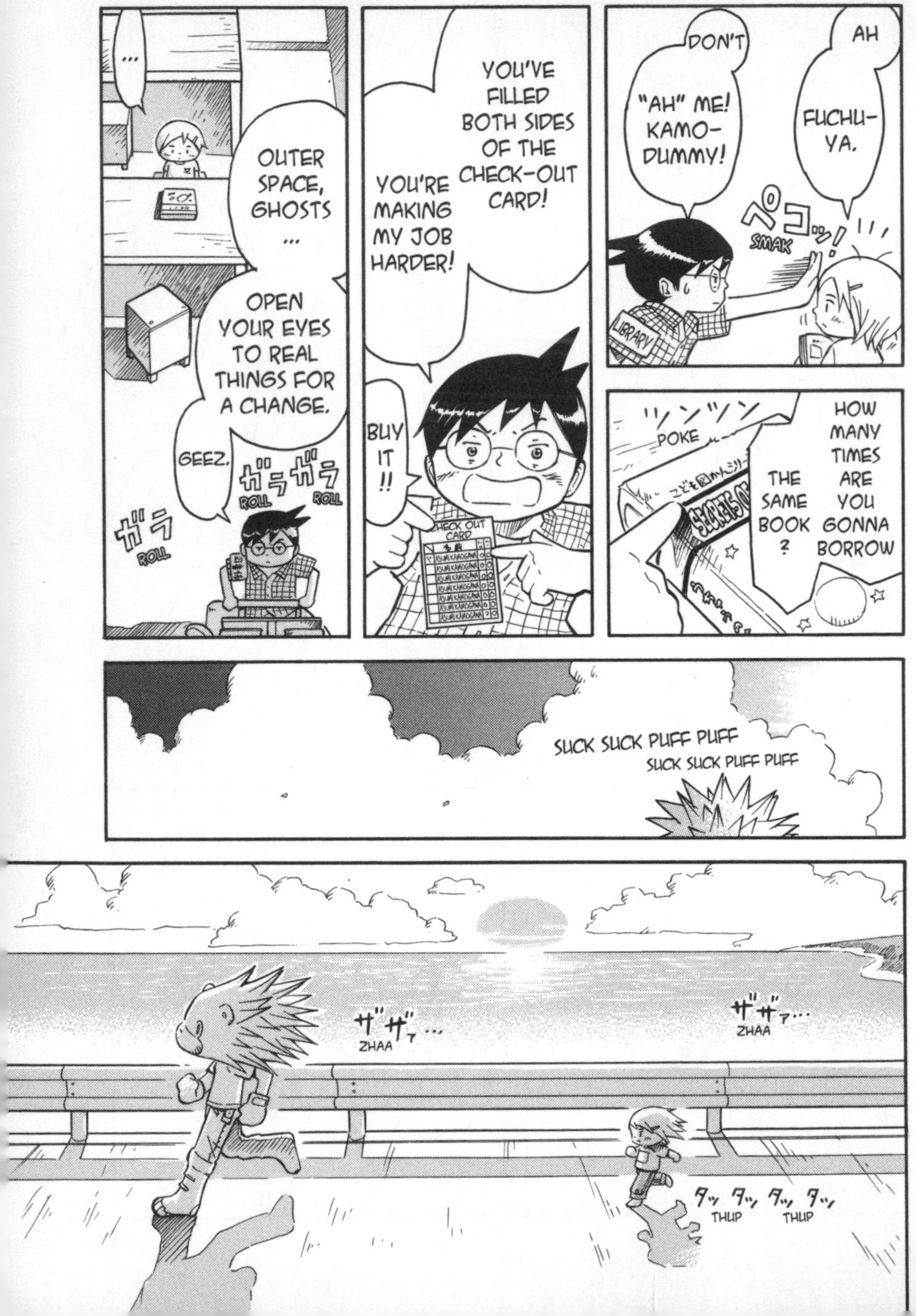
AH
FUCHU-YA.
DON'T
"AH" ME! KAMO-DUMMY!
SMAK
LIBRARY
HOW MANY TIMES ARE YOU GONNA BORROW
THE SAME BOOK?
POKE
YOU'VE FILLED BOTH SIDES OF THE CHECK-OUT CARD!
YOU'RE MAKING MY JOB HARDER!
BUY IT !!
CHECK OUT CARD
...
OUTER SPACE, GHOSTS ...
OPEN YOUR EYES TO REAL THINGS FOR A CHANGE.
GEEZ.
ガラガラ
ROLL ROLL
ガラ
ROLL
SUCK SUCK PUFF PUFF
SUCK SUCK PUFF PUFF
ZHAA
ZHAA
THUP THUP

SUCK
PUFF
...
タッ、タッ
THUP
タッタッタッ
THUP
PUFF PUFF
SUCK SUCK
トッ、トッ
THOP
トッ、トッ
THOP
HALT
ピタッ…
WHAT'S WRONG?
SHOULD I SLOW DOWN?
MR. LION?
HM?
WHY CAN'T ANYONE ELSE SEE YOU?
WHAT?

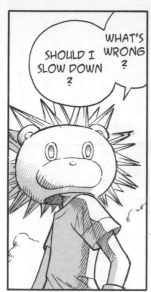

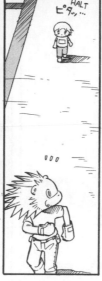

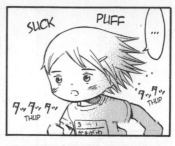

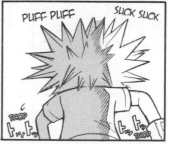

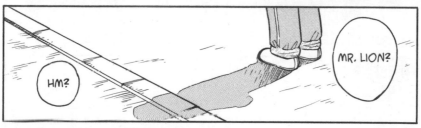

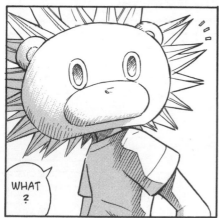

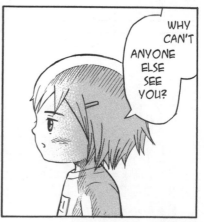

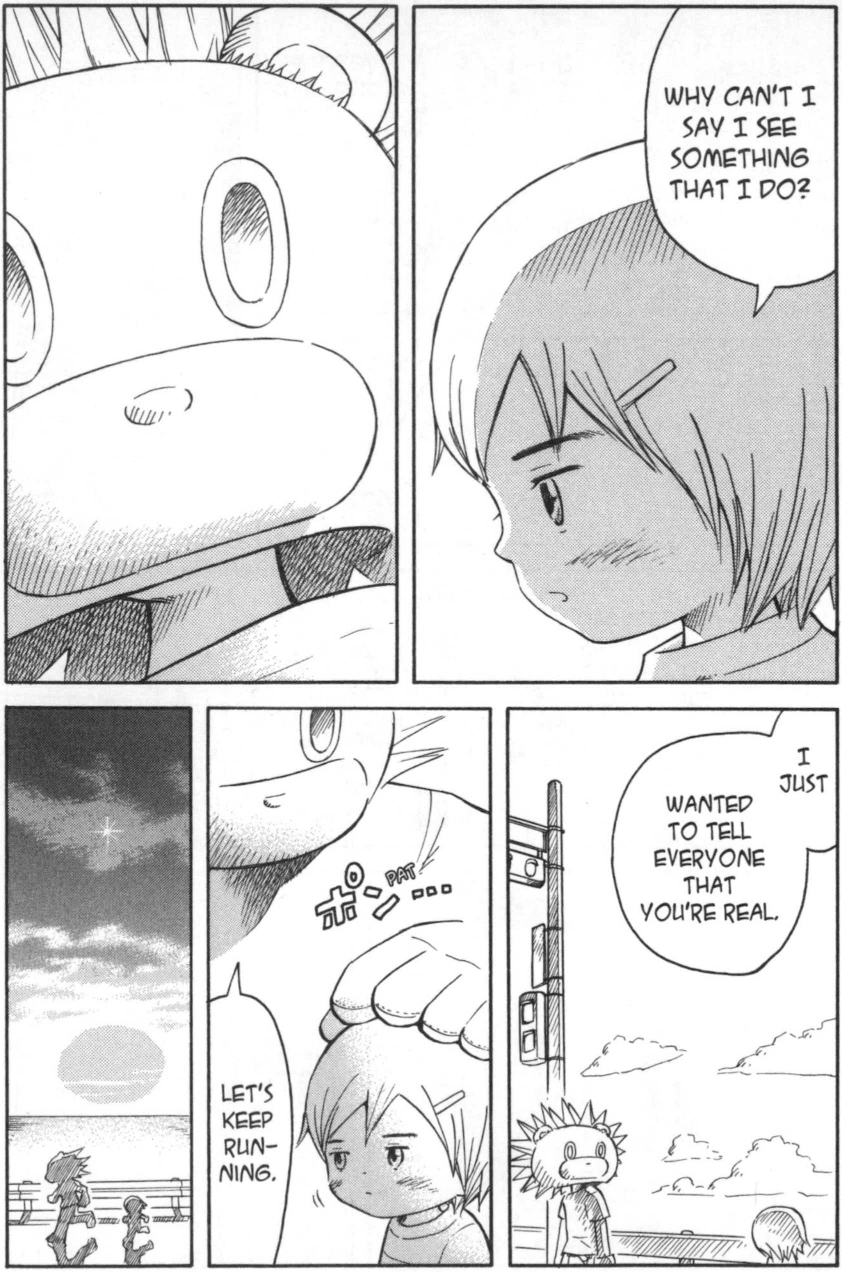
WHY CAN'T I SAY I SEE SOMETHING THAT I DO?
I JUST WANTED TO TELL EVERYONE THAT YOU'RE REAL.
ポン PAT...
LET'S KEEP RUN-NING.

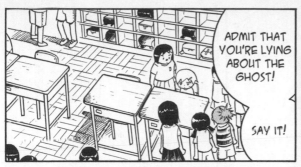

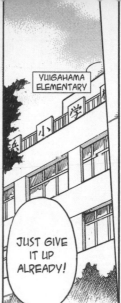

YUIGAHAMA ELEMENTARY
JUST GIVE IT UP ALREADY!
ADMIT THAT YOU'RE LYING ABOUT THE GHOST!
SAY IT!
...
DON'T JUST SIT THERE! SAY IT!
MISS SUZUNARI IS TELLING US TO MAKE UP WITH YOU
BUT YOU'RE SUCH A LIAR.
YOU EVEN SAID
YOU SAW YOUR DEAD MOTHER.
ガラッ
SLIDE
HOW AWFUL ...
LYING TO TRY AND MAKE EVERYONE FEEL SORRY FOR YOU.

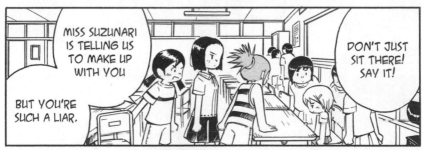

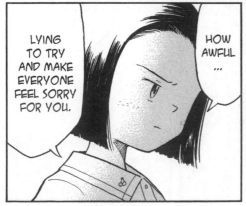

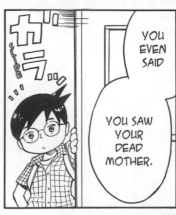

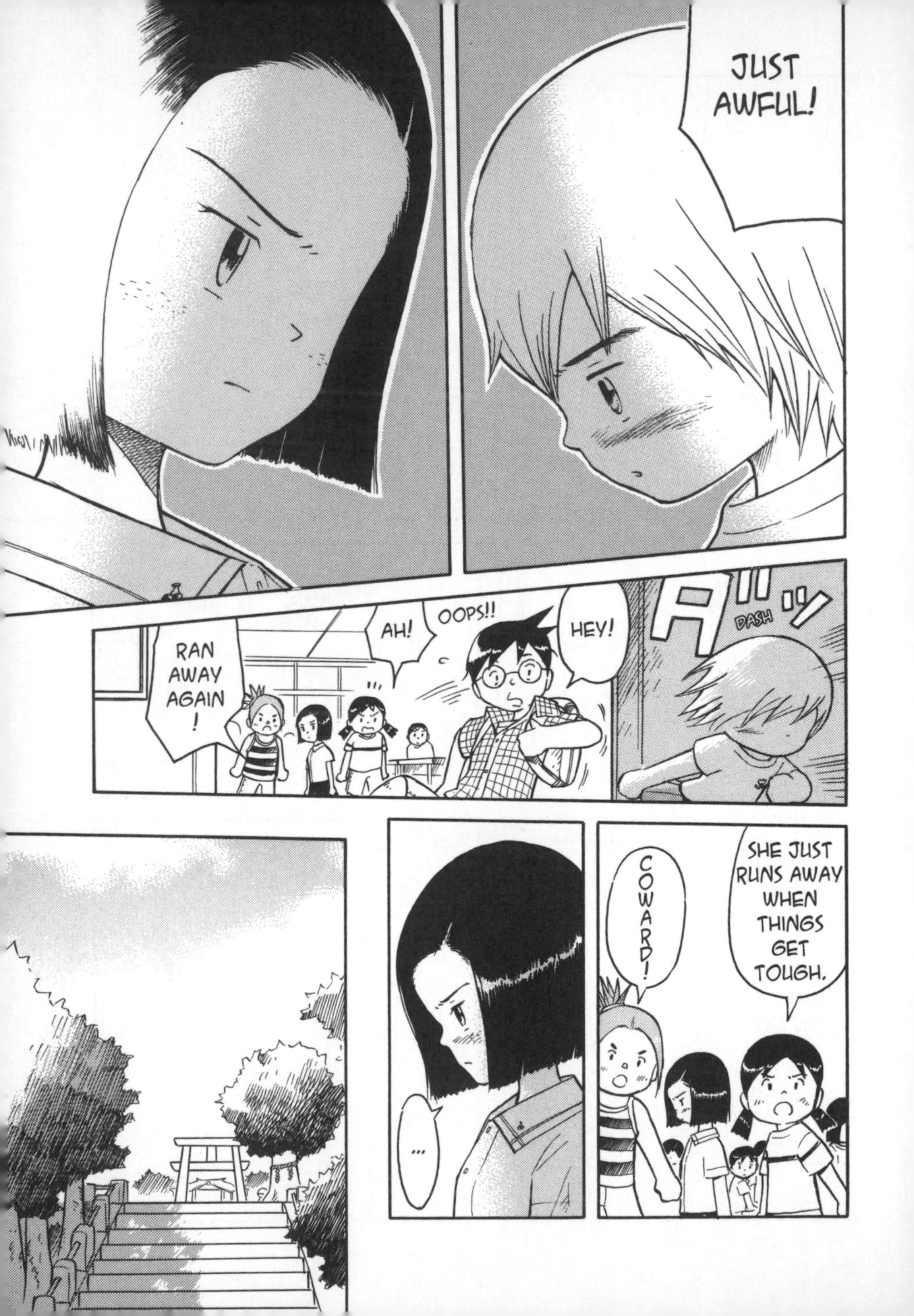
JUST AWFUL!
DASH
HEY!
OOPS!!
AH!
RAN AWAY AGAIN!
SHE JUST RUNS AWAY WHEN THINGS GET TOUGH.
COWARD!
...

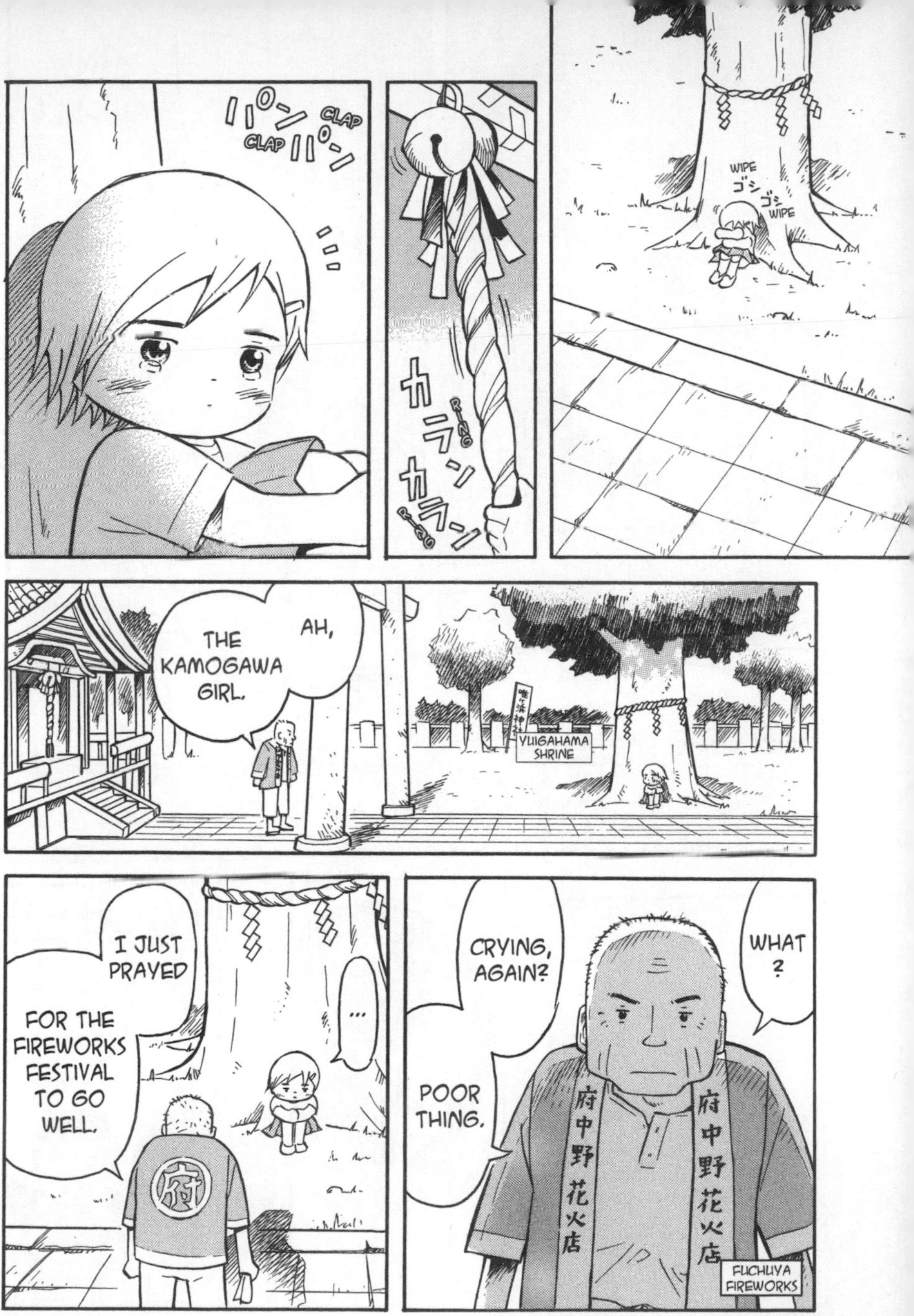
WIPE
ゴシゴシ
WIPE
カラン
RING
カラン
パーン
CLAP
CLAP
パーン
AH, THE KAMOGAWA GIRL.
唯ヶ浜神社
YUIGAHAMA SHRINE
WHAT?
CRYING, AGAIN?
POOR THING.
府中野花火店
府中野花火店
FUCHUYA FIREWORKS
...
I JUST PRAYED
FOR THE FIREWORKS FESTIVAL TO GO WELL.
府

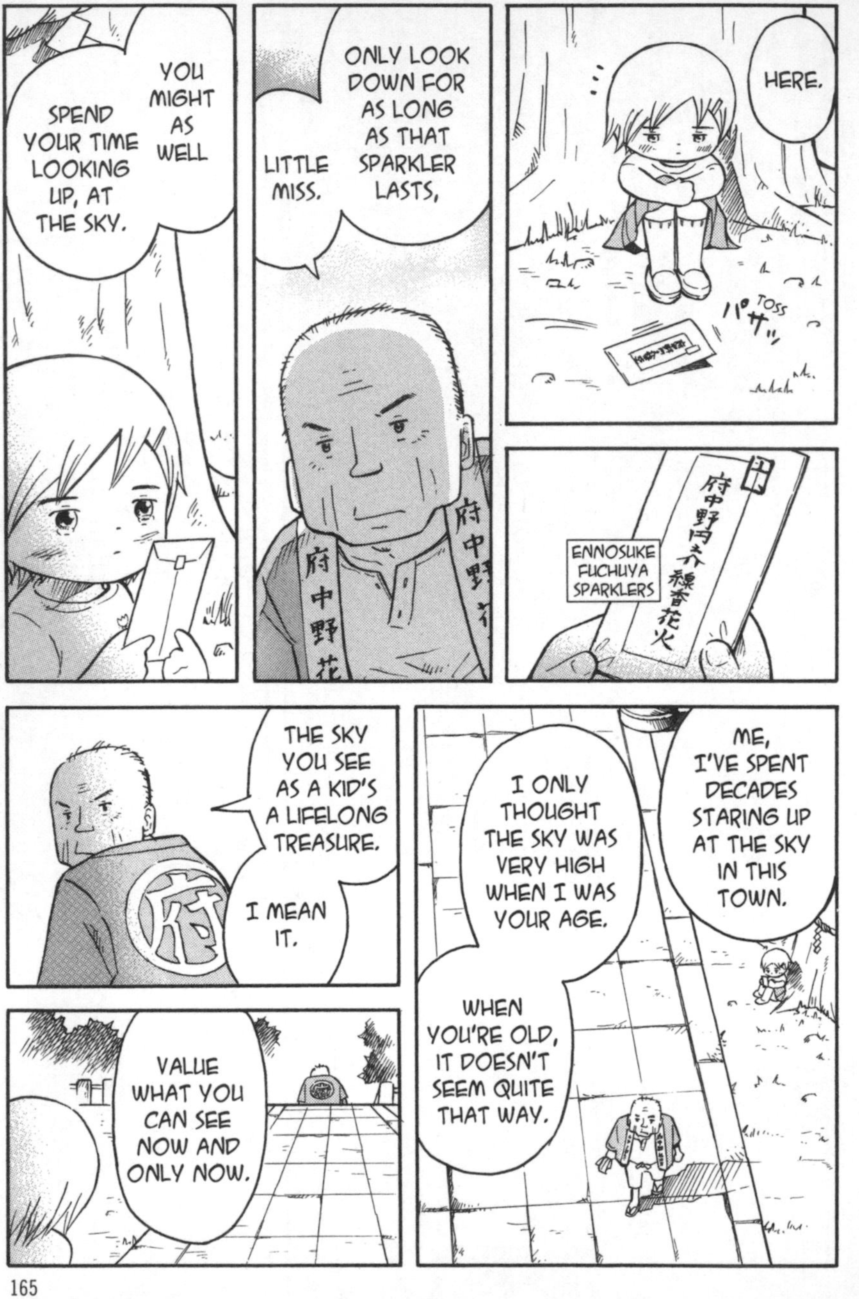
HERE.
パサッ
TOSS
府中野円介 線香花火
ENNOSUKE FUCHUYA SPARKLERS
ONLY LOOK DOWN FOR AS LONG AS THAT SPARKLER LASTS,
LITTLE MISS.
YOU MIGHT AS WELL
SPEND YOUR TIME LOOKING UP, AT THE SKY.
ME, I'VE SPENT DECADES STARING UP AT THE SKY IN THIS TOWN.
I ONLY THOUGHT THE SKY WAS VERY HIGH WHEN I WAS YOUR AGE.
WHEN YOU'RE OLD, IT DOESN'T SEEM QUITE THAT WAY.
THE SKY YOU SEE AS A KID'S A LIFELONG TREASURE.
I MEAN IT.
VALUE WHAT YOU CAN SEE NOW AND ONLY NOW.

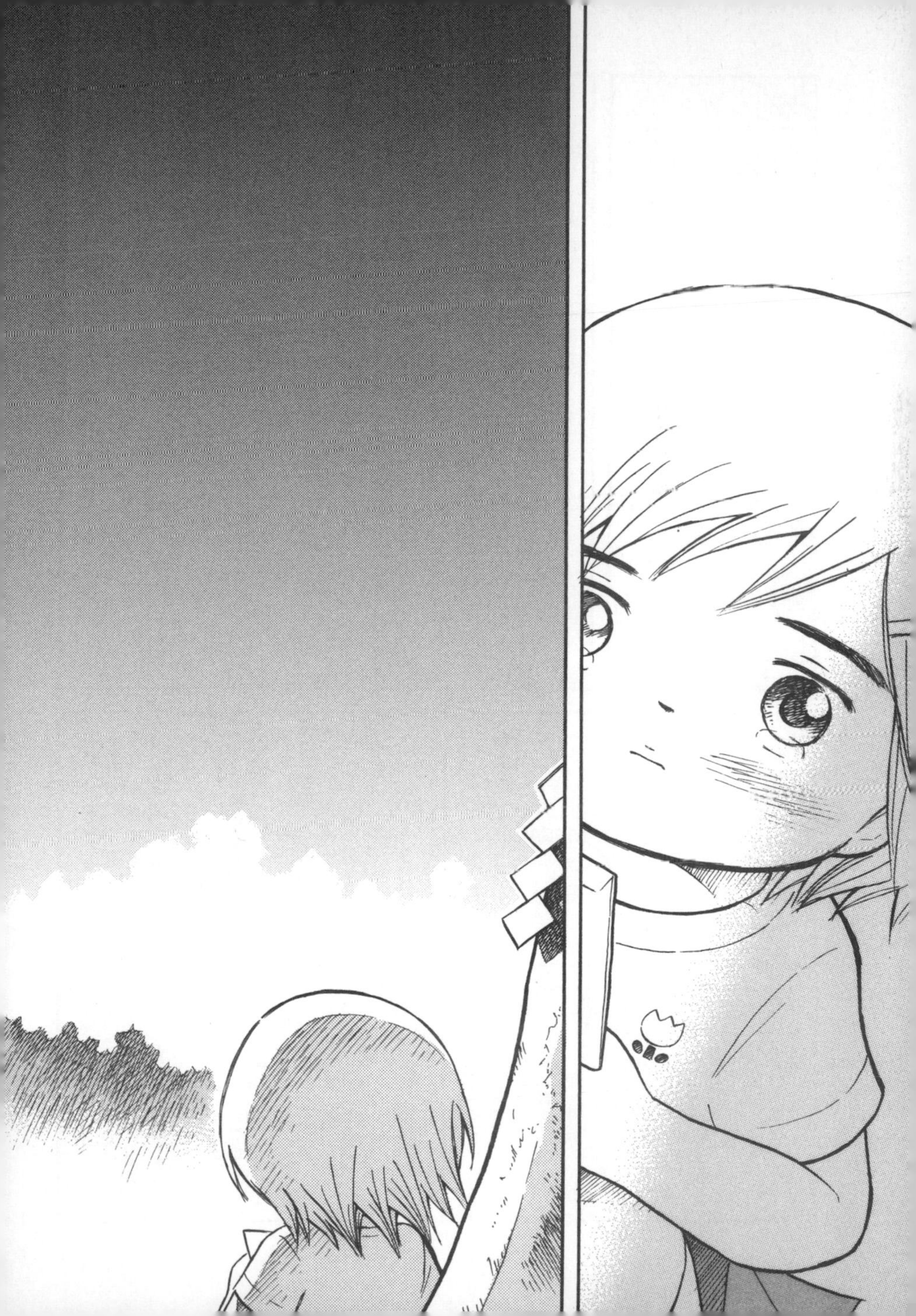

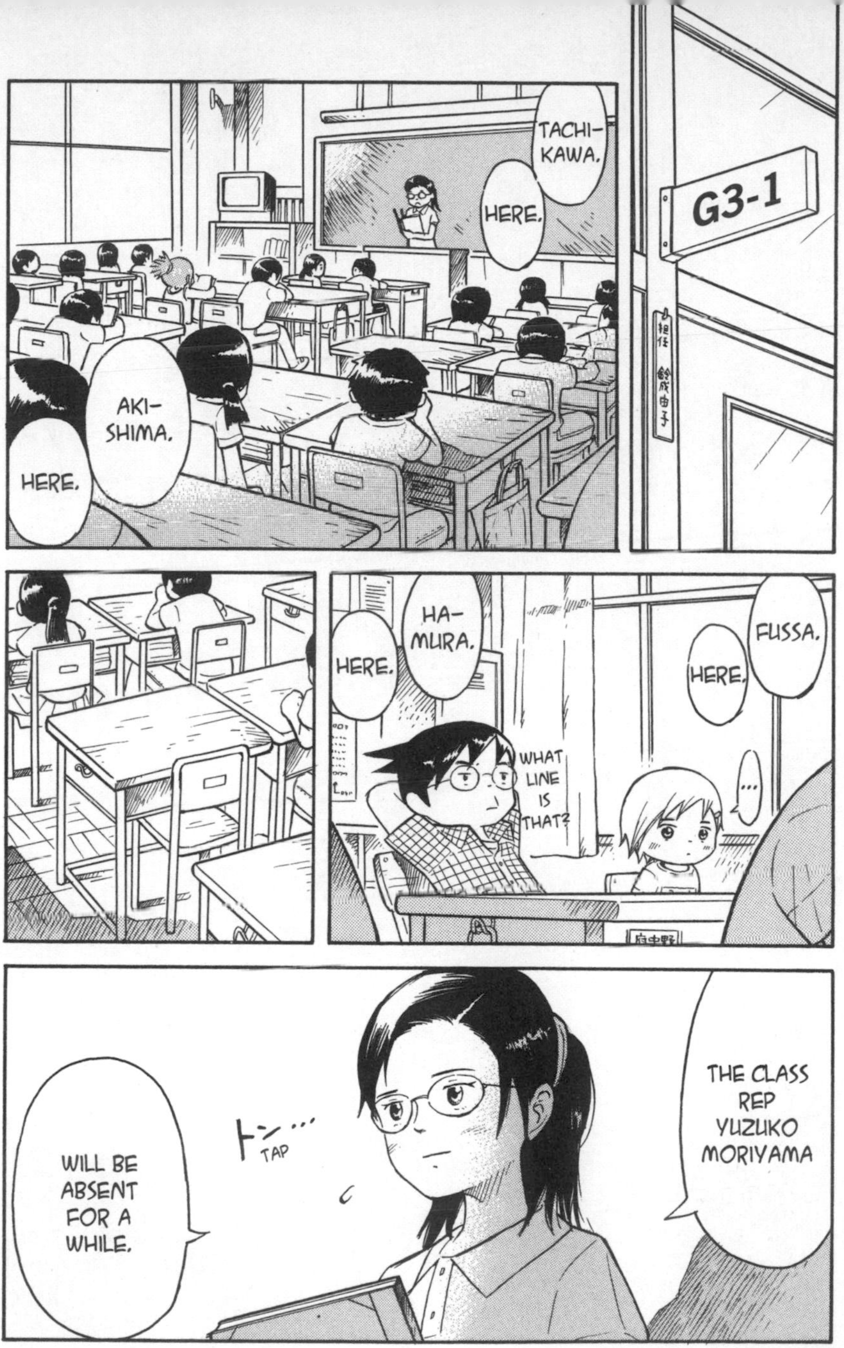
G3-1
TACHI-KAWA.
HERE.
AKI-SHIMA.
HERE.
FUSSA.
HERE.
HA-MURA.
HERE.
...
WHAT LINE IS THAT?
THE CLASS REP YUZUKO MORIYAMA
トン…
TAP
WILL BE ABSENT FOR A WHILE.

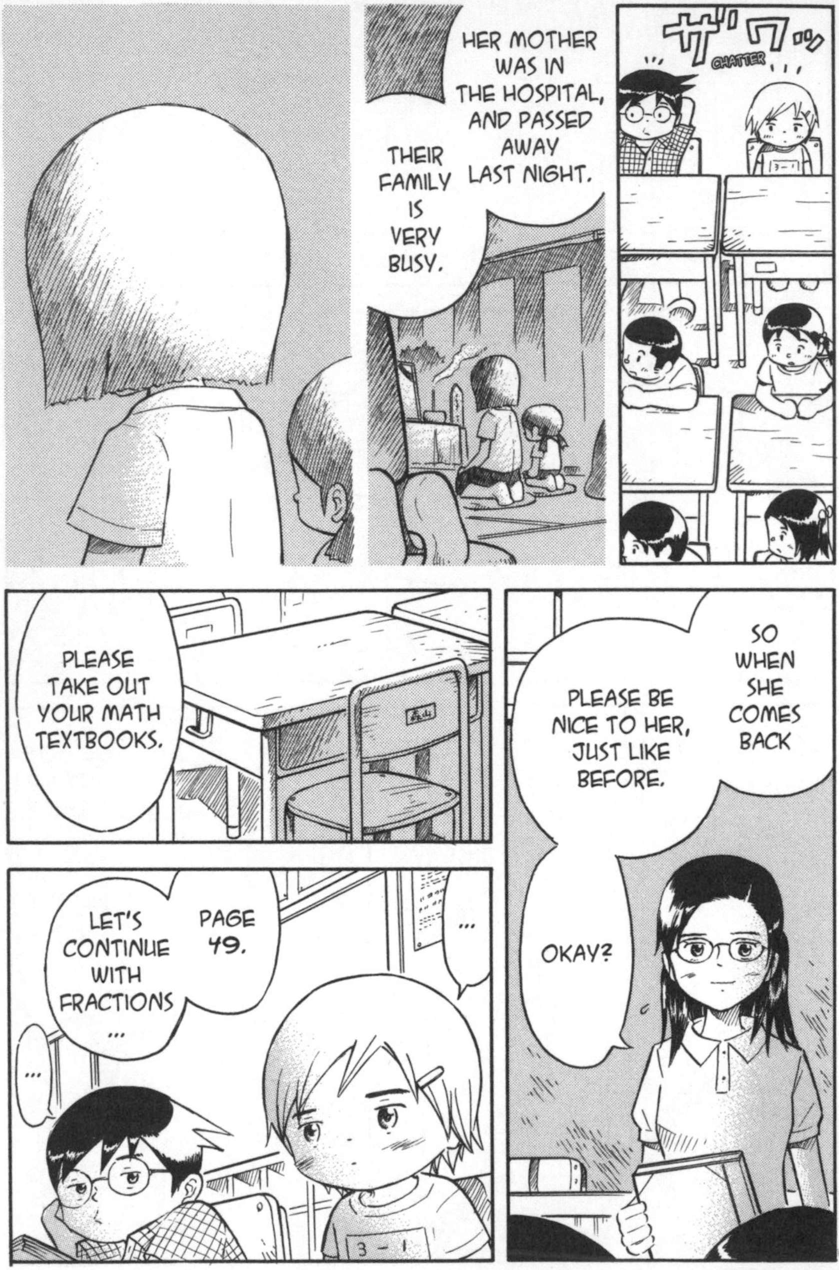
ザワッ
CHATTER
HER MOTHER WAS IN THE HOSPITAL, AND PASSED AWAY LAST NIGHT.
THEIR FAMILY IS VERY BUSY.
SO WHEN SHE COMES BACK
PLEASE BE NICE TO HER, JUST LIKE BEFORE.
OKAY?
PLEASE TAKE OUT YOUR MATH TEXTBOOKS.
...
PAGE 49.
LET'S CONTINUE WITH FRACTIONS ...
...

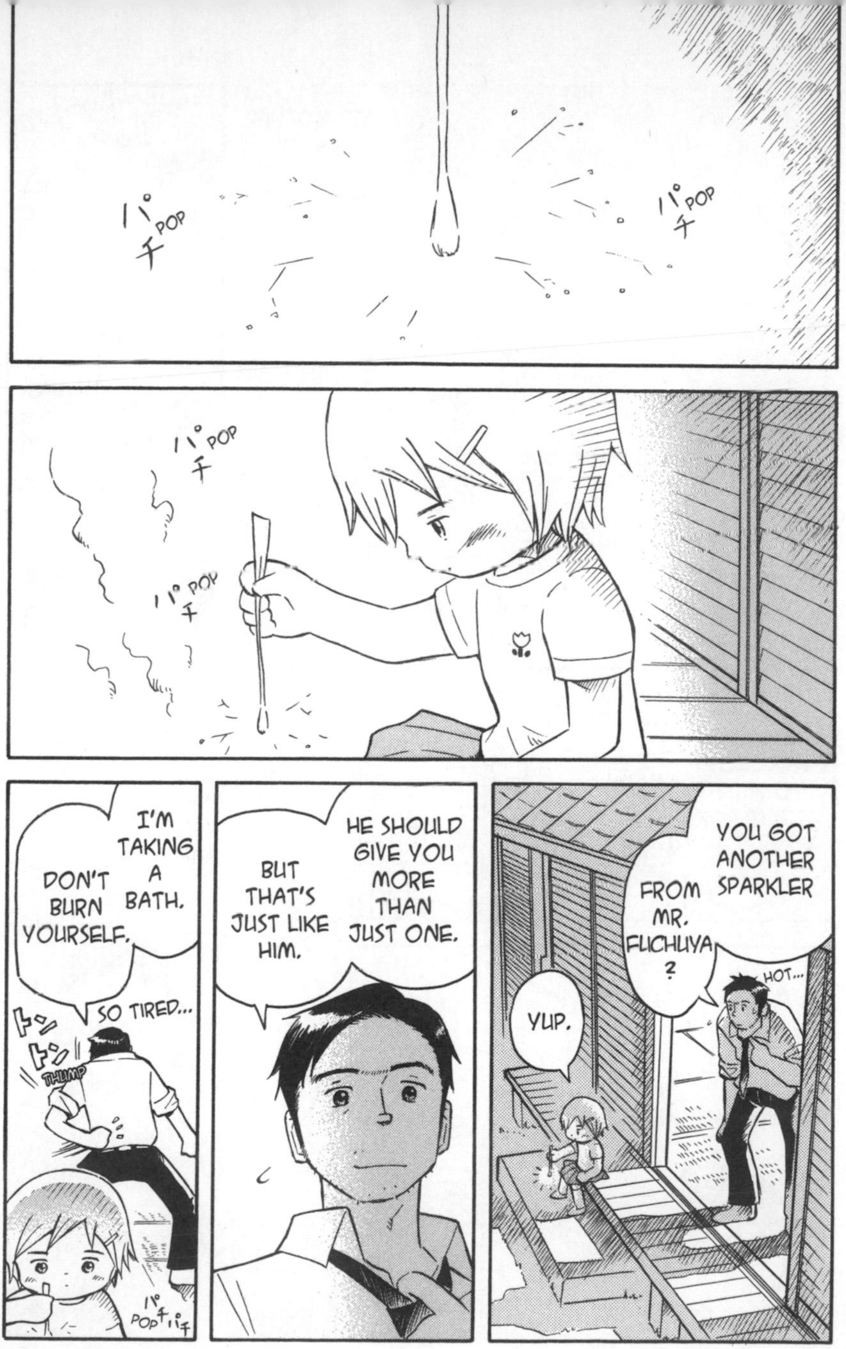
パチ POP
パチ POP
パチ POP
パチ POP
YOU GOT ANOTHER SPARKLER FROM MR. FUCHUYA?
HOT...
YUP.
HE SHOULD GIVE YOU MORE THAN JUST ONE.
BUT THAT'S JUST LIKE HIM.
I'M TAKING A BATH.
DON'T BURN YOURSELF.
SO TIRED...
THUMP
POP

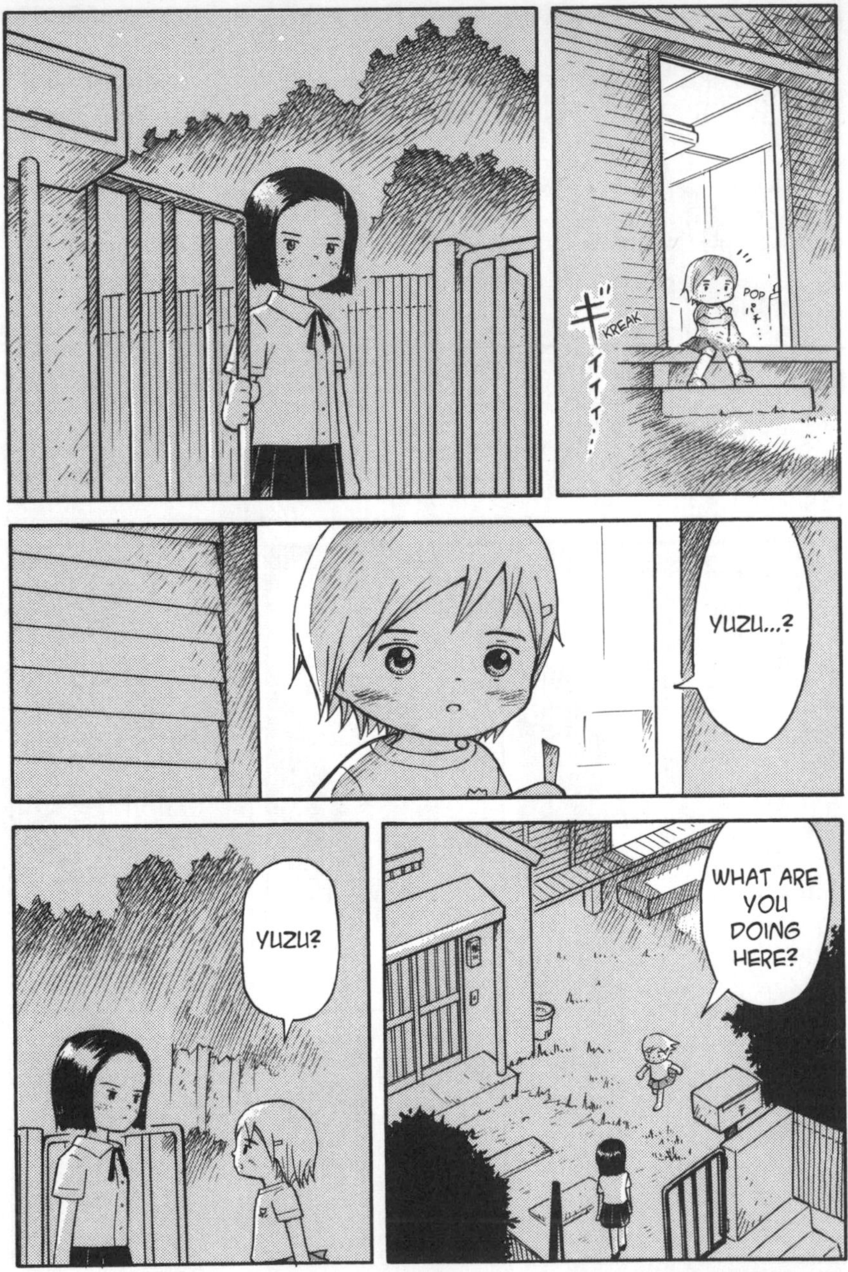
ギィィィ…
KREAK
POP
YUZU...?
WHAT ARE YOU DOING HERE?
YUZU?

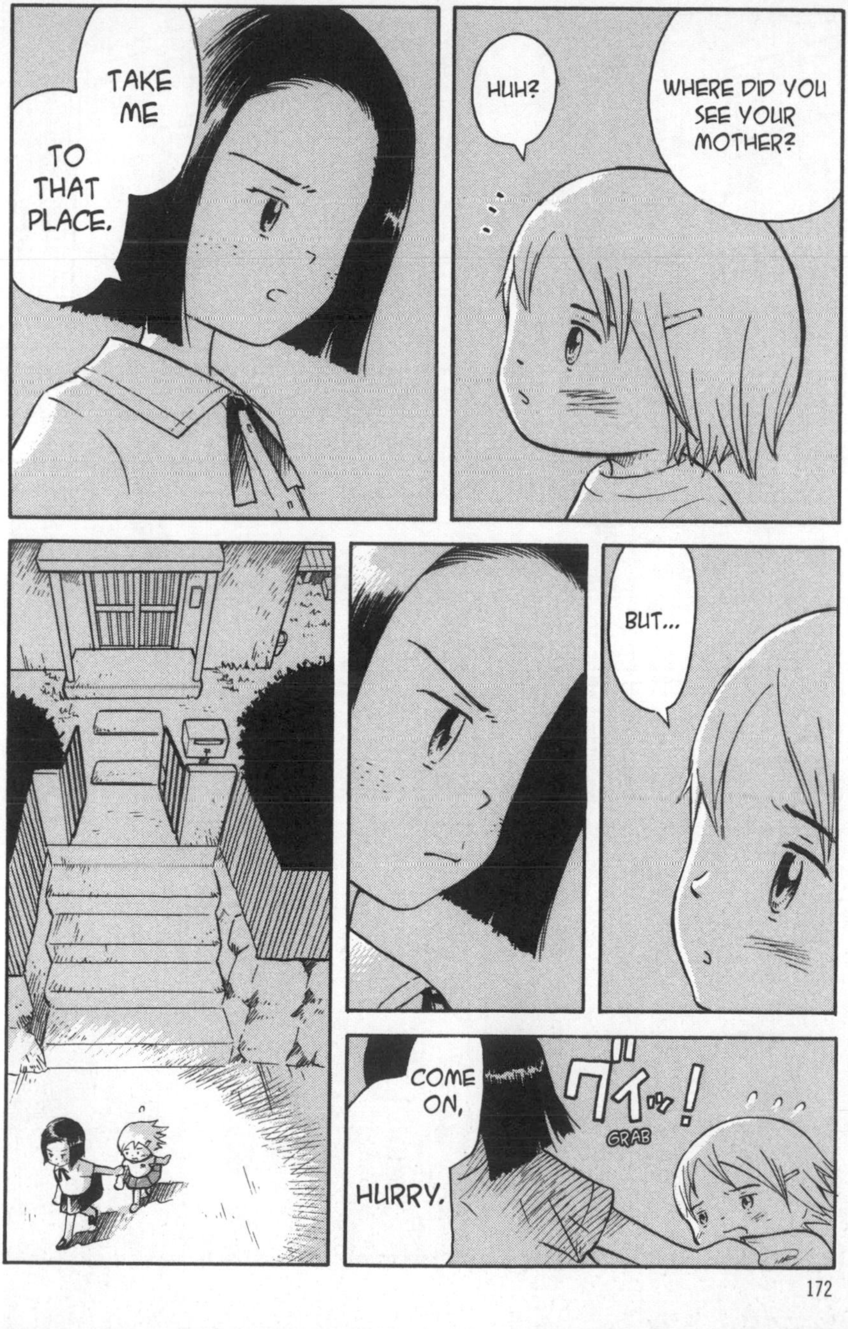
WHERE DID YOU SEE YOUR MOTHER?
HUH?
TAKE ME TO THAT PLACE.
BUT...
ヴィッ!
GRAB
COME ON,
HURRY.

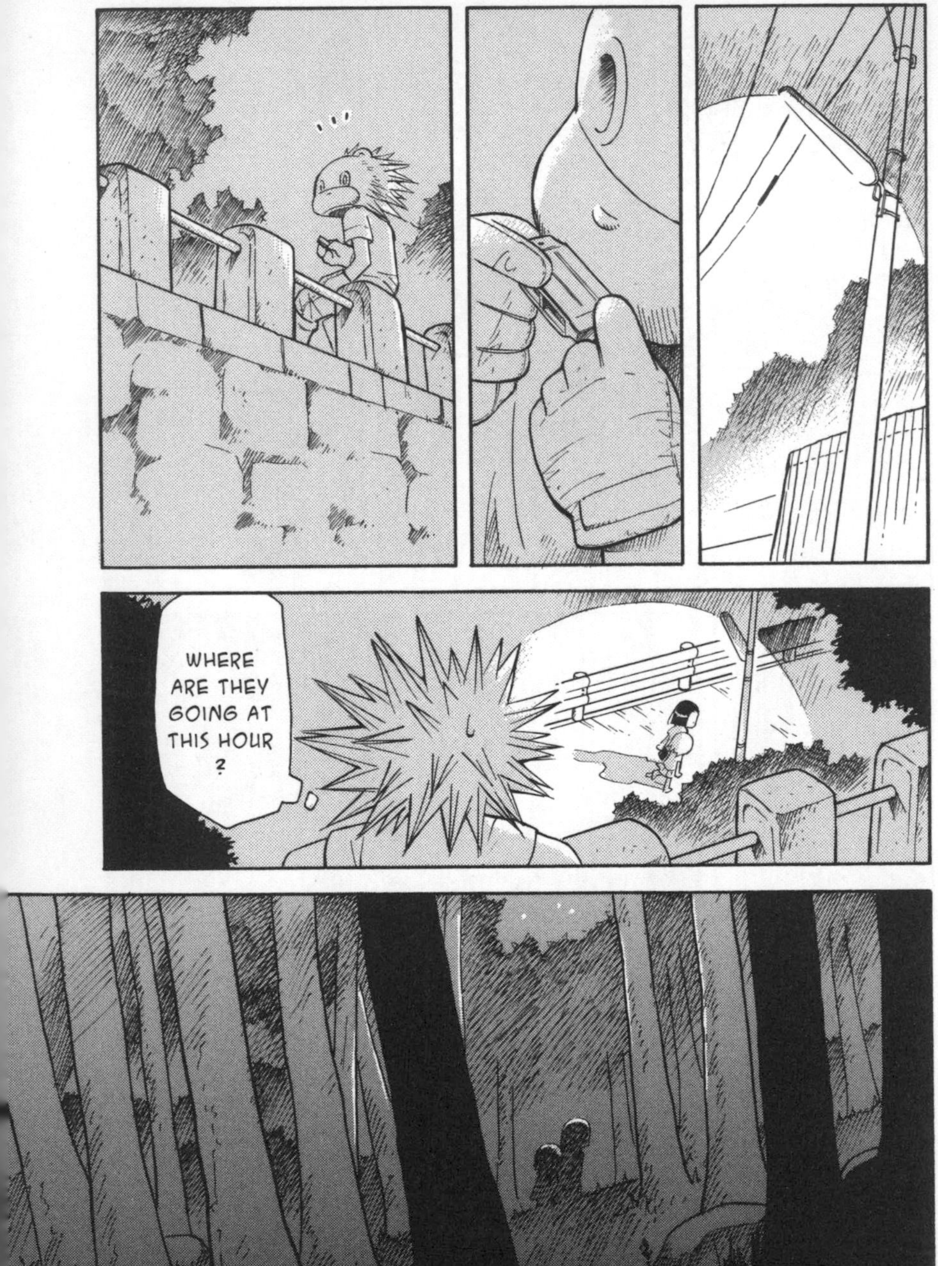
WHERE ARE THEY GOING AT THIS HOUR ?

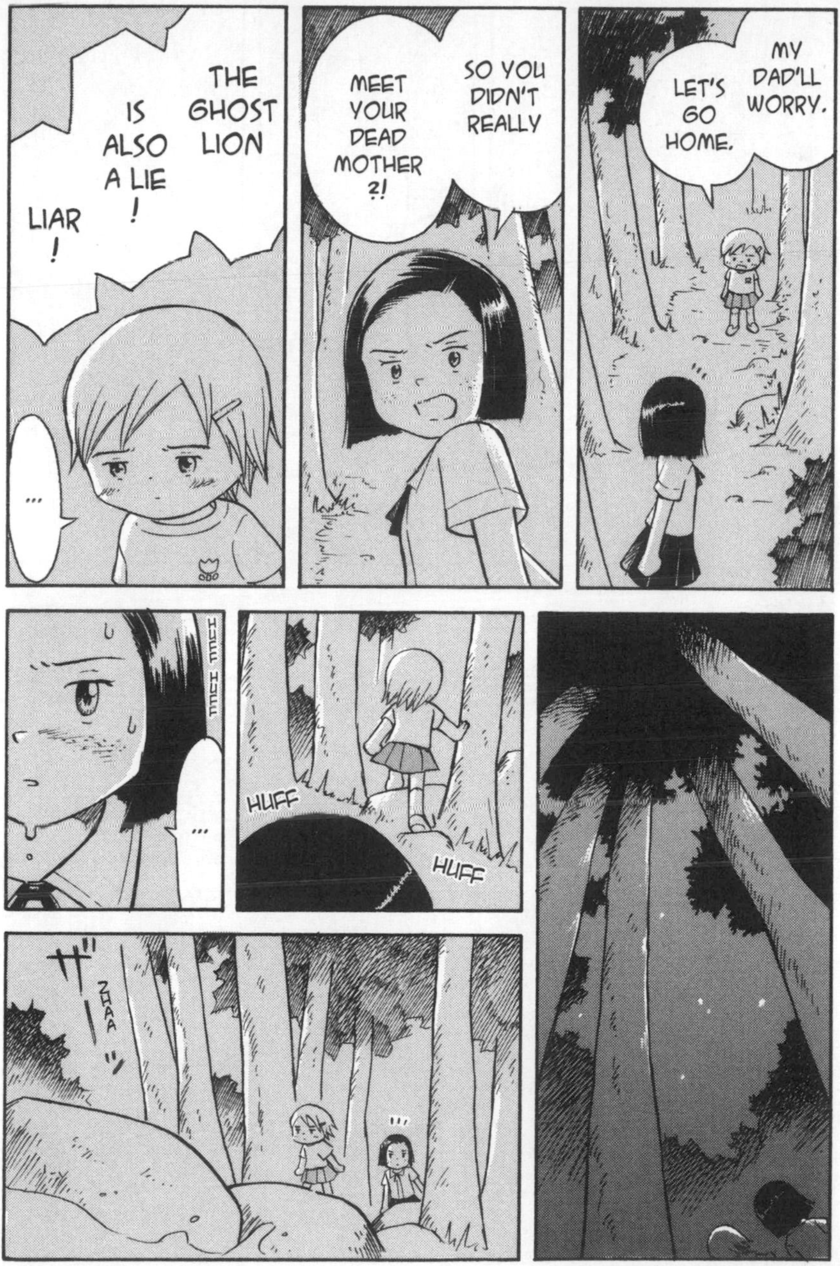
MY DAD'LL WORRY.
LET'S GO HOME.
SO YOU DIDN'T REALLY
MEET YOUR DEAD MOTHER?!
THE GHOST LION
IS ALSO A LIE!
LIAR!
...
HUFF
HUFF
HUFF HUFF
...
ZHAA
!!!

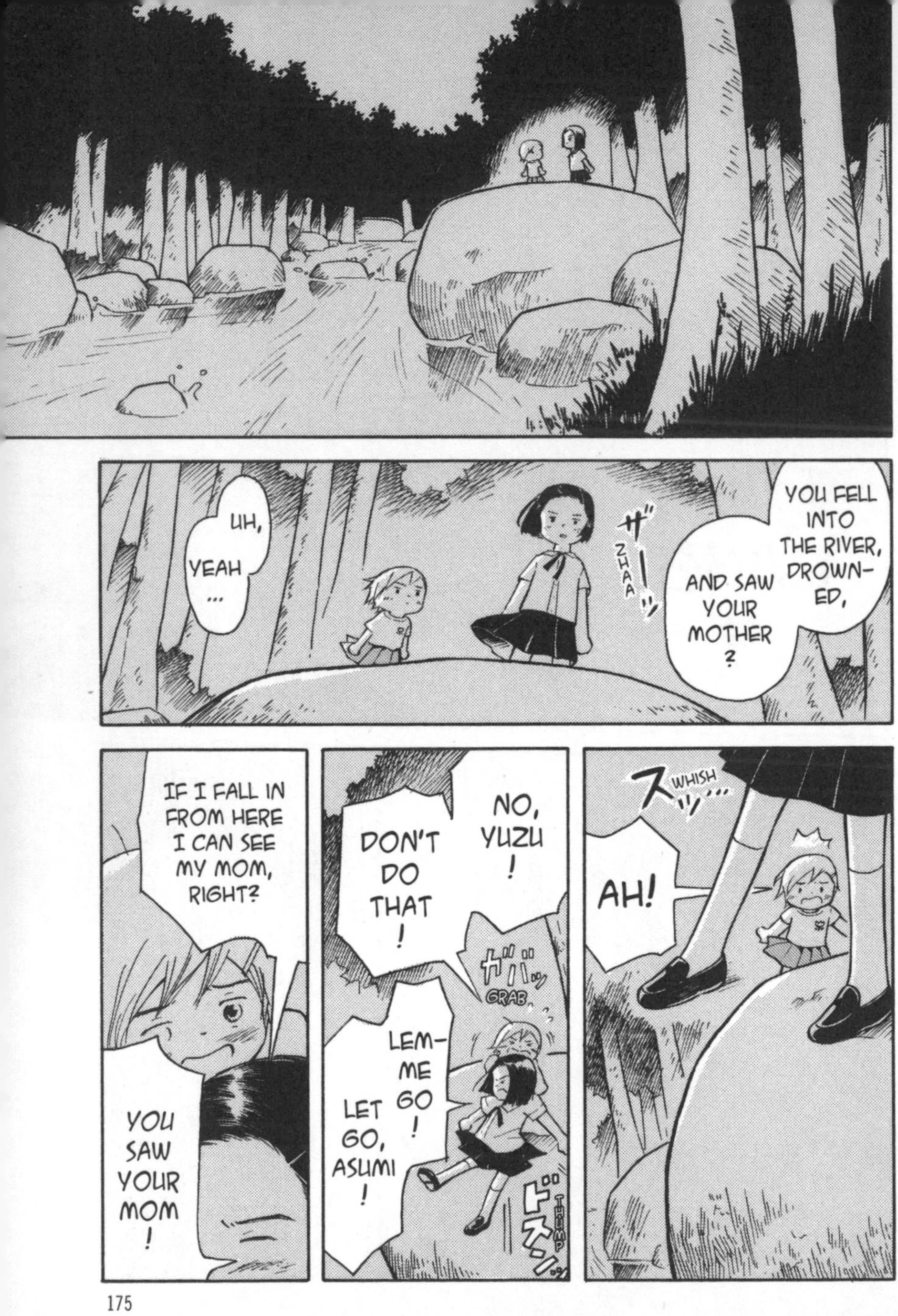
YOU FELL INTO THE RIVER, DROWNED,
AND SAW YOUR MOTHER?
ザーッ ZHAA
UH,
YEAH ...
スッ WHISH
AH!
NO, YUZU!
DON'T DO THAT!
ガバッ GRAB
LEMME GO!
LET GO, ASUMI!
ドスッ THUMP
IF I FALL IN FROM HERE I CAN SEE MY MOM, RIGHT?
YOU SAW YOUR MOM!

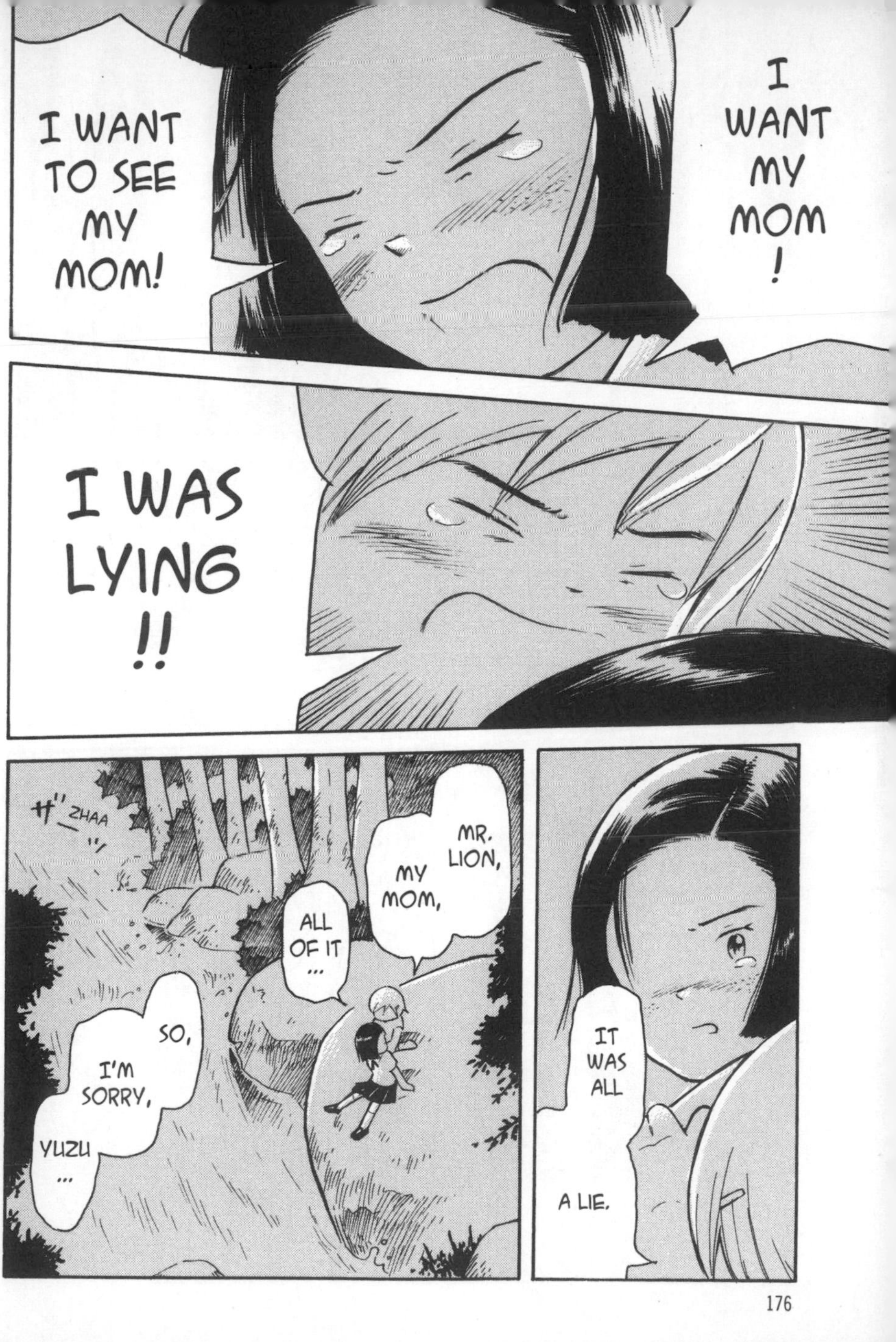
I WANT MY MOM!
I WANT TO SEE MY MOM!
I WAS LYING!!
IT WAS ALL A LIE.
ザッ ZHAA
MR. LION, MY MOM, ALL OF IT...
SO, I'M SORRY, YUZU...

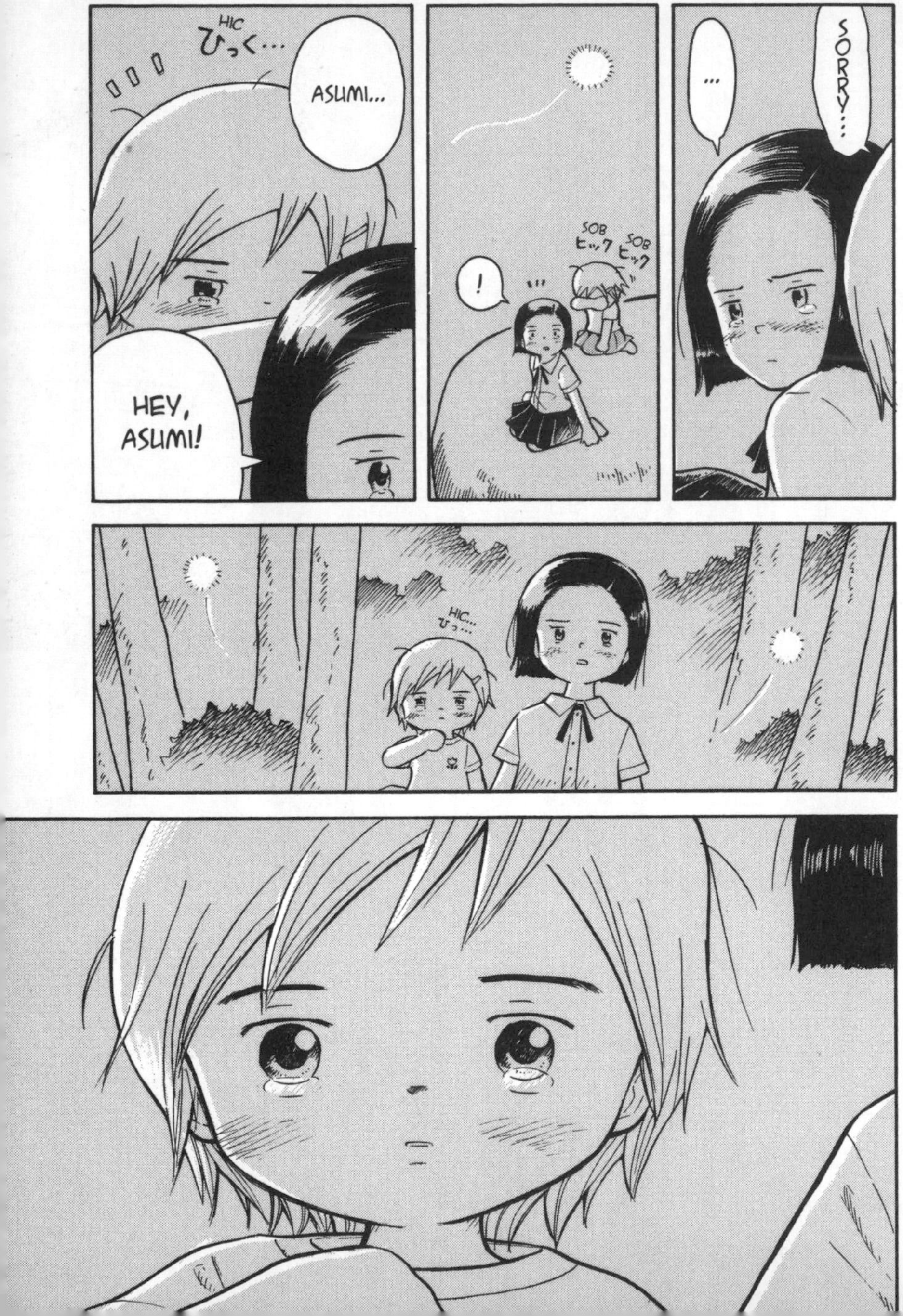
SORRY...
...
SOB
ヒック
SOB
ヒック
!
ASUMI...
HIC
ひっく…
HEY, ASUMI!
HIC...
ひっ…

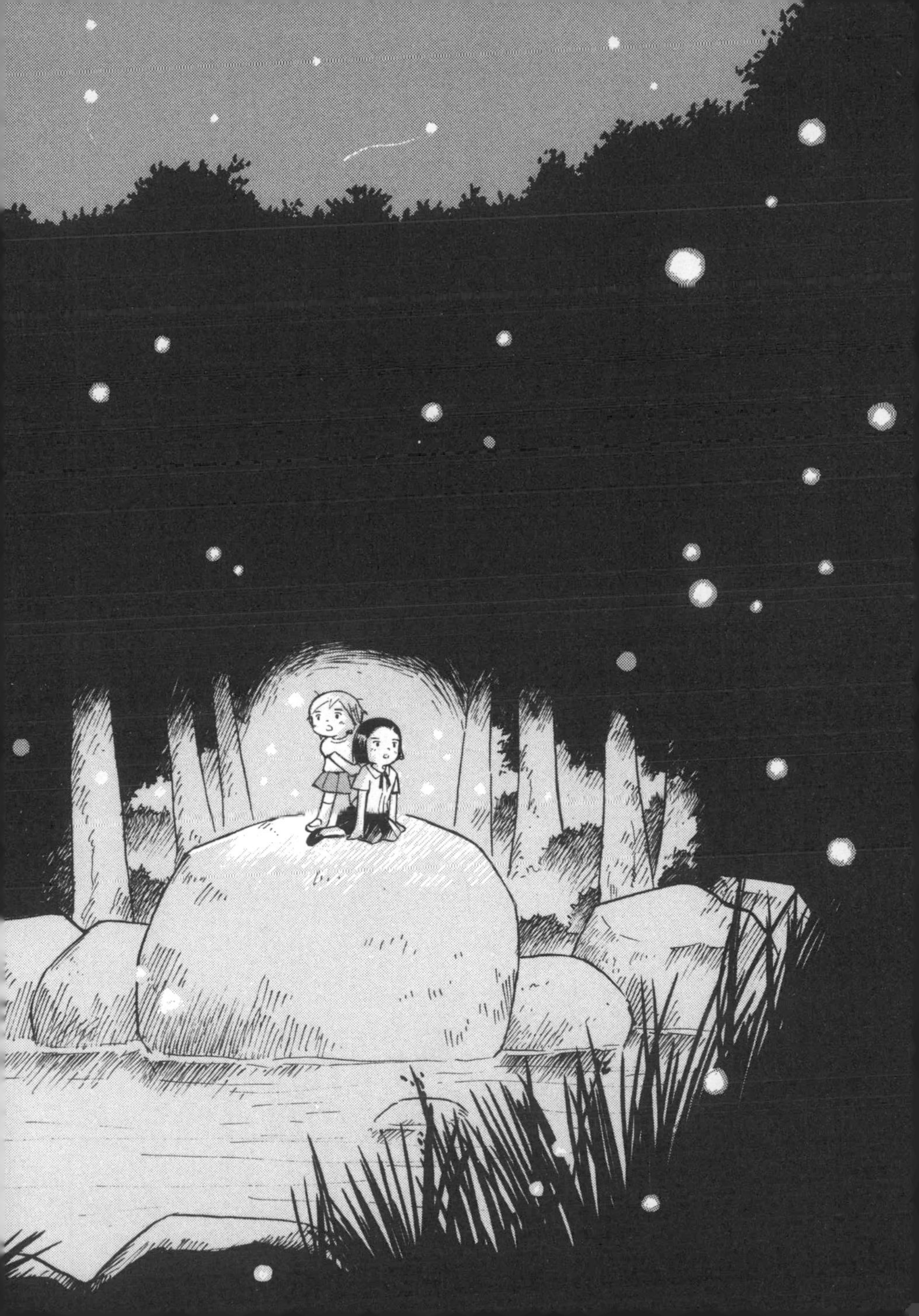

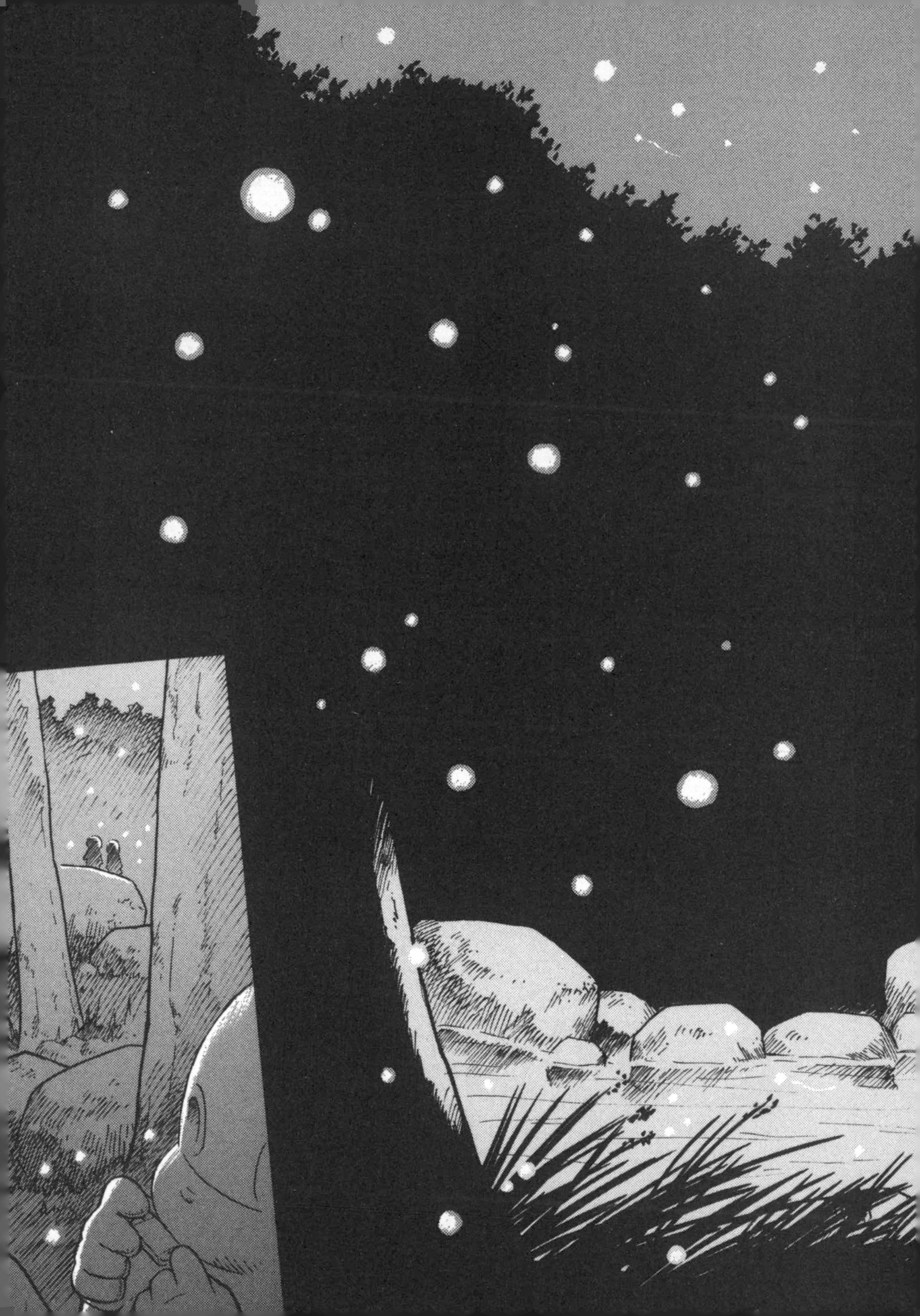

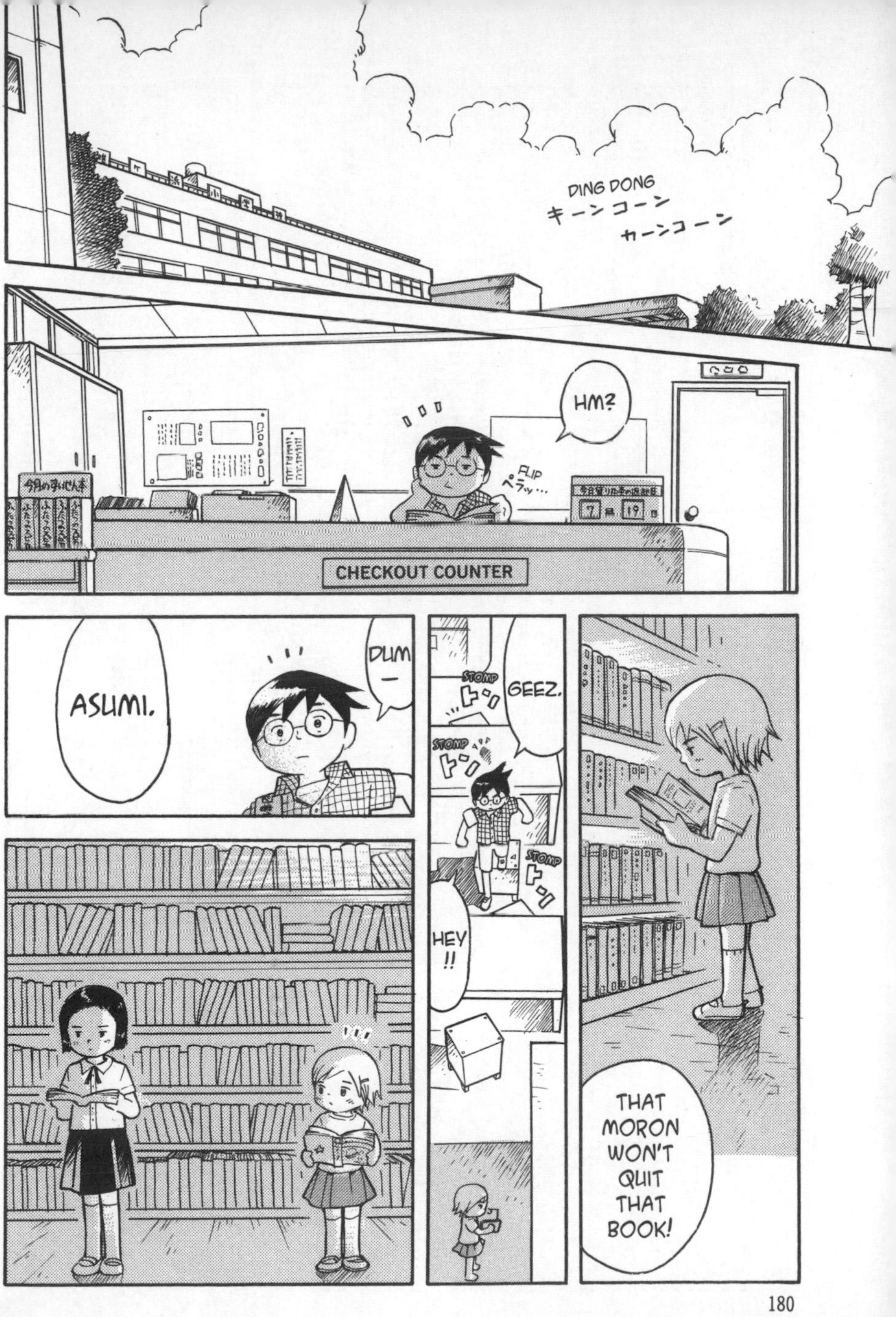
DING DONG
キーンコーン
カーンコーン
HM?
FLIP
ペラッ…
CHECKOUT COUNTER
THAT MORON WON'T QUIT THAT BOOK!
GEEZ.
STOMP
トッ
STOMP
トッ
STOMP
トッ
HEY!!
DUM
ASUMI.

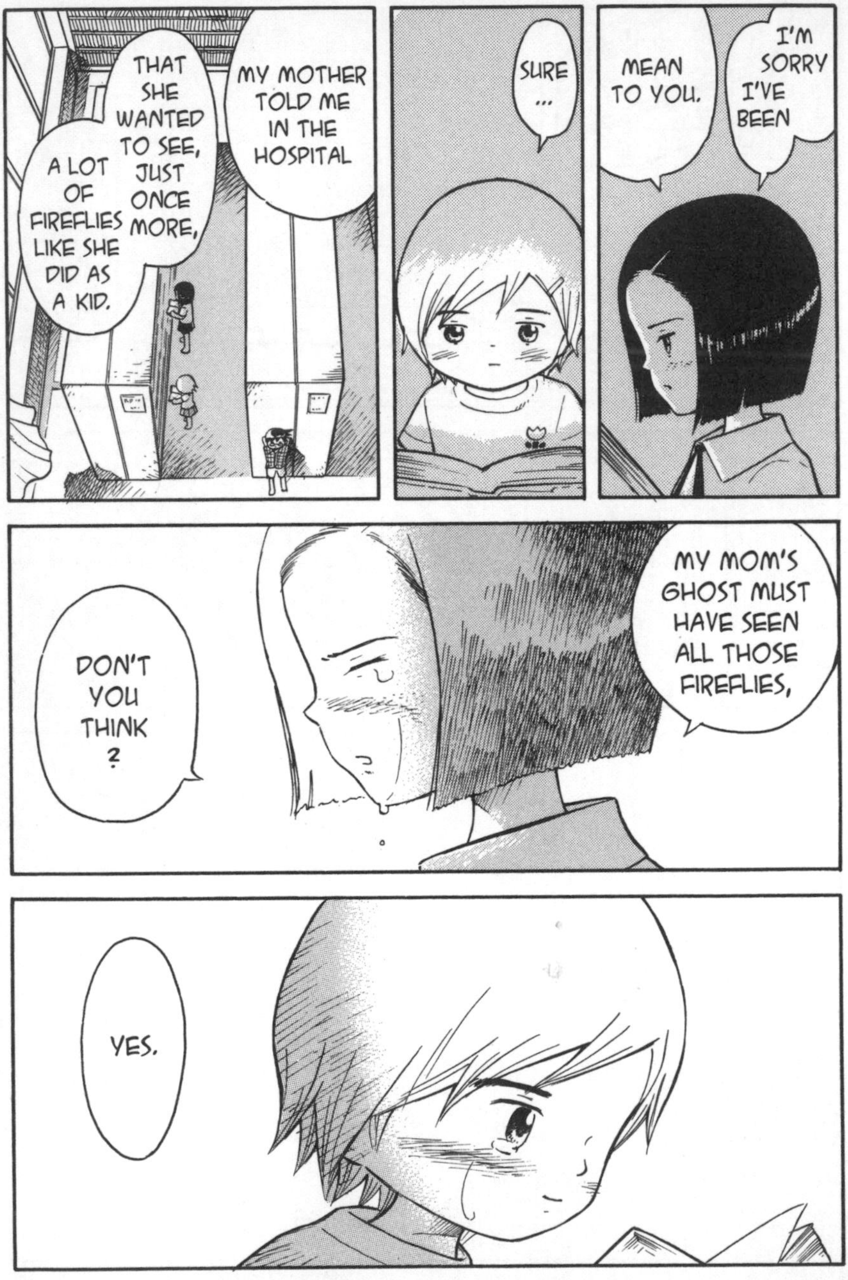
I'M SORRY I'VE BEEN
MEAN TO YOU.
SURE ...
MY MOTHER TOLD ME IN THE HOSPITAL
THAT SHE WANTED TO SEE, JUST ONCE MORE,
A LOT OF FIREFLIES LIKE SHE DID AS A KID.
MY MOM'S GHOST MUST HAVE SEEN ALL THOSE FIREFLIES,
DON'T YOU THINK?
YES.

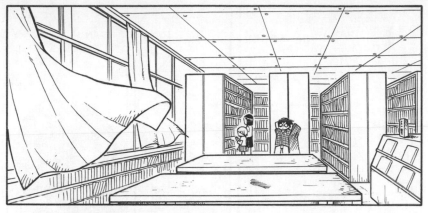

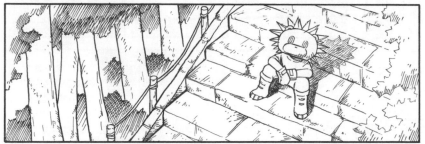

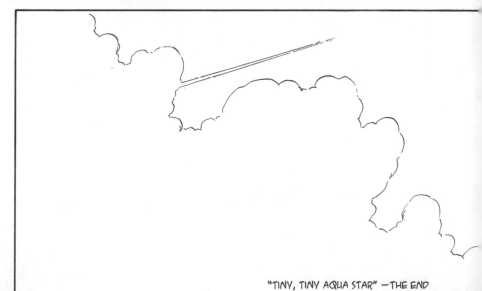

"TINY, TINY AQUA STAR" —THE END

ANOTHER SPICA

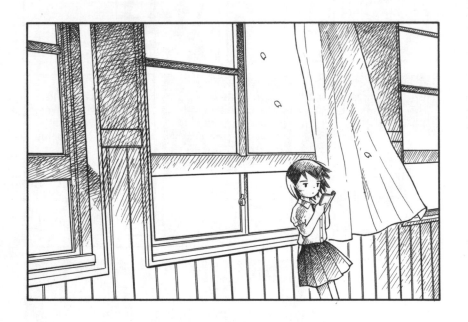

KOU YAGINUMA

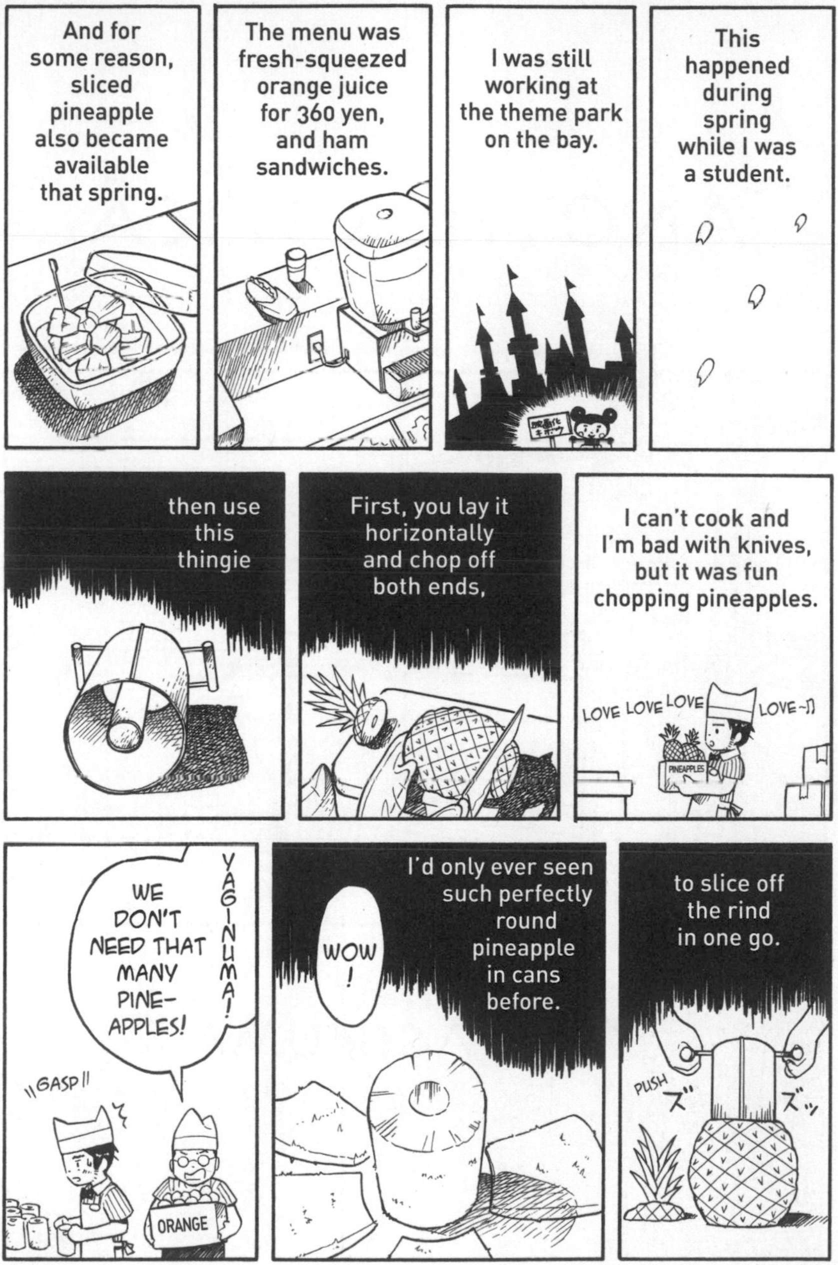
This happened during spring while I was a student.
I was still working at the theme park on the bay.
The menu was fresh-squeezed orange juice for 360 yen, and ham sandwiches.
And for some reason, sliced pineapple also became available that spring.
I can't cook and I'm bad with knives, but it was fun chopping pineapples.
LOVE LOVE LOVE LOVE~♫
PINEAPPLES
First, you lay it horizontally and chop off both ends,
then use this thingie
to slice off the rind in one go.
PUSH
ズ
ズッ
I'd only ever seen such perfectly round pineapple in cans before.
WOW!
YAGINUMA!
WE DON'T NEED THAT MANY PINE-APPLES!
GASP
ORANGE

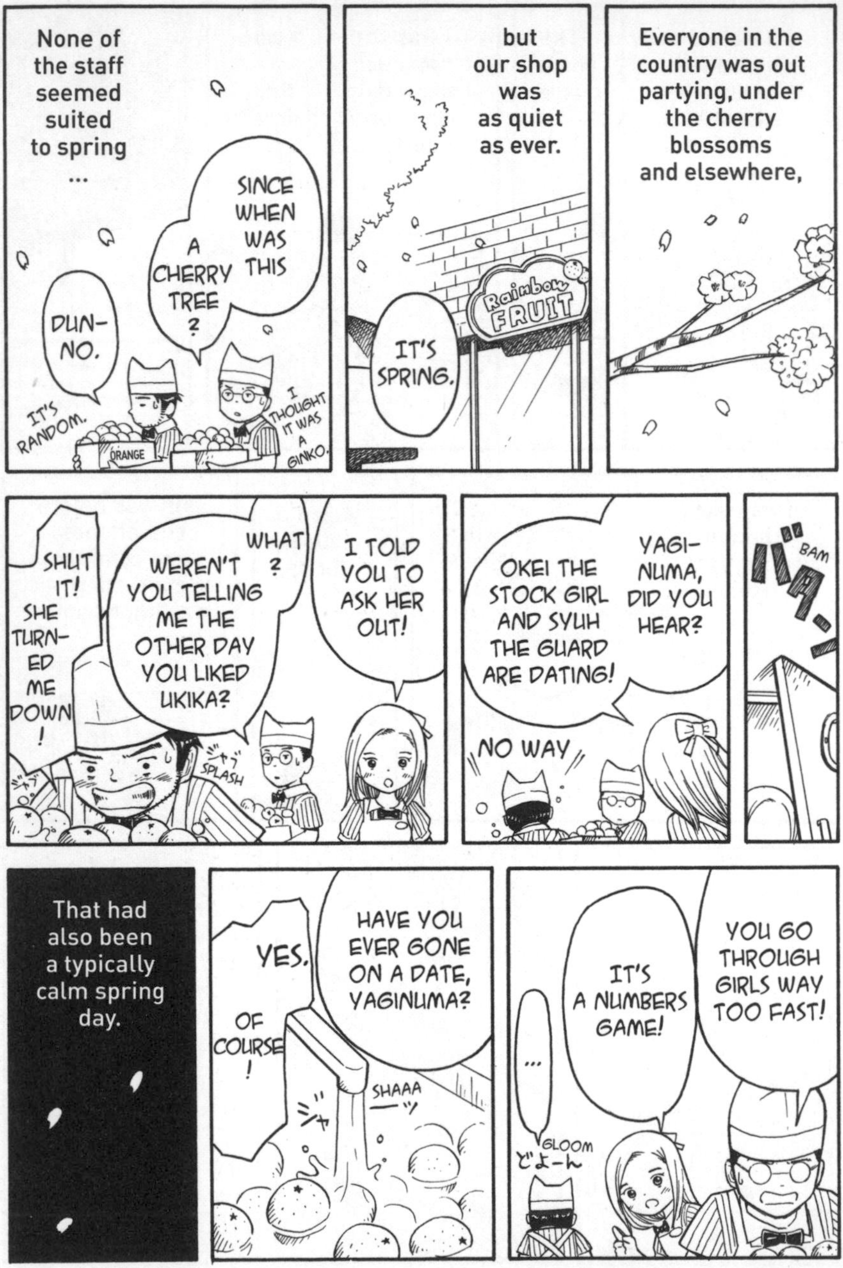
Everyone in the country was out partying, under the cherry blossoms and elsewhere,
but our shop was as quiet as ever.
IT'S SPRING.
Rainbow FRUIT
None of the staff seemed suited to spring ...
SINCE WHEN WAS THIS A CHERRY TREE?
DUN-NO.
I THOUGHT IT WAS A GINKO.
IT'S RANDOM.
ORANGE
BAM
YAGI-NUMA, DID YOU HEAR?
OKEI THE STOCK GIRL AND SYUH THE GUARD ARE DATING!
NO WAY
I TOLD YOU TO ASK HER OUT!
WHAT?
WEREN'T YOU TELLING ME THE OTHER DAY YOU LIKED UKIKA?
SHUT IT!
SHE TURN-ED ME DOWN!
SPLASH
YOU GO THROUGH GIRLS WAY TOO FAST!
IT'S A NUMBERS GAME!
...
GLOOM
どよーん
HAVE YOU EVER GONE ON A DATE, YAGINUMA?
YES.
OF COURSE!
SHAAA
That had also been a typically calm spring day.

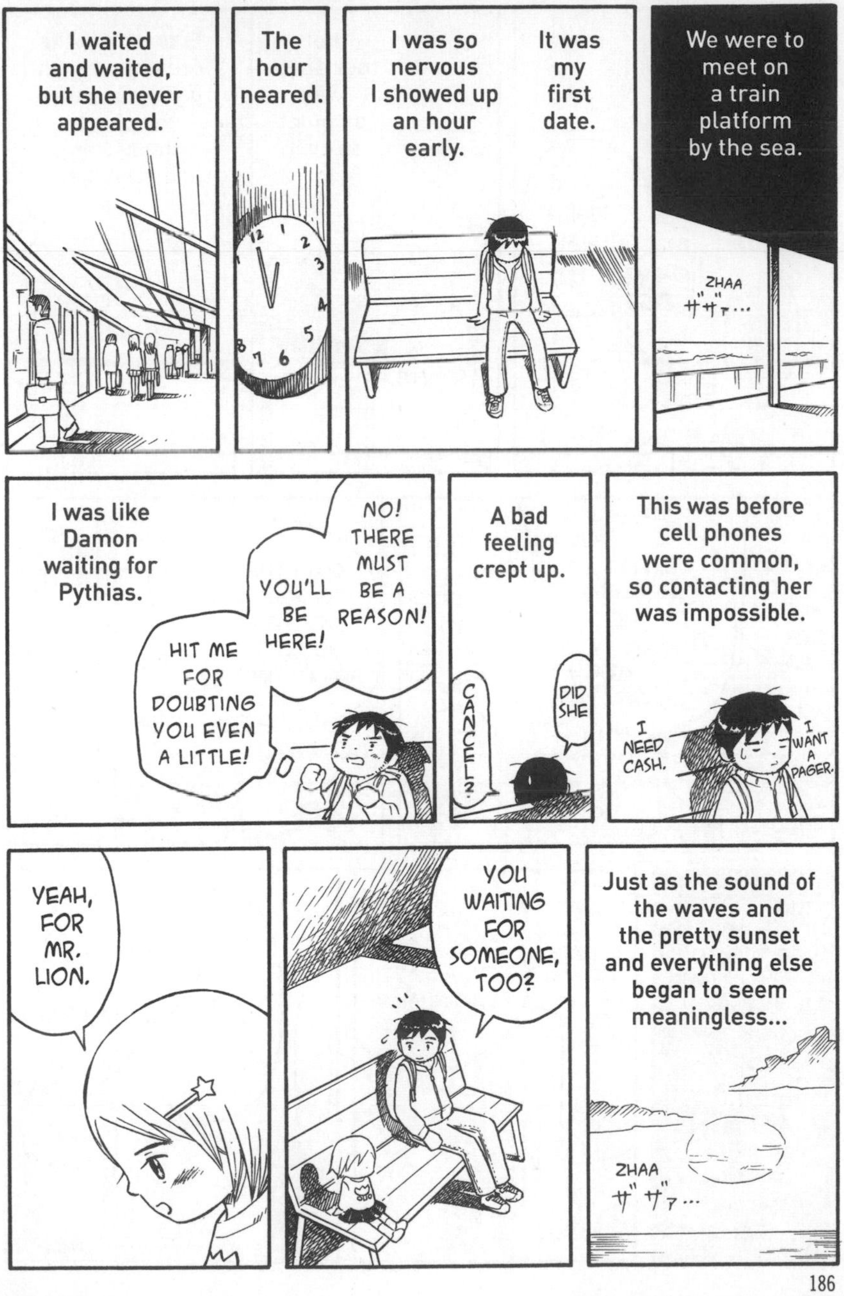
We were to meet on a train platform by the sea.
ZHAA
ザザァ…
It was my first date.
I was so nervous I showed up an hour early.
The hour neared.
I waited and waited, but she never appeared.
This was before cell phones were common, so contacting her was impossible.
I WANT A PAGER.
I NEED CASH.
A bad feeling crept up.
DID SHE
CANCEL?
NO! THERE MUST BE A REASON!
I was like Damon waiting for Pythias.
YOU'LL BE HERE!
HIT ME FOR DOUBTING YOU EVEN A LITTLE!
Just as the sound of the waves and the pretty sunset and everything else began to seem meaningless...
ZHAA
ザザァ…
YOU WAITING FOR SOMEONE, TOO?
YEAH, FOR MR. LION.

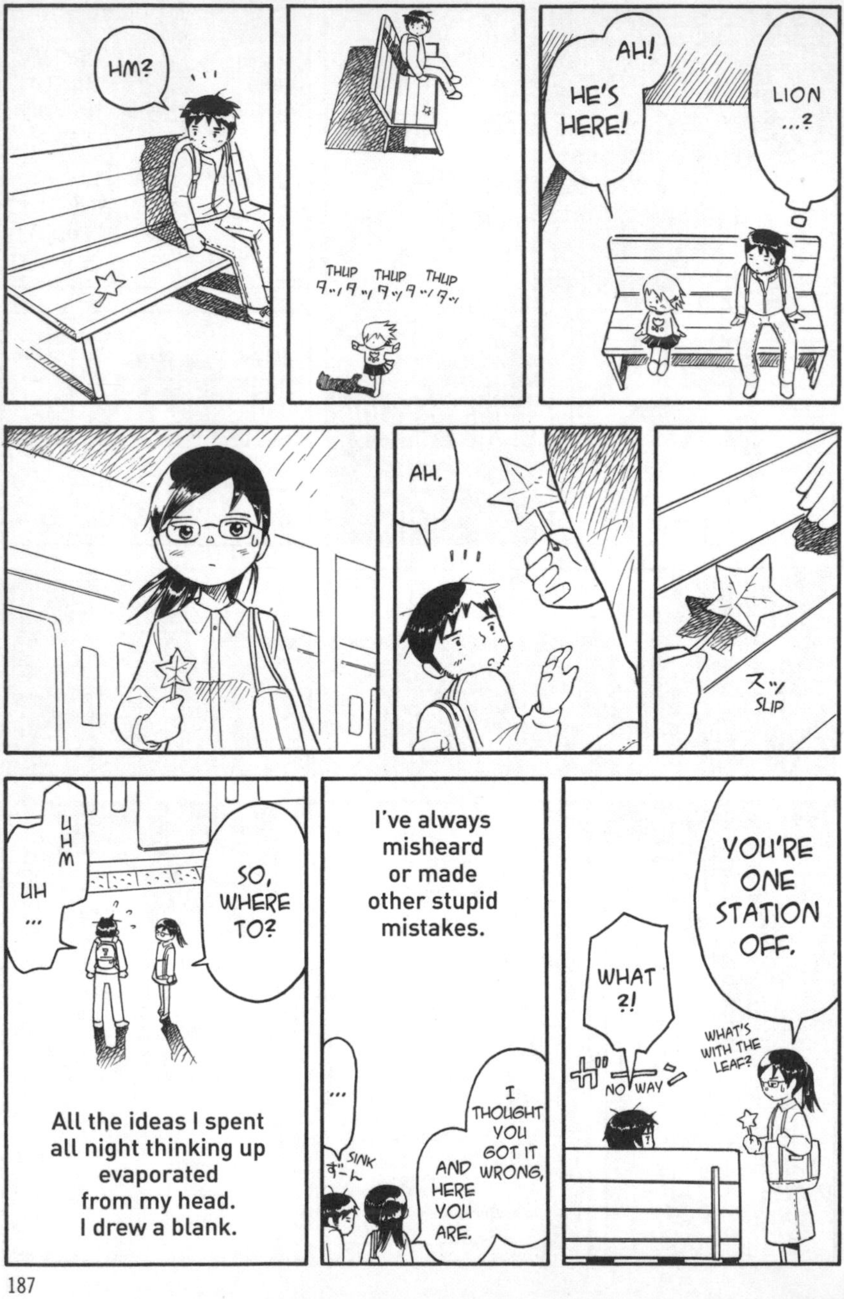
AH! HE'S HERE!
LION ...?
THUP THUP THUP
タッ/タッタッタッ/タッ
HM?
スッ SLIP
AH.
YOU'RE ONE STATION OFF.
WHAT ?!
WHAT'S WITH THE LEAF?
ガーン NO WAY
I've always misheard or made other stupid mistakes.
I THOUGHT YOU GOT IT WRONG, AND HERE YOU ARE.
...
SINK ずーん
SO, WHERE TO?
UHM
UH ...
All the ideas I spent all night thinking up evaporated from my head. I drew a blank.

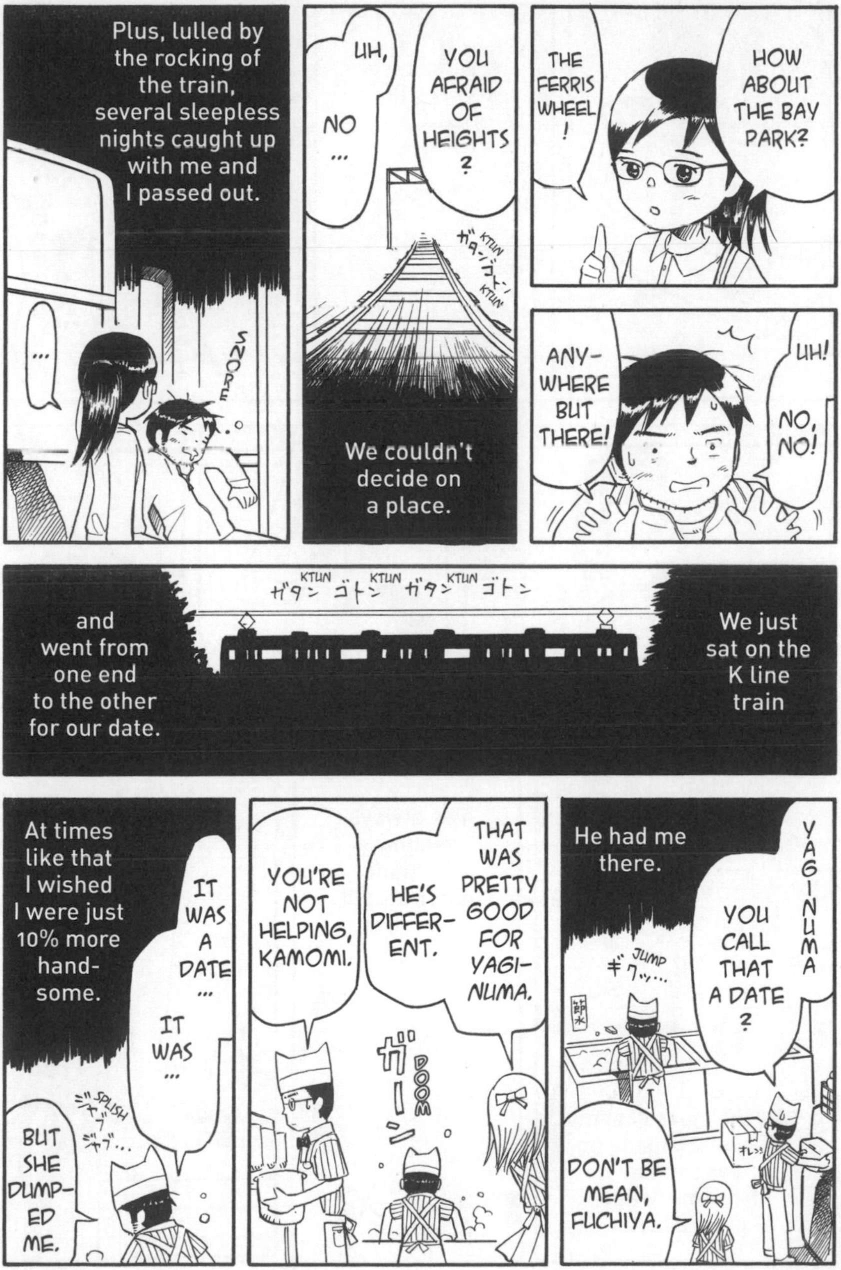
HOW ABOUT THE BAY PARK?
THE FERRIS WHEEL!
UH! NO, NO!
ANYWHERE BUT THERE!
YOU AFRAID OF HEIGHTS?
UH, NO...
KTUN KTUN
We couldn't decide on a place.
Plus, lulled by the rocking of the train, several sleepless nights caught up with me and I passed out.
...
SNORE
We just sat on the K line train
ガタン ゴトン ガタン ゴトン
KTUN KTUN KTUN
and went from one end to the other for our date.
YAGINUMA
YOU CALL THAT A DATE?
He had me there.
JUMP
DON'T BE MEAN, FUCHIYA.
THAT WAS PRETTY GOOD FOR YAGINUMA.
HE'S DIFFERENT.
YOU'RE NOT HELPING, KAMOMI.
DOOM
At times like that I wished I were just 10% more hand-some.
IT WAS A DATE...
IT WAS...
SPLISH
BUT SHE DUMPED ME.

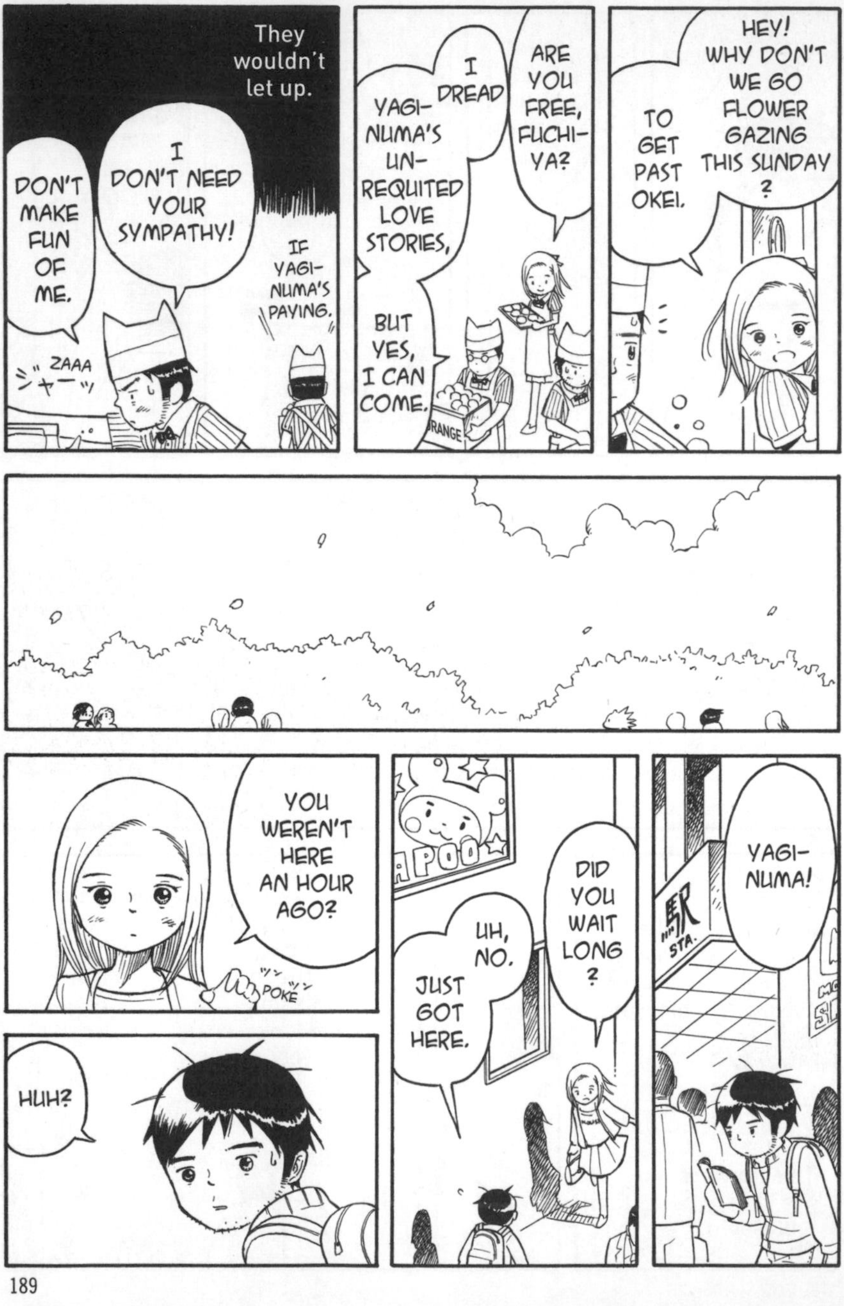
HEY! WHY DON'T WE GO FLOWER GAZING THIS SUNDAY?
TO GET PAST OKEI.
ARE YOU FREE, FUCHI-YA?
I DREAD YAGI-NUMA'S UN-REQUITED LOVE STORIES,
BUT YES, I CAN COME.
ORANGE
They wouldn't let up.
IF YAGI-NUMA'S PAYING.
I DON'T NEED YOUR SYMPATHY!
DON'T MAKE FUN OF ME.
ZAAA ジャーッ
YAGI-NUMA!
駅 STA.
DID YOU WAIT LONG?
UH, NO. JUST GOT HERE.
YOU WEREN'T HERE AN HOUR AGO?
ツン ツン POKE
HUH?

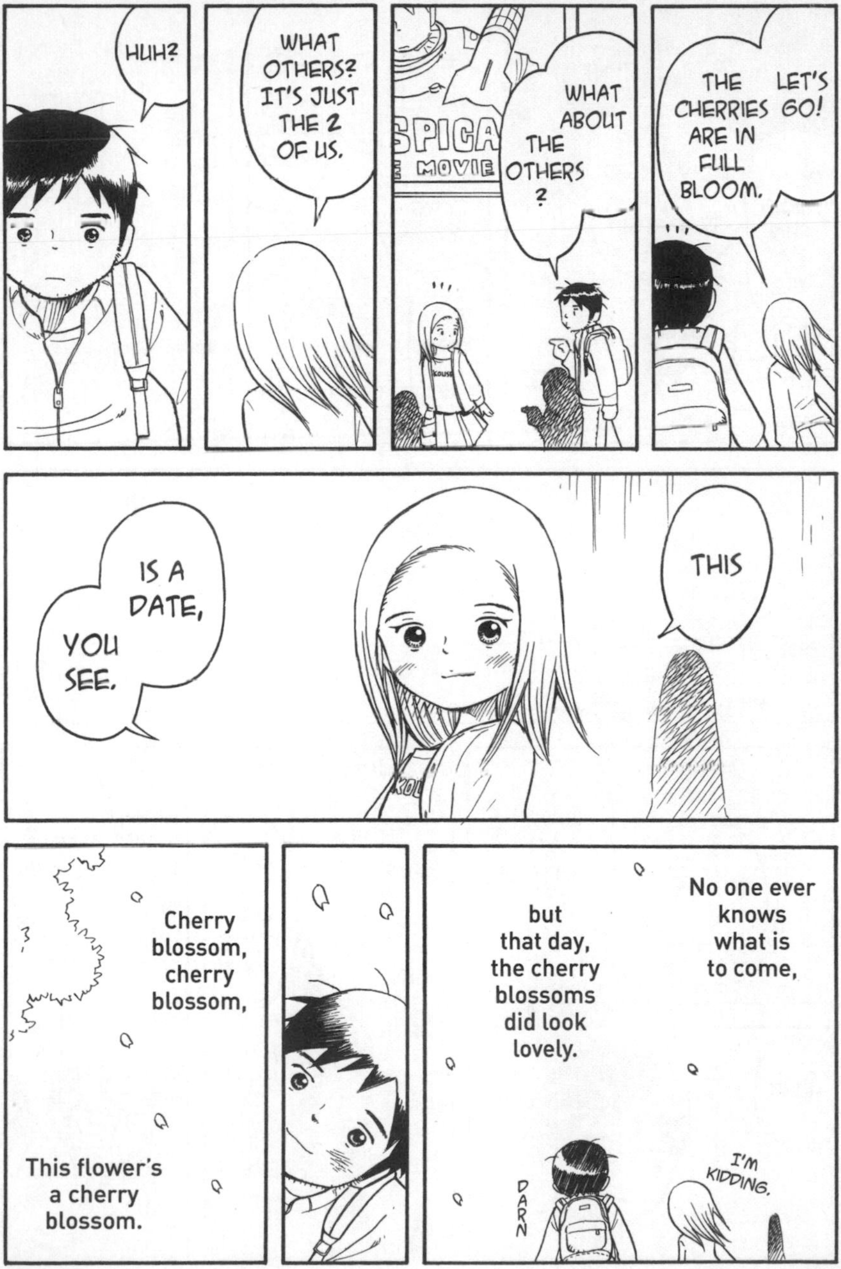
THE CHERRIES ARE IN FULL BLOOM. LET'S GO!
SPICA
MOVIE
WHAT ABOUT THE OTHERS?
WHAT OTHERS? IT'S JUST THE 2 OF US.
HUH?
THIS
IS A DATE, YOU SEE.
No one ever knows what is to come,
but that day, the cherry blossoms did look lovely.
I'M KIDDING.
DARN
Cherry blossom, cherry blossom,
This flower's a cherry blossom.

THE END

Notes on the Translation

P. 120

The character for Shu's first name means *autumn* and is commonly pronouced "aki." See also his T-shirt on pp. 112-14.

AUTUMN
"AKI" SUZUKI ?
IT'S READ "SHU."

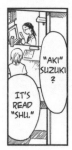

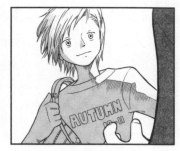

P. 133

The character "hama" in Yuigahama means *seashore*. The first character "yui" means *solitary* or *unique*. The "ga" is a connective. A real seashore region called Yuigahama exists in Kanagawa prefecture (as well as in neighboring Shizuoka). Though the "yui" is spelled with different characters, Asumi's hometown resembles the real area geographically.

THERE'S A "HAMA" IN THE NAME
SO THERE MUST BE A BEACH
IN YUIGA-HAMA.

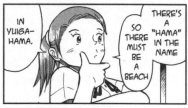

P. 168

While the attendance roll call consists of entirely plausible surnames, they happen also to be stations on the Oume line, which runs through the western half of Tokyo prefecture. Hence Fuchuya's quip.

FUSSA.
HERE.
HA-MURA.
HERE.
...
WHAT LINE IS THAT?

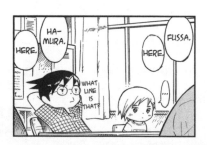

SO-ALB-723

Production - Hiroko Mizuno
           Tomoe Tsutsumi
           Christine Lee
           Rina Nakayama

Originally published in Japanese as *Futatsu no Supika 6*
by MEDIA FACTORY, Inc., Tokyo 2004
Futatsu no Supika first serialized in Gekkan Comic Flapper,
MEDIA FACTORY, Inc., 2001-2009

This is a work of fiction.

ISBN: 978-1-935654-03-2

Manufactured in Canada

First Edition

Vertical, Inc.
451 Park Avenue South, 7th Floor
New York, NY 10016
www.vertical-inc.com